Hume and Hume's Connexions

Hume and Hume's Connexions

Edited by
M. A. STEWART
and
JOHN P. WRIGHT

EDINBURGH UNIVERSITY PRESS

© Individual contributors, 1994

Edinburgh University Press Ltd
22 George Square, Edinburgh

Typeset in Linotronic Plantin
by Speedspools, Edinburgh, and
printed and bound in Great Britain
by the University Press, Cambridge

A CIP record for this book is available from
the British Library

ISBN 0 7486 0523 1

Contents

Notes on contributors   vii

Abbreviations   ix

Introduction   xi

1   The "affair" at Edinburgh and the "project" at Glasgow:
     the politics of Hume's attempts to become a professor   1
     ROGER L. EMERSON

2   Hume and Hutcheson   23
     JAMES MOORE

3   Hume and the invention of utilitarianism   58
     STEPHEN DARWALL

4   Hume and the natural lawyers: a change of landscape   83
     PAULINE C. WESTERMAN

5   Butler and Hume on habit and moral character   105
     JOHN P. WRIGHT

6   Hume, Reid and the science of the mind   119
     P. B. WOOD

7   Hume's doubts about probable reasoning: was Locke
     the target?   140
     DAVID OWEN

8   An early fragment on evil   160
     M. A. STEWART

9   Hume's historical view of miracles   171
     M. A. STEWART

10 Hume and the art of dialogue   201
    MICHEL MALHERBE

11 Hume and the madness of religion   224
    CHRISTOPHER BERNARD

12 Kant's critique of Hume's theory of faith   239
    MANFRED KUEHN

    Index   256

Notes on contributors

CHRISTOPHER BERNARD completed a Ph.D. thesis on Hume and the Imagination for St Andrews University in 1990 and has now qualified as a solicitor

STEPHEN DARWALL is Professor of Philosophy at the University of Michigan, and author of *Impartial reason* (Ithaca, NY 1983)

ROGER L. EMERSON is Professor of History at the University of Western Ontario, and author of *Professors, patronage and politics: The Aberdeen universities in the eighteenth century* (Aberdeen 1992)

MANFRED KUEHN is Associate Professor of Philosophy at Purdue University, and author of *Scottish common sense in Germany, 1768–1800* (Kingston, Ontario 1987)

MICHEL MALHERBE is Professor of Philosophy and Vice-President of the University of Nantes, has published annotated French translations of Hume's *Dialogues concerning natural religion* and *The natural history of religion,* and is author of *Kant ou Hume ou la raison et le sensible* (Paris 1980), and *La Philosophie empiriste de David Hume* (2nd edn, Paris 1984)

JAMES MOORE is Associate Professor of Political Science at Concordia University, Montreal

DAVID OWEN is Assistant Professor of Philosophy at the University of Arizona

M. A. STEWART is Professor of the History of Philosophy at the University of Lancaster, joint general editor of the forthcoming Oxford edition of the Philosophical, Political and Literary Works of David Hume, and editor of *Studies in the philosophy of the Scottish Enlightenment* (Oxford 1990)

PAULINE C. WESTERMAN lectures in the Philosophy of Law at the University of Groningen and at the Catholic University of Nijmegen

P. B. WOOD is a member of the History Department at the University of Victoria, British Columbia, and author of *The Aberdeen Enlightenment: The arts curriculum in the eighteenth century* (Aberdeen 1993)

JOHN P. WRIGHT is Professor of Philosophy at the University of Windsor, Ontario, and author of *The sceptical realism of David Hume* (Manchester 1983)

Abbreviations

AUL	Aberdeen University Library
EUL	Edinburgh University Library
GUA	Glasgow University Archives
GUL	Glasgow University Library
NLS	National Library of Scotland
SRO	Scottish Record Office
D (+ page no.)	*Dialogues concerning natural religion,* by David Hume, edited by N. Kemp Smith. 2nd edn (Edinburgh 1947)
E (+ page no.)	*Enquiries concerning human understanding and concerning the principles of morals,* by David Hume, edited by L. A. Selby-Bigge, revised by P. H. Nidditch (Oxford 1975)
Ess. (+ page no.)	*Essays moral, political and literary,* by David Hume, edited by E. F. Miller. Rev. edn (Indianapolis 1987)
GG (+ vol., page no.)	*The philosophical works,* by David Hume, edited by T. H. Green and T. H. Grose, 2nd edn (London 1882–6), in the 4-volume reprint (Aalen 1964)
H (+ vol., page no.)	*The history of England,* by David Hume, introd. W. B. Todd, 6 vols (Indianapolis 1983)
HL (+ vol., page no.)	*The letters of David Hume,* edited by J. Y. T. Greig, 2 vols (Oxford 1932)
NHL (+ page no.)	*New letters of David Hume,* edited by R. Klibansky and E. C. Mossner (Oxford 1954)
NHR (+ page no.)	*The natural history of religion,* by David Hume. In GG, vol. IV

T (+ page no.)   *A treatise of human nature,* by David Hume, edited
                        by L. A. Selby-Bigge, revised by P. H. Nidditch
                        (Oxford 1978). This volume includes Hume's
                        Abstract

Introduction

Over the past decade or so, a growing number of scholars have come to suspect that a good deal of twentieth-century commentary has misjudged David Hume's aims and achievements from having lost touch with the kinds of beliefs and concerns that motivated him and his contemporaries. Plainly, we should not underestimate the contributions that Hume has made to the progress of western thought, or discourage a historically well-informed comparison of his philosophical tenets and arguments with those current today. There would be little scholarship, and it would have less focus, if those who practised it did not engage at some level with the ideas they were studying, or were never prepared to extend those ideas to new applications. But neither should we underestimate the perils of the exercise.

Everyday observation and conversation give ready evidence of the human tendency to misinterpret and even reverse the meanings of others, to inflate the significance of isolated remarks, and to ascribe to people positions they did not advocate. Philosophers, like other habitual critics, need to identify and understand this tendency rather than just succumb to it. Once a prominent historical figure is brought into the service of some new philosophical fashion, the association is apt to outlive the fashion, and the older philosopher becomes a stereotype for a position he never espoused, in a controversy he never knew. It is now generally conceded that the "positivist" and "emotivist" Hume are of this genre; but these interpretations still survive in more mitigated forms that continue to distort the nature of the dialogue in which Hume was engaged. A profession that lives by shadow-boxing with its own contemporaries over views they do not hold is hardly one deserving of public support; no more is a profession that treats someone else's contemporaries in the same light.

The essays in this collection show that we can, nevertheless, go a fair way to bridge the gaps between the epochs if we will take the trouble to see where they lie. Our contributors illustrate the insights that can be gained for the interpretation of Hume's philosophy when we locate it at the heart of a living and vibrant debate in his own day. Hume and his near contemporaries serve as foils to one another, and to see this helps us to bring out the particular significance of their individual contributions. They were contesting a range of philosophical issues at a specific stage in the history of their development, and doing so against a changing background of developments in other related areas of interest, such as science, politics and religion. We should, therefore, look closely at how they formulated their problems, deployed their arguments and reacted to one another, if we are to achieve a proper understanding of their central philosophical concerns and learn from them what they themselves had to teach.

All the contributions to this volume represent new and significant research. The editors have selected essays which complement each other thematically and at the same time create a methodologically cohesive whole. Three main topic areas are addressed. The opening papers contribute to a substantial reappraisal of Hume's moral philosophy and of the tradition in which it has usually been placed. These are followed by a group which uses historical data to connect Hume's philosophy of mind with both his moral philosophy and his epistemology. A third group looks at his writing on religion in its literary and historical as well as its philosophical aspects. But cutting across these subject divisions are several recurring themes of Hume's thought, such as his use of human history, his natural-historical methodology, and his conviction that the same underlying mechanisms of the mind can explain a diverse range of human thinking, both speculative and moral, both within and beyond the arena of common life. On most of these themes the contributors are in broad agreement; where there is still divergence – for example, on the precise form of Hume's appeal to an experimental method – we can look to these papers to fuel a continuing, and now better informed, debate.

The first two essays complement each other in enabling us to compare the political and philosophical dimensions of Hume's failure to obtain a position teaching moral philosophy in the Scottish university system. This failure has traditionally been seen as the result of the religious intolerance of Hume's contemporaries – a view (it has to be said) that he himself encouraged. However, Roger L. Emerson's detailed study of the political alliances ranged for and against Hume in 1745 and 1752 reveals a far more complex set of factors. In the end, the political backing for Hume was too weak. But Emerson suggests that the support he received for these posts is as significant as the opposition he faced: the conventional religious duties that went with such positions would have been familiar to Hume and his supporters, and this should make us take a more cautious look at the relation between Hume's philosophical views and his practical attitudes to religious conformity.

The philosophical opposition to Hume in 1745 was spearheaded by
Francis Hutcheson, a fact that has never been satisfactorily squared with
the twentieth-century view that Hume's moral philosophy, and even his
epistemology, was heavily indebted to the sentimentalist theories of
Hutcheson. James Moore in his contribution contests this alignment,
taking his cue from the fact that the philosophies of Hutcheson and
Hume were perceived very differently in their own day. He contrasts
Hutcheson's strong alliance with Stoic moralists, with Hume's alliance
with philosophers writing in the Epicurean and Sceptical traditions. By
carefully identifying those materials that Hume added or revised in Book
III of *A treatise of human nature*, he enables us to reconstruct something of
what that work was like before Hume got into debate with Hutcheson in
1739–40. One consequence of his argument is that some of the passages
which are standardly used as proof of Hume's intellectual dependence on
Hutcheson are better seen as tactical revisions, charting a path that might
help bridge over deep differences.

Stephen Darwall also challenges some of the modern view of the relationship of Hume to Hutcheson in his examination of the role that Hume's
ideas played in the formation of Bentham's utilitarianism. Darwall shows
that Hume's use of moral-sense theory departs from Hutcheson's in a
way that leads to the utilitarian idea that the moral ranking of acts and
motives derives from the non-moral value of their consequences. He
argues that, in spite of some initial debt to Hutcheson's notion of moral
sense, Hume gives a psychological explanation of that sense in terms of
the pleasurable and painful states induced by the characters approved of
by it. Darwall is careful to point out that, while Hume himself is no
more a utilitarian than Hutcheson, he is of importance in the development
of the central conception of utilitarianism.

Since Hume's moral philosophy, and particularly his discussion of
justice, seems to use much of the idiom of the natural-law tradition, several
recent commentators have explored the possibility of interpreting his
account of morality in terms of that tradition. Pauline C. Westerman takes
issue with this, and argues from a detailed comparison of Grotius and Hume
that this new approach has had a distorting effect. The two thinkers may
employ much the same concepts, but it is for different purposes – Grotius
for purposes of justification, Hume for purposes of explanation. Grotius
uses an account of human nature to justify existing rules of justice; Hume,
to explain the institution of justice. Where Grotius seeks external criteria
that should regulate human behaviour, Hume investigates why people
actually follow the rules. There were, indeed, conflicting tendencies within
natural-law theory which paved the way for its own demise: thus,
Pufendorf showed that the demand for a more empirical account of human
nature together with the growing popularity of "evolutionary" theories

could not really be reconciled with natural-law doctrine. Hume's philosophy resolved these conflicts in a way, but the enterprise of natural law was undermined in the process, and replaced with a new programme.

In earlier writings on Hume, John P. Wright has stressed the influence of Cartesian psychophysiological models on Hume's epistemology. In his contribution to this volume, Wright argues that Hume derives from Joseph Butler a psychological account of the development of moral character, which he then applies in a distinctive way in his moral philosophy. This is based on the idea that, as we become accustomed to act in a certain way, the feelings which originally led us to act in that way become less sensible. Wright shows how this idea influences the account of calm passions in Book II of the *Treatise,* and how this differs from the account of calm desire in Hutcheson. He argues further that Butler's account of the development of habits is in the background of Hume's account of justice and the development of moral character in Book III and in the second *Enquiry.*

Drawing on Thomas Kuhn's suggestion that disciplines come to be shaped by certain paradigmatic works, P. B. Wood argues that the philosophy of mind in the Scottish Enlightenment came to be defined through two main influences. On the one hand, there is the natural-historical tradition exemplified in the writings of Locke and Butler, which had its roots in the methodological writings of Bacon. Wood makes important and novel claims about the natural history of mind as discussed by Hume. On the other hand, he argues that influences of the physiological psychology of Descartes and Malebranche, which survive in the writings of Locke and Hume, are only finally expunged by Reid. He is therefore able to show that Reid's well-known criticism of Hume is based on an informed understanding of where Hume was coming from, instead of the lack of understanding which some other recent historiography has credited him with.

Most work on Hume's so-called "problem of induction" has treated his account of the problem as resting on deductive principles. He is seen as denying that the principle of the uniformity of nature can necessitate our probable inferences. By putting Hume's sceptical argument concerning probability in the context of the non-formal model of rationality which was typical of the times, David Owen suggests a more plausible analysis. He argues that Locke was in part Hume's inspiration, in part his target. Locke had clearly set out the idea that our probable reasoning was based on conformity with past experience. According to Owen, Hume was arguing that the principle of the uniformity of nature could never serve as the "intermediate idea" required by reason as it was understood in the Lockean tradition.

New Hume manuscripts are a rarity, and it is even rarer for them to be secured for the instant benefit of scholars, instead of being taken out of circulation to become the playthings of mercenary traders. We should congratulate the National Library of Scotland on their success in buying the newly discovered early fragment on evil, and thank them for allowing it to be reproduced in facsimile in this collection. M. A. Stewart offers a close analysis of the content and dating of this remarkable document, to suggest that it may have been one of the "noble Parts" which was lost when Hume decided to remove theological provocations from the manuscript of his *Treatise*. Stewart shows that the fragment gives evidence of an early articulation of themes that Hume was to develop further in his *Dialogues concerning natural religion*, evidence which also confirms Philo's later role as Hume's own voice. Hume was working with an account of the attributes of the Deity which seems to have been distinctive to the natural theologians of the early eighteenth century.

In his extended study of another argument that Hume had removed from the *Treatise* on grounds of prudence, the argument of the essay 'Of miracles', Stewart sketches the origins in seventeenth-century English and French philosophy of Hume's use of the concepts of testimony and probability in assessing miracle reports. Contrary to other recent interpretations, Locke emerges as the strongest influence, the one who set the agenda in terms of which Hume conducts his own argument as an argument about the strength of historical evidence. In picking out themes to show this, Stewart includes a comparison with Hume's similar criteria for exposing the forgery of 'Ossian', but shows how Locke and Hume nevertheless end up on opposite sides in the debate on miracles, in virtue of their prior commitments for and against natural religion. Both Stewart and Owen have, therefore, in different contexts, stressed the importance of Locke's theory of probability as a significant influence on Hume.

Not only in the discussion of miracles, but in all Hume's writing on religion, there is clear literary artifice. Most attempts to provide a literary analysis of the *Dialogues* begin from later canons of literary criticism. Michel Malherbe's essay is important for its research into the conventions of dialogue in philosophy and natural religion in Hume's day and before. Malherbe makes particularly significant use of Shaftesbury's work on the use of popular literary forms for moral writing. He argues that, since Hume rejected Shaftesbury's prescription for moral writing, his resort to dialogue for natural religion calls for explanation. This lies in the way in which the speculative question of the "foundation" of religious belief by its very nature leads to unending controversy.

Hume's writing on philosophy and religion has natural links not only with his views on the nature of historical evidence, but with his actual historical writing. Christopher Bernard explores a significant connexion between Hume's philosophical and his historical work, by showing how

his historical studies of religion embody central principles of the philosophical psychology – of the imagination and the passions – developed in the
first two Books of the *Treatise*. Bernard discusses Hume's account of the
religious character, particularly as it is exemplified in *The history of England*
in the portrayals of the Lutheran Reformers, Becket, and Joan of Arc,
and he shows how Hume adapts ideas from Bayle and Locke in his
analysis of religious enthusiasm. He concludes by noting that, while
Hume shared with writers such as Calvin, Malebranche and Bayle the
view that we have a natural propensity to engage in activities that are
forbidden to us, he rejected their view that this tendency has its roots in
original sin. Hume argued instead that this psychologically grounded
propensity is most clearly manifested in a tendency of religious persons
to seek practices that pervert our natural moral feelings.

Like Bernard, Manfred Kuehn stresses Hume's view of the non-rational
or irrational sources of religious belief and its negative moral consequences.
Kuehn contrasts Hume's theory of irrational faith with Kant's belief in a
religion founded on reason alone, and argues that Kant's well-known
criticisms of Hume's theory of knowledge should be understood against
the background of their fundamentally different attitudes towards the
foundations of religion. Kuehn's essay is particularly valuable in deepening
our understanding of the nature of the points of agreement and disagreement between these two key philosophers of the eighteenth century. In
his conclusion, Kuehn argues that their differing views on the moral
relevance of religion depend on their differing conceptions of human
nature.

The editors are grateful to an international group of scholars who have
helped them in selecting papers and in providing additional feedback to
the contributors. These have included Annette Baier, Michael Barfoot,
John Biro, John Clayton, R. G. Frey, John Gill, Knud Haakonssen, Ian
Hacking, H. S. Harris, Vincent Hope, J. C. Laursen, Donald Livingston,
David McNaughton, David Norton and Peter Walmsley. Several contrib-
utors also offered valuable advice – Stephen Darwall, Roger Emerson,
James Moore, David Owen, Paul Wood. The editors would like to express
their appreciation, too, for the hospitality and facilities provided by two
institutions where the bulk of the editorial work was completed: the
Australian National University, where M. A. Stewart was a Visiting
Fellow in the Research School of Social Sciences in 1991–2, and the
University of Western Ontario, where John Wright was Hannah Visiting
Professor in the History of Medicine in 1992–3.

1

The "affair" at Edinburgh and the "project" at Glasgow: the politics of Hume's attempts to become a professor

ROGER L. EMERSON

In 1744–5, and then seven years later in 1751–2, David Hume sought and failed to get professorships at Scotland's leading universities. He was denied the moral philosophy chair at Edinburgh and then either the logic or moral philosophy post at Glasgow. Both cases were fairly typical appointments where politics, beliefs, merit and felt obligations mingled in ways now difficult to disentangle.

In what Hume called "my Affair at Edinburgh" (NHL 14), he was caught up in a complex political change which would almost certainly have scuppered his chances of employment had this not been done for him by Principal Wishart and the ministers of Edinburgh. In the second case, he attributed his failure to the then Duke of Argyll, who lacked the "courage to give the least countenance" to Hume and his friends (HL I, 164). Argyll and his political followers were involved in both cases but their roles have never been properly appreciated. To set the record a bit straighter is one intention of this essay. Another is to point to some of Hume's political connexions both during the 1740s and 1750s and thereafter.

The first thing one must understand about Scottish university appointments in the eighteenth century is that they were politicized, and that the politicians concerned with them were intent upon controlling every office of profit and honour in the kingdom. The more one controlled, the greater one's prestige, power and ability to manage affairs in ways useful to oneself and one's associates or masters in London. The privilege of managing Scottish affairs for the ministry in London had been sought since c.1714 by two competing Scottish factions – the Squadrone and the Argathelians.[1] Both were Whiggish in outlook, but their territorial bases and leaders were very different.

The Squadrone interest was successively led by the Duke of Montrose (1714–15), the Duke of Roxburgh (1716–25), the Marquis of Tweeddale (c.1740–46). It enlisted the support of the Earls of Aberdeen, Errol, Findlater and Seafield, Crawford, Rothes, Hopetoun, Marchmont, Stair, Viscount Arbuthnot, and other lesser noblemen and lairds. From the gentry came the party's managers, usually advocates with fairly broad acres, like Mungo Graham of Gorthy, Robert Dundas of Arniston, Robert Scott, Andrew (later Sir Andrew) Mitchell of Thirleston, Thomas Hay of Huntington and Robert Craigie of Kilgraston. The members of this faction were united by blood as much as by ideas, and by a lust for office as much as by principle. The Squadrone's geographical base ran from Glasgow and Dunbartonshire in the West through the central belt to the Lothians, Linlithgowshire, Fife and the Borders. It had few Highland adherents, although some individuals around Aberdeen were in this party.[2]

The Argathelian faction was led by John Campbell, second Duke of Argyll, from c.1705 to 1738, when he broke with the Walpole ministry and went into opposition. During those years its principal manager was the Duke's younger brother, Archibald Campbell, Earl of Ilay. He in turn was ably served after 1724 by an Edinburgh lieutenant, Andrew Fletcher, Lord Milton, a judge of the Courts of Session and Justiciary. In 1738, Ilay, who disliked his brother, remained loyal to Walpole's government and continued to manage an Argathelian rump.

After Walpole's fall in 1742, both brothers were again in the government, but Ilay lost the control of the Crown's Scottish patronage and with it the management of much else. In 1743, however, he regained a good deal of unofficial power when his brother died and he inherited the Argyll estates and title. These lands began around Glasgow and extended in a broken way from the Kintyre peninsula to Wester Ross and out to remote Hebridean islands. Argyll was not the only Highland magnate in this connexion; there were other men with northern estates, and more whose lands lay in Perthshire, the central belt, Ayrshire and the Lothians. In easy relation with them were some Jacobite lairds and many talented Whig gentlemen such as Duncan Forbes of Culloden, Charles Erskine of Tinwald, Sir Gilbert Elliot of Minto, and by the 1740s many of the bright young men at the bar like Henry Home of Kames.

The Argathelian ranks also included by the 1740s many of Scotland's most interesting intellectuals. Colin MacLaurin, Robert Simson, most of the learned physicians, and later the Edinburgh literati gathered about David Hume and William Robertson belonged to this connexion. So too did a majority of the kingdom's professors by 1761, when Ilay died. The Squadrone had its intellectuals too – George Turnbull, James Thomson, Tobias Smollett – but they tended to live in London or elsewhere in England. Only Robert Wallace by the 1740s had both a first-rate mind and a Scottish address.

During the period the Argathelians managed government affairs in Scotland, from c.1725 to 1742, Ilay packed the offices of state, the courts, the Kirk and most corporations with men loyal to himself and his brother. When John Hay, fourth Marquis of Tweeddale, replaced him in

1742 as the Crown's chief Scottish agent, he found throughout the kingdom entrenched resistance to his regime. Tweeddale was slow in establishing his network of control. By 1743, however, he had correspondents in most areas of Scotland and in all of its important corporations, including the universities. He tried to organize effective factions in the colleges, but only at St Andrews and at Marischal College in Aberdeen did he achieve substantial control. At Glasgow, vacancies did not occur frequently enough to allow the Squadrone to create a clear majority in the college meeting. Old Argathelians also remained loyal to Ilay, who looked after his Alma Mater.

At Edinburgh, control of the university had to be exercised through the Town Council, which was the legal patron of most of the chairs.[3] Between 1742 and 1745 the Squadrone never managed to wrest the Council from Argathelian hands.[4] It could not, therefore, dominate the university, although it sought to do so. Hume's projected appointment in 1744–5 became another occasion in which the contending factions struggled. This did not much matter in the long run, because the great crisis of the '45 showed Tweeddale and his friends to be less effective, active and clever than Ilay and his. By early 1746, Ilay had returned to power. That he would do so was not altogether obvious in 1745, and Hume's case was one of several in which the Squadrone succeeded for the moment in breaking up an entrenched interest. There were others which deserve notice for what they say about the politics of university appointments.

Both of the Aberdeen universities experienced conflicts between 1733 and 1745 which were stirred up and sustained by outsiders.[5] These allowed politicians to test local support and to try to dominate the colleges which had useful assets – patronage, votes, places and even land or feudal superiorities which might be bought.

At St Andrews, where the Argathelians had almost no faction in the colleges, Thomas Tullideph was picked by Tweeddale as one of his chief advisers on church matters. The reward for this service was a royal chaplaincy and the post of Moderator, which carried a handsome gratuity and bestowed upon its holder the greatest honour in the gift of the Kirk.[6] The unification of the arts colleges, though not achieved until 1747, had been a Squadrone initiative.

At Glasgow, Squadrone and Argathelians supported different candidates for the seven chairs filled between 1740 and 1746.[7] In some cases the aid was covert, but in others – where success was more sure – it was open and victory was claimed. Two of these cases involved men who figure in Hume's candidacy and its failure. Bailie Gavin Hamilton of Edinburgh had helped to secure from the Squadrone leaders Glasgow's regius chair of botany and anatomy for his cousin Robert in 1742.[8] A year later the bailie lobbied on behalf of another relative, William Leechman, who was chosen professor of divinity.[9]

At Edinburgh, Hamilton was to lead the fight against Hume in the Council and Leechman was to aid and abet those who aspersed Hume's morals and religious orthodoxy. Both almost certainly saw themselves as paying off political debts as they helped to defeat Hume's friends. This is not to say that there were no other reasons for opposition to Hume's candidacy held by Hamilton, Leechman or their friend, Francis Hutcheson. It is in the nature of such events to be overdetermined. M. A. Stewart, James Moore and David Raynor have quite rightly pointed to philosophical reasons for opposition to Hume's candidacy, while both Stewart and Richard Sher have found others which might broadly be termed ideological. Like Raynor, J. D. Mackie pointed to irritations of a more personal sort, which could be amplified in Edinburgh because of other personal relationships which Sher has traced. Perhaps Hume would have been better off had he been less critical of Hutcheson's philosophy and had he never called Leechman, Hamilton's relative, a "rank Atheist". What was surely a jesting remark could not have seemed funny once the sermon to which it referred became evidence for those who sought to bar Leechman himself from his Glasgow professorship.[10] Given this record, politicians would and did intervene in Edinburgh University appointments. How they did so was determined by the constitutions of the university and the burgh and by political arrangements in both Scotland and London.

Politicians managed Edinburgh University through the Town Council, and the Council through the elections held each autumn. Because the "set of the burgh",[11] or its constitution, prescribed complex election rules, it was difficult to change the Council's membership radically or quickly. Each year the Council co-opted a few new members. To wrest control from one faction, inducements had to be given to merchants and tradesmen to vote as new political managers wished them to do. Tweeddale in the 1740s lacked the wherewithal to give these. He never had a completely free hand in Scotland, and in 1744 found himself with less disposable patronage than Ilay had had or still had even without the support of the Crown.[12] That partly explains why in 1742, when Ilay was clearly losing power in London, John Coutts, an Argathelian, could win the Lord Provost's place in Edinburgh. He kept it two years and could not be dislodged by Squadrone men. He was followed in 1744 by his friend and protégé, Archibald Stewart. Both were probably more attached to the second Duke than to Ilay, but after 1743 they counted as members of Ilay's party.[13] One compelling bit of evidence for that is the fact that Coutts between 1744–51 was a director of the Royal Bank of Scotland; this, like the British Linen Company (later Bank) in which he also invested, was an adjunct to the Argathelian political machine.[14] Coutts and Stewart knew to whom they belonged and in whose interest they ran the Council and the city. When they picked their friend David Hume for the chair of moral philosophy, everyone who cared would also have known that he was the Argathelian candidate.

In 1744, Hume would also have been seen as potentially the last in a series of men recently helped to chairs by this connexion. Ilay had played no role in those events which can be clearly documented; indeed, he may not have lifted a finger. Did he need to interfere openly, when his friends would pick only people who had the connexion's interest at heart?[15] In only one case in the early 1740s had a Squadrone man clearly been picked. That occurred in February 1745, and involved Kenneth Macken-zie, a relative of Thomas Hay who was Tweeddale's Edinburgh lieutenant. He was nominated by the Faculty of Advocates for the chair of civil law, along with a second candidate who would not serve. The Advocates – more sensitive to political pressures than the merchants and tradesmen – had done "the right thing" and given the councillors Hobson's choice. The Council chose Mackenzie as its professor, but seems to have extracted as its price a large donation to the Edinburgh Workhouse![16]

It is significant that, in the appointment just before Hume's case, the Squadrone candidate had been chosen, but partly out of respect to the Faculty of Advocates which had named him. When Hume was put up as a candidate for the moral philosophy chair, he knew whence his strength came and he undoubtedly knew that Ilay's enemies would be his. He could not, however, expect much help from Ilay that would be direct and open. Hume's reputation as a sceptic would ensure that some Argathelians would find his candidacy difficult to swallow. Among them would be the university's principal, William Wishart, and others outside Edinburgh like Hutcheson. Ilay would not openly care to back Hume against the wishes of useful and prestigious members of his queue. Neither was Hume the sort of person in whom Ilay was likely to show much interest. Tweeddale, on the other hand, could not openly oppose Hume's candida-ture, because it was only too likely, until March of 1745, that Provost Coutts's friend would be elected. If the Marquis were to put his prestige on the line, it would be over a bigger matter than this appointment. Neither patron was to be openly engaged, but Tweeddale's friends worked behind the scenes to defeat Hume, and Tweeddale knew they were doing so.

That Ilay too was also active behind the curtain can be inferred from the actions taken by his clerical adviser, Patrick Cuming, and various members of his party. If that inference is incorrect, it still follows that Ilay's friends believed he would countenance their activities, as he must have done since they extended over many months, and appointments such as this were invariably of interest to Ilay. Did Hume have any claim to better treatment? I think not.

That is clear when one asks about Hume's own personal friendships. His correspondence shows that in 1744 he had friends in both political camps and others who were Jacobites. George Carre of Nisbet was a Squadrone office-holder and the political manager of his family's Berwickshire interests. It was to him that Hume applied when seeking the patronage of the Earls of Haddington and Marchmont in 1739.[17] Both earls had ties to the Squadrone. Hume's oldest friend, William Mure of Caldwell, had ties to Squadrone families, and when he entered the House of Commons in 1742 it was as an opposition Whig.[18] This was his stance in 1746 when Ilay returned to power, and until 1754 Mure was something of an independent in a world which had little use for them. Later, his independence would precipitate a famous quarrel between Ilay and his nephew, the third Earl of Bute, whose affairs in Scotland Mure looked after. One should also remember that, before the denouement of the bid for the chair at Edinburgh, Hume had been employed by Sir James Johnstone of Westerhall on behalf of the Marquis of Annandale. Sir James had opposed Argathelian candidates in Dumfriesshire and had done so with the Annandale influence.[19]

Hume was also friendly with Argathelians who stuck with the second Duke rather than Lord Ilay after 1738. Among these were James Oswald of Dunnikier and Archibald Stewart, whom Ilay in 1746 was not unhappy to see prosecuted for his lame defence of Edinburgh during the '45.[20] The only member of Ilay's party to whom Hume was close in 1744 seems to have been Henry Home of Kames. Kames had cast his lot with the Argathelians by 1732 or so, but only in 1752 would he get his reward, when he put on the gown of a senator of the College of Justice.[21] Only Hume's friendship with Coutts and Stewart gave him a claim to consideration. They were not among Ilay's favourites – and their friend was not the sort of person whom Ilay was known for befriending.

Ilay (now the third Duke) and Lord Milton tended to favour people like themselves – practical improvers, men with technical and technological interests, chemists, botanists, physicians, natural philosophers, mathematicians, scientists, bankers and moderate clerics – people who were sensible and could be trusted to do the reasonable thing.[22] In 1744–5 it is doubtful that Hume would have seemed to them to belong in this category. Certainly, many of his subsequent essays did not suggest that he did. In those, he shared Argyll's and Milton's common interests in banking, economic policy and politics, but distrusted mercantilism, paper money, state direction of economic matters and beggar-your-neighbour policies. There is little reason to believe that Hume did not already hold those opinions. The Duke and Milton did not. They understood politics very well, but they also lacked Hume's interest in liberty and virtue. Hume's 1742 judgement on Sir Robert Walpole as "not virtuous", "not equitable" in engrossing power, and no friend to either "liberty" or "learning" (Ess. 574–6), was likely to have been his judgement on Walpole's friends and servants such as Ilay and Milton.

It is also difficult to think that Hume would have had greater respect for Argyll as an amateur chemist, apothecary, and even quack. Hume was no avid botanist, and certainly no architectural dabbler planning in 1743–4 to build the first great Gothic-revival building in Scotland.[23] Hume might admire patriotism, but the Duke's was designed to protect the Scottish national identity;[24] Hume and his friends aimed at changing that into something which could be called North British and which required assimilation to English polite standards. Neither the Duke nor the philosopher much liked "high-flying" clergymen, but Argyll often had occasion to placate and use those who most threatened Hume's peace and his aspirations. In a city like Edinburgh, Hume's opinions would have been common knowledge among the élite. There is little reason to think that he and Argyll would have gotten on well together in 1744, or that the Duke would have found Hume a man worth protecting if it cost much effort. Hume would be Coutts's or Stewart's problem, a problem largely created by Dr John Pringle's unwillingness to resign.

When Coutts put Hume forward as a candidate for this place in the summer of 1744, he believed Pringle intended to resign and would do so quickly. In fact, Pringle did intend to resign but not that year, and he did not do so until March 1745. What has to be accounted for is his timing and procrastination. There is too little known about this to allow definitive judgements and certain explanations, but one can make surmises about his motives and reasons for doing what he did and when he did it.

Pringle's was a Squadrone family, one which had benefited from patronage secured through this connexion. One of his uncles, Robert Pringle, had been an under-secretary of state, secretary of war, and general factotum to the Duke of Roxburgh and his friends during the 1720s. Other uncles and cousins had judicial jobs gained through the Squadrone party. One relative, Francis, was a professor at St Andrews who had been given the first refusal of an Edinburgh professorship in 1734 when the Squadrone interest was strong enough to secure this.[25] Francis chose to remain at St Andrews, but John Pringle's own professorship was probably obtained in the same way and in the same year.[26]

Pringle had also been a more recent recipient of favour. In 1742 he had gone to war as personal physician to the Earl of Stair. His Lordship, a Squadrone man who had been hated by the second Duke, was the commanding general of the forces in Flanders. He managed to have Pringle made first an army doctor and then, in 1744, Physician-General. This plum gave Pringle a guinea a day while on active service and a life pension of half that sum when retired. His army position would also open up to him a London practice and preferment which led eventually to positions in the Royal Household. There could be few questions about resigning such a position and giving up such prospects to return to the salary and perquisites of an Edinburgh professor. (The professorial salary was £102, which he might have been able to raise by private classes to about £130.) Pringle would resign, but it would make no sense for him to make life easy for his friends' political opponents, among whom must be counted Provost Coutts. The only considerations weighing against the resignation of his Edinburgh post were personal ones. He spoke Scots, felt gauche, and his girlfriend was in Edinburgh. As he wrote to Andrew Mitchell, "I would rather have her ⟨than⟩ the best practice in London".[27] Skilfully protracting negotiations while he sorted out his feelings would allow Squadrone sympathizers on the Council to organize opposition to Coutts's plans and give Tweeddale's friends an opportunity to influence the appointment of a successor. Delay would also benefit those who taught for him, George Muirhead and William Cleghorn, to whom Pringle probably felt under some obligation.

Pringle had further inducements not to hurry his departure. Staying on would irk Principal Wishart, whom Pringle had seen since the autumn of 1742 as the instigator of a campaign to oust him. Since Wishart was an Argathelian, whose party was or seemed to be on the skids, delay would lessen the chance that Wishart would himself obtain the moral philosophy chair which it was clear he wanted.[28] If Pringle wished to play politics with the appointment, then keeping the principal's hopes alive would pit him against Coutts and Hume, thus setting members of Argyll's clique against one another. That might be to the advantage of the Squadrone, as, indeed, it turned out to be.

We do not know if Pringle yet knew Hume personally,[29] but he would almost certainly have known the *Treatise* and the *Essays*, since both touched on subjects which he taught. Probably he disapproved of Hume's metaphysics and epistemology; he may also have found the moral theory too analytical and areligious. Pringle was close to Colin MacLaurin and was likely at this date to have shared his friend's suspicion of sceptics and of those who distrusted rational religion and the Newtonian arguments which upheld it. On the other hand, Pringle admired Shaftesbury and Bacon, and taught a course to which historical facts were not seen as irrelevant.[30] There is no indication that he procrastinated because he objected to Hume's candidacy on principle, or that any personal animus against Hume coloured his calculations.

Pringle may have had another reason to keep the Town Council in suspense. When he was appointed in 1734, the Argathelian Council had subjected him to an unusual form of public trial of his abilities, and special rules governing his conduct as a professor had been prescribed to him.[31] These precluded his devoting much time to medicine, the subject that really interested him. Procrastinating after he had offered to resign embarrassed Provost Coutts and his party. Pringle may have been paying back an old and rankling indignity. For whatever reasons, his actions made political sense. In the long run they benefited his political friends, hurt the Argathelian interest and helped to ensure the selection of one of his deputies, William Cleghorn, as the next incumbent. Pringle was a clever man and quite likely saw the consequences of his actions.

His successor, Cleghorn, belonged to an important academic family whose political allegiances had shifted away from the Argathelian connexion. His maternal grandfather, William Hamilton of Airdrie, had once opposed Argyll but in 1727 had made his peace with the Campbell brothers. By 1730 Ilay had bestowed upon him the Principalship of Edinburgh, a post in which he served until his death in 1733. Hamilton had a large family. Cleghorn's mother married a well-off Edinburgh brewer but one of her sisters did rather better. She married James Balfour of Pilrig. Their son, another James, was to write against David Hume's philosophy and to succeed Cleghorn in the moral philosophy chair in 1754. The principal's son, Robert, in 1744 was a notable cleric, who in 1754 became professor of divinity. Another son, Alexander, emigrated to Annapolis, Maryland and is remembered in American history for his writings. To us, the most interesting of the principal's children is Gavin, who became an Edinburgh publisher and bookseller.[32] In 1744 he was first bailie in Edinburgh, clearly an important man on the Town Council and one who, as we have seen, had secured patronage for relatives in Glasgow. In 1744 he hoped to secure Pringle's place for his nephew. He expected and he got Squadrone support in his efforts, but only as the affair drew to its conclusion.

Hamilton's cause was most helped by that self-interested but Hume-fearing Argathelian, Principal Wishart. By late 1742, Wishart had told some of the councillors that he would like to combine the duties of principal and professor of moral philosophy. Wishart was prepared to give up his Edinburgh church and, therefore, to accept a cut in salary to realize his end. More importantly, doing this would create a vacancy worth more to politicians on the Council who controlled the patronage to the city church livings than the philosophy chair was worth. The principal wished to resume instruction in Latin and he hoped to relate morals more closely to religion. Bailie Hamilton was not the only councillor to know of the plans, but no one in the Council greeted the offer with much interest or favour and Wishart did not push it. Pringle had learned of it through other correspondents by November 1742, but his continuing to employ deputies other than the principal suggests that he had no interest in furthering this backward-looking scheme. By the winter of 1744–5 the principal and Bailie Hamilton had come to an agreement. Wishart would work for the election of the bailie's nephew; but if Cleghorn's candidacy faltered, or if by chance the chair was offered to the principal, he reserved the right to seek it or accept it as God's providential gift.[33]

Wishart's aid to Cleghorn came in two forms. He rallied the Edinburgh clerics to oppose Hume, and it was he and they who presumably (perhaps we should say "providentially") raised "the accusation of Heresy, Deism, Scepticism, Atheism &c." of which Hume complained to his friend Mure of Caldwell (HL I, 57). Wishart's agitation may have extended to Glasgow, since, in the same letter, Hume noted that Hutcheson, whom he had hitherto regarded as a friend, "entertains a bad opinion of my orthodoxy" and is "unwilling that I should be Professor of Ethics in Edinburgh". Just a month earlier, Hutcheson had written to Sir Gilbert Elliot of Minto declining to stand himself as a candidate for the post, but recommending seven young men whom he thought to be more fit than Hume. One was Cleghorn. All were eventually placed in university chairs – three by the Argathelians and at least two by the Squadrone – before Argyll's death in 1761.[34]

Between July 1744 and the election to the chair on 5 June 1745, Hutcheson, his nominees, Hume, Wishart and, at the end of the day, a couple of other men would all be considered as candidates in the field. Hume, Wishart and Cleghorn were only the betting favourites. Hume claimed that during the summer of 1744 the "Authority of all the good Company in Town" vindicated his morals and religious beliefs (HL I, 58). As that discussion went on, two other significant developments were also occurring.

The Duke of Argyll's influence was increasing in Scotland. After the second Duke's death in 1743, the third Duke gathered up his and his brother's supporters and unified the party which had been split since 1738. He also embarked upon the building programme at Inverary. He needed a residence, but this was also an improving project with political dimensions. It meant jobs and money to some Edinburgh craftsmen and it meant favours to be distributed in Glasgow and the West. Exactly the same effects came from the creation by Lord Milton, between 1742 and 1746, of the British Linen Company.[35] Tweeddale and his friends could take no comfort in those developments, and they were shocked at the reception accorded Argyll when he came north during the summer of 1744. In August he held court at Holyroodhouse, where he had a right to reside, and where "great numbers of all ranks (as lord Garlies sayd) clean and unclean" attended his levees. Included among them were the Lord Provost, Coutts, "and some of the Baillies who had not noticed him the last time he was in Scotland". This strengthened Coutts's position and weakened the Squadrone generally. So too did Argyll's ability to secure some Crown patronage for his protégés.[36] Most thought it would not be long before the Scottish political regime would change. That impression was probably deepened by the increasing unrest amongst Jacobites and the rumours about French activity in the Minch and the Highlands.

As Argyll's fortunes rose generally, Provost Coutts's tended to sag after the summer of 1744. He got caught up in a contentious dispute over the filling of an Edinburgh pulpit. Half the parishioners disliked the candidate whom Coutts imposed and the Edinburgh ministers voted to install him by only eight to seven. Many clerics had found reasons to oppose him. That case came to its end in the spring of 1745 as the final vote on Hume's professorship neared. *Le bon David* looked to be a far less eligible candidate by the beginning of April than he had been in the previous autumn.[37]

After months of dithering and silence, Pringle resigned his professorship in March 1745; the Council received his letter of 19 March on the 27th. A week later, it seems to have tried to compromise matters in a way which would satisfy the interests of most parties: it elected Francis Hutcheson as professor of moral philosophy.[38] Hutcheson was an Argathelian; he was pious; he had a splendid reputation; and the Squadrone supporters could not attack this appointment which would exclude Hume. At the same meeting Bailie Hamilton, who presided, asked that the city's ministers be convened to give their *avisamentum* concerning the appointment of Hutcheson. Hamilton may have been doing something a bit tricky by asking for this only after the appointment had been made. He knew the clerics would not object to Hutcheson and that no risk had been run. He may also have known that they would ask the Council hereafter to "order the Ministers' advisamentum to be held prior to any Choice, and that Such advisamentum Should be taken by the whole Councill and not by a Committee, as heretofore has been the practice".[39] (This practice was to be adopted in Hume's case and to work very much to his disadvantage.) The ministers approved of Hutcheson, who was then sent a letter of appointment. He replied to Hamilton on 8 April, noting that his prompt reply was made possible because he "had heard of [the Council's] design some time agoe, and thus had full leisure to consider it". Someone not on Hume's side had clearly been soliciting Hutcheson for days, if not weeks or months, but he would not serve. Being informed of this, the Council produced other names, not recorded in their minutes, for the consideration of the ministers.[40]

While all that was going on, outside the Council chambers the charges against Hume of "Scepticism, Heterodoxy & other hard Names, which confound the ignorant" revived and were clearly doing damage (HL I, 59–60). Hume solicited support from friends who might influence councillors; among them were Lord Elibank and Charles Erskine whom Argyll had recently made a judge. The other side was doing the same thing. Tweeddale's Edinburgh manager, Thomas Hay, wrote the Marquis that letters had gone to old Berwickshire neighbours of Hume asking them to write to wavering councillors. "I hope if Provost Coutts is bafled in these two instances" – the other was a job in a tax office – "it will waken his interest considerably."[41]

The Squadrone agents had come late to this fight, but they recognized that they now had a chance to win and that doing so would be politically important. For that reason, Hay's agent promised his Lordship on 16 April that "no assistance that can be given Baillie Hamilton & his freinds shall be wanting".[42] That clearly had been his policy for some time. It had also worked. By late April, Coutts had found an alternative compromise candidate to Hume, just in case. This was "Mr Law of Elvingston",[43] the son of a former holder of the chair much admired by Principal Wishart. Law was a minor Argathelian politician and a relative of the Squadrone Solicitor-General, Robert Dundas.[44] The prudence of that move must have been apparent by the end of the month. Letters from Berwickshire had swung at least one councillor to Bailie Hamilton's party. By mid-May Thomas Hay was optimistic, although the votes were close. By the end of the month it was reported that Lord Elibank had wooed back to Hume another councillor by getting the man's brother a job in the Navy. The issue was too risky openly to involve Tweeddale. However, Hay did expect the Marquis to agree with a remark indicative of the tenor of Edinburgh debate, that Hume, Coutts, Elibank and their party were "all too wise to enter into the Vulgar mistake of Christianity". They also had at their disposal too much power and largesse, "which will be a great drawback till your Lordship stand on a better footing".[45]

The slippage of Coutts's support and his waning enthusiasm for Hume's candidacy can also be inferred from the decision of the Council to seek the advice of the Edinburgh ministers *before* formally choosing a professor. To seek prior approval for David Hume was to give away the store. At the meeting on 10 April, Coutts's friends did get consideration of the whole matter deferred for some weeks.[46] This allowed Hume, now in England acting as tutor to the Marquis of Annandale, to be consulted. His response is very likely what Henry Home chose to publish as *A letter from a gentleman to his friend in Edinburgh* (NHL 15). It appeared in the fourth week in May, only days before the ministers met to consider Hume's candidacy.[47] The pamphlet did not work. The defence of Hume's morals and orthodoxy did not convince the ministers, who voted him down on 28 May, but it did show how much Hume wanted the professorship. "Twelve of the 15 Ministers of this City", wrote Hay to Tweeddale, "gave their avisamentum against Mr. Hume." Three voted for him: Patrick Cuming, Argyll's adviser on church matters; Alexander Webster, the "high-flying" leader of the Kirk's evangelical wing, and Robert Wallace, the Squadrone's own chief clerical manager.[48] The latter's vote disappointed and angered Hay, who attributed it to evangelical leanings which Wallace did not in fact possess. Hume found Wallace's conduct "noble & generous" (NHL 15).

By 29 May Hume's game was up, even though the Council that day put off its election until 5 June when more of Coutts's party was likely to be present. On 1 June Hume wrote to Henry Home asking that his name be withdrawn from consideration.[49] In effect Coutts had already done this. Again Thomas Hay is interesting.

> And as for Provost Couts, that he may defeat Mr. Cleghorns party at any rate, He has yester night [31 May] offered his interest to Principal Wishart whose friends are now laying themselves out for it & yet it is not many days since the Principal & Mr. Couts were at great variance publickly.[50]

Indeed, according to Hay, Coutts had said in the Council that he thought that some of the ministers who rejected Hume "had never read the pamphlets whence people had taken a bad impression of him". This remark clearly had nettled some of his colleagues. Hume had lost out by the end of May, but Hay was not yet sure that Cleghorn would win. That victory was essential to the Squadrone men, and they continued to seek it.

If the first week in June was unpleasant for Hume, it was equally so for Principal Wishart. The providence of God had led Coutts to support Wishart's pretensions to the chair, but what the ex-provost gave the Lord took away. Wishart, the new Argathelian candidate, seems to have been accused of bad faith by members of the Council who favoured Cleghorn. What was worse, the councillors seem to have ignored Coutts and treated Wishart's candidacy with scorn and disdain. In a long justification to be read to the Council, the principal vindicated his conduct. It was probably unread and unheard.[51] On 6 June, Thomas Hay again reported to Tweeddale. This time he could crow a bit.

> Mr. Cleghorn prevailed over Principal Wishart yesterday by a majority of 6 or 7. Provost Couts thought it necessary for him to move for a delay till Provost Steuarts arrival upon which the Deacon Conveener said with some warmth that he did not understand what the motion meant unless Provost Steuart was to have the absolute direction of the town Council. . . . I fancy Provost Couts's party is broken & after the two late overthrows it may be less difficult to defeat him than it has been hitherto.[52]

By the time Hay finished his letter, political realism had returned – he deplored Tweeddale's inability to find enough patronage and spoils to cement the Squadrone's power. It was a tacit admission of their party's weakness and one which displayed their ineptitude as well as their lack of personal and official resources.

Hume attributed his Edinburgh failure to the accusations of "Heresy, Deism, Scepticism, Atheism, &c." levelled against him. Wishart, his Edinburgh cabal, and Professors Hutcheson and Leechman of Glasgow had activated "the bigotry of the clergy and the credulity of the mob", which in turn affected the jobbing councillors if they did not in fact form part of it (HL I, 56–62). Hume did not criticize Bailie Hamilton or think ill of Cleghorn. They were seeking their own interest and he could hardly fault them for that. Hume was grateful to Coutts and Stewart and he certainly had reason to think well of Argyll. His party had sustained Hume's cause, and their clerical manager, Patrick Cuming, had even voted Hume's fitness as a professor – hardly a popular or politic act, but explicable as an act of party loyalty. It was from Argathelians that Hume had been given support and had found it, even though men like Wishart had been longer in the party.

It is not surprising, therefore, that after 1745 Hume should have become more involved with members of this faction. There are no more friendly letters to Squadrone men, other than to Robert Wallace, in his surviving correspondence. From 1748 on, he began to consult Argathelians about his works and he presented a set of them to Argyll, jokingly remarking that the Duke was in his debt since they were not dedicated to him (HL I, 111–13).[53] In February 1752, Hume complained bitterly when "the Squadrone" tried to exclude him from the Keepership of the Advocates' Library (HL I, 165). Once again he complained against the cry of deism, atheism, etc., as the Squadrone and the bigots "entered into a regular concert and cabal". In later years he and his friends were to ridicule the principal villains, Robert Dundas the elder and younger.[54] The fight for the Edinburgh chair put Hume in Argyll's camp and gave him some grudging respect for the Duke. That made his second academic disappointment at Glasgow in 1752 all the sharper.

Hume's candidacy for the Glasgow chair of logic in 1751–2 was promoted and urged under very different conditions.[55] There most college livings were in the gift of the college corporation. They were filled by the masters afforced by the rector and dean. In 1751–2 there were no private patrons, and no other corporations in the burgh save the Presbytery which could influence elections. The Crown appointed to six of the fourteen chairs. By 1751 Ilay was pretty clearly again in charge of Scottish minor politics. At Glasgow he had chosen or not vetoed eight of the twelve professors who would consider Hume's appointment.[56] Glasgow as Ilay's Alma Mater was also the college whose interests were closest to his heart. Its masters were accustomed to seeking and taking his advice about appointments and they almost always gave him the last word. He had certainly been consulted about the five professors appointed between 1746 and 1752.

But Glasgow was not altogether his bailiwick. The second Duke of Montrose remained its chancellor in 1751–2 and the rector was a Lanarkshire gentleman tied to the Squadrone, Sir John Maxwell of Pollock. Three or four of the professors' loyalties ran in the same direction, including those of Hume's old opponent, William Leechman. This was a divided institution with a minority capable of making trouble. Principal Campbell was something of an evangelical and could not be expected warmly to welcome a man like Hume. Finally, the Glasgow Presbytery exercised the same rights of enquiry into a candidate's morals and orthodoxy which the ministers in Edinburgh had used to scupper Hume's chances. If Hume's friends were to get him elected, they had to find a majority for him in the college, in an electoral body which included the rector, dean, principal and three or four masters whose opposition might be expected.[57] Then they would have to secure the approval of a Presbytery which had intervened in university affairs several times between 1717 and 1743. This was a fairly tall order. It must have been clear early on that it could not be met without considerable political pressure being brought to bear. In the end, Ilay did not wish to struggle over this. The "project" which William Cullen had concocted late in 1751 had failed by 21 January 1752 (HL I, 163).

Argyll's precise role in this case cannot be ascertained. There is no correspondence about Hume's project in Lord Milton's surviving papers, which do contain materials on every other Glasgow appointment from 1745 to 1761 when the third Duke died. Argyll was probably solicited by Hume's friends in London and by others who wrote directly to him.[58] It is unthinkable that he should not have been consulted, since earlier he had been in on the appointment of Adam Smith;[59] Hume certainly believed he had been, and that he had been scared off by "the violent and solemn remonstrances of the clergy" (HL I, 164). On 8 February 1752, four days after Hume wrote that to his friend John Clephane, Cullen reported that the Duke was still pondering Glasgow appointments: "The folkes here [Edinburgh?] who have sollicited the D. of Argyll about our professorships have as yet received no other answer but that he must consult the College before he gives opinion."[60] The plurals indicate that Argyll was thinking of a number of deals involving the chairs of history, oriental languages, logic and moral philosophy. Such complex transactions took time to work out.

Consultations were still continuing when on 29 April the Faculty set 6 May as the date for the selection of a professor of logic.[61] On that date the masters unanimously chose James Clow. His election was almost certainly one dictated by Argyll's political needs. He was placating old enemies because his position in London was not as firm as it was in Scotland.[62] Clow was either the son or a relative of Montrose's former chamberlain and the former tutor of Lord Garlies who controlled two of the towns in the Wigton burgh's district. Clow's election would not ruffle the ministers. It would please Montrose and it gave the college a competent man. The appointments to the other chairs of William Ruat, George Muirhead and Adam Smith would not be questioned, and the college would be less divided than if Hume had been chosen.

Hume would have understood all this very clearly. That he did so is suggested by a comment which he made to Adam Smith in 1759. He reported that Ilay, to whom he had just conveyed Smith's gift of *The theory of moral sentiments*, "is more decisive than he uses to be in its favour. I suppose he either considers it as an exotic" – a plant – "or thinks the author will be serviceable to him in the Glasgow elections" (HL I, 305). The remark is slighting and humorous, but it also suggests that the Duke's realism had been learned, if not appreciated, by a somewhat naive and idealistic philosopher.

Hume's "affair" and "project" shed light on his career in several ways. They show him by 1744 to be clearly involved with the Argathelian party in Scotland, the party to which he looked for patronage in 1751–2 and from which he secured it in the latter year. By about that time this was also becoming the party of the Moderates and of the Edinburgh literati whom Hume was to amuse and lead until his death in 1776. Argyll's political allies and friends in London included General James St Clair under whom Hume served during 1746–9, Lord Hertford under whom Hume acted in France, and General Henry Seymour Conway (Hertford's brother) who made Hume under-secretary of state. The latter was married to a daughter of the fourth Duke whom Hume probably visited in his years of retirement in Scotland (HL II, 361–2). By 1746, certainly by 1752, he seems to have learned that the patronage this connexion could dispense to him was not academic, but military and civil.

Hume's efforts to become a professor should also make us ask again what his own religious position really was. To qualify for either post Hume would have had to sign the Westminster Confession, and at Glasgow lead his students in prayers. His attendance at church would have been expected or required. Had his backers not thought that he could have fulfilled these parts of the jobs they hoped to secure for him, they could hardly have put him forward. They knew him at least as well as we do and believed him religious enough to become a professor. So too did Robert Wallace and Alexander Webster, who had no political motives to vote for him in the company of Edinburgh ministers. Their actions may have given Hume a better opinion of some clerics, just as these affairs may have increased the realism with which he approached historical and political topics. Finally, both attempts to become a professor show the limits of toleration in Scotland of a man such as Hume was. Argyll, who had done so much to promote enlightenment in Scotland, could not in 1752 advance such a man in the universities, but, outside them, his party could and did protect Hume and foster his career.

NOTES

1. The nature of Scottish university politics is discussed at length in R. L. Emerson, *Professors, patronage and politics: The Aberdeen universities in the eighteenth century* (Aberdeen 1992).
2. The best accounts of the Argathelians and the Squadrone during these years are in J. S. Shaw, *The management of Scottish society, 1707–1764* (Edinburgh 1983), and A. Murdoch, *The people above* (Edinburgh 1980).
3. The University of Edinburgh was a less independent corporation than has usually been imagined by its historians. For an account of the placement of its medical professors, see R. L. Emerson, 'Medical men, politicians and the medical schools at Glasgow and Edinburgh, 1685–1830', in *William Cullen and the eighteenth-century medical world*, ed. R. Passmore and others (Edinburgh 1992), 190–219.
4. *The House of Commons, 1715–1754*, 2 vols, ed. R. R. Sedgwick (London 1970), I, pp. 398–9; II, p. 447; *The lord provosts of Edinburgh, 1296 to 1932*, ed. T. B. Whitson (Edinburgh 1932), pp. 68–70.
5. Emerson, *Professors*, pp. 59–70.
6. Tullideph was the choice of Robert Craigie of Glendoick, the Lord Advocate and MP for Wick (Thomas Hay to Tweeddale, 8 May 1742; Tullideph to Tweeddale, 9 June 1744: NLS, MSS 7047, fo. 18; 7062, fo. 89).
7. R. L. Emerson, 'Politics and the Glasgow professors, 1690–1800', in *The Glasgow Enlightenment*, ed. A. Hook and R. B. Sher (Edinburgh 1994), ch. 1.
8. Gavin Hamilton and probably his brother, William, were described to Tweeddale as men "who both behave very well" and who might "deserve some regard in the competition" for the Glasgow chair of anatomy. Later it was the bailie "who negotiates for his cousin" who was described as a friend (Robert Dundas to Tweeddale, 15 April 1742; Hay to Tweeddale, 1 May 1742: NLS, MSS 7046, fo. 61; 7047, fo. 3).
9. Leechman's appointment in 1743 was not strictly a party matter: both Argathelians and Squadrone divided along religious lines. The Moderates, who favoured Leechman, were led by Francis Hutcheson, while the Evangelicals, whose candidate was John MacLaurin, were marshalled by Principal Campbell. Leechman himself sought the support of the Duke of Montrose who was a Squadrone supporter and chancellor of the university, of Tweeddale and his aide, Andrew Mitchell MP, and of Hume's friend, William Mure MP, who was no Argathelian and can probably be described as an independent. MacLaurin's backers at Glasgow sought help from Argyll. (Hay to Tweeddale, 26 and 29 November 1743; Archibald Campbell of Succoth to Lord Milton, December 1743: NLS, MSS 7059, fos 62, 70; 16591, fo. 199.)
   It is not known if Argyll intervened; Tweeddale did not do so directly, perhaps because the election "seems to be made a matter of conscience". There is no question but what the Squadrone men had opposed MacLaurin because of

his involvement in the "Cambuslang wark" (1743). The previous election in 1740 had also split the masters, but at that time Argyll had probably supported MacLaurin (Principal Campbell and Profs Johnstone, Dick and Rosse to Lord Milton, 1740: NLS, MS 16582, fo. 51). In the two elections the parties divided as follows:

	1740	1743
Neil Campbell, Principal	MacLaurin	MacLaurin
William Anderson, Ecclesiastical history	Potter	MacLaurin
Charles Morthland, Oriental languages	?	Leechman
George Rosse, Humanity	MacLaurin	Leechman
Alexander Dunlop, Greek	?	Leechman
John Loudoun, Logic	Potter	MacLaurin
Francis Hutcheson, Moral philosophy	Potter	Leechman
Robert Dick, Natural philosophy	MacLaurin	MacLaurin
Robert Simson, Mathematics	Potter	Leechman
William Forbes, Law	MacLaurin	MacLaurin
Thomas Brisbane, Anatomy	?	———
Robert Hamilton, Anatomy	———	Leechman
John Johnstone, Medicine	MacLaurin	MacLaurin
John Graham of Dougalston, Rector	Potter	———
George Bogle of Daldowie, Rector	———	Leechman

Those whose names have been italicized were Squadrone appointees or normally allied themselves with that party.

10. HL I, 32–52; NHL 10–14; M. A. Stewart, *Warmth in the cause of virtue* (forthcoming); R. B. Sher, 'Professors of virtue', in *Studies in the philosophy of the Scottish Enlightenment*, ed. M. A. Stewart (Oxford 1990), at pp. 105–14; J. Moore, 'Hume and Hutcheson', this volume; D. R. Raynor, private correspondence and unpublished papers; J. D. Mackie, *The University of Glasgow, 1451 to 1951* (Glasgow 1954), p. 202.

11. *Set of the city of Edinburgh with the acts of Parliament and Council relative thereto* (1783).

12. Shaw, pp. 58–85, 158–63.

13. Stewart entered the House of Commons in 1741 as a member of "the Duke of Argyll's Gang", the MPs loyal to the Duke but not to his brother or to Walpole's ministry (Sedgwick, I, p. 447).

14. N. Munro, *History of the Royal Bank of Scotland, 1727–1927* (Edinburgh 1928), p. 399; NLS, MS SB350. Coutts in 1744 held shares in the Edinburgh Linen Co-partnery, which Lord Milton (Deputy Governor of the Royal Bank) in that year undertook to expand into a national company whose patronage power would lie outside the influence of the Squadrone politicians (S. G. Checkland, *Scottish banking: A history, 1695–1973* (Glasgow 1975), pp. 94–6). By 1746 Coutts was a director of the British Linen Bank, a place he held until his death in 1750 (C. A. Malcolm, *History of the British Linen Bank* (Edinburgh 1950), p. 209). Neither he nor Stewart seems to have been a stockholder in the Bank of Scotland, a bank scarcely half the size of the Royal Bank at that time (SRO, GD 18/5881–2; Checkland, pp. 68–9, 84–5).

15. Those placed at the university from 1732 to 1744 with the approval of the Argathelians included James Smith, John Gowdie, William Kirkpatrick,

George Abercrombie, John Erskine, William Wishart II and Patrick Cuming. That Ilay's friends were active is clear from Lord Milton's correspondence: NLS, MSS 16568, fo. 180; 16564, fos 90–98; 16571, fo. 123; R. Wodrow, *Analecta* (Edinburgh 1842–3), IV, pp. 96, 104, 138; A. Grant, *Story of the University of Edinburgh* (London 1884), II, pp. 314–15. In another six cases candidates were picked by private patrons, with whose rights Ilay did not normally interfere, or by professors in whose choices he probably acquiesced. There may have been great reluctance to appoint John Pringle in 1738 and John Stewart in 1742, at least in part because their families had opposed the Argathelians in the past.

16. Hay to Tweeddale, 19 February 1745: NLS, MS 7065, fo. 77. Hay thought that this would not have happened had the Faculty of Advocates, whose right it was to present a short list, and the professors involved acted differently.

17. HL I, 36; Shaw, pp. 48, 54.

18. His wife was the daughter of James Graham of Easdale; his old tutor, William Leechman, came from a family dependent upon the Baillies of Jarviswood, themselves related to the Earls of Marchmont and the Marquis of Annandale (Sedgwick, I, pp. 427–8; II, pp. 282–3).

19. Sedgwick, II, pp. 181 (Mure), 314–15, 447 (Johnstone).

20. Hugo Arnot, *History of Edinburgh* (1789), p. 223. Stewart was Lord Provost in 1745 and Hume wrote a pamphlet in his defence.

21. R. L. Emerson, 'Henry Home, Lord Kames' in *Dictionary of literary biography*, CIV, ed. D. T. Siebert (Detroit 1991).

22. Emerson, 'Medical men', p. 199.

23. On the Duke as builder, see I. G. Lindsay and M. Cosh, *Inverary and the dukes of Argyll* (Edinburgh 1973). Hume thought the Goths "inferior to the Romans, in taste and science", and probably found Inverary Castle too ornate, even disgusting (Ess. 98, 192–3).

24. The cases for this viewpoint with regard to Argyll and Lord Milton have been made by Murdoch and Shaw.

25. The unsolicited offer was made to Francis Pringle some time before 30 March 1734, on which date he replied to those who made it – an *ad hoc* committee drawn from the Council, the Court of Session, the Faculty of Advocates and the Society of Writers to the Signet. He thanked particularly David Scott of Scotstarvit, an opposition MP in 1741, and Walter Pringle, Lord Newhall, who may have been his brother and was certainly a Squadrone man. The delegate of the Faculty of Advocates was Robert Dundas, who belonged to the same connexion. So too did Walter Pringle of Torsonce, whom he also thanked. Three other Pringles then belonged to the Faculty and at least one to the Society of Writers. The period 1733–4 was one in which Scottish opposition to Walpole was at a height and effective. The humanity chair at Edinburgh when Francis Pringle turned it down went to John Ker, another Squadrone man. (Commonplace book of Francis Pringle, St Andrews University Archives; Shaw, p. 61; *Minute book of the Faculty of Advocates*, ed. J. M. Pinkerton (Edinburgh 1980), II, p. 148; *The Faculty of Advocates in Scotland, 1932–1943*, ed. F. J. Grant (Edinburgh 1944), pp. 173–5; *Records of the Baron Court of Stichill, 1655–1807*, ed. G. and C. B. Gunn (Edinburgh 1905), pp. 231–2.)

26. The special rules imposed on Dr Pringle when he came to his chair should be seen in the context of party fights (EUL, College Minutes, 10 January, 19–25 February 1734).

20 *Hume and Hume's connexions*

27. S. X. Radbill, 'John Pringle', in *Dictionary of scientific biography*, ed. C. C. Gillispie (New York 1970–80); Pringle to Mitchell, 6 July 1743: British Library, Add. MS 6861, fo. 192. I owe the latter reference to M. A. Stewart.
28. Pringle to Mitchell, 18 November 1742: British Library, Add. MS 6861, fo. 172; Wishart, shorthand 'Letter or speech, intended . . . June 5 1745': EUL, MS La. II/115. I owe these references and a transcription of Wishart's shorthand to M. A. Stewart.
29. Pringle helped found the Philosophical Society in 1737 and Hume was certainly a member by c.1750 (R. L. Emerson, 'The Philosophical Society of Edinburgh, 1748–1768', *British journal for the history of science* 14 (1981), 143–8). Robert Wallace's paper on population was delivered to the society before 1745 and subsequently expanded into a book-length exposition which Hume in 1751 said Wallace "was pleas'd lately to communicate" to him (NHL 29). If Hume was a member of the Society earlier he might have heard or read the paper and still have written what he wrote about the book.
30. John Pringle, 'Lectures from Cicero': EUL, MS Gen. 74D; *id.*, *Six discourses*, with Life by Andrew Kippis (London 1783), pp. vii, lxviii, lxxxi; [Robert Henderson], 'Short account of the University of Edinburgh', *Scots magazine* 3 (1741), p. 373.
31. See n. 26.
32. Sher, pp. 106–12.
33. Wishart, 'Letter or speech'.
34. Francis Hutcheson to Gilbert Elliot, Lord Minto, 4 July 1744: NLS, MS 11004, fo. 57. This letter allows one to infer that Elliot had tried to induce Hutcheson to accept the chair. The persons named as fit candidates were: Thomas Craigie, then professor of Hebrew (1741) at St Andrews and later professor of moral philosophy (1746) at Glasgow; Robert Trail, later professor of oriental languages (1761) and divinity (1761) at Glasgow; Robert Pollock, later professor of divinity (1745) and principal at Marischal College; William Ruat [or Rouet], later professor of oriental languages (1745) and ecclesiastical history (1752) at Glasgow; James Moor, later professor of Greek (1746) at Glasgow; William Cleghorn; and George Muirhead, later professor of oriental languages (1752) and humanity (1754) at Glasgow. Craigie, Trail and Cleghorn had support from Squadrone politicians, while Pollock, Ruat and Muirhead at some time served patrons belonging to the Squadrone faction. Muirhead had also served as Pringle's deputy at Edinburgh.
35. Shaw, pp. 155–63.
36. John Inglis to Tweeddale, 3 August 1744; Argyll to Tweeddale, September 1744; Robert Dundas to Tweeddale, 20 November 1744: NLS, MSS 7063, fos 72, 147; 7064, fo. 89. Argyll was able to name officers in the Independent Highland Companies and got a judge's gown for Charles Erskine.
37. Alexander Arbuthnott to Tweeddale, 16 April 1745: NLS, MS 7065, fo. 157. The procedure for selecting Edinburgh ministers is given by R. B. Sher, 'Moderates, managers and popular politics in mid-eighteenth century Edinburgh', in *New perspectives on the politics and culture of early modern Scotland*, ed. J. Dwyer and others (Edinburgh 1982), at pp. 180–83.
38. Council minutes, 3 April 1745.
39. Council minutes, 10 April 1745.
40. Council minutes, 10 April 1745.
41. Hay to Tweeddale, 23 and 30 April 1745: NLS, MS 7065, fos 168, 181.
42. See n. 37.

43. Hay to Tweeddale, 23 April 1745: NLS, MS 7065, fo. 168.
44. *Ibid.* In 1755 Law became sheriff-substitute in Haddington (Grant, p. 121).
45. Arbuthnott to Tweeddale, 30 April 1745; Hay to Tweeddale, 30 April 1745, 26 June 1745, 6 June 1745: NLS, MSS 7065, fos 180, 181; 7066, fos 71, 115.
46. Council minutes, 10 April 1745.
47. *Edinburgh evening courant*, 21 May 1745; Council minutes, 22 May 1745.
48. Hay to Tweeddale, 1 June 1745: NLS, MS 7066, fo. 85.
49. Hume also had sent a letter to Provost Stewart, probably before the end of May, announcing his intention of remaining with the Marquis, "but, unluckily, before my friends in Edinburgh could be inform'd of my resolutions, the matter was brought to an issue, and by the cabals of the Principal, the bigotry of the clergy, and the credulity of the mob, we lost it" (HL I, 62; cf. NHL 15).
50. See n. 48.
51. Wishart, 'Letter or speech'.
52. Hay to Tweeddale, 6 June 1745: NLS, MS 7066, fo. 115. There were thirty-three on the Council if all attended. The "two overthrows" were the defeats of Hume and Wishart.
53. In this letter to Charles Erskine, Lord Tinwald, dated 13 February 1748, Hume said that his works were not for "the Duke of Argyle", but for "Archibald Campbell, who is undoubtedly a Man of Sense & Learning" and not merely a political figure to be flattered. See also 'Memorandum about a dedication to Mr John Home', 21 January 1757: NLS, MS 16700, fo. 189, which shows Lord Milton was consulted over the proposed dedication of Hume's *Four dissertations*.
54. The Hume candidacy was part of the background to the casting in 1760 of Robert Dundas as Bumbo in *Sister Peg*, a pamphlet probably written by Adam Ferguson, with perhaps some input from other of Hume's friends.
55. J. Coutts, *History of the University of Glasgow* (Glasgow 1909), p. 312. There is no very hard evidence that Hume's friends were seeking to put him in the logic chair, but that was a likelier posting than the more sensitive chair of moral philosophy. The latter was held by Thomas Craigie who was known to be dying. Adam Smith had held the logic chair since January 1751 but Craigie seems to have favoured him as his own successor.
56. Emerson, 'Politics'.
57. Those who could be expected to oppose Hume's appointment were the Duke of Montrose (Chancellor), Sir John Maxwell (Rector), Principal Campbell, William Leechman (dean of faculty and professor of divinity), William Anderson (professor of ecclesiastical history), and perhaps Robert Hamilton (professor of anatomy and botany). In Argyll's party one could count William Ruat (oriental languages), George Rosse (humanist – but also inclined to the evangelicals), James Moor (Greek), Adam Smith (logic), Robert Dick (natural philosophy), Robert Simson (mathematics), perhaps Hercules Lindsay (law), and William Cullen (medicine).
58. Gilbert Elliot of Minto is likely to have been involved in this business. Cf. Smith to Cullen, November 1751, in *Correspondence of Adam Smith*, ed. E. C. Mossner and I. S. Ross (Oxford 1977), pp. 5–6; J. Thomson, *Account of the life, letters and writings of William Cullen*, 2 vols (Edinburgh 1859; 1st edn 1832), I, p. 606.
59. Draft, William Cullen to [Adam Smith?], n.d. (1751–2): GUL, MS 2255/11.
60. Cullen to Robert Simson, 8 February 1752: GUA, MS 26223. There is much

evidence in the papers of Lord Milton, Simson, Cullen and others which supports the view that Argyll had in mind complex changes which Hume's appointment would have complicated.

61. GUA, Faculty Minutes, 29 April, 6 May 1752.
62. Shaw, pp. 177–8; S. Bricke, 'The Pelhams vs. Argyll', *Scottish historical review* 61 (1982), 157–65.

2

Hume and Hutcheson

JAMES MOORE

I. A QUESTION OF INFLUENCE

In the opinion of many distinguished historians of philosophy in the past half-century, the most important formative influence upon the moral philosophy of David Hume, and perhaps on Hume's philosophy as a whole, was the work of his senior contemporary, Francis Hutcheson. This scholarly opinion derives in large part from the work of Norman Kemp Smith, who in 1941 argued that "Hume, under the Influence of Hutcheson, entered into his Philosophy through the Gateway of Morals".[1] On Kemp Smith's account, the inspiration for Hume's philosophy may be traced to an insight which he drew from Hutcheson's writings very early in life. It was that virtue and vice are perceived not by reason but by feeling or sentiment, that moral judgements are made by the instinctive, not the cogitative or rational parts of our nature. Hume took up this Hutchesonian theme and applied it not just to moral judgements, but to all judgements of matter of fact and existence, to all subjects of belief as distinct from knowledge. In extrapolating Hutcheson's naturalistic theory of morals to the understanding, Hume carried Hutcheson's teaching much farther than Hutcheson himself would have allowed. But despite the more radical uses which Hume made of Hutcheson's ideas – to address problems of belief in causal connexions, in the continuity of the external world and the self – Hume remained faithful to Hutcheson's naturalism, particularly in ethics. Hume's moral philosophy was the least original and, perhaps for this reason, the most stable part of his philosophy.[2]

Others have interpreted the achievements of the two philosophers differently, without doubting that Hutcheson's writings provided the source of what was most distinctive in the moral philosophy of Hume. David Raphael has described Hume as "Hutcheson's friend and spiritual son in moral theory".[3] His construction of the relationship between Hutcheson and Hume appears to have been worked out independently of Kemp Smith's interpretation. Raphael took them to have been empiricists in morals, committed to the view that moral distinctions are perceived by an internal sense analogous to the external senses and especially to aesthetic sensibility. He noted the many arguments against rationalist philosophers like Samuel Clarke which Hume appeared to have learned from the writings of Hutcheson. He has more recently indicated that he subscribes to Kemp Smith's account of the origins of Hume's philosophy.[4]

Arthur Prior took an even stronger position: "There is little or nothing in Hume's moral philosophy that cannot be traced to Hutcheson, but in Hume it is all more clear and pointed."[5] Both, in Prior's view, were early critics of the naturalistic fallacy in ethics. They recognized that judgements concerning right and wrong, virtue and vice, cannot be derived from judgements concerning truth and falsehood. They understood the autonomy of moral discourse: that propositions which contain an 'ought' can only be derived from others which contain an 'ought'. This was the compelling consideration which led them to conclude that moral judgements and distinctions must be made by a moral sense.

More recently, David Norton has advanced a different understanding of Hume's indebtedness. He has challenged the naturalist and empiricist readings of Hutcheson's and Hume's moral theories, arguing that Hutcheson was a realist in his moral theory. And, "making allowances for differences of terminology and emphasis", it was a version of this moral realism that Hume made the distinguishing feature of his moral philosophy.[6] Both philosophers, in Norton's view, held a theory of moral perception in which sensible ideas of actions bring before the mind other ideas of qualities of character, of virtue and vice, which represent an external or objective world. Hutcheson called these "concomitant ideas"; he used the term to refer to primary qualities, to extension, duration, number, and sometimes also, although more rarely, to ideas of virtue and vice. Hume did not use the same term; but, Norton argues, he subscribed to something like this realist moral epistemology. When we observe or contemplate a person's character, we experience feelings of moral pleasure or moral pain, and these signify or represent real qualities, virtues or vices, in the character we have before our minds.[7] Thus, Norton concludes, Hume was indeed influenced by Hutcheson: it is merely the nature of that influence which has been misunderstood. Although he was a sceptic in metaphysics, Hume remained, in his moral philosophy, a common-sense moralist, allied, with Hutcheson, in the refutation of Hobbes, Mandeville and other sceptics.

We find, then, a consensus, based, to be sure, on different lines of reasoning, that Hutcheson exercised a formative and lasting influence upon Hume's thinking and writing. But notwithstanding the weight of scholarly opinion in support of this reading, there are other considerations which give one grounds for scepticism. Hutcheson's initial response to the philosophy outlined in Hume's draft of Book III of the *Treatise* was generally and deeply disapproving. His many reservations about Hume's work may be gleaned from Hume's letter to Hutcheson of 17 September 1739. Hume expressed his disappointment that Hutcheson should have reacted so negatively to his treatment of morals (HL I, 32–5). He defended his very different understanding of the role of the moral philosopher; his appreciation of the kinds of questions it was appropriate to ask in moral philosophy; his theory of justice; his inclusion of natural abilities among the virtues. The differences between them, in the minds of both philosophers, were neither few nor insignificant.

Secondly, it has been observed by many of the same scholars who think that Hume's moral philosophy was originally or fundamentally Hutchesonian, that Hume also appears to have been a Hobbist in various aspects of his moral philosophy,[8] an orientation which is not easily reconciled with his alleged attachment to the views of Hutcheson.

Thirdly, it is odd that Hutcheson should have vigorously opposed Hume's attempts to secure an appointment as a professor of moral philosophy in Edinburgh, if he considered Hume an ally or follower in moral philosophy. It must be said that Hume himself found Hutcheson's behaviour extraordinary at this juncture; he thought that whatever philosophical differences might pertain between Hutcheson and himself, the senior philosopher ought to have the candour to respect his qualifications and his ability for the position (HL I, 58).

Finally, there is the circumstance that Hume's contemporaries – James Balfour, Adam Smith, Thomas Reid, Adam Ferguson – considered his views in moral philosophy to be basically different from Hutcheson's. The same opinion prevailed among scholars in the nineteenth century. The tendency to align and elide their work together may derive from our own preoccupations in moral philosophy (with naturalism, intuitionism as opposed to empiricism, the naturalistic fallacy, moral realism); and these may not have been the questions which were of first importance to Hutcheson or Hume. I shall argue that their moral philosophies were indeed very different in origin and inspiration, that in crucial respects their views on moral subjects were directly opposed.

II. THE LETTER TO A PHYSICIAN

Commentators conventionally begin their interpretations of Hume's moral philosophy with his own account of its origins, in his letter to a physician of 1734; Kemp Smith, in particular, thought this contained evidence of Hume's indebtedness to Hutcheson.[9] I submit that it reveals two important and enduring features of Hume's moral philosophy which were not prompted or inspired by Hutcheson. In both cases, Hume's ideas would prove to be opposed to the ideas of the older philosopher.

First, Hume told the physician how he had undermined his mental health by attempting to mould his character in accordance with the moral ideas of the ancient Stoics:

> being smit with their beautiful Representations of Virtue & Philosophy . . . I was continually fortifying myself with Reflections against Death, & Poverty, & Shame, & Pain, & all the other Calamities of Life. (HL I, 14)

This exercise "contributed more than anything to waste my Spirits". It also left him profoundly sceptical of the ideas of virtue and vice found in the writings of the Stoics. Hume mentions that he had been reading Cicero, Seneca and Plutarch. Seneca and Plutarch were unambiguously Stoic in their morals. Cicero was an eclectic; his compositions drew upon different schools of moral philosophy which he represented by different spokesmen in his dialogues. Hume was to adopt many of Cicero's arguments, particularly those ideas of virtue and vice which Cicero drew from the teachings of the Epicureans and Sceptics. Some of Hume's most notable differences with Hutcheson turned upon their different readings of Cicero. Hutcheson, it should be added, took Cicero to have been a Stoic, and preferred those works of Cicero's in which the Stoics had the better of the argument.

Secondly, Hume told the physician that, once his health had improved, he was able to recognize more precisely what he had found unsatisfactory in the writings of the ancient moralists.

> I found that the moral Philosophy transmitted to us by Antiquity, labor'd under the same Inconvenience that has been found in their natural Philosophy, of being entirely Hypothetical, and depending more upon Invention than Experience. Every one consulted his Fancy in erecting Schemes of Virtue & of Happiness, without regarding human Nature, upon which every moral Conclusion must depend. This therefore I resolved to make my principal Study, & the Source from which I would derive every Truth in Criticism as well as Morality. (HL I, 16)

This points to the principal contribution Hume thought he could make to moral philosophy. Unlike Hutcheson, who thought that ancient moralists, most notably the Stoics, had discovered the distinction between virtue and vice, Hume thought the ideas of virtue and happiness conceived by all the ancient sects were merely hypothetical or fanciful, like their ideas of the natural or physical world. In making his own moral distinctions, Hume would insist that moral ideas must be based upon experience. His "principal Study" would be "human Nature, on which every moral Conclusion must depend". The language of this part of the letter clearly prefigures the title and subtitle of the work which issued from this project: *A treatise of human nature: Being an attempt to introduce the experimental method of reasoning into moral subjects.*

This was the origin or inspiration of Hume's moral philosophy. It was an attempt to revise or reduce the insights of the moral philosophers of antiquity to an experimental science of morals. In effecting this revision or reduction, Hume drew upon or appropriated or took over the insights of a particular tradition of moral philosophy. This was the tradition of the Epicureans, a tradition of moral philosophy revived particularly by French writers of the seventeenth and eighteenth centuries.

III. THE EPICUREAN TRADITION IN MORALS

There were at least two distinct Epicurean traditions in morals available to Hume. One was the frivolous, popular tradition in which Epicureans were perceived to be lovers of sensuous pleasure: the tradition represented by the character of the Franklin in the *Canterbury tales,* who

> lived for pleasure and had always done,
> For he was Epicurus' very son,
> In whose opinion sensual delight
> Was the one true felicity in sight. (tr. Coghill)

This tradition was for the most part a fiction, a caricature, a product of the critical imagination of Stoic and Augustinian opponents of Epicurus and his school.[10]

In opposition to this construction, a more authentic or faithful reading of the great Epicurean moralists of antiquity – Epicurus himself, Lucretius, Horace – had been rendered in the seventeenth century by Gassendi, by St Evremond, by the Baron des Coustures and, in his own very singular way, by Hobbes. This tradition, the substantive tradition of Epicurean morals, was adapted by Pierre Bayle and became identified, no doubt because of its association with the work of Bayle, as the morality of the sceptics or the Pyrrhonians in the early eighteenth century.[11] The principal topics and themes developed by Hume in Parts II and III of Book III of the *Treatise* derive from this tradition: (a) the distinction between justice and the natural virtues; (b) the state of nature; (c) the convention to abstain from the possessions of others; (d) the argument that virtues are approved because of their usefulness and agreeableness; (e) the idea that sympathy reinforces our approval of qualities which are useful and agreeable.

Let us turn first to the distinction between justice and the natural virtues. Horace made this distinction very clearly in his Epicurean satires on the teachings of the Stoics:

> Nature alone is incapable of distinguishing what is just and what is not, in the same way that natural instinct acquaints us with what is good and what is bad.[12]

Cicero represented the distinction between justice and the natural virtues in the discourses of Torquatus, the Epicurean spokesman in *De finibus*

bonorum et malorum. While some virtues (wisdom, fortitude, temperance)
are always a source of pleasure, the same is not the case with justice. The
"insatiable desire of some Men after Riches, Luxury, Honour, Dominion"
is such that

> nothing but a severe Punishment inflicted on them by the Laws is
> able to stop their Career. True Reason therefore directs all Men of
> Sound Judgement to observe the rules of Justice, Equity and Fidelity,
> which are the best means to procure to ourselves the good Esteem
> and Love of others, which is absolutely necessary to render our lives
> Pleasant and Sedate.[13]

St Evremond consistently distinguished between justice and the natural
virtues. He observed that, whereas justice is absolutely necessary for the
institution and preservation of society, people have little inclination to
act from this principle. There is always an agreeable motive to act out of
kindness, generosity, liberality, friendship. Justice, which is indispensable
for social life, is none the less an annoyance; only necessity obliges us to
act justly.[14] It was among the most important insights of Epicurus, St
Evremond thought, that he insisted upon this difference between justice
and the natural virtues.[15]

Secondly, Hume's account of the state of nature, as a condition in
which human nature is severely disadvantaged in comparison with the
easier, more felicitous condition of animals, was a persistent refrain in
the philosophy of Epicurus and his followers. Epicurus "seem'd to be
prepossessed in favour of Brutes on the score of their easier way of
Living".[16] Lucretius, Horace, Diodorus all depicted the natural state
of mankind as one of inferiority to the animal world.[17] Cicero thought
the same, Gassendi recalled,[18] and the same passage is later reproduced
by Hume to show that Hobbes was not the first moralist to take a
bleak view of the natural condition of mankind without society (E
189–90).

Thirdly, it was the view of Epicurus and of his followers, including
Hume, that society originated in a convention to leave everyone in possession of his things.

> This then was the first Knot or Tie of Societies, which as it supposed
> that every Person might have something belonging to him, or what
> he might call his own, either because he was the first possessor of it,
> or because it was given him, or because he had it by way of exchange,
> or because he acquired it by his Industry; I say, this was the first
> Knot which confirmed to every private Person the possession of that
> which he thus challenged as his own.[19]

This was the origin of society. It also marked the origin of property and
justice. In the absence of this agreement among men to abstain from the
things of others, there would be neither justice nor injustice. Again, this

was the view of Cicero;[20] and among modern moralists, it was the opinion of Gassendi (reflecting the ideas of Epicurus) and of Bayle:

> the love of tranquillity, and diffidence, led men soon to this mutual convention, that each would be content with what he had occupied, and this was the origin of thine and mine.[21]

Fourthly, Epicurean moralists perceived the virtue of justice to be derived from nothing but its utility. "Justice is nothing in itself", Epicurus said. "Mankind, united in Society, discovered the Utility and Advantage of agreeing among themselves." "Epicurus was much in the right", added the Baron des Coustures, "when he asserted that it was Society that first discover'd the Utility of Laws."[22] "Cicero treats excellently upon this subject", said Gassendi, noting the passage in *De officiis* where Cicero asserts that

> there is nothing truly useful but what is Just and Honest, and nothing Just and Honest but what is truly useful; these are reciprocal, and whoever endeavours to separate 'em offers at the most pernicious thing that can befall human life.[23]

Finally, Epicurus and his followers observed that, once the laws had curbed and regulated differences of temperament, it was possible for some, at least, to live in sympathy with one another. The Baron des Coustures continues his reflection:

> He [Epicurus] therefore extols the happiness of those, who, either by Nature, or by the Precepts of Wisdom, have found themselves disposed to an *harmonious Sympathy*; and who have observ'd that certain Medium that could fix their Tempers and unite their Minds, by which means they found out the Secret of living peaceably and agreeably.[24]

Thus much of Hume's account of justice and the natural virtues in Book III of the *Treatise* may be traced to his reading of moral philosophers, ancient and modern, in the Epicurean tradition. Hume's originality as a moral philosopher did not consist in the invention of such principles of morals as utility and agreeableness, the convention to abstain from the possessions of others, sympathy with other proprietors, etc. His contribution was to have introduced a way of explaining these ideas in a manner that was more logical, more credible, better grounded in experience. This was what he meant by his claim that he had introduced the experimental method of reasoning into moral subjects.

IV. THE EXPERIMENTAL METHOD IN MORALS

In the Introduction to the *Treatise*, Hume advises the reader that the "only solid foundation" of a science of human nature lies in "experience and observation" (T xvi). While others may have "begun" to establish this foundation, Hume had a very precise conception of how it should proceed, as is shown by his clarification of these terms at the beginning of Book I.

First, by 'observation' he meant 'perception'; and all perceptions, we are told, may be divided into impressions and ideas. The problem he set for himself was to explain how any idea – of space or time, of necessary connexion, of virtue or vice – may be traced to corresponding impressions. The difference between an idea and an impression was typically the greater liveliness or vivacity of the impression.

> [A]ll our simple ideas proceed either mediately or immediately, from their correspondent impressions.

> This then is the first principle I establish in the science of human nature; nor ought we to despise it because of the simplicity of its appearance. (T 7)

Secondly, in explaining the relation of ideas and impressions, Hume appealed to experience, to the manner in which ideas are associated with or naturally related to other ideas. The experience of ideas related to others by resemblance, contiguity and causation prompts the imagination to conceive a particular idea in a livelier, more vivacious manner. This project is carried over into Book II, where Hume explains how ideas of property and riches, beauty and deformity, may be traced to impressions of pride and humility, when the object of the impression is self; love and hatred, when the object of the impression is another. These impressions are reinforced by sympathy, which enlivens our ideas of self and others, and explains, in part, our approval of qualities which are useful and agreeable to self and others. The "experiments" he there employed "to confirm this system" led him to consider ideas of persons and things as we find them naturally related or associated in the imagination.

Thirdly, Hume also thought that the imagination may be misleading, particularly when associations of ideas of persons and things are less than uniform. In these circumstances, experimental reasoning requires the correction of imagination by judgement, which regulates misleading associations of ideas by reducing the same associations to general rules.

Let us consider, as an example of experimental reasoning in morals, Hume's account of the idea of justice. We have no idea of justice, Hume thought, as long as we remain in a state of nature. In that condition there is no natural instinct or natural affection, and no association of ideas of persons and things which would impress upon us the idea of justice. The natural state of mankind is a condition of scarcity, weakness and instability (T 484–5). Hume's depiction of the state of nature derives, as we have seen, from the Epicurean tradition. And the remedy Hume proposed for this condition was also the classical remedy of Epicurus, reiterated by Gassendi and by Bayle: a convention of abstinence from things which are connected or associated with others. It was the recognition that such abstinence was useful which fostered or generated (or mothered, as Horace put it) the idea of justice. Thus far, Hume's theory of justice was not original.

But his analysis becomes highly original when he explains that such conventions allow us to *believe* that others will be just in their behaviour. And this belief prompts us to conceive the idea of justice in a more lively or vivid manner.

> The effect, then, of belief is to raise up a simple idea to an equality with our impressions, and bestow on it a like influence on the passions. This effect it can only have by making an idea approach an impression in force and vivacity. (T 119)

As long as justice remains merely an idea, it has no influence on human behaviour. But when the idea has the force of an impression it may exercise a controlling influence upon the passions. We believe that most persons in a given society will be just, that they will abstain from the possessions of others, because we understand that others, like ourselves, have an *interest* in observing the conventions of social behaviour. And this interest is firmly grounded in human nature. It is nothing but the direct and violent passions of avarice and ambition regularized and redirected by the conventions and rules of justice.

The significance of Hume's contention that the idea of justice, properly understood, may have the force or liveliness of an impression, is that it provided an answer to one of the questions or problems posed for moral philosophers and jurists by Hobbes in chapter 13 of *Leviathan* (1651). How could anyone depend upon others to behave with restraint, in the absence of government and fear of punishment, when the greater part of mankind is avaricious and ambitious, motivated by desire for gain and love of glory? Hume's theory of belief provided a way of explaining how people come to behave rationally, how they come to be naturally obliged, without government or fear of punishment by God or some other superior power (as Pufendorf, for one, had explained it).[25] The obligation derives from our understanding that adherence to conventions or general rules of behaviour will serve our interests, our passions of avarice and ambition, more effectively than an irregular and uninhibited indulgence of those passions. Repeated experience of the advantages of conventional or regular behaviour reinforces this belief in the utility of justice. And the idea of justice is further enlivened and reinforced by the sympathetic approval of others. Thus sympathy with others provides a second source of obligation to observe the conventions and rules of justice, a moral obligation which further enlivens the natural obligation or interest we have in adhering to the rules of justice.

The general impression or belief that our interests will be better satisfied by justice than injustice is also explained, more specifically, by the imagination, and the manner in which ideas of persons and things are associated in the mind. We tend naturally to associate an idea of a person and an idea of those things with which we find him constantly conjoined; we understand these things as his possessions. But it is also possible for us to separate a person from his possessions in the imagination, and also in our conduct. As long as we remain in our natural condition or state of nature, we have no interest in thinking or doing otherwise. For property is a species of *causation* (T 506);[26] and in any causal relation, the cause may be separated from the effect. We only connect the two ideas constantly when the contingent connexions between men and things are stabilized in the imagination by judgement, which makes possession a general rule. Then we have an interest in respecting the property of others; but the source or origin of this impression is artificial or conventional.

A similar correction of the natural principles of the imagination is made in the origin of government. The natural tendency of the imagination to prefer the *contiguous* to the remote prompts many to imagine that it is in their interest to neglect and violate the rules of property and society. This tendency is redirected and remedied by judgement, when there is an agreement of judgements that it is in the interest of people in society for the rules of justice to be executed or enforced by rulers. Rulers make it the immediate interest of subjects to observe these rules; and the interest of rulers is secured by the benefits of political office, by wealth and fame, which are made readily available to rulers in any well-contrived establishment or constitution (T 534–5). Finally, the imagination is also led by the *resemblance* of persons with one another to make comparisons. And comparisons of this kind are productive of conflict, particularly among the proud (T 596).[27]

Why did Hume think it a legitimate or appropriate vocation for the moral philosopher to employ the experimental method of reasoning to amend or revise Epicurean ideas in moral philosophy? One clue to this may be found in the natural philosophers who were considered authoritative at the University of Edinburgh when Hume was a student there. In his final year of study (1724–5), Hume had attended the natural philosophy class of Robert Steuart and subscribed to the recently founded Physiological Library, a collection at that time of some 400 volumes.[28] Three features of the published catalogue of this class library are worth noting.

First, it begins with forty-two items by Robert Boyle, whose influential revision of the atomistic ideas of the natural philosophy of Epicurus and his modern followers was clearly accorded special authority. Boyle did not like to be called an Epicurean, because of the anti-religious connotations of the name; he endeavoured to reconcile his experimental and theoretical science with arguments for the truth of natural and revealed religion.[29] Secondly, the largest collection of works by other authors appears under the heading 'Natural and experimental philosophy', where the first work listed is Lucretius's *De rerum natura*; the collected works of Gassendi in Latin, and the abridgement in French by Bernier, are included; as is Hobbes's work on Body. Thirdly, the catalogue concludes with a section on natural and revealed religion; this begins with Cicero's *De natura deorum,* and includes the writings of various natural theologians who were attempting to derive ideas of the being and attributes of God from evidence of design in the creation, the project of the Boyle Lectures in the early eighteenth century.

Hume had thus been introduced to experimental method in a context where he would have been expected to apply it to other areas of experience. But as he later acknowledged, he was overcome by sceptical doubts concerning its applicability to religion before he had reached the age of twenty (HL I, 154). As the sceptic in his *Dialogues concerning natural religion* was later to argue, the creation was not an appropriate subject of observation or experiment. There was one occurrence, the creation of the universe, and no observations of the same order to which it might be related which would make an impression on the mind (D 149–50). "A total suspence of judgment is here our only reasonable resource" (D 186–7). In his scepticism concerning religion, Hume found himself at odds with most of his contemporaries; among them, his senior contemporary, the professor of moral philosophy at Glasgow.

V. HUTCHESON ON THE EPICUREAN TRADITION

While Hume may have considered it an appropriate vocation of the moral philosopher to find better reasons for believing the moral distinctions of the Epicureans and Sceptics than they had discovered for themselves, a different fashion in moral philosophy had established itself, in Dublin and in Glasgow. There the ideas of Hutcheson had gained the ascendancy, and those ideas were very different from Hume's. Whereas Hume thought the moral philosophies of the ancients were fanciful or hypothetical, lacking an adequate basis in experience, Hutcheson looked directly to the ancients for an account of the foundations of morality. On the title-page of his *Inquiry into the original of our ideas of beauty and virtue* (1725), he declared that in this book "the Ideas of *Moral Good* and *Evil* are establish'd, according to the Sentiments of the Antient *Moralists*".

But Hutcheson was always clear that there was one school of moral philosophers among the ancients which he opposed, that of the Epicureans. He made this point in the second edition of the *Inquiry* (1726),[30] and in a letter the same year to the *Dublin weekly journal.*[31] He distinguished two views of morality in his *Illustrations upon the moral sense* (1728), "The one that of the old *Epicureans,* as it is beautifully explained in the first Book of *Cicero, De finibus*; which is revived by Mr. *Hobbes,* and followed by many better Writers". The other is the view of moralists like himself, "that we have a *moral Sense* or Determination of our Mind, to *approve* every *kind Affection* either in our selves or others".[32] It is not surprising, then, to find that Hutcheson differed from Hume on all those matters which Hume took over from writers in the Epicurean tradition.

1. Hutcheson made no distinction between justice and the natural virtues. He held rather that the idea of virtue is always *natural*, in that it is always amiable and agreeable to the moral sense.

2. He considered talk of the state of nature, as employed by Hobbes and Pufendorf, an abuse of words. The term should rather denote the most perfect condition which human beings may attain by the exercise of the faculties implanted in their nature. Certainly, he wrote, in his inaugural lecture on the natural sociability of mankind, "this most perfect state rightly takes the name of natural".[33] But the term 'state of nature' had become so debased, not only by moral philosophers, but also by Reformed theologians who considered it the fallen state (between the state of innocence and the state of grace), that he preferred to speak instead of the state of liberty, or state of freedom from human government.

3. Hutcheson did not find it difficult to justify the rights of men to life, liberty, reputation and the property on which they had laboured. He saw no need for conventions, rules or artificial restraints to ensure that they would be just in their dealings with one another. The only difficulty in Hutcheson's thinking on the subject of rights is that he justified them in a number of different ways, depending on the context in which he wrote. In his *Inquiry*, he held that ideas of obligation and rights could be derived from that natural or instinctive benevolence which always brings to mind the idea of virtue. In his compend for students, *Philosophiæ moralis institutio compendiaria* (1742, revised 1745), he supposed that rights might also be recognized and secured by attending to what he there called the divine moral law. In *A system of moral philosophy*, written for the most part by 1737 but not published during his lifetime, he understood rights and obligations to be part of a system, presided over by the Creator. There is a difficulty, I believe, in reducing these several accounts to one account. It is sufficient to observe that rights, for Hutcheson, were always natural or instinctive, never artificial or conventional.

4. Hutcheson thought human nature so designed that we cannot fail to approve certain qualities of character, namely benevolence or kind affection. It was not the utility or agreeableness of these qualities that prompts us to approve them. It was rather that, when we perceive a benevolent or public-spirited citizen, a charitable neighbour, an affectionate father, the idea of virtue comes immediately to mind. And when we calculate the benefits which follow from a particular action, we do so simply to discover the measure of the benevolence or kind affection which prompted the

action. We do not approve of qualities which are merely useful to ourselves and others, such as a mean-spirited industriousness. And we do approve of qualities which are not useful or advantageous to ourselves, such as the courage and public spirit of an enemy (*System*, I, p. 81). Our approval depends upon nothing but our perception of morally relevant qualities of character, e.g. benevolence or kind affection.

5. Hutcheson found no place for sympathy in his system: "sympathy could never account for that immediate ardour of love and good-will which breaks forth toward any character represented to us as eminent in moral excellence" (*ibid.*, p. 48). The idea of sympathy was an invention of the Cyrenaics and Epicureans to allow them to reduce all fellow-feeling, kind affection and benevolence to the indirect and private pleasure of the percipient (pp. 39–47). This was inconsistent with the experience of moral agents and persons of virtue.

VI. HUTCHESON'S REACTION TO BOOK III AND HUME'S REPLY

Hutcheson was introduced to Hume and his writings early in 1739 through the initiative of Henry Home, who had sent Hutcheson Books I and II of the *Treatise* through a third party. Hutcheson's initial response was encouraging, but he had not yet studied the text with care.[34] On the strength of this introduction, David Hume sent Hutcheson a draft of Book III, his treatment of morals. Hutcheson replied in a letter, now lost, but known to us from Hume's reply. Hutcheson found himself in basic disagreement with Hume on a number of points:

1. Hume's moral philosophy lacked "Warmth in the Cause of Virtue". Hume replied that this was no accident: he was a metaphysician, engaged in an abstract enquiry concerning the principles of morals; he was not a practical moralist or advocate of virtue, as Hutcheson was. Hume thought that his abstract metaphysics might be of use to a practical moralist, in the same way that an anatomist might be of service to a painter or sculptor. The two enquiries were complementary, but must not be confused: "I am persuaded that a Metaphysician may be very helpful to a Moralist; tho' I cannot easily conceive these two Characters united in the same Work" (HL I, 33).

2. Hutcheson observed that Hume's understanding of human nature depended upon an inadequate idea of what is natural. Hume had made no attempt to explain why human beings were created. Hume replied that the question of why they had been created did not permit a philosophical response. Such questions were endless, and "quite wide of my Purpose".

3. Hutcheson was concerned that Hume had described justice as an artificial virtue and therefore as something unnatural. Hume answered that he had never called justice "unnatural", only artificial. He cited

the authority of Horace, and suggested that Grotius and Pufendorf would have been more consistent if they had agreed with Horace that justice has its origin not in nature, but in utility.

4. Hutcheson contested Hume's inclusion of natural abilities among the virtues. Hume replied that their differences on this question might be merely verbal. There were surely many qualities which might be considered virtues. It was important to avoid the kind of narrowness that made benevolence the only virtue (as Hutcheson had done in his *Inquiry*). One of the merits of Cicero's delineation of the virtues in *De officiis* was that, unlike the author of *The whole duty of man*, Cicero recognized many qualities and abilities as virtues (HL I, 34).

Two other differences between them were remarked by Hume in a postscript. He recommended that Hutcheson consider only the tendencies of qualities of character to be useful to self and others, not the "actual Operation" or consequences of actions, "which depends on Chance". This would allow Hutcheson to recognize that our approval or disapproval of actions and characters derives from nothing but sympathy. Given Hutcheson's diffidence about utility and sympathy, and his concern to calculate the measure of benevolence in particular actions and characters, it is remarkable that Hume should have imagined that Hutcheson might be receptive to this recommendation.

Hume thought also that Hutcheson would surely agree that virtue can never be its own motive. There must be another motive, distinct from the virtue which prompts us to act. Cicero had proved this point against the Stoics, in the fourth book of *De finibus*. But again, Hutcheson had been concerned to prove just the opposite point: that there are kind affections and benevolence in human nature; these qualities are recognized to be virtues; and they prompt us to act without the assistance of other motives and passions. The presence of such additional motivation would merely weaken or subtract from the virtue of the action or character. Besides, there were other texts of Cicero's, and other ways of reading the texts of Cicero recommended by Hume. These were matters which Hutcheson would attempt to make clear to Hume in due course.

A seventh and fundamental difference between them, which had far-reaching implications, comes to light in a later letter. Hume thought, remarkably, that Hutcheson must agree with him that we can never know the sentiments or feelings of the supreme being:

> since Morality, according to your Opinion, as well as mine, is determin'd merely by Sentiment, it regards only human Nature and human Life. . . . What Experience have we with regard to superior Beings? How can we ascribe to them any Sentiments at all? They have implanted those Sentiments in us for the Conduct of Life like our

bodily Sensations, which they possess not themselves. I expect no
Answer to these Difficultys in the Compass of a Letter. (HL I, 40)
It is well that Hume expected no answer to these difficulties in a letter;
for he does not seem to have received a letter from Hutcheson on this
subject. Nor did Hutcheson ever draw the sceptical inference concerning
superior beings which Hume would have had him draw. In his early
writings, he thought it a legitimate inference from a human nature which
is dignified by benevolence and a moral sense, that God must be a
benevolent God. He was at the same time careful to distinguish his kind
of theological morality from the moral theology of Reformed theologians
and moralists, who insisted that veneration or regard for the Deity was
necessary to make an action virtuous (*Inquiry*, pp. 95–7, 274–6; *Essay*,
pp. 202–3, 322–3). In his compend, he takes a more orthodox view:

> Since then God must appear to us as the Supreme excellence, . . . no
> affection of soul can be more approved than the most ardent love
> and veneration towards the Deity, with a steddy purpose to obey
> him, . . . along with an humble submission and resignation of ourselves
> and all our interests to his will, with confidence in his goodness.

He also writes:

> [T]he nature of virtue is . . . as immutable as the divine Wisdom and
> Goodness. Cast the consideration of these perfections of God out of
> this question, and indeed nothing would remain certain or immut-
> able.[35]

In *A system of moral philosophy*, evidence for an original and divine mind
is discovered in the order or system of the creation. The presence of
benevolence and a moral sense in human nature shows that God must be
benevolent, and when actions are motivated by veneration for the Deity
as well as benevolence, the virtue of such actions is enhanced. Hutcheson
finds that the sorrows of the human condition (more in evidence in the
System than in his other writings) are compensated by attending to the
benevolence and other attributes of the Deity. He dismisses the question
whether a society of atheists is possible as "a needless inquiry". "The
experiment . . . has never yet been made." And the removal of religion
would lead to the dissolution of the strongest obligations which make
society possible (*System*, I, pp. 174–84). In all of Hutcheson's systems or
constructions of his moral philosophy, it was always possible to make the
inference that God is a benevolent God. In this respect, as in many
others, his moral philosophy differed profoundly from Hume's.

Were their differences irreconcilable? Hutcheson may well have pre-
sumed so. But Hume seems to have thought that there were certain
respects in which their approaches to moral subjects might be made to
agree; or, at least, that they might be recognized to be mutually supportive
or complementary. "I intend to make a new Tryal if it be possible to

make the Moralist and Metaphysician agree a little better" (HL I, 33). Hume set himself to work on this project in the months which followed their initial exchange.

VII. ALTERATIONS TO THE MANUSCRIPT OF BOOK III

Between September 1739 and March 1740, Hume made substantial revisions to the manuscript of Book III of the *Treatise*. He wrote to tell Hutcheson that the text had been "pretty much alter'd since you saw it", and "I flatter myself that the Alterations I have made have improv'd it very much both in point of Prudence and Philosophy" (HL I, 36–7). From Hume's letters of 17 September 1739 and 4 and 16 March 1740, it is possible to identify at least four sections of Book III which were written or altered or revised during the months which followed Hutcheson's initial reaction. Many of the replies set out in Hume's first letter found their way into the altered text of Book III.

Hume's first difference with Hutcheson – that he was a metaphysician, not a practical moralist (an anatomist of human nature, not a painter) – appears in the 'Conclusion' of the book, Part III, Section VI. Hume sent Hutcheson the revised Conclusion, "that you may see I desire to keep on good Terms even with the strictest & most rigid" (HL I, 37). Their second difference, over the term 'natural', provided the occasion for an extended discussion of the meaning of 'nature' in Part I, Section II, 'Moral distinctions deriv'd from a moral sense'. Hutcheson's third difficulty with Hume's morals, the description of justice as an artificial, not a natural virtue, was addressed at length in Part II, Section I, 'Justice, whether a natural or artificial virtue?' In the same section, Hume elaborated the observation, taken over from Cicero, that the motive which prompts one to behave in a virtuous manner must be distinct from the quality which is perceived as a virtue. Hume had advised Hutcheson that he would make this argument more convincingly in an altered version of the text (HL I, 35).

Another passage that Hutcheson would not have seen in the manuscript of 1739 was communicated to him by Hume in his letter of 16 March 1740. There Hume sought Hutcheson's advice "in a Point of Prudence". Hume had "concluded a Reasoning" with a statement that compared virtues and vices with sounds and colours; they were "not Qualitys in Objects but Perceptions in the Mind" (HL I, 39). This is the conclusion Hume drew from his extended argument against deriving ideas of virtue and vice from reason in Part I, Section I ('Moral distinctions not deriv'd from reason'). He did not rehearse for Hutcheson the reasoning which had led him to this conclusion; nor did he attempt to situate this passage in the context of any text that Hutcheson had already read. His announcement that he had "concluded" this reasoning suggests that Part I, Section

I had just been finished and had formed no part of the draft which had
been read by Hutcheson in the summer of 1739. It appears rather that
Hume wrote this section, together with the two sections which followed
it, and the Conclusion, between September 1739 and March 1740, to
address issues which were primarily of concern to Hutcheson and moralists
who thought like him.

What did Hume hope to accomplish by altering or revising his treatment
of morals in this way? To persuade Hutcheson that virtue could never be
its own reward, that sympathy must be the source of moral approval and
disapproval, that nothing entitles us to attribute sentiments to superior
beings, Hume would have to appeal to principles or sentiments they held
in common. It was in this spirit that he argued, in support of Hutcheson,
that moral distinctions are not derived from reason (III. i. 1), but the
arguments which he employed were sceptical arguments, very different
from the moralistic and Stoic considerations advanced by Hutcheson.
Hume could also agree that moral distinctions or ideas of virtue and vice
were discovered by a moral sense (III. i. 2), although he had a different
understanding of the moral sense from Hutcheson's. The articulation of
these differences now allowed him to explain, more distinctly than before,
why justice was not a natural but an artificial virtue (III. ii. 1). But in
none of this was he writing as a follower of Hutcheson's. In casting
himself in the role of the anatomist, and in assigning Hutcheson the part
of the painter, Hume was also advising Hutcheson that his own *Treatise
of human nature* was more profound and more accurate, if not as elegant
or eloquent as the productions of the senior philosopher.

VIII. DIFFERENCES CONCERNING THE ROLE OF REASON

Although Hume advertised to the reader that the third Book of the
Treatise was "in some measure independent of the other two", he expressed
none the less his conviction that the three Books, taken together, formed
a system, which would become more persuasive and mutually supportive
as it proceeded (T 455). He also advised that the question of how moral
distinctions are made may be reduced to the question whether it is by
our ideas or our impressions that we distinguish between virtue and vice.
In morals, as in questions relating to the understanding and the passions,
the first principle of the science of human nature was that ideas must be
traced to their corresponding impressions.

Once Hume had made clear that his book on morals was part of a
system that included the understanding and the passions, he began to
fashion an argument that would lend support – albeit qualified support –
to Hutcheson's critique of moral theories which attempted to derive
distinctions between virtue and vice from reason alone. Hutcheson had
argued his case against these theories most distinctly and consecutively in

his *Illustrations upon the moral sense*. In the first three sections of that work, he examined successively the ideas of three leading advocates of the theory that reason alone discovers moral distinctions: John Locke, Samuel Clarke and William Wollaston. The sequence of Hume's discussion in Part I, Section I follows Hutcheson's *Illustrations* closely and reinforces the succession of themes in Hutcheson's work.[36] Hume's choice of antagonists (not named in the text, but they would be named in a subsequent defence of this section)[37] was the very selection of philosophical opponents that Hutcheson had made. The arguments of the two philosophers terminated in the same nominal conclusion: that moral distinctions are made not by reason but by a moral sense.

But despite the structural resemblance of the two discussions, it soon becomes clear that the aims or objectives of the two philosophers were far from identical or even entirely compatible. The gravamen of Hutcheson's complaint against Locke, Clarke and Wollaston was that they had failed to recognize the relevance of those particular qualities of character (benevolence and kind affection, or their opposites, malice and disaffection) which always brought before the mind the ideas of virtue and vice. Hume's differences with the same philosophers derived from more sceptical considerations, from an appreciation of the limitations of reason as exercised in human understanding and in conduct, themes elaborated in the two earlier Books of the *Treatise*.

Hutcheson had observed, in opposition to Locke and his followers, that it was not reasonableness that prompts us to act morally; it was rather the benevolence or kind affection of the agent. And it was the perception of these qualities in the character of the agent or actor that prompts an observer to form an attendant idea of virtue (*Illustrations*, sec. I). Hume agreed with Hutcheson, as opposed to Locke and others, that it was not reason or reasonableness which prompts people to act morally. But his explanation of this incapacity was not that virtuous conduct can only be prompted by virtuous motives; it was the more sceptical reflection that reason, strictly speaking, does not prompt us to act at all (T 457–8). He had already proved in Book II that reason is and ought only to be the slave of the passions (T 415). This is a locution Hutcheson never employed;[38] the phrase is an echo, rather, of Bayle[39] and Mandeville.[40]

Secondly, Hume agreed with Hutcheson's contention that ideas of virtue and vice cannot be discovered by reason in the relations or fitnesses of things, as Clarke, for one, had argued. Hutcheson had remarked the absurdity of supposing that virtues and vices may be discovered in relations of ideas, for such relations might pertain to inanimate objects, as well as persons; in that case, there would be no reason to exclude from "the Class of Virtues, all the practical Mathematicks, and the Operations of

Chymistry" (*Illustrations*, p. 248). Hume concurred with this reasoning; he merely illustrated it more vividly, observing that if virtue and vice could be discovered in relations of ideas, then one might discover murder, even parricide, in the world of plants, as when a parent tree is deprived of nourishment by a sapling generated from its seed (T 463–8). Hume also reinforced Hutcheson's criticism of the entirely abstract character of the relational theory of morals. They differed, however, in their understanding of what had been overlooked in Clarke's theory. Hutcheson thought that what had been neglected were those qualities of character (benevolence and kind affection or their opposites) which we perceive in moral agents. Relations are merely ideas, which accompany our perceptions of objects when we compare them. But to form an idea of virtue or vice, one must perceive something more substantial than relations of ideas; one must perceive kind affection or benevolence, which we find, not in any comparison of ideas, but in qualities which are perceived in the characters we observe or apprehend. Hume thought otherwise; it was not those particular qualities of character so much and so singularly admired by Hutcheson which the relational theory had neglected or ignored. It was a particular feeling, an impression as opposed to an idea, which allows us to distinguish virtue from vice; this feeling cannot be accounted for by relations of ideas, demonstrable or probable.

Thirdly, Hume's scepticism concerning reason was also manifested in his rejection of Wollaston's theory that virtue and vice may be discovered by reason in the truths or falsehoods which are signified by assertions or actions (understood as assertions). Hutcheson had maintained that, however true or false an assertion or an action might be, one discovers the speaker or the actor to be virtuous or vicious only when one considers whether his speech or action was motivated by benevolence or kind affection (*Illustrations*, sec. III). Hume's difficulty with Wollaston's theory was again of a more sceptical order. It was that the true causes of actions are often unknown. An observer may often mistake the motivation of an agent, just as a scientist may make erroneous inferences from his observations of phenomena in the physical world (T 461–2n.). This last sceptical consideration, like the last of his sceptical reflections on Clarke's theory, would also apply to Hutcheson's own ideas of virtue and vice, inasmuch as those ideas depended upon an accurate perception of the motives or affections of the agent.

It has become evident, then, that as Hume elaborated his own arguments against the reasonable, the relational and the truth-signifying theories of virtue, his way of agreeing with Hutcheson and supporting that philosopher was carefully qualified. Hume was prepared to underline Hutcheson's misgivings about the theories of his rationalist opponents. But he expressed his support in a manner that was consistent with his own sceptical reflections on the role of reason in the realms of the understanding and the passions, and these sceptical reflections applied in some degree to the ideas of Hutcheson as well. This becomes still more evident when one considers the very different roles they assigned reason in moral life.

In *Illustrations upon the moral sense*, having illustrated the errors of Locke, Clarke and Wollaston in sections I to III, Hutcheson outlined his own understanding of the role of reason in section IV. He distinguished four roles or employments for reason in moral conduct. They were (a) to know that some actions and affections are always considered virtuous or vicious; (b) to know that the quality of character which is approved is always benevolence or kind affection; (c) to know what actions provide evidence of kind affection or benevolence in the agent; and (d) to know how self-interest may motivate people to perform the sorts of actions they would have undertaken if their conduct had been motivated by benevolence or kind affection (pp. 275-6).

Hume's understanding of the role of reason in conduct would have excluded, categorically, every one of the four roles assigned to reason by Hutcheson.

The first employment of reason, to know that some actions and affections are always considered virtuous, was confirmed, Hutcheson thought, by "*Experience* and *History* . . . in all Nations". Hume did *not* think that the same actions and affections are always approved. He thought that experience and history show that mankind is always directed in its approval or disapproval of conduct and character by the same *principles* or *sentiments* of morals: "there never was any nation of the world, nor any single person in any nation, who was utterly depriv'd of them" (T 474). Hume's emphasis was upon the uniformity of the sentiments or principles of moral approval and disapproval: the principles of usefulness and agreeableness to oneself and to others. This uniformity of sentiments or principles was entirely consistent with variations and changes in the qualities of character and the forms of conduct which are in fact approved. Hutcheson's understanding of the universality of our ideas of virtue and vice made no allowance for such variation and change. The same qualities of character had always been and would always be approved or disapproved; this was, for Hutcheson but not for Hume, the first conclusion of reason.

Hume also disagreed with the second of the roles assigned to reason by Hutcheson: to know that the quality which is approved is always benevolence. There were many other qualities which Hume took to be virtues. He had already registered his disagreement with Hutcheson on this matter in his first letter: "were Benevolence the only Virtue no Characters cou'd be mixt, but wou'd depend entirely on their Degrees of Benevolence" (HL I, 34).

Thirdly, it formed no part of Hume's conception of reason in morals that it should inform us of those actions which provide real evidence of benevolence or kind affection in the agent. Hutcheson had supposed that this was the question that had been addressed by all writers on natural and even civil law (*Illustrations*, p. 276). This was not Hume's understanding of the laws of nature, as he called the conventions or general rules of conduct on which human society depends. The conventions to abstain from the possessions of others, together with the conventions of promise-keeping and transferring property by consent, were none of them evidence of benevolence or kind affection. They were contrivances or means which permitted the satisfaction of the passions of interest and ambition, of pride and love of esteem.

> Society is absolutely necessary for the well-being of men; and these [conventions] are as necessary to the support of society. Whatever restraint they may impose on the passions of men, they are the real offspring of those passions, and are only a more artful and more refin'd way of satisfying them. (T 526)

Accordingly, the fourth employment Hutcheson found for reason – to know how self-interest may motivate people to act as they would have acted, if their actions had been prompted by benevolence – was not a problem for Hume. Hume assumed that men would always be motivated by interest in any case (T 534). The challenge for moral reasoners was to find ways of directing these interests in a manner that would be useful and agreeable to oneself and others; conduct prompted by benevolence and kind affection formed no part of these considerations, except in so far as good nature and benevolence are themselves perceived to be useful and agreeable (T 603–4).

Hume's conception of the proper use of reason in conduct was expressed by him, very clearly and succinctly, in the course of his own critique of the reasonableness criterion for moral distinctions:

> [R]eason, in a strict and philosophical sense, can have an influence on our conduct only after two ways: Either when it excites a passion by informing us of the existence of something which is a proper object of it; or when it discovers the connexion of causes and effects, so as to afford us means of exerting any passion. These are the only kinds of judgment, which can accompany our actions; or can be said to produce them in any manner. (T 459)

The first of these uses of reason, to discover the proper objects of the passions, had been the subject of Book II of the *Treatise*. There Hume had explained at length how the various passions, indirect and direct, are related to their proper objects (to self and others) by associations of ideas, of persons in their relations with one another and with things. The second use of reason, to discover the means which allow us to exert these passions, was one of the dominant themes of Book III. In Part II and Part

III of Book III, Hume set out the conventions, or general rules, or probable connexions of causes and effects, which one must follow in order to live in society; enjoy the advantages of justice and property; the benefits of promises kept; the security afforded by governments. It was reason or judgement which suggested the means of exerting the indirect and direct passions of pride and love of esteem, of interest and ambition, which were so directly destructive of human relations in the absence of these rules and conventions and the benefits they afforded.

What of another use of reason, which Hume had described as the first principle of the science of human nature, the discovery of the impressions from which our ideas derive? This first principle of experimental reasoning was itself ultimately a matter of feeling or sentiment, as Hume had argued in various passages in Book I. In the same manner, it also made sense, he thought, to understand the liveliness or vivacity of moral judgements as impressions. And this was another possible area of agreement or affinity with Hutcheson, who also thought that moral judgements depended upon feeling or sensibility or, as Hutcheson preferred to call it, a moral sense.

IX. SYMPATHY AND THE MORAL SENSE

There have been different theories about Hutcheson's (and, it is supposed, by implication, Hume's) use of the term 'moral sense'. Kemp Smith thought that the moral sense was understood by both philosophers to have been a natural instinct, an original and therefore a natural part of the constitution of human nature.[41] Raphael thought Hume had been misled by Hutcheson's analogy between moral sense and aesthetic sensibility or the sense of beauty. The analogy obscured the authoritative or imperative nature of moral judgements, particularly judgements relating to obligations. Hume recognized this deficiency, and so conceived a theory of artificial virtue to permit himself an idea of obligation, albeit one lacking in force or moral authority.[42]

David Norton has called attention to another dimension of the moral sense, as both Hutcheson and Hume understood it. He has described this feature as moral realism, or common-sense morality. In all perception, Hutcheson thought, we distinguish between sensible ideas, which refer to our own inner experiences, sensations of colour, taste, smell; and other ideas, which he called "concomitant ideas", which refer to external things, to extension, motion, rest. In moral perception, Hutcheson made a similar distinction between perceptions of actions or qualities of character, and the ideas of virtue or vice which attend or accompany these perceptions, and which may be considered analogous to the concomitant ideas of perception. In Norton's view, Hume took over Hutcheson's theory of moral perception (not his theory of non-moral perception), by contending that the feelings we experience when we observe certain qualities of character signify or represent an external reality, namely the virtues or vices of the character we observe.[43]

There are instructive insights in each of these interpretations; the last, in particular, recognizes an important characteristic of the moral sense, as Hutcheson (though not Hume) understood it. There would appear to be an anomaly, however, in Hutcheson's comparison of non-moral and moral perception. Whereas the concomitant ideas in non-moral perception refer to external things, the concomitant ideas of moral distinctions, of virtue and vice, do not; they are internal sensations, like the sensations of taste and smell. Of course, they are also real ideas, not illusions; and they come to mind only when we perceive qualities of character or actions, which are indeed ideas of things external to the perceiver (*Illustrations*, p. 283). Hume clearly thought it was Hutcheson's opinion that the ideas of virtue and vice were sensible ideas, comparable with tastes and smells. His letter of 16 March 1740 makes it plain that he took this to be Hutcheson's view, and that they were in agreement on this point. This was the conclusion which followed from his argument, and Hutcheson's, that ideas of virtue and vice were not discovered by reason.

> Take any action allow'd to be vicious . . . The vice entirely escapes you, as long as you consider the object. You never can find it, till you turn your reflexion into your own breast, and find a sentiment of disapprobation, which arises in you, towards this action. Here is a matter of fact; but 'tis the object of feeling, not of reason. It lies in yourself, not in the object. (T 468–9)

Thus far, Hutcheson and Hume were in agreement: moral distinctions were objects of sentiment or feeling, not of reason. Unlike Hutcheson, however, Hume thought there was no attendant or concomitant feeling or sentiment of virtue or vice. There was one idea only before the mind: an idea of an action or a character or a quality. In order for it to be conceived as a virtue or a vice the idea must have the liveliness or the vivacity of an impression, but the enlivening must be of a particular kind. Moral ideas are distinguished from other lively ideas, in part, by the circumstance that they are ideas of the usefulness and agreeableness of certain qualities of character: of justice, fidelity, allegiance, generosity, greatness of mind. Of course, the recognition that a character or an action is useful requires the exercise of judgement or reasoning. But this is reasoning in the service of the passions. Virtue and vice are among the principal causes or subjects of pride and humility, love and hatred. By reasoning experimentally, by discovering the various associations or connexions of persons and things which prompt us to feel one or another of these passions, and by discovering the artificial institutions and arrangements which allow us to exert these passions, we form a lively idea or impression of the kinds of conduct and the qualities of character which are useful and agreeable.

It may still be asked why utility pleases. Hume's answer, in the *Treatise*, was that we sympathize with characters who are useful and agreeable, and with persons who are associated with others who have useful and agreeable qualities. The merit of understanding the moral sense in terms of sympathy was that sympathy can also be explained experimentally, as an enlivening of our ideas when we find ourselves in association with persons who are connected with us by resemblance, contiguity and causation. Of course, sympathy, like belief, must also be regulated by general rules, derived from judgement and experience. Otherwise, we would always be more impressed by the qualities of the persons who are closest to us, or who most resemble us, or who are connected with us in other ways. This is why moral obligations based on sympathy must follow upon natural obligations, on interest regularized by conventions or general rules. If sympathy with others were the only source of obligation, then Hume's theory of obligation would indeed lack force or authority. In making natural or interested obligations of first importance for the social institutions of property, contracts and government, Hume was attempting to ensure that the obligations which maintain society would be strong enough to counter the force of the violent passions (of avarice, ambition, etc.). Hume corrected his original text in a way which emphasized that interested obligation is the basis of society; sympathy, however, is the source of the moral obligation which supports this interest.[44]

In ordering the priorities of obligation in this way Hume was following the priorities of the Epicurean tradition, where people might achieve a harmonious sympathy with one another, only after they have been united in society for reasons of interest or utility. It is sometimes supposed that Hume's employment of the idea of sympathy was designed to counter or oppose the ideas of Hobbes and other moral Sceptics and Epicureans. But it is worth remarking that sympathy was first introduced in the *Treatise* in the discussion of pride and humility, to account for the love of fame (II. i. 11). It figures most prominently in the discussion of love and hatred, in an explanation of our esteem for the rich and powerful (II. ii. 5). Hume was concerned to explain, as Hobbes was, the psychological phenomena of desire for glory and desire for gain.

Sympathy, finally, was not an instinct, Hume explained, in the Conclusion of Book III:

> Those who resolve the sense of morals into original instincts of the human mind, may defend the cause of virtue with sufficient authority; but want the advantage, which those possess, who account for that sense by an extensive sympathy with mankind. (T 619)

The advantage of sympathy, in this respect, was that it allows us to reflect on the principles which prompt us to be sympathetic. As he put it, in the Conclusion and again in a later letter to Hutcheson, it approves of itself upon reflection: no doubt because it allows us to enter into the feelings of others and share their judgements about the usefulness and agreeableness of characters and conduct; and those judgements in turn reinforce our own sentiments concerning the same actions and characters. And it was a further merit of the principle of sympathy that, unlike any attempt to understand the moral sense as a natural or original instinct of human nature, sympathy did not have to be explained in terms of the end or design or purpose of human nature.

X. JUSTICE AND BENEVOLENCE

It was clear to both philosophers, from the beginning of their corres-
pondence, that they disagreed fundamentally on the subject of justice and injustice. Hutcheson complained that Hume's theory made justice unnatural (HL I, 33). Hume countered that the sentiment of justice was not unnatural in several of the meanings of that Protean term: it was not miraculous, or unusual, but merely artificial (T 473–5, 477). He appealed to the authority of Horace: utility was the mother of justice and equity (HL I, 33). Hutcheson preferred the authority of the natural jurists, Grotius and Pufendorf; they had derived their ideas of justice, rights and obligations from the law of nature, which they understood as the duty of natural sociability. Hutcheson too was convinced of the natural sociability of mankind. But he did not understand natural sociability as Pufendorf, in particular, understood it, as the necessity for mankind to live in society as the only remedy for our natural poverty (*indigentia*) and weakness (*imbecillitas*).[45] He maintained that people are naturally motivated to act in a spirit of benevolence, for the public interest or the general good;[46] And he derived from the natural motive of benevolence ideas of natural rights and obligations.

Hutcheson's best known account, at least prior to the 1740s, was contained in the final section of his *Inquiry*, where he argued that our ideas of rights and obligations are derived immediately from the natural virtue of benevolence without the sanctions of law enforced by every man (Grotius and Locke) or by superior powers (Pufendorf). For the moral sense is so constituted that we cannot help but feel uneasiness or displeasure when we fail (or see others fail) to act from the motive of benevolence. We feel a sense of obligation to act benevolently, quite apart from any law or rule, however enforced. And this sense of obligation is enhanced when we recognize that general or public benevolence increases our own innocent pleasure and satisfaction. Indeed, he considers that "the principal Business of the *moral Philosopher* is to show, from solid Reasons, 'That *universal Benevolence* tends to the Happiness of the *Benevolent*'" (*Inquiry*,

p. 252). It is never the business of the moral philosopher to discover obligations which are consistent with, or somehow further, selfishness and self-love, and their attendant passions.

The same moral sense, which discovers an obligation to act from a motive of benevolence, recognizes also a right to act from the same motive. Whenever an action or a possession or a claim *"would in the whole tend to the general Good*, we say that any Person in such Circumstances has *a Right to do, possess, or demand that Thing"* (p. 256). Hutcheson distinguished (as Grotius and Pufendorf had done) between perfect rights, when an action, claim or possession is of such necessity for the public good that it must be enforced; and imperfect rights, which are not of such necessity, and so need not be enforced. He had his own reason for maintaining this distinction. He wished to underline the virtue of imperfect rights, such as the right to the kind or charitable offices of another; as compared with perfect rights, such as the right to life, to property, to demand performance of contracts. The latter were absolutely necessary, inasmuch as their violation or neglect is always productive of misery; but the former, although not so necessary, have always more virtue in them because they demand more benevolence (pp. 268–9).

Hutcheson's theory that virtue and rights stand in an inverse relationship – the greater the virtue, the more imperfect the right – may derive from his employment of a vocabulary of rights which was designed (by the natural jurists) to distinguish between the just and unjust use of force, not between degrees of virtue and of vice, which was Hutcheson's main concern. But he was not deterred by the paradoxical aspect of his theory of rights. He made use of it, to observe that it is not the highest degree of virtue or benevolence which prompts us to secure the rights of others and ourselves. The motive which prompts us to secure the rights of life and property is not public or general benevolence; it is the stronger attractions of private or particular benevolence, of natural affection for family and friends, of gratitude, even some measure of self-love: these are the motives which prompt us to secure perfect rights (pp. 263–4). Thus it is benevolence, general and public, or particular and private, which provides the natural source or origin of our ideas of justice, rights and obligation.

Hume's differences with the natural jurisprudence tradition were more fundamental and far-reaching. In Sections II–XI of his discussion 'Of justice and injustice' (T 484–569), Hume addressed the principal topics of the natural jurisprudence tradition as Pufendorf had presented them: the origin of justice and property, the rules that determine property, the obligation of promises, the origin of government; and Hume accounted for these rights and obligations in a manner very different from Pufendorf and his many annotators and supplementers. He traced the origin of these ideas to our experience that it was in our interest to abstain from the possessions of others, keep promises, obey governments. The source of these impressions of interest was not natural: there was no natural instinct which would prompt us to be sociable, in the manner required by Pufendorf, i.e. which would prompt us to agree to leave others in possession of the things they have occupied, to do what we have contracted to do, to obey superior powers. The unrestrained passions of mankind, pride in property and riches, love of fame and esteem, would prompt us rather to seize the possessions of others, break promises, and claim power for ourselves. It is only by an artificial restraint and redirection of these passions, that the same passions restrain themselves; making it in the interest of all who seek to satisfy their pride, their love of fame and esteem, to observe the artificial rules and conventions of justice, property, contracts and allegiance.

This was the theme of the successive sections of Hume's treatment of justice and injustice. His discussion had the effect of reversing the priorities of Grotius and Pufendorf: they had identified the dictum of Horace, which Hume thought the epitome of his own position, as the very position they were arguing against in their treatises on natural law.[47] In tracing ideas of rights and obligations to impressions of utility or interest, Hume undermined the Stoic foundations of the natural-law tradition, making the "laws of nature" consistent with the moral psychology of the Epicureans and Sceptics. It was a corollary of this far-reaching critique of the natural jurists that Hume should have found himself in entire disagreement with the theory of justice proposed by Hutcheson.

Hume's differences with Hutcheson on the subject of justice were enunciated clearly and succinctly in Part II, Section I of Book III. Every one of the three arguments in this section appears to have been written in response to positions taken by Hutcheson. Hume was concerned, first of all, that Hutcheson's theory of justice and other virtues was a version of the Stoic theory that virtue may be considered its own motive or reward. This seemed to Hume, as it had seemed to Cicero, to leave virtue and moral life without a satisfactory motive or source in human nature.

Cicero had remarked, in an exchange with Cato, that the Stoics leave themselves "without a source and starting point for duty and for conduct", adding that it is not right to suppose that "there is a single principle which must cover both the springs of action and the ultimate Goods" (*De finibus*, IV. xvii, tr. Rackham). This was, for Hume, a serious deficiency in Hutcheson's moral philosophy: benevolence was both the motive or spring of action and the ultimate good. But there were many passions and affections which are considered to be virtuous, and the end or good or virtue of the passion always lies beyond itself. Parental affection is a virtue, not for its own sake, but because it prompts us to care for our children. Benevolence is approved, not because it is benevolence, but because it prompts us to relieve the distressed and afflicted. Besides, there are other virtues, where the motive is not natural or instinctive; and this is the case with justice. There is no natural instinct to abstain from the possessions of others, or to repay a loan; yet these activities are virtuous. Therefore the motives which prompt us to respect the possessions of others, repay loans, perform what we have contracted to do, must also be virtuous. Since these motives are not natural or instinctive, they must be artificial or conventional in origin. This was the first of the three arguments contained in this section (T 477–80).

Hutcheson might well have replied to Hume's first point that he had never written that regard for virtue was the motive that prompts us to be virtuous or just. It was always benevolence, general and public, or particular and private, which is considered a virtue by the moral sense. He might have asked further why anyone should care for children, relieve the distressed, respect the possessions of others, if it were not that human nature is so constituted or designed that failure to act benevolently brings to mind an idea of vice; and our conduct is justly deplored by ourselves as well as others, when we fail to act in a benevolent spirit.

Hume devoted the second argument of this section to an examination of the claim that public or general benevolence should be considered the origin or motivation of justice. The difficulty is that "That is a motive too remote and too sublime to affect the generality of mankind, and operate with any force in actions so contrary to private interest as are frequently those of justice and common honesty" (T 481). This was one of the traditional criticisms made by Sceptics and Epicureans of the moral psychology of the Stoics. But the same psychology was also inconsistent with the experimental account of the passions outlined in the previous book of the *Treatise*. For "there is no such passion in human minds, as the love of mankind, merely as such":

> But in the main, we may affirm, that man in general, or human nature, is nothing but the object both of love and hatred, and requires some other cause, which by a double relation of impressions and ideas, may excite these passions. (T 481–2)

In Book II, Hume had argued that a passion must have an object, which is either oneself or another; and the object must be associated or related in the imagination with ideas of other persons or things: it is only in relation to particular persons and things that we feel passions which have an influence on our conduct (T 329–32).

Hutcheson would not have disagreed in the case of justice, particularly in that part of justice which concerns perfect as distinct from imperfect rights. He acknowledged that public or general benevolence was too weak a motive to prompt people to secure the rights of property and performance of contracts for themselves and others. It was private or particular affection for family, friends and neighbours which prompts us to have regard for justice. But the problems with private benevolence or affection were also insuperable in Hume's view. For we are obliged to respect the possessions of and repay loans to persons for whom it is impossible to feel any natural affection or private benevolence: profligate scoundrels, wretches, persons whom one cannot help but despise. They have a right, however, to their possessions, to the return of money or objects they have loaned. Our motive to behave justly with respect to such persons cannot be particular or private benevolence, or natural affection. We behave justly in such cases because we understand that it is in our interest and in the interest of others to observe the rules and conventions of justice. This interest is the only motive strong enough to counter the passions that would prompt us to behave instinctively. This interested motivation, then, is not natural or instinctive; it derives from artificial arrangements, or conventions, or rules which regulate the passions and the imagination of people in society (T 482–4).

Hume's and Hutcheson's position on the origin or derivation of the ideas of justice and property remained directly opposed. Three years later, on receiving a copy of Hutcheson's Latin compend, Hume recalled their continuing disagreement concerning the origin of justice, not without exasperation that Hutcheson seemed oblivious to the merits of Hume's reasoning:

> You sometimes, in my Opinion, ascribe the Original of Property & Justice to public Benevolence, & sometimes to private Benevolence towards the Possessors of the Goods, neither of which seem to me satisfactory. You know my Opinion on this head. (HL I, 47)

XI. THE APPENDIX

Hume returned to his differences with Hutcheson one last time in the *Treatise*, to reiterate his position on matters on which they differed. He took the opportunity to restate his views in the Appendix after Book III. The opening statement of the Appendix, "There is nothing I wou'd more willingly lay hold of, than an opportunity of confessing my errors" (T 623), would have recalled to Hutcheson Hume's letter of a few months before, in which he said "I admire so much the Candour I have observd in Mr Locke, Yourself, & a very few more, that I woud be extremely ambitious of imitating it, by frankly confessing my Errors" (HL I, 39). In the text, Hume acknowledged that "I have not been so fortunate as to discover any very considerable mistakes in the reasonings deliver'd in the preceding volumes" (T 623). There was, to be sure, an exception – personal identity. Hutcheson had had reservations about a theory of personal identity, similar to Hume's, some years earlier.[48] It is not unreasonable to think that he would have repeated these reservations to Hume, who seems, again, to have been attempting to revise his very different philosophy to accommodate, so far as this was possible, Hutcheson's concerns.

But on other subjects, Hume remained adamant. One of these was belief, where he was also at pains to emphasize the analogy between belief and other sentiments of the human mind (T 623–7). What is the nature of belief? Is it a distinct idea or feeling of the reality of an object which we conjoin with our idea of it? Or do we simply perceive the idea in a more lively or vivacious manner? Hume argued that it must be the latter. He offered two preliminary reasons: first, we have no abstract idea of existence; secondly, if belief consisted in a separate idea, we might believe anything at all, since the imagination is able to conjoin and separate ideas at whim. But if belief is a more lively or vivacious manner of conceiving an idea, this can be explained, experimentally, i.e. by a natural relation or association of ideas prompted by a present impression. The analogy with moral perception is evident. It is erroneous to suppose that we have an idea or sentiment of virtue which we conjoin or annex to our perceptions of actions and qualities of character. We perceive the virtue or the vice of actions and of qualities of character when these ideas impress themselves upon us in a particularly lively or vivacious manner. Hume offered four additional considerations in support of his theory of perceptions (and by analogy moral perceptions).

1. We have no experience or immediate awareness of this additional feeling or impression.
2. It is simpler to suppose that the feeling of conviction is merely the manner in which the idea is perceived than to suppose that this feeling of belief (or of virtue) is a separate impression.
3. The cause of this feeling of conviction or belief can be explained. It is "nothing but the idea of an object, that has been frequently conjoin'd, or is associated with a present impression. This is the whole of it" (T 626).
4. One can explain the influence of belief upon the passions by supposing that belief is nothing but an idea conceived in a particularly lively or vivacious manner. For ideas enlivened in this way make an impression. And the passions are nothing but impressions of sensation or reflection. No separate idea or feeling is required to account for this influence.

The differences between Hume and Hutcheson on this point are therefore fundamental; and they apply to every aspect of human nature – the understanding, the passions and morals. If a separate or distinct or concomitant idea of existence or of virtue was required to account for belief or for moral distinctions, the capacity to conceive such ideas would have to be explained. Hutcheson never hesitated to explain the faculty or power to conceive moral and other ideas by the providence of a generous or benevolent Deity; but in Hume's view, as we have seen, this was not a satisfactory or even a philosophical answer to the problem.

XII. THE EPIGRAPH

In the epigraph prefixed to Book III of the *Treatise*, Hume quoted the following lines from Lucan's *Pharsalia*:

> ... Duræ semper virtutis amator,
> Quære quid est virtus, et posce exemplar honesti.[49]

This was a plea addressed to Cato by his lieutenant, Labienus. Cato was urged to consult the oracle of Jupiter Ammon, on the outcome of the civil war between the forces of Pompey (whom Cato supported) and Caesar. Cato's soldiers had been wearied, crossing the African desert, by heat, sandstorms, snakes and thirst. Now they had arrived, by chance or fate, at a temple which housed an oracle, still active, and famed for its wisdom. Here was an opportunity, or so Labienus thought, to discover whether their efforts, the hardships they had suffered, the war itself, had been justified. But Cato, as Lucan tells the story, was offended by this appeal. He saw no need to consult an oracle to discover virtue. He was himself the model of an honourable man.[50]

It is sometimes supposed that Hume's use of these lines as the epigraph to Book III was a signal to his readers that he was, like Hutcheson, a defender of the cause of virtue. But the context permits a different interpretation. Hume was identifying with Labienus, who had uttered the appeal which Hume recited. It was an appeal to a Stoic lover of stern virtue, a contemporary Cato, to ask what virtue is, and bring before his mind a model of an honourable man. There may have been other Catos among Hume's acquaintances. But the most famous lover of Stoic virtue among them must surely have been Hutcheson. It seems not implausible to suppose that Hume was directing this plea to Hutcheson, and to lovers of stern virtue like Hutcheson, to reconsider their idea of virtue and their idea of an honourable man. For Hume, as for Labienus, the answer was not obvious; it would require an oracle to pronounce on the matter. In Hume's mind the oracle would appear to have been Book III of the *Treatise*.

XIII. CONCLUSION

From this examination of the differences between them, and of the alterations Hume made to the manuscript of the *Treatise* to persuade Hutcheson of the merits of Hume's approach, it is possible to draw a number of conclusions. One is that Hume's moral philosophy was not at all Hutchesonian in origin or inspiration: it derived rather from a tradition of moral philosophy, the substantive Epicurean tradition adopted by Bayle and other modern sceptics, which was opposed by Hutcheson in all the separate expressions of his moral philosophy. Secondly, one can explain the apparent anomaly that Hume's account of the passions and the virtues should have exhibited certain affinities with Hobbes's moral psychology. Hume was clearly responding, in parts of Book III, to problems that had been posed by Hobbes; and he was writing within a tradition of moral philosophy that included Hobbes. Thirdly, one may now recognize how the alterations Hume made to Book III have conveyed the misleading impression that he was a Hutchesonian in his moral philosophy. He was attempting to find areas of agreement with Hutcheson so that he could persuade the senior philosopher to revise his thinking on the subject of virtue and vice in light of Hume's more scientific understanding of the subject. Fourthly, one can better appreciate, in this light, why Hutcheson should have been so diffident of Hume's philosophy, why he should have exerted himself "to the utmost of his Power" to prevent Hume from being appointed to a chair in moral philosophy (HL I, 58). Finally, and most importantly, it allows one to comprehend Hume's moral philosophy within the framework of his philosophy as a whole, and so to recognize it as part of an integrated view of human nature, which included the understanding and the passions.[51]

NOTES

1. N. Kemp Smith, *The philosophy of David Hume* (London 1941), p. 12, subtitle.
2. *Ibid.*, p. 562.
3. D. D. Raphael, *The moral sense* (Oxford 1947), p. 46.
4. D. D. Raphael, 'Hume's critique of ethical rationalism', in *Hume and the Enlightenment*, ed. W. B. Todd (Edinburgh 1974), p. 14.
5. A. N. Prior, *Logic and the basis of ethics* (Oxford 1949), p. 31.
6. D. F. Norton, *David Hume: Common-sense moralist, sceptical metaphysician* (Princeton 1982), p. 132.
7. Norton, p. 131.
8. Prior, pp. 31–2; Raphael, 'Hume's critique', p. 16; Norton, pp. 147–8.
9. Kemp Smith, pp. 14–20.
10. T. F. Mayo, *Epicurus in England (1650–1725)* (Dallas 1934), p. xvii: "popular opinion . . . has insisted upon regarding Epicureanism as a crude and scandalous pursuit of pleasurable sensation. This very usual misinterpretation . . . has more in common with the sensationalism of Aristippus and the Cyrenaic School than with what Epicurus actually taught."
11. Bayle's endorsement of the morals of Epicurus and his disciples (see below, n. 16) was thought by one of his eighteenth-century critics to have been inconsistent with his Pyrrhonism. Jean-Pierre de Crousaz, *Examen du pyrrhonisme ancien et moderne* (1733), pp. 411ff., thought that Bayle, as a Pyrrhonian, should have been entirely indifferent in his moral judgements; instead he endorsed, in practice, the principles of the Epicureans. Hume parodied the frivolous Epicurean tradition in his essay 'The Epicurean' (Ess. 138–45). But in the two *Enquiries*, he was prepared to regard the moral principles of

Epicurus himself as consistent with his own scepticism, with certain qualifications, e.g. with regard to self-love.

12. Horace, *Satires*, I. iii. 111ff. Hume had appealed to the authority of Horace, "one of the best Moralists of Antiquity", in his letter to Hutcheson (HL I, 33), citing Horace's pronouncement, a few lines earlier (98), that utility itself is the mother of justice and equity.

13. Cicero, *De finibus bonorum et malorum*, I. xvi. This passage was quoted at length by Pierre Gassendi in his work on the morals of Epicurus. I follow an English translation of Bernier's abridgement of the works of Gassendi, *Three discourses of happiness, virtue and liberty. Collected from the work of the learn'd Gassendi by Monsieur Bernier. Translated out of French* (1699), pp. 74–5. Bernier's abridgement of Gassendi would have been available to Hume as a member of the Physiological Library. See below, n. 28.

14. St Evremond, 'Des belles-lettres et de la jurisprudence', from 'A Monsieur le Maréchal de Créqui, etc.', in *Oeuvres en prose*, 4 vols, ed. R. Ternois (Paris 1962–9), IV, p. 135.

15. St Evremond, 'Sur l'amitié', *Oeuvres*, III, pp. 310–11. Hume regarded St Evremond as a writer of insight on the subject of the virtues. See T 599, E 237 and 251–2.

16. *Epicurus's morals. Translated from the Greek by John Digby, esq. with comments and reflections taken out of several authors* (1712), p. 145. Many of these comments derive from remarks made by the Baron des Coustures, in *La Morale d'Epicure, avec des réflexions* (1685). This work was reviewed enthusiastically by Pierre Bayle, in *Nouvelles de la république des lettres* (January 1686), art. IX, reprinted in *Oeuvres diverses* (1727), I, 474–6. It was Bayle's view that the morals of Epicurus were much better adapted to human nature than the ideas of the Stoics: "Les idées d'Epicure sont beaucoup plus proportionnées à notre état, . . . les autres n'étoient que francs Comédiens" (p. 475). See also *Dictionnaire historique et critique* (2nd edn 1702; English translation by Pierre Desmaizeaux, 1734–8), s.v. 'Epicurus', esp. Remark M. Hume was, of course, an avid reader of Bayle's writings during the period in which he composed his *Treatise*. See letters to Michael Ramsay, March 1732 (HL I, 12); 26 August 1737 (*Archiwum historii filozofii i mysli spolecznez* 9 (1963), pp. 133–4).

17. The relevant passages from these authors were reproduced by Pufendorf, in his description "of the Natural State of Man". See Samuel Pufendorf, *Of the law of nature and nations . . . To which are added all the large notes of Mr Barbeyrac* (1729), II. ii. 2, pp. 102–5. Pufendorf's ambivalent relation to the Epicurean tradition in morals has been examined by Fiametta Palladini, in 'Lucrezio in Pufendorf', *La cultura* 19 (1981), 110–49, and *Samuel Pufendorf discepolo di Hobbes: Per una reinterpretazione del giusnaturalismo moderno* (Bologna 1990).

18. Cicero, *Pro sexto*, I. 42; Gassendi/Bernier, p. 322. The same passage is cited by Pufendorf, p. 104.

19. Gassendi/Bernier, p. 318.

20. Cicero, *De officiis*, I. vii. This passage is also cited by Pufendorf, IV. iv. 8, p. 370.

21. Bayle, 'Du tien et du mien', in 'Nouvelles lettres critiques sur l'histoire du Calvinisme', *Oeuvres diverses*, II, p. 280. See also E. Labrousse, *Pierre Bayle. II: Hétérodoxie et rigorisme* (The Hague 1964), p. 477.

22. *Epicurus's morals*, p. 147.

23. Gassendi/Bernier, pp. 332–4, citing Cicero, *De officiis*, III. v.

24. *Epicurus's morals*, p. 158.
25. Pufendorf, II. iii. 20, pp. 143–6.
26. See also *A dissertation on the passions* (1757), GG IV, 151n.: "Property . . . is a species of *causation*. It enables the person to produce alterations on the object, and it supposes that his condition is improved and altered by it. It is indeed the relation the most interesting of any, and occurs the most frequently to the mind."
27. Hume's observation appears to have been a refinement of a less elegant remark of Mandeville's. See Bernard Mandeville, *The fable of the bees*, 2 vols, ed. F. B. Kaye (Oxford 1924), I, p. 124.
28. *The Physiological Library. Begun by Mr. Steuart, and some of the students of natural philosophy in the University of Edinburgh, April 2. 1724* (EUL, MS De 10.127). See M. Barfoot, 'Hume and the culture of science in the early eighteenth century', in *Studies in the philosophy of the Scottish Enlightenment*, ed. M. A. Stewart (Oxford 1990), 151–90.
29. Robert Boyle, *The Christian virtuoso: Shewing, that by being addicted to experimental philosophy, a man is rather assisted, than indisposed, to be a good Christian* (1690). Cf. E. J. Dijksterhuis, *The mechanization of the world picture*, tr. C. Dikshoorn (Oxford 1961), p. 436: "Like Gassend, [Boyle] is a practical atomist. However, he avoids any terms connected with the word atom, nor does he like to be called an Epicurean, because of the associations with a special world-view implied in the word."
30. Francis Hutcheson, 'Alterations and additions made in the second edition of the Inquiry into beauty and virtue' (1726), p. 20.
31. 19 February 1726; reprinted in James Arbuckle, *A collection of letters and essays on several subjects*, 2 vols (1729), I, 394–407.
32. *An essay on the nature and conduct of the passions and affections. With Illustrations on the moral sense* (1728), pp. 207–8, 211.
33. Hutcheson, *De naturali hominum socialitate oratio inauguralis* (1730), p. 8. I follow an unpublished translation made by Michael Silverthorne.
34. I. S. Ross, 'Hutcheson on Hume's *Treatise*: An unnoticed letter', *Journal of the history of philosophy* 4 (1966), 69–72.
35. From the English translation, *A short introduction to moral philosophy* (1747), pp. 21–2.
36. Raphael, 'Hume's critique'.
37. *A letter from a gentleman to his friend in Edinburgh* (1745), p. 30.
38. Norton, p. 100, n. 5.
39. Bayle, 'Réponse aux questions d'un provincial', in *Oeuvres diverses*, III, p. 521, and the article 'Eve', in *Dictionnaire historique et critique*, Remark F. See also Labrousse, pp. 79–80, n. 35, and p. 475, who links the theme of the servitude of reason to the passions to the Augustinian as well as the sceptical dimension of Bayle's thought.
40. Bernard Mandeville, *An enquiry into the origin of honour, and the usefulness of Christianity in war* (1732), 2nd edn, introd. M. M. Goldsmith (London 1971), p. 31: "All Human Creatures are sway'd and wholly govern'd by their Passions, whatever fine Notions we may flatter our Selves with; even those who . . . strictly follow the Dictates of their Reason, are no less compell'd so to do by some Passion or other, that sets them to Work, than others, . . . whom we call Slaves to their Passions."
41. Kemp Smith, pp. 45, 149.
42. Raphael, *Moral sense*, p. 98.

43. Norton, pp. 131–2.
44. In its fullest version, the correction reads: "*Self-interest* is the original Motive to the *Establishment* of Justice: but a Sympathy with *public* Interest is the Source of the *moral* Approbation, which attends that Virtue. This latter Principle of Sympathy is too weak to controul our Passions; but has sufficient Force to influence our Taste, and give us the Sentiments of Approbation or Blame." (T 670, referring to 499–500).
45. Pufendorf, *On the natural state of men,* tr. M. Seidler (Lewiston, NY 1990), pp. 112–16.
46. Hutcheson, *De naturali hominum socialitate,* pp. 11–13.
47. Horace, *Satires,* I. iii. 98; Hugo Grotius, *Rights of war and peace* (London 1738), Preliminary discourse, sec. XVII, p. xx; Pufendorf, *Law of nature and nations,* II. iii. 10, p. 128.
48. Hutcheson to Wm Mace, 6 September 1727: *European magazine* 14 (1788), 158–60.
49. "Lover always of stern virtue, ask what virtue is, and call for a model of the honourable man" (*Pharsalia,* IX. 563). Most modern editions read *saltem* ("at least") for *semper* ("always").
50. "There is humour in Labienus's naïveté. Standing before his eyes is the exemplar he would have Cato ask about – Cato himself" (F. M. Ahl, *Lucan: An introduction* (Ithaca, NY 1976), p. 264).
51. This essay was written while I was a Simon Research Fellow at the University of Manchester.

3

Hume and the invention of utilitarianism

STEPHEN DARWALL

When the act happens, in the particular instance in question, to be productive of effects which we approve of, much more if we happen to observe that the same motive may frequently be productive, in other instances, of the like effects, we are apt to transfer our approbation to the motive itself, and to assume, as the just ground for the approbation we bestow on the act, the circumstance of its originating from that motive.

Bentham[1]

'Tis evident, that when we praise any actions, we regard only the motives that produced them, and consider the actions as signs or indications of certain principles in the mind and temper. The external performance has no merit. We must look within to find the moral quality. . . . After the same manner, when we require any action, or blame a person for not performing it, we always suppose, that one in that situation shou'd be influenc'd by the proper motive of that action, and we esteem it vicious in him to be regardless of it.

Hume[2]

The ideas we have come to think most central to utilitarianism did not assume their familiar shape before Bentham. Bentham was not the first in the history of ethics to advance the greatest-happiness principle as a normative doctrine. Hutcheson had already written that "that action is best, which procures the greatest happiness for the greatest numbers";[3] and, among others, Cumberland had put forward a broadly utilitarian doctrine within the framework of natural law.[4] But Bentham invented *philosophical utilitarianism*, to use Scanlon's helpful phrase.[5] He was the first to advance a utilitarian normative ethic on the basis of the philosophical conception of morality's nature which would become distinctive of the utilitarian tradition. He was the first to argue that facts concerning the (non-moral) good of persons provide the only rationale (or "extrinsic ground", as he called it) for a normative ethical view, and to argue for utilitarianism on this basis.[6]

Compare Hutcheson. One of Hutcheson's main aims in the *Inquiry concerning the original of our ideas of virtue or moral good* was to exhibit how any moral proposition involves irreducible, distinctively moral, ideas (which he called "approbation" and "condemnation", respectively). These ideas, he maintained, naturally arise only when we contemplate the actions and affections of moral agents. "MORAL GOODNESS denotes our Idea of *some Quality apprehended in Actions, which procures Approbation, attended with Desire of the Agents Happiness*" (*Inquiry*, intro.; R I, 261). And by 'action', he means not what Hume calls an "external performance", but the realization in action of an "affection" or motive. There *is* a sense, he believes, in which acts that actually *produce* happiness are morally good, namely, as an alternative for choice considered independently of motive. But this sense is derivative. What makes such acts worthy of moral choice is that they realize that at which morally good motives aim. For Hutcheson, facts about individual well-being never provide a rationale by themselves for thinking an action worthy of moral choice, since such facts simply concern what he calls "natural", and what we might call non-moral, goodness. Any grounding for the proposition that action is morally choiceworthy to the extent that it realizes happiness must relate such action to the distinctive ideas of morality. And these apply, in the first instance, to motive and character, and only derivatively to action.

This, if we may speak anachronistically, turns Bentham on his head. Bentham argued that the most fundamental approval is directed to the existence of pleasurable, and the absence of painful, *states*, and that we transfer this approval to acts and to motives we think realize these states. Sometimes, because we transfer our approbation from its usual effects to the motive itself, we "assume, as the just ground for the approbation we bestow on the act, the circumstance of its originating from that motive". But this is an error. Ultimately, the rationale for our evaluations of both acts and motives is the happiness or unhappiness to which they lead.

It is well known that Hume took some of the main lines of his sentiment-alist meta-ethic from Hutcheson's theory of the moral sense, although, as I shall show, important details have not been well recognized. And, like Hutcheson, Hume held that moral approbation concerns only motive and character in the first instance. Indeed, in one way he went even farther in this direction, since Hutcheson maintained that acts acquire a kind of moral value, choiceworthiness, considered independently of motive. Hume's position was that "the external performance has no merit"; approbation is only of action as a "sign or indication of certain principles in the mind or temper". "When we require any action, or blame a person for not performing it", what we require is never an action *per se*, but a person's being properly moved: "we always suppose, that one in that situation shou'd be influenc'd by the proper motive of that action, and we esteem it vicious in him to be regardless of it" (T 477).[7] An action *can* be performed "from a certain sense of duty", but this happens only when a person "who feels his heart devoid of" a virtuous principle does something characteristic of it, "in order to acquire by practice, that virtuous principle, or at least, to disguise to himself, as much as possible, his want of it" (T 479). The action itself has no merit, not even derivatively.

This all seems even farther from Bentham than Hutcheson was, but it is only part of the picture. In what follows I aim to show that elements of Hume's moral philosophy constitute a radical departure from Hutcheson, in the direction of a view that, like philosophical utilitarianism, seeks a basis for a normative moral doctrine in propositions about non-moral good. It is well known that Hume argued that "reflexions on the tendencies of actions have by far the greatest influence, and determine all the great lines of our duty" (T 590).[8] But it is also generally noted by commentators that he contrasts these with "immediately agreeable" virtues. Even here, however, it can be shown that he meant to argue that approbation of the trait derives from thoughts of the natural (non-moral) goodness which the trait realizes or causes. None of this was lost on Bentham. He wrote that, when he read the *Treatise,* he "felt as if the scales had fallen" from his eyes; he "learned to see that *utility* was the test and measure of all virtue".[9]

Second, Hume urged that the distinction "usual in all systems of ethics . . . betwixt *natural abilities* and *moral virtues*", which Hutcheson had made the very foundation of his moral philosophy, is "merely a dispute of words" (T 606).[10] Hutcheson could hold that thoughts of the felicific tendencies of acts provide no independent rationale for the moral assessment of acts and motives because he believed such thoughts do not yet engage the fundamental, distinctively moral ideas. But Hume put in question the very category Hutcheson thought fundamental. And once this was done, a path was cleared to the idea that, if an external ground can justify the approval of a trait, it can also justify the approval of an act. A non-moral rationale for a moral ranking of acts was no longer blocked by the thought that any answer to the question of what a person morally should do can only be based on propositions involving fundamental moral notions that apply, in the first instance, only to motive and character.

Thus Hume emerges as a crucial transitional figure in the development of utilitarianism. In fact, as I shall show, Hume's very presentation of his ideas in the *Treatise* reflects this. While much has been written on Hume's ethics, commentators have generally failed to grasp the details of Hume's debt to Hutcheson in his initial presentation of the theory of moral sentiment at the beginning of Book III of the *Treatise,* and the conflicts between this, more Hutchesonian version of the theory and further developments which take Hume in the direction of Bentham.[11] Necessarily, therefore, they have failed to grasp the true nature of Hume's transitional role.[12]

I aim to correct this. I sketch the main outlines of Hutcheson's moral philosophy in section I, and show, in section II, the uncanny resemblance between it and Hume's initial presentation of his positive meta-ethics. Section III describes Hume's psychology of moral sentiment, and section IV shows how this, together with Hume's rejection of Hutcheson's distinctively moral value, clears the space for philosophical utilitarianism to occupy.

I should make clear that I am not claiming in any of this that Hume himself was a utilitarian of any sort. As he responded to Hutcheson's complaint that the *Treatise* "wants a certain Warmth in the Cause of Virtue", his primary project was descriptive and analytical: to provide an "Anatomy" of the human mind (HL I, 32–3). Whereas the philosophical utilitarian is concerned to advance a rationale or ground for a normative ethical doctrine, Hume's project was primarily to describe the complex patterns of our normative views as they are actually realized in human psychology. His major claim was that the psychology of moral sentiment is *in fact* one in which thoughts of the pleasure and pain which contemplated traits are believed to produce give rise to approbation and blame. Unlike Bentham, he was unconcerned to argue that these are the only philosophically respectable grounds for approving traits or, *a fortiori*, acts. Partly for this reason, surely, Hume was also utterly unattracted by maximizing utilitarian normative doctrines.

I. HUTCHESON AND THE DISTINCTIVELY MORAL IDEAS

Hutcheson is most famous for the theory of the moral sense. Since he accepted Locke's dictum that every simple idea requires a sense to receive it, this simply follows for him from his contention that moral notions all involve irreducible, distinctively moral ideas. Throughout the Introduction and section I of the *Inquiry,* Hutcheson gives example after example, in an effort to convince readers who will "consult their own Breasts" that we distinguish a peculiarly moral goodness from "natural" goodness. The perception of pleasure, together with the idea that something can raise it "mediately, or immediately", is sufficient to give us the notion of "natural Good". But no construction out of this idea can give us the concept of moral goodness; this requires a different irreducible idea, which we have owing to moral sense. Contemplating the "kind Affections of rational Agents", we spontaneously have (through moral sense) the idea of a kind of goodness which cannot be reduced to the tendency of such affections actually to produce natural good – whether to us as observers, or to the beneficiaries of kindness.[13]

The thesis that ideas received by moral sense form the basis for judgements of a peculiarly moral kind of good and evil was prominent in Hutcheson's *Inquiry* from the first edition. It was not, however, until the third edition, published in 1729, that its entire force and theoretical role became clear. In the earlier editions, Hutcheson defined 'moral goodness' and 'moral evil' at the outset of the *Inquiry* in the following terms:

> The Word MORAL GOODNESS, denotes our Idea of *some Quality appre-hended in Actions, which procures Approbation, and Love toward the Actor, from those who receive no Advantage by the Action.* MORAL EVIL denotes our Idea of *a contrary Quality, which excites Aversion, and Dislike toward the Actor, even from Persons unconcern'd in its natural Tendency.* (*Inquiry*, 1st edn, intro.; SB I, 69)

But beginning with the third edition, these definitions are substituted:

> The Word MORAL GOODNESS, in this Treatise, denotes our Idea of *some Quality apprehended in Actions, which procures Approbation, attended with Desire of the Agents Happiness.* MORAL EVIL denotes our Idea of *a contrary Quality, which excites Condemnation or Dislike.* Approbation and Condemnation are probably simple Ideas which cannot be farther explained. (*ibid.*, 3rd edn, intro.; R I, 261)

And whereas he had characterized moral sense in earlier editions as "a Determination of our Minds to receive amiable or disagreeable Ideas of Actions, when they shall occur to our Observation, antecedently to any Opinions of Advantage or Loss to redound to our selves from them", this gives way, from the third edition on, to: "a Determination of our Minds to receive the simple Ideas of Approbation or Condemnation, from Actions observed" (I. viii; R I, 269).

Hutcheson thus moved from describing the sentiments felt through moral sense in relatively vague terms that might refer to responses caused by contemplating many things other than the actions and motives of moral agents, to using terms apparently selected to pick out precisely these.[14] 'Approbation' still appears, but it is now clear that he intends a particular sort of approbation, a simple idea that is distinct from, say, the pleasure which a person with what Hutcheson later called "publick Sense" feels for the happiness of others or whatever might cause it.[15] And 'Condemnation', with its full judicial overtones, replaces the more general 'Aversion'.[16] Thus Hutcheson's considered view is that moral good and evil are distinguished from the natural good and evil that might result from them, by virtue of the fact that contemplation of the former spontaneously causes simple ideas distinctive of morality, approbation and condemnation respectively, whereas contemplation of the latter only gives rise to ideas of different kinds.

Now if the fundamental moral notion is of a kind of value that can be realized only in "Affections of rational Agents" considered intrinsically (I. i; SB I, 73; R I, 264), one may well wonder how Hutcheson gets to an act-utilitarian normative ethic. Everything in Hutcheson's ethics relates back to the fundamental moral ideas received by moral sense, and the major link is his thesis that every morally good affection is an instance of benevolence, and that the morally best motive is universal benevolence.[17] He takes it, moreover, that interpersonal quantitative assessments of happiness or natural good are unproblematic and that universal benevolence aims at the greatest happiness overall. The amount of overall good a person actually produces on an occasion is, he thinks, a function of the degree of the agent's virtue (i.e. benevolence) and her "ability", in which he evidently includes her knowledge of opportunities to do good. Thus in the earlier editions of the *Inquiry*, he writes "$M = B \times A$"; where M is the "*Quantity* of *publick Good*", B is the degree of benevolence, and A is the degree of the agent's ability to do good (III. xi; SB I, 110). Here we should note two things. First, the degree of the agent's virtue just is the degree of her benevolence, irrespective of what good that motive will actually cause or tend to cause. Disability in doing good does not disable moral goodness. Second, if we hold ability fixed, an agent's moral goodness varies with the actual "Moment of Good" she produces. The morally best agent aims at producing the greatest happiness overall.

This is why Hutcheson says that "in comparing the *moral Qualitys* of Actions, in order to regulate our *Election* among various Actions propos'd . . . we are led by *our moral Sense*" to think that "*that Action* is *best*, which procures the *greatest Happiness* for the *greatest Numbers*" (III. viii; R I, 283–4).[18] *Moral choiceworthiness*, the "moral Quality" of acts relevant to an agent concerned with "*Election* among various Actions propos'd", is distinct from the moral goodness consisting in a benevolently motivated action's capacity to "procure Approbation". Moral sense approves directly of universal benevolence. And the choiceworthiness of acts that tend to produce the greatest overall natural good derives from the fact that such action achieves that at which moral goodness aims.

Similar remarks hold for Hutcheson's theory of rights, a utilitarian account which rivals Mill's in its subtlety. Hutcheson titles the section in which he discusses rights, 'A Deduction of some Complex moral Ideas, viz. of Obligation, and Right, Perfect, Imperfect, and External, Alienable, and Unalienable, from this Moral Sense'. And he begins by reminding his readers of "the *true Original* of moral *Ideas*, *viz. This moral Sense of Excellence in every Appearance, or Evidence of Benevolence*" (VII. i; R I, 292). "From this Sense too", he writes, "we derive our Ideas of RIGHTS."

> Whenever it appears to us, that a *Faculty of doing, demanding, or possessing any thing, universally allow'd in certain Circumstances, would in the whole tend to the general Good*, we say that one in such Circumstances has *a Right to do, possess, or demand that Thing*. And according as this Tendency to the *publick Good* is *greater* or *less*, the *Right* is *greater* or *less*. (VII. vi; R I, 297)

Like his view of the morally eligible, Hutcheson's account of rights is utilitarian without being grounded in philosophical utilitarianism. On the contrary, since the idea of a right is a complex moral idea, any rationale for a claim of right must go via the fundamental moral ideas. That certain conventions of "doing, demanding, or possessing" things would realize the greatest good, constitutes a rationale for a claim of right only when it is conjoined with the premise that the morally best character aims at the greatest good.

To summarize: for Hutcheson, the moral approbation of acts and motives cannot derive from approbation of their effects, as Bentham would later hold. Indeed, in the specific sense in which Hutcheson used the term to refer to the simple idea received by moral sense, *approbation* is never felt when contemplating anything other than motives or actions as involving them. It is because we feel approbation, properly so called, when we contemplate benevolence that we approve derivatively of acts and institutions that achieve that at which benevolence aims, and not because we approve of this state that we approve acts and characters that tend to achieve it.

It may seem odd to find the thought that an aim has moral value being entertained independently of any thought of the moral value of its object.[19] It is, of course, unproblematic that benevolence can be thought morally praiseworthy in a way that happiness itself cannot. What may seem puzzling is that moral praise of benevolence could be ungrounded in the premise that overall happiness is morally valuable and choiceworthy in itself. Hutcheson compounds the puzzle, indeed, by insisting that all morally good motives (in fact, all rational motives) implicitly regard action (and motive) as having only *instrumental* value to the production of natural goods.[20] Even so, in Hutcheson's framework the positive regard we feel for the happiness of others is a response of "publick Sense", not one of moral sense. What moral sense approves is benevolence, not its object.

II. HUME'S HUTCHESONIANISM

This position is unquestionably distant from the view on which Hume settles, both in the *Treatise* and in the *Enquiry*. Most obviously, it requires a substantial line to exist between evaluations that are distinctively moral and those that are not, whereas Hume argues even in the *Treatise* that the distinction is purely verbal (T 606). And in the *Enquiry*, his project, he says, is to "analyse that complication of mental qualities, which form what, in common life, we call *Personal Merit*", explicitly avoiding the terms 'moral good' and 'virtue'.[21]

None the less, when Hume first presents his meta-ethics in the *Treatise*, this aspect of his considered view is nowhere in evidence, and the similarity to Hutcheson's moral sentimentalism is striking indeed. Part I of Book

III, 'Of virtue and vice in general', is devoted to the source of "moral distinctions". And even if it is supposed that in Section I Hume simply assumes a distinction "usual in all systems of ethics" in order to show that it cannot be given a rationalist grounding, he appears to make the *same* assumption in presenting his own view in Section II, where he argues that "moral distinctions [are] deriv'd from a moral sense".[22] His contention there is not that some general category of merit can be grounded in sentiment, but that "decisions concerning moral rectitude and depravity" and "moral good and evil" can.

There is, in fact, a marked contrast between the terms Hume uses to describe the sorts of evaluation with which he is concerned in Part I of Book III of the *Treatise* and those of later sections and of the *Enquiry*. In the *Treatise*, Hume frequently uses such negative moral terms as 'criminal', 'wrong', 'guilt', 'moral deformity', 'iniquity', and, most frequently, 'moral evil' – terms which carry the same judicial overtones of culpability, lacking adequate excuse, as Hutcheson's 'Condemnation'. In later sections, and especially in the *Enquiry*, however, these terms occur much less frequently. Hume there uses what he regards as general terms of approbation and disapprobation – 'merit' and 'demerit', 'virtue' and 'vice' – arguing, as we have seen, that only as a verbal matter can we distinguish a peculiarly moral disapprobation.[23]

And there are other, more specific similarities to Hutcheson in *Treatise* III. i. In considering the objection that "if virtue and vice be determin'd by pleasure and pain", then "irrational" or "inanimate" objects "might become morally good or evil" (T 471), Hume makes two responses, each of which is characteristically Hutchesonian.[24] He says, first, that not "every sentiment of pleasure or pain, which arises from characters and actions, [is] of that *peculiar* kind, which makes us praise or condemn" (T 472). The similarity to Hutcheson's thesis that moral good and evil, when contemplated, cause the fundamental, distinctively moral pleasures and pains of approbation and condemnation can hardly be coincidental.[25]

Hume's second reply is more complex, and must be quoted at some length.

> *Secondly*, We may call to remembrance the preceding system of the passions, in order to remark a still more considerable difference among our pains and pleasures. Pride and humility, love and hatred are excited, when there is any thing presented to us, that both bears a relation to the object of the passion, and produces a separate sensation related to the sensation of the passion. Now virtue and vice are attended with these circumstances. They must necessarily be plac'd either in ourselves or others, and excite either pleasure or uneasiness; and therefore must give rise to one of these four passions;

which clearly distinguishes them from the pleasure and pain arising
from inanimate objects, that often bear no relation to us. (T 473)

Evidently, Hume thinks there is something about the way virtue and vice
relate to love and pride, and hate and humility, respectively, that enables
him to respond to the objection, but it takes some care to see exactly
what it is. Note first that Hume distinguishes between the "separate
sensation", pleasurable in the case of virtue, painful in the case of vice,
which is caused by their contemplation, and the distinct "sensation[s] of
the passion" to which these pleasures and pains give rise – the sentiments
of love or pride and hatred or humility. The "preceding system of the
passions" to which Hume refers is, of course, his double-relations theory
of the indirect passions. According to this, the pleasurable sensation felt
in contemplating, say, another's virtue, causes love towards that person.
It does so because a double relation obtains among the relevant ideas and
impressions. The first is between the ideas of the object of love, the
other, and of its cause, the contemplated quality of *his*; and the second
between the impressions of the "separate" pleasurable sensation felt in
contemplating his virtuous quality and the pleasurable sensation of love
itself.

But how exactly does this respond to the objection? How does it show
that on Hume's account of moral distinctions it is not true that a quality
of any inanimate object can be morally good or evil so long as it can
"excite a satisfaction or uneasiness"? We may grant Hume that, since the
object of love is "some other person", qualities of inanimate objects will
not generally cause love and hatred. But the question remains, why does
that show that these qualities are not morally good and evil so far as
Hume's account is concerned?

Hume must be thinking that something about the fact that only pleasures
and pains of the former kind do *cause* love and hatred makes only the
former criteria of virtue and vice. But, again, nothing in the notion that
virtue is such that its contemplation causes pleasure, even a peculiar kind
of pleasure, makes this further consideration relevant.[26] It would be
relevant only if for a quality to be a virtue or vice it were not sufficient
for its contemplation to produce pleasure or pain, even of a peculiar
kind, but also necessary that its contemplation give rise, respectively, to
love or hatred. That is, it would be relevant, only if Hume meant to be
embracing both conjuncts of Hutcheson's definition of moral goodness as
"some Quality apprehended in Actions, which procures Approbation,
and Love toward the Actor" (*Inquiry*, intro.; SB I, 69).[27]

Thus, Hume's two replies are both Hutchesonian, the first explicitly,
the second implicitly. Inanimate objects cannot be morally good or evil,
first, because contemplating their qualities does not cause the peculiar
pleasures "which make us praise or condemn", and, second, because it

does not cause love, as contemplating morally good traits does.[28] So not only does Hume initially present his meta-ethics within a framework that is Hutchesonian in its trappings, by assuming Hutcheson's distinction between natural and moral good, and by using Hutcheson's term 'moral sense' to refer to the source of the latter idea. He also *appears* to adopt Hutcheson's ideas about the relation between moral good and evil and sentiment, in detail, when he argues in Part I that his account of the basis of moral distinctions is not vulnerable to the sort of objection he had himself posed to the rationalists.

III. APPROBATION DE-MORALIZED

Having answered the objection to his own satisfaction, Hume turns, without pause, to a project that sets him straightway on a course utterly different from Hutcheson's, and that leads him ultimately to a position much closer to Bentham's in the passage quoted at the beginning. "It may now be ask'd *in general*", Hume writes, "concerning this pain or pleasure, that distinguishes moral good and evil, *From what principles is it derived, and whence does it arise in the human mind?*" (T 473). Hume immediately rejects Hutcheson's answer, that it comes from a sense that is an "*original* quality" and part of our "*primary* constitution" (see also II. i. 7, T 296). He is driven to this conclusion by two things. For one, he simply disagrees with Hutcheson that every motive and trait of which we approve on reflection is a form of benevolence. This must be false, he thinks, if for no further reason than that we also approve of justice, and justice cannot be resolved into benevolence, as he shows in Part II.[29] But actually, justice is only a special case. A careful survey of the traits found worthy of praise, Hume thinks, yields a daunting list, few of which are forms of benevolence. If the moral sentiment were to be explained by an "original" sense, then it would have to be originally constituted to be sensitive to every virtue (and vice) on the list. And, second, even if this were possible, Hume is bound to prefer simpler explanations by his guiding aim in the *Treatise* to apply "experimental philosophy to moral subjects" (T xvi). To proceed otherwise "is not conformable to the usual maxims, by which nature is conducted, where a few principles produce all that variety we observe in the universe" (T 473). It is necessary, therefore, to "find some more general principles, upon which all our notions of morals are founded" (T 473).

Hume believes he has a simpler explanation, although it takes somewhat different forms in the *Treatise* and in the *Enquiry*. In the *Treatise*, the explanation proceeds in terms of sympathy (in that work's special sense) with the good consequences of virtues, both immediate and remote. The *Enquiry*'s explanation is a bit different, featuring what Hume there calls "humanity" or benevolence. The explanations share the same structure, however, proceeding roughly as follows. When we contemplate a (virtuous) trait, we are led by an association of ideas to consider the pleasurable states produced or realized by that trait, either in the agent himself or in others "with whom he has any commerce" (T 590). Through sympathy or humanity we come either to have similar pleasurable feelings ourselves (*Treatise*), or to be pleased at the pleasurable feelings of those we are drawn to consider (*Enquiry*). This pleasure is disinterested. Therefore, we feel disinterested pleasure in contemplating the trait. Therefore, we feel the moral sentiment in contemplating the trait. Therefore, the trait is a virtue.

Before proceeding, I should note that these are not the only explanations Hume offers. In the *Treatise,* he also writes that "we always consider the *natural* and *usual* force of the passions" when we find traits virtuous or vicious (T 483; see also 488). Thus, we will count a parent's lacking in the usual degree of parental affection a vice, and this, apparently, independently of any thought of the ill effects, immediate or remote, of this lack. Since my object is to uncover aspects of Hume's thought that led in the direction of philosophical utilitarianism, I shall simply ignore this and some other complicating features.

The *Treatise* explanation of why virtues are approved by reflection on their immediate and remote effects is advanced primarily in Part III, although it relies on earlier remarks about sympathy from Book II and Hume's account of the "moral obligation" to justice in Part II of Book III. "To discover the true origin of morals", he writes at the beginning of Part III, "and of that love or hatred, which arises from mental qualities, we must take the matter pretty deep, and compare some principles, which have been already examin'd and explain'd" (T 575). The most important of these is sympathy. As numerous commentators have noted, what Hume means by sympathy is a psychological mechanism that changes ideas of feelings into (approximately) the feelings themselves.[30] One of the ways it is supposed to work is as follows. On seeing, say, a wince of pain, one is led, by an association of ideas, to the idea of the pain one takes to have caused it. The wincer will be related in some degree to oneself. Perhaps she will be one's acquaintance, or one's sister, or perhaps only a fellow human being. Depending on how closely she is related, "the impression of ourselves", which "is always intimately present with us", will infuse the idea of (her) pain more or less with *its* force and vivacity. This converts the idea of (her) pain into an impression; it becomes "the very passion itself" (T 317).[31]

Now Hume believes he can already explain on principles firmly established earlier in the *Treatise* why the thought of a motive or trait leads naturally to the thought of effects it tends to cause. What the principle of sympathy provides is a way of explaining why, when these effects are pleasurable, the *idea* of the effect will be transformed into a pleasurable *impression*. Hume's reasoning is enthymematic, but it must proceed from here in something like the following fashion. Since, when such a motive or trait is contemplated disinterestedly, there is a "separate sensation" of pleasure, which, because it is caused by a quality in a person, generates either love or pride (by the theory of double relations), this explains why we regard the motive as virtuous or the trait as a virtue.

But what exactly is the relation between the pleasures generated directly by sympathy with, say, the pleasures a trait is believed to bring about, and the pleasure which Hume identifies as approbation of the trait? Hume is not clear on this point. There are places where he seems almost to say that any disinterested pleasure felt on contemplating a trait is the moral sentiment. Thus: "every thing, which gives uneasiness in human actions, upon the general survey, is call'd Vice, and whatever produces satisfaction, in the same manner, is denominated virtue" (T 499). If so, then the pleasure directly generated by sympathy may just *be* the moral sentiment.

But Hume also says things that suggest a different model. "All the sentiments of approbation, which attend any particular species of objects", he writes, "have a great resemblance to each other, tho' deriv'd from different sources; and, on the other hand, those sentiments, when directed to different objects, are different to the feeling, tho' deriv'd from the same source" (T 617). This suggests that approbation is not simply felt on the occasion of disinterestedly contemplating a trait, but has the trait *as object*. If so, since the pleasures generated directly by sympathy with a trait's effects do not have the trait as object, they cannot themselves be approbation.

To take this line, Hume would need some account of how the sympathetically generated pleasures none the less *cause* approbation. He does not give one in the *Treatise*, but there is no reason why he could not. Indeed, some kind of double-relations mechanism, like the one he invokes to explain the indirect passions, might be available to explain approbation as well.[32] Thinking of a trait believed to have pleasurable consequences causes a "separate sensation" which is pleasurable, namely, the one directly generated by sympathy, and this resembles the pleasurable impression of approbation. Second, the idea of the object of approbation, the trait, resembles the idea of its cause (either the trait itself, or the effects, considered as effects of *this* trait). Thus, reflection on the (believed) pleasurable effects of a trait produces approbation of the trait, either because sympathetically generated pleasures constitute approbation, or because they cause it.

The claim that approbation can arise from thinking about a trait's pleasurable effects is made, first, for the artificial virtues, relying on points already established in Part II. In these instances, at least, "reflecting on the tendency of characters and mental qualities, is sufficient to give us the sentiments of approbation and blame" (T 577). From there Hume proceeds to consider the natural virtues. And here he may appear to restrict the role of sympathy in establishing traits as virtues. Thus he writes that "*most* of those qualities, which we *naturally* approve of, have actually that tendency, and render a man a proper member of society" (T 578).[33] The reason for Hume's caution is that there are traits that are, he thinks, not simply "useful", but "immediately agreeable".[34] Thus, "wit, and a certain easy and disengag'd behaviour, are qualities *immediately agreeable* to others" (T 590).[35] He cautiously concludes that, therefore, moral sentiments "may arise either from the mere species or appearance of character and passions, or from reflexion on their tendency to the happiness of mankind" (T 589).

This may be taken to suggest that immediately agreeable traits cause approbation in a spectator when contemplated in themselves, without any sympathy with pleasures the trait itself realizes or produces. But while Hume sometimes gives the impression that this is his view, in actuality it is not. One place this can be seen is in the well-known set of passages about correction of sentiment and the general point of view.

Hume originally raises the problem of intersubjective agreement in connexion with judgements of useful traits by sympathy. Since sympathy works on a principle of psychological distance – we sympathize more with the feelings of those to whom we are closer (they are more closely related to the impression we always carry of ourselves) – this creates a problem of calibration, owing to the different distances from the moral observer to the persons whom an observed trait tends to benefit or harm. Although I cannot "feel the same lively pleasure from the virtues of a person, who liv'd in *Greece* two thousand years ago, that I feel from the virtues of a familiar friend and acquaintance", yet "I do not say, that I esteem the one more than the other" (T 581).

Hume explains this by the fact that we are in the habit of judging vice and virtue, not by the pleasures we actually have when we contemplate personal qualities, but by those we would have if "we remain'd in one point of view". Only if we can fix on "some *steady* and *general* points of view; and always, in our thoughts, place ourselves in them, whatever may be our present situation" can we hope to agree in our judgements with each other, and with ourselves over time.

Hume actually makes a quite definite proposal about which point of view would be best for these purposes, although it is almost never discussed by commentators.[36] "Being thus loosen'd from our first station, we cannot afterwards fix ourselves so commodiously by any means as by a sympathy with those, who have any commerce with the person we consider" (T

583). His suggestion, as he reiterates in several places, is that judgements of vice and virtue are made by sympathizing with the effects of traits on those most immediately affected by them in "that narrow circle" in which the agent moves (T 602).[37]

Now the relevance of this discussion for our purposes is that Hume makes this same proposal for calibrating judgements of traits that are "immediately agreeable". Indeed, the structure of Hume's categories of virtue, most prominently in the *Enquiry* but also in the *Treatise*, makes it clear that by virtues that are immediately agreeable, Hume generally means, not traits that are immediately agreeable *when contemplated by an observer or judge*, but traits that are either immediately agreeable to the person himself or to those who have commerce with him. The immediate pleasure is one that is *experienced by those who actually engage the trait*, either by exercising it or by having intercourse with those who do, and even then not necessarily through contemplating it.[38] When we approve of "another, because of his wit, politeness, modesty, decency, or any agreeable quality which he possesses", "the idea, which we form of their effect on his acquaintance, has an agreeable influence on our imagination, and gives us the sentiment of approbation" (E 267). He concludes, in the *Treatise*, that

> however directly the distinction of vice and virtue may seem to flow from the immediate pleasure or uneasiness, which particular qualities cause to ourselves or others; 'tis easy to observe, that it has also a considerable dependence on the principle of *sympathy* so often insisted on. We approve of a person, who is possess'd of qualities *immediately agreeable* to those, with whom he has any commerce; tho' perhaps we ourselves never reap'd any pleasure from them. We also approve of one, who is possess'd of qualities, that are *immediately agreeable* to himself; tho' they be of no service to any mortal.[39]

Even with "immediately agreeable" traits, therefore, the moral sentiment arises in a spectator by reflection on pleasures the trait is believed to bring about. If the trait is immediately agreeable to others, then a spectator will approve it because she sympathizes with the immediately agreeable pleasures of those who may actually encounter the person with the trait. And if the trait is immediately agreeable to the person who has it, then a spectator will approve it because she sympathizes with pleasure the trait itself realizes in that person. In either case, a spectator's (pleasurable) approbation is not an intrinsic response to contemplating the trait, but a response generated by sympathy with other pleasurable states she believes likely to be caused or realized by it.

It follows, then, that for every Humean virtue, approbation in a spectator results from reflection on pleasurable states the virtuous trait is believed likely to bring about.[40] We have been following the *Treatise* account, but nearly identical things can be said of the line Hume takes in the *Enquiry*. Substituting humanity for sympathy simply means that the spectator's reflective pleasures are generated by fellow-feeling rather than by *Treatise*-sympathy. Everything else remains the same. Now this does not mean that Hume thinks, as Bentham would later, that naturally good consequences are the initial *objects* of approbation, and that this approval then gets transferred to acts and motives by an association of ideas. On the contrary, Hume consistently held, like Hutcheson, that we approve traits and motives such as love, the *desire* for others' natural good, rather than naturally good states themselves. His disagreement with Hutcheson rather concerned how approbation comes to have this (and other) objects.

Hume was in no doubt that his theory of the origins of the moral sentiment was a radical departure from Hutcheson. In a letter to Hutcheson he wrote:

> I desire you to consider, if there be any Quality, that is virtuous, without having a Tendency either to the public Good or to the Good of the Person, who possesses it. If there be none without these Tendencys, we may conclude that their Merit is derivd from Sympathy. (HL I, 34–5)

He might have added that not only could he explain the existence of a separate disinterested sensation when we contemplate traits we believe to produce or realize pleasurable states; he could also explain why we love those who have them. But actually, Hutcheson and Hume were as divided about love as they were about the nature of the moral sentiment. Hutcheson had written that, unlike genuine virtues such as "Honesty, Faith, Generosity, Kindness", natural goods, such as "Houses, Lands, Gardens, Vineyards, Health, Strength, Sagacity", procure "no Love at all toward the Possessor, but often contrary Affections of *Envy* and *Hatred*" (*Inquiry*, 1st edn, intro.; S I, 70).[41] Hume disagreed, as his double-relations theory required that he should. The contemplation of "natural goods" causes love, when they belong to another (and pride, when they are one's own). Nor need they be qualities of the person. They can be possessions, such as "houses, gardens, equipages" (T 357).[42] Contemplating these generates, by sympathy or humanity, a pleasurable sensation which resonates with the pleasurable sensation of love, as does the idea of *the other's* possessions or qualities resonate with the idea of love's object. So even though Hume agreed with Hutcheson that virtue causes love, he held that this does not restrict its scope in the way Hutcheson had supposed. In particular, Hume believed, it could not support the distinction Hutcheson wanted it to: one "usual in all systems of ethics . . . betwixt *natural abilities* and *moral virtues*" (T 606).

This actually raises something of a problem for Hume. Not even Hume was willing to count a fine house as among a householder's virtues, even though contemplating it causes pleasures, by sympathy or humanity, which may seem indistinguishable from those caused by contemplating character traits, and even though contemplating either causes love.[43] He explicitly restricts virtue and vice, merit and demerit to "mental qualities" that produce certain "peculiar sentiments of pain and pleasure" "by the survey or reflexion" (e.g. T 574–5). Presumably, the "peculiar" sentiment must be approbation itself. It is simply a truth of human psychology, Hume must think, that when we contemplate, first, a person's wit, and then, her fine house, the former causes a peculiar sentiment of approbation directed to her wit, while the latter does not cause a similar sentiment directed to her house. And this, even though the pleasures generated by sympathy are no more distinguishable than those of different virtuous traits, though both cause love, *and* though whatever double relations between impressions and ideas hold in the one case would seem to hold also in the other.[44]

Of course, even if Hutcheson could have been convinced that all virtuous traits have a tendency to good, he could never have accepted that this is what *makes* them morally good, since this tendency is only a fact about natural goodness. But, then, Hume does not really say that a tendency to good is what makes a trait a virtue. With Hutcheson, he consistently asserts that the only thing that can do this is approbation of the trait, together with love of the agent.[45] But, Hutcheson must have thought, if sympathy with the natural goods a person's "mental qualities" are apt to realize is sufficient to cause Humean approbation, then causing Humean approbation cannot be what makes a trait morally good.

IV. SLOUCHING TOWARDS BENTHAM

Ironically, the very reason that would have forced Hutcheson to reject Hume's account of the moral sentiment – that it was based entirely on sympathy with natural goods – is what especially suited it to Bentham's philosophical purposes. Bentham's problematic was almost the reverse of Hutcheson's. In his view, it is a *problem* for constructive moral and political discourse that participants frequently put forward views which they base on no more secure foundation than their own intuitive moral convictions or feelings. In the first two chapters of *An introduction to the principles of morals and legislation*, Bentham argues that the principle of utility is the unique solution to this problem.

Consider, first, how he describes the principle of utility. "The principle here in question", he remarks, "may be taken for an act of the mind; a sentiment; a sentiment of approbation; a sentiment which, when applied to an action, approves of its utility, as that quality of it by which the measure of approbation or disapprobation bestowed upon it ought to be governed" (*Principles*, p. 1n.). As Bentham is thinking of it, the principle of utility is less a "first-order" moral proposition, than a thesis about the form that moral thought and discourse should itself take. It puts forward what he calls an "extrinsic ground" or "external standard", not for conduct directly, but for *approving* conduct. Again, it approves of an action's utility, as "that quality by which the measure of approbation or disapprobation bestowed upon it ought to be governed". By calling the standard which the principle of utility imposes on moral thought and discourse "extrinsic" or "external", Bentham means to convey that it is fully independent of the approbation of conduct which it is taken to recommend, and can, therefore, be uncontroversially applied even by people who have sharply conflicting moral views.[46]

"The various systems that have been formed concerning the standard of right and wrong", Bentham writes, "all of them [consist] in so many contrivances for avoiding the obligation of appealing to any external standard" (*Principles*, p. 8). The "obligation" here is an intellectual or philosophical one. All previous systems of ethics, Bentham believes, are guilty of simply "prevailing upon the reader to accept of the author's sentiment or opinion as a reason for itself" (*Principles*, p. 9). In a remarkable footnote, he attempts to illustrate how the major modern British ethical theories – Hutcheson's "moral sense", Reid's "common sense", Price's "rule of right", Clarke's "fitness of things", among several others – merely amount to devices that give the appearance of making claims that are entitled to the respect of others, but without anchoring them in any justification that could command rational assent. The reader is rather induced, or "prevail[ed] upon" to accept the author's sentiment or opinion as self-evident.

We need not concern ourselves too much here with why Bentham thinks that participants in moral and political debate undertake an "obligation" to appeal to an external standard in justifying their moral positions. I think it can be argued that one reason is that he regards such an obligation as a necessary condition of *liberal* public moral debate. When people make a moral claim on others, he suggests, but are unwilling to offer a reason for so doing that others could be expected to accept without already sharing the same moral views, this is implicitly coercive. Thus he writes of earlier theories:

> The mischief common to all these ways of thinking and arguing (which, in truth, as we have seen, are but one and the same method, couched in different forms of words) is their serving as a cloke, and pretence, and aliment, to despotism; if not a despotism in practice, a despotism however in disposition: which is but too apt, when pretence and power offer, to show itself in practice.[47]

And when he considers an objector asking "But is it never, then, from any other considerations than those of utility, that we derive our notions of right and wrong?", he responds:

I do not know: I do not care. Whether a moral sentiment can be originally conceived from any other source than a view of utility, is one question: whether upon examination and reflection it can, in point of fact, be actually persisted in and justified on any other ground, by a person reflecting within himself, is another; whether in point of right it can properly be justified on any other ground, by a person addressing himself to a community, is a third. The two first are questions of speculation: it matters not, comparatively speaking, how they are decided. The last is a question of practice: the decision of it is of as much importance as that of any can be. (*Principles*, p. 9n.)

These passages indicate that Bentham's own version of philosophical utilitarianism may itself have been situated in a larger, "liberal pragmatist" programme in moral and political philosophy. Taken with other passages in the first two chapters of the *Principles*, they suggest that Bentham thinks considerations of utility are uniquely suitable as a basis for non-coercive public moral and political debate. First, because they concern, to use Hutcheson's terms, natural and not moral good, they qualify as "external" or "extrinsic" grounds; they provide a morally uncontroversial basis for settling moral and political controversy. Second, they can form a basis for *practical* moral debate because, unlike any competing external ground, they engage the "two sovereign masters", pleasure and pain, which motivate all action.[48]

Whatever his own deeper philosophical motivations for doing so, Bentham clearly put forward the view that intuitive moral convictions about what a person should do require an independent rationale and that considerations of utility are uniquely suited to provide this. This is why I say that the reason why Hutcheson could not have accepted Hume's account of the moral sentiment – that it rested entirely on considerations of natural goodness, none of which engaged the distinctively moral ideas – is what suited it to Bentham's purpose: it pointed the way to what Bentham could regard as a suitably independent, "external" rationale.

There is virtually no reason to think that Hume would have agreed with this use of his ideas. As he understood human psychology, the objects of approbation never include naturally good effects, but only motives and traits of character and, derivatively, acts as signs of these. Most importantly, Hume agreed with Hutcheson that we approve such motives as love, the desire for the good of others, rather than natural goodness itself. And moreover, Hume believed that while we approve of traits we think have utility, this is not properly a philosophical ground or justification for our approval – as if approbation were ours to award on the basis of the best arguments as we see them. No such justification is needed or possible. We approve of useful and agreeable traits, he thinks, not because we are convinced these are good intellectual grounds for approving of them, but simply because, when we have thoughts of what such traits are apt to accomplish, this causes us to approve the traits and love those who have them. Thus the question that pushes a philosophical utilitarian such as Bentham towards act-utilitarianism – why, if what grounds the approbation of traits is utility, it should not also ground the approbation of acts directly – does not arise for Hume.

Still, even if Hume would not have been attracted by philosophical utilitarianism, he played a crucial role in preparing the way for this view. From Bentham on, the utilitarian tradition would generally take the position that moral claims – both of right and of moral good – require a rationale, and that the only philosophically respectable rationale consists in the (non-moral) value that acts and motives realize or produce. By arguing that convictions about the moral goodness of motives are themselves anchored in thoughts of the pleasurable states these bring about, Hume made an explicit argument against Hutcheson's view that moral approbation of motive and character is psychologically basic. And his argument could be read, by those with a different philosophical agenda, to suggest that what he thought psychologically more basic is also more fundamental in the order of justification. Thus did Hume open up a space for philosophical utilitarianism even if he did not himself occupy it.[49]

NOTES

1. *Introduction to the principles of morals and legislation*, ch. 2, sec. 19, in *The works of Jeremy Bentham*, 11 vols, ed. J. Bowring (Edinburgh 1838–43), I, p. 11. Later references will be to this edition.

2. T 477; see also 575.

3. Francis Hutcheson, *An inquiry into the original of our ideas of beauty and virtue* (1725), p. 164. Much of this first edition is reprinted in *British moralists*, 2 vols, ed. L. A. Selby-Bigge (Oxford 1897). The fourth edition (1738) is excerpted in *British moralists, 1650–1800*, 2 vols, ed. D. D. Raphael (Oxford 1969). Hereafter, my quotations will reflect the text of Hutcheson's third edition revision (1729) unless otherwise indicated; references will be included to section numbers and, when possible, to volume and page numbers in Selby-Bigge (SB) or Raphael (R); the latter is also cited for certain other sources.

   Bentham is sometimes said to have first encountered the greatest-happiness principle in Cesare Beccaria's *Dei delitti e delle pene* (1764): "la massima felicita divisa nel maggior numero". See, e.g., the translation by H. Paolucci (*On crimes and punishments*, Indianapolis 1963), p. 8n.

4. "Reason dictates to everyone as the end his own happiness joined with the happiness of others." Although rarely read these days, Cumberland's *De legibus naturæ* (1672) was an important work in the modern natural-law tradition. An English translation (*A treatise of the laws of nature*) by John

Maxwell was published in 1727. This passage comes from an excerpt translated by Raphael at R I, 100.

Various writers, such as John Gay, Bishop Berkeley and John Brown, elaborated utilitarian doctrines within a theological voluntarist interpretation of natural law.

5. T. M. Scanlon, 'Contractarianism and utilitarianism', in *Utilitarianism and beyond*, ed. A. Sen and B. Williams (Cambridge 1982), p. 108.

6. See, e.g., *Principles*, p. 8. On the distinction between moral and non-moral good, see W. K. Frankena, *Ethics* (Englewood-Cliffs, NJ 1963), pp. 47–8.

7. This may help to explain an otherwise puzzling passage in Hume's letter to Hutcheson of 17 September 1739, responding to some criticisms Hutcheson had made of his manuscript of Book III of the *Treatise*. Hume mentions an argument of Cicero's which he takes to show that "to every virtuous Action there must be a Motive or impelling Passion distinct from the Virtue, and that Virtue can never be the sole Motive to any Action. You do not assent to this; tho' I think there is no Proposition more certain or important" (HL I, 35). Since both propositions Hume here mentions were explicitly defended by Hutcheson in his writings, it is hard to reconstruct exactly what the dispute was. Hutcheson had held both that every (non-derivatively) morally good action was so by virtue of realizing a form of benevolence (which he held to be a natural motive) and that the sense of moral goodness can never be by itself a motive. In the *Essay*, he argued that desires are only raised by the prospect of pleasure, either to the agent or to someone else, and that, therefore, moral sense can only motivate by making vivid the contemplative pleasure one would make possible if one were to act on the motive of benevolence. See *An essay on the nature and conduct of the passions and affections*, 3rd edn (1742), pp. 62, 305. Perhaps, then, the dispute concerned the matter mentioned in the text.

8. Hume's talk of the tendencies of actions here, rather than those of motives or traits, should not be taken as evidence that he is departing from the view referred to above. In the cases he has in mind, the good consequences of the motives come primarily through the good consequences of the actions they motivate.

9. *Principles*, pp. 268–9n.

10. Although he continued to hold that only "mental qualities" are objects of approbation and therefore have merit. On this see the last several paragraphs of Section III.

11. Commentators have often appreciated the general nature of Hume's debt to Hutcheson, especially as this involves Hume's criticisms of Clarkean rationalism. On the latter, see, e.g., B. Stroud, *Hume* (London 1977), pp. 10, 251, 263–4.

12. Thus Norman Kemp Smith, whose pioneering work on the importance of Hutcheson's influence on Hume was a great achievement of scholarship, lists the "main differences" between them "apart from Hume's less 'warm' method of writing about morals, and his view of the 'natural' as not resting directly on final causes", as "(1) his view of natural abilities as virtues, (2) his contention that regard for virtue can never be the sole 'motive' to any action [see n. 7 above] . . . and (3) his refusal to allow that moral distinctions, resting as they do on grounds peculiar to human nature, allow of any theological application" (*Philosophy of David Hume* (London 1941), p. 42n.).

Scholars sometimes show a tendency to attribute to Hume Bentham's view that we judge a trait morally good if it usually has good consequences because we feel approbation for the general good. But this is not Hume's view. Like Hutcheson, he reserves the term 'approbation' for a sentiment felt in contemplating motive and character, and never uses it to refer to pleasure felt in contemplating the general good. Thus, Kemp Smith queries Hume: "why . . . does it come about that public good is morally approved?" (p. 148, see also 196). Stroud makes the same error: "The well-being of particular people and the flourishing of society and mankind generally must be things which themselves give me pleasing sentiments of approbation" (*Hume*, p. 196).

Several scholars have written on both Hutcheson's and Hume's ethics without fully recognizing the tensions I describe here. See, e.g., D. D. Raphael, *The moral sense* (London 1947); and V. M. Hope, *Virtue by consensus* (Oxford 1989). F. C. Whelan remarks on Hume's transitional role between Hutchesonian moral-sense theory and Benthamite utilitarianism, but fails to appreciate the tensions between these and, thus, within Hume's own text. See *Order and artifice in Hume's political philosophy* (Princeton 1985), p. 215.

13. Usually, Hutcheson is primarily concerned to show that moral approval is disinterested, i.e. with the former claim. But he also argues that "as soon as any Action is represented to us as flowing from *Love, Humanity, Gratitude, Compassion,* a *Study* of the good of others, and an ultimate Desire of their Happiness . . . we . . . admire the lovely Action" (*Inquiry*, I. ii; R I, 265. See also I. iv; SB I, 77–8).

14. Although, it should be noted, Hutcheson does not say that approbation and condemnation have the affections and actions of agents *as objects*. He simply says that these ideas are "procur'd" by apprehending qualities of actions or affections. Actually, even here he says that the qualities themselves procure approbation and condemnation, although it is clear enough that he means via their contemplation.

15. Hutcheson writes that pleasure at the happiness of others must be different from moral approbation "since many are strongly affected with the Fortunes of others, who seldom reflect upon *Virtue, or Vice,* in themselves, or others, as an Object". See *Essay*, pp. 5–6.

16. It is worth noting that there was a robust tradition in this period of describing the internal sanction of conscience as "self-condemnation". Thus, e.g., Samuel Clarke: "For whoever acts contrary to this sense and conscience of his own mind is self-condemned" (R I, 202). And the Cambridge Platonist, Benjamin Whichcote: "Self-condemnation I take to be the very life of Hell" (*Select sermons* (1698), p. 62).

17. "BENEVOLENCE is a Word fit enough in general, to denote the internal Spring of Virtue. . . . But to understand this more distinctly, 'tis highly necessary to observe, that under this Name are included very different Dispositions of the Soul. Sometimes it denotes a *calm, extensive Affection,* or Good-will toward all Beings capable of Happiness or Misery: Sometimes, 2. A calm deliberate Affection of the Soul toward the Happiness of certain smaller Systems or Individuals; such as Patriotism, or Love of a Country, Friendship, Parental-Affection. . . . Now tho' all these different Dispositions come under the general Character of Benevolent, yet as they are in Nature different, so they have different Degrees of Moral Beauty. The first Sort is above all amiable and excellent." (*Inquiry*, 4th edn, III. vi; R I, 282.)

18. He also says that "*Dignity,* or *moral Importance* of Persons, may compensate Numbers", but since the moral importance of any character is equal to "the

Quantity of *publick Good* produc'd by him", this is not an independent criterion (*Inquiry*, III. viii and xi; R I, 283, 285).

19. I am indebted to Holly Smith for impressing this on me.

20. On this, see the *Essay*.

21. E 173. Cf. the remark in Appendix IV, 'Of some verbal disputes', that "on all occasions, where there might arise the least hesitation" in calling something which is appropriately the object of esteem and praise "morally good", because it is a natural ability, "I avoided the terms *virtue* and *vice*" (E 312).

22. This, of course, was Hutcheson's favoured formulation of his view. Hume's readers could have been expected to catch the reference.

23. "A blemish, a fault, a vice, a crime; these expressions seem to denote different degrees of censure and disapprobation; which are, however, all of them, at the bottom, pretty nearly of the same kind or species" (E 322). Even here, however, Hume cannot bring himself to claim that the species of "censure and disapprobation" *is* the same. This passage, which comes at the end of the *Enquiry*, bears an interesting relation to a similar passage at the end of the *Treatise*, where Hume notes what must be a puzzling fact in the face of his theory of sympathy-generated approbation: namely, that a convenient house and virtuous character, though both tend to produce utility and are approved by reflection on the utility they tend to produce, none the less "cause not the same feeling of approbation" (T 617). "There is something very inexplicable", he adds, "in this variation of our feelings; but 'tis what we have experience of with regard to all our passions and sentiments." I shall discuss this further below.

   Another point that deserves comment is that while Hume frequently uses 'blame' and 'censure' throughout both the *Treatise* and *Enquiry*, both these terms can carry the sense of unfavourable criticism that does not imply guilt, and he plainly uses them in this sense.

24. As he notes, this objection is like one Hume himself levels against the view that moral distinctions are grounded in the relations between ideas at T 466-7.

25. Granted, Hume also says in the next sentence but one that "'Tis only when a character is considered in general, without reference to our particular interest, that it causes such a feeling or sentiment, as denominates it morally good or evil". This might be thought to show that he believes it sufficient for a sentiment to be a moral sentiment, or sufficient at any rate for it to be a sentiment that establishes merit, that it be felt on a disinterested contemplation of traits. While that is Hume's considered view, all he says here is that it is a necessary condition. Granted again, Hume had already written on the preceding page: "since the distinguishing impressions, by which moral good or evil is known, are nothing but *particular* pains or pleasures; it follows, that in all enquiries concerning these moral distinctions, it will be sufficient to shew the principles, which make us feel a satisfaction or uneasiness from the survey of any character, in order to satisfy us why the character is laudable or blameable". But in itself this is not inconsistent with a Hutchesonian reading of "pleasure or pain . . . of that *peculiar* kind, which makes us praise or condemn" either. If it were true, as Hutcheson believes, that the only pleasures and pains we are moved to feel when we contemplate motives and actions disinterestedly are the fundamental, peculiarly moral ideas, then the two passages would have consistent Hutchesonian readings. Thus in section I of the *Inquiry* Hutcheson apparently believes that the main competitor to his theory of

moral sense is the thesis that we can only be pleased and pained by contemplating actions from self-love.

26. Unless, of course, the peculiar kind of pleasure just is one that causes (or is accompanied by) love, but then this virtually amounts to accepting Hutcheson's definition of moral goodness, to be discussed presently.

27. Cf. "Actions themselves, not proceeding from any constant principle, have no influence on love or hatred, pride or humility; and consequently are never consider'd in morality"; and "To discover the true origin of morals, and of that love or hatred, which arises from mental qualities . . ." (both from T 575). As with the passage just discussed from Part II, Hume conjoins these passages to a discussion of how, according to his theory of double relations, the pleasurable contemplation of personal qualities will cause love. Again, as in the earlier passage, this can only show that actions are "consider'd in morality" just in so far as they are seen to proceed from a constant principle, contemplation of which causes love or hatred, if it is already assumed that it is of the nature of virtue and vice to cause love and hatred respectively. At T 614, Hume calls "approbation or blame" a "fainter and more imperceptible love or hatred".

28. Actually, the two replies mix Hutcheson's formulation from the first and second editions of the *Inquiry* with that from the third and later editions. It is the latter, recall, in which the simple ideas of approbation and condemnation are explicitly mentioned, but these editions substitute "Desire of the Agents Happiness" for "Love toward the Actor". Moreover, Hume distinguishes between love and desire for the beloved's happiness. See T 367.

29. That this is so had already been argued forcefully against Hutcheson by Butler, both in Sermon XII and in 'A dissertation upon the nature of virtue' (R I, 374–7, 383–6).

30. See, e.g., Stroud, pp. 196–8. As Stroud points out, this has the impossible consequence that sympathy with a toothache produces a toothache. He suggests that Hume might be understood as proposing that sympathy produces feelings of the "same general affective quality as those we observe or contemplate".

31. The main discussion of sympathy in the *Treatise* occurs at pp. 316–21.

32. I am indebted for this suggestion to Geoffrey Sayre-McCord.

33. As the context makes clear, "that tendency" is the tendency to the good of mankind. Also: "moral distinctions arise, in a great measure, from the tendency of qualities and characters to the interest of society, and . . . 'tis our concern for that interest, which makes us approve or disapprove of them. Now we have no such extensive concern for society but from sympathy" (T 579).

34. This distinction is even more prominent in the *Enquiry*, where Hume divides all virtues into qualities (a) "useful to ourselves"; (b) "immediately agreeable to ourselves"; (c) "useful to others"; and (d) "immediately agreeable to others".

35. And other traits are immediately agreeable to the person who has them. On this, more below.

36. Here and throughout the rest of this paragraph I am indebted to Louis Loeb. I am told that Dorothy Coleman discussed this aspect of Hume's views in a paper for the 1988 meetings of the Hume Society in Marburg.

37. In this last passage the suggestion is explicitly made for traits Hume calls "good", and which he contrasts with "greatness of mind" (a point I am grateful to Annette Baier for pointing out). The passage on p. 583 does not seem to be similarly restricted, however. See, however, A. C. Baier, *A progress of sentiments* (Cambridge, MA 1991), p. 213.

Relativization to the narrow circle is not explicit in the *Enquiry*, although it is suggested by passages at E 269, 276 and 278. Hume gives no rationale for selecting this particular point of view except that "being thus acquainted with the nature of man, we expect not any impossibilities from him" (T 602). Needless to say, it has a substantial effect on his list of virtues and vices. For example, "when we enumerate the good qualities of any person, we always mention those parts of his character, which render him a safe companion, an easy friend, a gentle master, an agreeable husband, or an indulgent father. We consider him with all his relations in society; and love or hate him, according as he affects those, who have any immediate intercourse with him" (T 606).

It is worth noting that, on the most literal interpretation of the proposal, it does not actually solve the problem, since different individuals will obviously sympathize more or less with those in the narrow circle depending on their distance from them. This would be different if Hume meant to propose that we consider what sentiments we would feel were we to place ourselves in the point of view of those in the narrow circle. But while he does speak of placing ourselves in "some *steady* and *general* points of view", what he specifically proposes is "sympathy with those, who have any commerce with the person we consider" (T 581–3). And on Hume's theory of sympathy this is a different matter.

38. Thus, some qualities "are denominated virtuous from their being *immediately agreeable* to the person himself, who possesses them. Each of the passions and operations of the mind has a particular feeling, which must be either agreeable or disagreeable. The first is virtuous, the second vicious" (T 590).

Note, Hume thinks that there are some cases where simply to become aware of a trait is to be engaged by it. The "engaging endearments" of love are immediately agreeable to any spectator. But even here Hume says that the immediate pleasure of spectators derives from sympathy with the pleasures of the lovers themselves: "the very softness and tenderness of the sentiment, its engaging endearments, its fond expressions, its delicate attentions, and all that flow of mutual confidence and regard, which enters into a warm attachment of love and friendship: it will be allowed, I say, that these feelings, being delightful in themselves, are necessarily communicated to the spectators, and melt them into the same fondness and delicacy. The tear naturally starts in our eye on the apprehension of a warm sentiment of this nature" (E 257). See also E 260; T 604, 611.

39. T 590. And while no "views of utility or of future beneficial consequences" need precede approbation of immediately agreeable traits, "the same social sympathy, we may observe, or fellow-feeling with human happiness or misery, gives rise to both" (E 260).

40. Again, ignoring complicating factors of Hume's view such as the "natural and usual force of the passions" criterion at T 483.

In a deliciously ironic twist, Hume makes the following apparent exception: "there is also a certain *je-ne-sçai-quoi* of agreeable and handsome, that concurs to the same effect. In this case, as well as in that of wit and eloquence, we must have recourse to a certain sense, which acts without reflexion, and regards not the tendencies of qualities and characters. Some moralists account for all the sentiments of virtue by this sense. Their hypothesis is very plausible. Nothing but a particular enquiry can give the preference to any other hypothesis" (T 612). The irony, of course, is that Hume is saying that the best case for an "approbative sense" is a decidedly *non-moral* one. This reverses Hutcheson's position. Note also that this would not really be an exception, since it, too, would have to be subject to corrective sympathy with the immediately agreeable pleasures of those in the narrow circle.

41. For an excellent study of Hutcheson that stresses the role of love, see W. Leidhold, *Ethik und Politik bei Francis Hutcheson* (Freiburg and Munich 1985).
42. Is this not written with an eye on Hutcheson?
43. David Norton points this out in *David Hume: Common-sense moralist and sceptical metaphysician* (Princeton 1982), p. 115.
44. A double relation would exist between the pleasurable sensation of contemplating the house and the pleasurable sensation of approbation, and between the idea of object of the sentiment (the house) and the idea of its cause (the contemplated house).
45. Explaining the existence of an impression through other psychological mechanisms does not, Hume says, make the impression any less simple. Thus, pride is a simple impression, even though it can be explained by a psychological mechanism, and not as an original quality of the mind (T 277). More generally: "Ideas never admit of a total union, but are endow'd with a kind of impenetrability, by which they exclude each other, and are capable of forming a compound by their conjunction, not by their mixture. On the other hand, impressions and passions are susceptible of an entire union; and like colours, may be blended so perfectly together, that each of them may lose itself, and contribute only to vary that uniform impression, which arises from the whole. Some of the most curious phænomena of the human mind are deriv'd from this property of the passions" (T 366).
46. Of course, even if it is morally uncontroversial which act will maximize utility, it will not be uncontroversial that this should dictate, or even bear on, our approbation of acts, i.e. our view of what a person morally should do. Bentham's hope is to use the fact that utility will be uncontroversial in the first sense in a philosophical argument to settle controversy of the second sort. On this, see the next three paragraphs.
47. *Principles*, p. 9n. And earlier he says of someone who would put forward "his own *unfounded* sentiments", i.e. unfounded in an extrinsic ground, "let him ask himself whether his principle is not despotical" (p. 3).
48. "Admitting any other principle than the principle of utility to be a right principle, . . . let him [its proponent] say whether there is any such thing as a *motive* that a man can have to pursue the dictates of it: if there is, let him say what that motive is, and how it is to be distinguished from those which enforce the dictates of utility: if not, then last let him say what it is this other principle can be good for?" (*Principles*, p. 4)

Ross Harrison describes Bentham's argument for the principle of utility in the first two chapters of the *Principles* as designed to display its necessary role in a "public language of evaluation", but he does not mention Bentham's stress on avoiding "despotism", without which the argument for an "external standard" does not get off the ground. See *Bentham* (London 1983), pp. 183–94.
49. Research on which this essay is based was conducted with the support of a fellowship from the National Endowment for the Humanities.

4

Hume and the natural lawyers:
a change of landscape

PAULINE C. WESTERMAN

I. INTRODUCTION

One of the more conspicuous features of Hume's treatment of morals in the *Treatise* is his frequent use of vocabulary drawn from the natural-law tradition. To those who are acquainted with the works of Grotius or Pufendorf, all sorts of familiar themes recur. Hume deals with the nature of promises and obligation; he accounts for the origins of private property and justice, and he even refers explicitly to three laws of nature (T 469, 484, 516, 526).

This gives rise to the question of how far Hume's moral philosophy can be read as a genuine continuation of natural-law theory. Hume scholars are divided over this. Forbes thinks that Hume's philosophy can be characterized as a modern version of natural-law theory.[1] According to his interpretation, Hume's innovation was to present a secular and empirical account of human nature. Haakonssen claims that Hume's theory gives a more refined, more sociological version of the fundamental principles of natural law.[2] More recently, Buckle's study of the natural-law tradition and private property argues an even closer affinity between Hume and the natural lawyers.[3] On the other hand, there are scholars who argue that Hume was not a natural lawyer at all. Moore, for instance, contends that Hume's philosophy can be regarded as the sceptical answer to an ongoing debate between sceptics and natural lawyers.[4]

The relationship between Hume and the natural lawyers is hard to assess. Although his moral philosophy is presented in the manner of many natural lawyers and deals with a range of topics traditionally found in their theories, Hume scarcely mentions the works of his supposed illustrious "forerunners".[5] Apart from a well-known footnote in Appendix III of the second *Enquiry* where he quotes Grotius (E 307), references to Pufendorf and Grotius are conspicuous by their absence. His glancing reference to both in a letter to Hutcheson in 1739 (HL I, 33) is not of a kind that constitutes proof that he had seriously studied either. If Hume was aware that he made an important contribution to natural-law theory, he seems not to have acknowledged the achievement.

In this essay I shall advocate a different approach to this matter. If Hume reacted to natural-law doctrine, we should be aware that he did not merely react to the works of Grotius and Pufendorf proper, but to a standard body of knowledge into which their theories had been incorporated. By the time Hume became acquainted with the natural-law tradition, the writings of Grotius and Pufendorf were no longer at the avant-garde of political thought, but they were used as textbook material and reiterated verbatim during classes. There is no reason to think James Balfour, who taught moral philosophy at Edinburgh in the 1750s, was untypical in this: he "either read straightforward lectures on Pufendorf or did not lecture at all", and was thereby following a syllabus established by earlier professors like William Law and John Pringle.[6] The success of natural-law theory and its subsequent propagation and proliferation did not, however, leave the theory untouched. In the process, these once novel and contested doctrines lost their subtle nuances and ambiguities. What once counted as problematic was discarded, whereas new problems arose that were not even contemplated by the natural lawyers. Their successors are therefore confronted with a landscape which is fundamentally different from the one that they themselves initially explored. In this respect, the fate of political theories is comparable to that of scientific theories.[7]

We may compare the situation Hume was in to that of social scientists today. The latter may or may not have read Marx, but they use the concepts of "class structure" or "alienation" because these are integrative and uncontested elements of social theory today. They do not think it necessary to cite Marx each time they use these concepts, and are hardly likely to engage in a lengthy critique of Marxist theory, since their subject is a different one. Least of all will they think of themselves as having "improved" or "amended" Marxist theory. They use these categories as tools that are part of the tacit background knowledge of the profession and that serve as a framework for modern sociological research. But our present-day sociologist lives in a landscape very different from Marx's.

Similarly, if we encounter in Hume's philosophy such natural-law topics as "human nature", "laws of nature", "the origin of justice and property", "the obligation of promises", we should keep in mind that he may be using these notions with the same freedom that our social scientist today uses one-time Marxist notions. He is not necessarily interested in a critique of natural law, or promoting his theory as a better version of natural law, but he may still be using these tools to clarify the problems he was addressing. To understand *how* Hume used the tools that were initially invented by Grotius or Pufendorf, and for what purposes, we must compare the landscape Grotius and Pufendorf inhabited with the landscape that surrounded Hume. Hume's treatment of human nature and justice reveals that the core of natural-law doctrine had been undermined. His moral philosophy can be seen as the culmination of various conflicting tendencies within natural-law doctrine that paved the way for its own demise.

To establish this contrast, it is worth while to take a look first at seventeenth-century natural-law theory, its basic assumptions and the problems it addressed. I want to draw attention to two fundamental tenets. The first is the natural lawyers' use of human nature as the starting-point for the derivation of moral principles. The second concerns the function these moral principles are supposed to perform. In sections II and III, I shall deal with changes in the concept of human nature, and in sections IV to VI with the function of moral principles. On both fronts, drastic changes occur; these can shed light on Hume's moral philosophy, which will be analysed in sections VII to IX. An overall assessment of these developments will occupy sections X and XI.

II. HUMAN INCLINATIONS

It is an assumption shared by all natural lawyers, their differences notwithstanding, that it is possible to derive natural laws from a description of human nature. Human nature is the starting-point for an analysis of eternally valid precepts. We should keep in mind, however, that natural lawyers do not traditionally refer to a *factual* description. Thomas Aquinas did not refer to what people really do or really want in everyday life, but to human nature as designed by God. He referred not to actual behaviour, but to our inclinations; and these inclinations had been implanted by God as the architect of the universe. So Aquinas's description of human nature contains a normative element in itself. There was for him no conflict between description and prescription. People may err as to what their aim should be, or as to how they might achieve it, but this did not really affect the way their inclinations were designed by God. At a deeper level one could see that people were designed to strive for the good life, and for knowledge of God.[8]

For Grotius, things were more problematic than that. Contrary to Aquinas, he did not conceive of natural law as merely a different way of arriving at eternal truths that could equally be found in the Scriptures. He thought that natural law was the only way to build up consensus in a society that was deeply divided. Amid the turmoil of contesting countries and conflicting systems of belief, he wanted to gain access to universally valid laws of nature without having to dwell on God's intentions for mankind. He had to suppose that we could dispense with the religious hypothesis, since he wanted to establish a basis for international law which would be universally acknowledged by different religious and ideological groups. His claim that the eternal laws of nature are valid even when we avoid supposing that there is a God who governs the universe changed the order of demonstration.[9] Instead of describing the universe and human nature as the result of a divine design, Grotius had to derive the design from a description of human nature.

In this respect the well-known analogy between morals and mathematics is revealing for the situation Grotius was in.[10] Pufendorf, Locke and countless more minor figures all repeated the idea that from human nature alone certain immutable standards and rules can be deduced, in the same way that from the existence of a triangle alone the indubitable proposition can be deduced that its three angles are equal to two right angles. The analogy is meant to illustrate that moral reasoning can be as indubitable and self-evident as geometry. But it also served as a proof that by contemplation of human nature alone one could discover moral principles. Even without the religious hypothesis, the idea could be upheld that a normative element is contained within the description of human nature. For indeed, a triangle is a triangle if and only if its three angles can be equated to two right angles. In similar vein, man is human if and only if he is social and rational.

III. AN EMPIRICAL ACCOUNT OF HUMAN NATURE

For Grotius's successors it became increasingly difficult to maintain this position. Hobbes's account of human nature could not be simply discarded. In the post-Hobbesian period it was no longer thought to be a satisfactory strategy to abstract from the actual behaviour of human beings, and to uphold the idea that, although people looked like rectangles or pentagons, they were essentially triangles if you looked more closely.

It is very interesting to read Pufendorf's account of natural law, for it is marked by profound inconsistencies – inconsistencies that can be understood as a response to conflicting demands. On the one hand, Pufendorf saw himself as Grotius's successor. He echoed Grotius's demand for a new science of morals, which should be autonomous and free from interference by theologians and politicians. In the Preface to *De jure naturæ et gentium* he warns the theologians not to meddle with this subject, since it is not "proper for such men to lay claim to a greater authority in such matters than belongs to those who make a profession of this study" (tr. Oldfather, pp. vii–viii). And he adds: "Let the cobbler stick to his last." The basis for this new science was to be found in a thorough investigation of human nature. That for Pufendorf human nature remained the point of departure for any science of morals can be gathered from his frequent assertions that God plays only an indirect role. God can only alter the law of nature by changing human nature (I. iii. 5).

On the other hand, Pufendorf could not disentangle himself from Hobbesian psychology.[11] He asserts that man is essentially weak, depraved and selfish. But apparently, this realistic description could not be reconciled with the idea that human nature is a starting-point for the discovery of fundamental moral principles. A truly "empirical" account of human nature cannot by itself lead the way to natural laws.

Pufendorf's solution is far from convincing: contrary to his idea that God can change natural laws only by changing mankind, Pufendorf claims that it is ultimately God's *command* to be sociable and lead a social life. This reintroduction of a voluntarist approach to natural law paved the way for exactly those theological disputes that Grotius (and Pufendorf) had wanted to avoid. Apart from that, the normative element that had once been included *within* the description of human nature had been torn apart from human nature. Human nature had to be *supplemented* with God's command; and this threatened the whole enterprise of deducing natural laws from human nature alone.

Hobbes's influence, however, was all-pervasive. Together with the Cartesian theory of the passions it paved the way for an ever-growing awareness that human nature should be described as realistically as possible. That is why Spinoza, to mention just one example, in his political work bitterly complains about philosophers:

> In fact they conceive men, not as they are, but as they would like them to be. The result is that they have generally written satire instead of ethics, and have never conceived a political system which can be applied in practice; but have produced either obvious fantasies, or schemes that could only have been put into effect in Utopia, or the poets' golden age, where, of course, there was no need of them at all.[12]

Things were no different for Hume. The whole first section of the first *Enquiry* is dedicated to a critique of the moralizing philosophy. Hume advocates careful research into "the secret springs and principles, by which the human mind is actuated in its operations" (E 14). His plea for a more experimental method can therefore be seen as a continuation and elaboration of an ideal that was pervasive throughout the seventeenth and eighteenth centuries.[13]

For Spinoza, however, this more realistic description of human nature was not an ideal as such. It served as a necessary *means* to develop a realistic theory of society. The same can be observed in Hume. Both the *"poetical* fiction of the *golden age"* and the *"philosophical* fiction of the *state of nature"* are rejected on the ground that the situation of man and society should be conceived as "a medium amidst all these extremes" (E 188–9). Justice can only be understood if we adopt an account of man as neither angels nor monsters. And in Section IV of the second *Enquiry* Hume repeats the criticism that was by then well known, that the assumption that man was a thoroughly rational being, with sufficient "sagacity" and "strength of mind", would render political society superfluous

(E 205). Spinoza's assertion that in a golden age there would be no need for a political system is echoed by Hume, who asserts that if people had possessed the rationality ascribed to them by philosophers, "there had never, in that case, been any such thing as government or political society".

It is understandable that Hume from his own standpoint (and Spinoza from his) would think that he had a more adequate theory of morals than Grotius, just as social scientists now think they see things in a better way than their illustrious forerunners. The failures of the founding father of natural law were ascribed to his inability to disentangle himself from Aristotelian phraseology; a handicap Hume was now freed from, thanks to "a more experimental method".[14] But Hume had not seen why it was that Grotius and Pufendorf had failed to provide for a genuinely realistic account of human nature. For them human nature served as a starting-point for a derivation a priori of universal natural laws. And within the framework of this attempt, one had to refer *either* to a highly idealized account of human nature in which the normative element is included (Grotius's solution), *or* to a more realistic version for which one had to pay the price of introducing an extra element: God's commands (Pufendorf's solution).

Why, then, did Hume not find himself in the same awkward position as Pufendorf? How could he afford the luxury of a more empirical description of human nature without endangering the whole project of natural law? To answer this, we must turn to the second crucial tenet of natural law: the function that is performed by universally acceptable laws of nature.

IV. ETERNAL STANDARDS

Once more we should turn to Aquinas as a point of reference against which subsequent developments in natural-law theory can be appreciated. To Aquinas, natural laws formed a part of the all-embracing eternal law, which could be known and discovered by human reason, and which served as a set of fixed criteria by which positive laws could be judged and evaluated. Given man's inclinations, human institutions and laws were to be judged according to their ability to realize man's proper ends. Confronted, for instance, with the problem of private property, Aquinas could easily point to the limits of this institution. Theft could be justified if private property exceeded the limits within which it could contribute to the good life.

It is clear, however, that by removing the religious hypothesis, Grotius had to do without these clear limits and criteria. As we have seen, his idea of man was a rather abstract concept. He tells us only that man is essentially a social being, from which it was very difficult to derive criteria by way of a priori reasoning alone. It cannot be shown – conceiving of man simply on the model of the triangle – whether private property is justified or not.

That Grotius was aware of this problem is clear from his assertion that sometimes institutions cannot be deduced from natural law (and from human nature, which is the mother of natural law), which nevertheless can be found all over the world. In this case, he writes, these institutions must be understood as the products of human free will: "For whatever cannot be deduced from certain principles by a sure process of reasoning, and yet is clearly observed everywhere, must have its origin in the free will of man" (Prolegomena, par. 40). In dealing with these institutions he will rely on the reports of ancient writers or on biblical sources.

What we see here is very odd. The whole enterprise of a priori reasoning is abandoned and replaced by conventional a posteriori argument as soon as the really important institutions have to be justified. Now, human institutions are understood within a historical framework, and it is by investigating the origins of these institutions that a justification is sought. Grotius makes use of anthropological reports and biblical sources in order to contrast the current civilized world with an earlier barbarian state.

The state of nature figured not as a Hobbesian fiction, to get insight into the true nature of the human species as it is without governments and institutions; it served him rather as a device to contrast refined manners and luxury with the material misery of primitive society. The establishment of private property, of positive laws and of society itself, was all treated as a series of historical events, as crucial developments within an ongoing process of civilization. It was stressed that these institutions were established *gradually*; not by a "mere act of will" (*De jure belli ac pacis*, II. ii. 5). The transition point between the state of nature and civilized society was not marked by explicit consent, but by a gradual and tacit agreement. The whole argument in fact boils down to the assertion that these institutions are the product of human artifice, and that they can be seen as useful *additions* to natural law.

But if one reads Grotius's account of private property, it is clear that these historical accounts, although they were meant as justifications, offer very little in this regard. The only point of analysis where natural law comes in is in the concept of *consent*. Consent is a crucial notion, of course, since according to natural law only those laws are justified which are the product of consent. "Consent" is the thin thread with which the positive laws are linked with natural laws. The indirect nature of this link is clearly expressed by Grotius:

> [S]ince it is a rule of the law of nature to abide by pacts, out of this source the bodies of municipal law have arisen. . . . [T]he mother of

municipal law is that obligation which arises from mutual consent; and since this obligation derives its force from the law of nature, nature may be considered, so to say, the great-grandmother of municipal law. (Prolegomena, pars 15–16)

But although the notion of consent was a crucial thread, it conflicted with his desire to provide an adequate historical account. Grotius knew that there never was a moment at which all people willingly and consciously "consented". So he struggled to reconcile a realistic historical account (tacit, gradual, implicit) with the requirements of the great-grandmother.

What we see here is that it proved increasingly difficult to link the most important steps in the history of mankind to natural laws, or to their primary source: human nature. On the whole, we have to conclude that these accounts are far more successful as *explanations* than as *justifications*.[15]

V. MAN'S ARTIFICE

For Pufendorf, it was even harder to establish eternal principles by which positive laws and institutions could be justified. Despite his claims to the contrary, the major institutions of society could not be justified by referring to the depraved and weak nature of man. They could only be justified by referring to God's command. Yet, he obviously did not want to base his entire system of natural law on God's command alone, thereby obstructing the whole enterprise. In order to be a natural lawyer, he had to argue from human nature, but how?

His solution was an extension of Grotius's historical arguments. He emphasized man's *artifice* rather than human *nature*. Hence Pufendorf's theory that moral entities are the product of *imposition*.[16] The ultimate foundation for man's artifice can be found in God's decision to leave some matters for man to decide. In the case of private property, for instance, Pufendorf consistently argued that the biblical notion of "community of things" had to be understood in a negative way: God had given people the right to decide for themselves how to organize property (IV. iv. 2).

Related to this view is Pufendorf's distinction between so-called hypothetical and absolute commands. Absolute commands are laws that apply to all, "without regard for any institution formed or introduced by men". Hypothetical commands, on the other hand, "presuppose some state or institution formed or accepted by men" (II. iii. 24). Examples of hypothetical commands are those that concern private property. In a culture where there is no such thing as private property, these laws of nature are, of course, silent (IV. ii). They operate only in societies where private property has been established. Significantly, Pufendorf was mainly interested in hypothetical laws. It is to these that all eight books of his main *opus* are dedicated.

The proper business of natural lawyers, justification, was thereby reduced to the domain of hypothetical laws, whereas the primary institutions and most important laws are mainly explained. Only by the notion of consent could these explanations serve as justifications at the same time.

VI. CONVENTIONS

It is not surprising that subsequent philosophers, who advocated realism, thought that these historical explanations formed the most fertile part of natural-law theory. What they did not see was that these historical explanations had very little to do with the proper business of natural law: providing for a justification of existing laws and practices in the light of eternal laws of nature, that arise from human nature.

And indeed Hume himself must have thought that the only worthwhile element in his natural-law predecessors was these historical accounts. Not surprisingly, the only explicit reference to Grotius in Hume's moral philosophy is precisely to his historical account of the origin of property (E 307n.) The very paragraph in which Hume makes this reference is a telling one: he is trying to account for the origin of property and is stressing its gradual development. It is developed by "a sense of common interest; which sense each man feels in his own breast, which he remarks in his fellows, and which carries him, in concurrence with others, into a general plan or system of actions, which tends to public utility". And in order to stress the tacit nature of this "general plan", Hume gives the example of two men pulling the oars of a boat. They do this "by common convention for common interest, without any promise or contract". In the same way, "speech and words and language are fixed by human convention and agreement" (E 306). He repeats here – by means of the same examples – views which he had already explained in the *Treatise* (T 490).

If we compare Grotius's historical account and the one Hume is providing here, there are striking similarities. Both stress that an institution such as private property is not established by "a mere act of will", and both emphasize the gradual nature of these developments.

But at the same time there are two important differences. Hume gives a historical explanation not only of private property or some primary institutions; he is *extending* his explanation to *justice itself*. And that is something the natural lawyers would not have dreamt of doing. For them, justice was embodied within eternal and perpetual laws, which were independent of human conventions. They allowed for institutions such as private property to be artificial and man-made conventions (as useful additions to the laws of nature), but they never thought of justice itself as something that ultimately rested on conventions.[17]

But for Hume justice derives its existence only from the fact that it is embedded in society. Time and again he stresses that justice derives its utility from the fact that society is always a "medium amidst extremes", in which there is neither abundance nor extreme misery, and whose members are neither angels nor criminals. Consequently, Hume argues that in extreme cases of emergency, where normal conditions are absent, such as in a shipwreck, justice immediately loses significance (E 186).

It is clear that the conventional character of justice should not be taken in the Hobbesian sense. Hume does not merely assert that there is no justice or injustice prior to the original covenant. His claim is stronger: only within the framework of society are there such things as promises and the obligation to keep them. Talk about "consent" as the origin of government is for Hume "entirely erroneous" (T 542). In Hume's view, the original covenant or contract cannot be regarded as establishing justice, since such a contract presupposes the very existence of certain fundamental rules of justice.

Hume explicitly asserts that justice is a man-made device to cope with a world of relative scarcity and limited benevolence. It is therefore a so-called artificial and not a natural virtue: "the sense of justice and injustice is not deriv'd from nature, but arises artificially, tho' necessarily from education, and human conventions" (T 483).[18]

Given that Hume extended Grotius's treatment of the primary institutions of society to the very rules of justice themselves, it is at once clear that there is a second major difference in the historical accounts of the natural lawyers and Hume's own. For we have seen that there was a certain confusion in the works of natural lawyers as to the status of their historical accounts. They were clearly meant as justification and explanation at the same time – explanation in the sense that they honestly sought to discover how and why these institutions had been created; justification in the sense that these institutions were ultimately connected to natural law by the mere fact that they were consented to. The notion of consent linked these institutions to the great-grandmother of human nature.

But in Hume's philosophy it is precisely this notion of consent that is firmly placed within the limits of existing society. It is therefore impossible for him to justify the positive rules of justice, property and its attending obligations by referring to laws of nature. The thin thread that once connected positive and natural laws together is cut off. And not only is it *impossible* for Hume to justify existing laws and practices; it is clearly not what he *wanted* to do. Hume is not dealing with questions of whether private property can be justified, or under what conditions theft is justified.[19] He was no lawyer. He had abandoned his law studies, because he "found an insurmountable Aversion to every thing but the pursuits of Philosophy and general Learning" (HL I, 1).

Hume does no more than what he announced he would do:

> We now proceed to examine two questions, viz. *concerning the manner,*
> *in which the rules of justice are established by the artifice of men*; and
> *concerning the reasons, which determine us to attribute to the observance*
> *or neglect of these rules a moral beauty and deformity.* (T 484)

And in dealing with the first question he talks about the way human
conventions arise. That his explanations serve no other purpose than
explanation alone can also be gathered from his dismissing of the state of
nature as "a mere fiction" (T 493). Grotius could not dispense with the
state of nature. It served as a fixed point for contrasting and justifying
the advantages of civilized society.[20] The misery of the primitive state
was an important element of an explanation that served as a sort of
justification at the same time. For Hume, however, the notion of the
state of nature only impeded a realistic and adequate historical explanation.

VII. HUME'S LAWS OF NATURE

If Hume's historical accounts are no longer tied to natural law and can
therefore be regarded as no more than explanations, what are we to think
of his notion of "laws of nature"? Hume introduces the term at the end
of III. ii. 1 (T 484). If he puts justice itself firmly in the category of
human inventions, what then is the meaning of 'natural'?

There is no ambiguity here. Hume several times warns the reader what
he understands by 'natural'. We can speak of "laws of nature", he says,
if "by natural we understand what is common to any species, or even if
we confine it to mean what is inseparable from the species" (T 484).
Conventions can be said to be "natural" only in the sense that they are
established by mankind, who has the natural capacity to create conventions.
In the same sense language can be said to be "natural", since it derives
its existence from our natural capacity for speech. This particular meaning
of 'natural' does not preclude language and justice from being considered
man-made, artificial conventions.

The fact that Hume, in the same passage, describes mankind as an
"inventive species", naturally able to establish conventions, does not make
him a natural-law theorist, and it is a misinterpretation to suggest that he
somehow keeps the options open for some kind of natural law, or basic law,
standing above positive law (Haakonssen, p. 20). All he does is to point out
that the rules of justice are established in order to cope with the human
condition. In this sense it is certainly true that, for Hume, the laws "are not
in any way *derived* from statements about human nature, they are *caused* by
certain elementary features of human nature" (Haakonssen, p. 37). And
precisely by saying that the laws are *caused* by human nature, he was far
removed from natural-law doctrine. For we have seen that natural-law
thinkers share the basic assumption that eternally valid moral principles
should be *justified* by human nature. That is why "consent" formed the

single thread between human nature and the important ("absolute") positive laws. If the relationship between human nature and human institutions
had been merely a causal one, as it is in Hume, there would have been no
problem in connecting the primary institution and its laws to the great-
grandmother of human nature. It is the justificatory role of human nature
that made it so difficult to connect with positive laws. And it is the
justificatory role of human nature that is responsible for the inconsistencies
in Pufendorf when he tried to give a genuinely empirical account of
human nature.

Hume, on the other hand, can deal much more freely with human
nature. An example of this can be found in the 'Dialogue', where Palamedes
raises the problem that what is called a vice in one culture is regarded as
a virtue in another. "How shall we pretend to fix a standard for judgments
of this nature?" he exclaims. The *I*-figure retorts that the situation is not
as hopeless as that. Universal principles can be found "by tracing matters
. . . a little higher". The idea is captured in a beautiful image: "The
Rhine flows north, the Rhone south; yet both spring from the *same*
mountain, and are also actuated, in their opposite directions, by the *same*
principle of gravity" (E 333).

But what is the status of these principles? What does Hume mean by
'principles'? Is he speaking of universal "test-principles", to use the
modern term (Haakonssen, pp. 43–4)? If so, and if indeed these principles
serve as criteria for justice, then they tell people how they *should* act. But
clearly, that is not Hume's point. For in another passage in the 'Dialogue',
Hume clarifies the concept of higher principles by asserting that "the
principles upon which men reason in morals are always the same; though
the conclusions which they draw are often very different" (E 335–6).

Clearly, then, Hume does not take these principles as normative criteria
for our moral judgements, but as principles underlying those judgements.
Whereas Grotius and Pufendorf went to great lengths to argue that we
should not look (a posteriori) to the moral judgements people make, and
that the principles of natural law are independent of these, Hume argues
the other way round: he is trying to attack the relativist position by
claiming that at the bottom of man's moral distinctions is a certain
consensus regarding the main principles. But these judgements are not
taken as justifying norms. They serve Hume only as an indication that
there is a certain uniformity in some fundamental moral distinctions
people make. If he asserts that utility is a universal principle, he means
that sympathy with utility is always at the bottom of the moral distinctions
people make. He does not mean that we *ought* to argue in accordance
with public interest; and given his view that 'ought' cannot be derived
from 'is', this is an important distinction.

For Hume, human nature provides the key only to understanding how artificial institutions could originate. We might say that in Humean philosophy human nature is used as an *explanans* in order to understand how the convention of justice became established. And considering it as an *explanans*, Hume is free to describe it as realistically as possible. He can afford the luxury of a genuinely empirical and realistic account of human nature, because he is not trying to discover and/or justify a set of eternally valid laws. Certainly, both he and the natural lawyers stress the features of human nature, and in both philosophies an analysis of human nature plays an important role in the analysis of justice. But these superficial similarities should not obscure the fact that Hume's account serves quite a different purpose from the earlier ones.[21] The road (from human nature to rules of justice) may look similar, but it runs through an entirely different landscape.

VIII. SELF-LOVE

The fact that for Hume human nature serves as an *explanans* in explaining the origins of justice, and not a point of reference by which the rules of justice can be justified, opens up a wide range of possibilities that were not accessible to the natural lawyers. Hume, unlike the natural lawyers, could for instance point to *self-love* as the origin of justice. Speaking of the rules of justice, Hume asserts:

'Tis self-love which is their real origin; and as the self-love of one person is naturally contrary to that of another, these several interested passions are oblig'd to adjust themselves after such a manner as to concur in some system of conduct and behaviour. This system, therefore, comprehending the interest of each individual, is of course advantageous to the public; tho' it be not intended for that purpose by the inventors. (T 529)

Justice is here the unintended outcome of a gradual development, which is paradoxically at odds with the selfish motives of society. We have seen why Grotius and Pufendorf could not deal so freely with man's selfish interests. Although they shared Hume's ideas of a gradual development of some primary social institutions, they had to found these institutions upon consent, which formed the indirect link to human nature. They *had* to preserve that link, since they tried to provide for a justification of these institutions. Hume, on the other hand, merely dealing with the question of how the *positive* rules of justice had been established, could do without this concept, and consequently could enquire more honestly into the real motives people have for establishing certain social rules.

It has been claimed that this theory of justice as an "unintended consequence" can be considered as "one of the boldest moves in the history of the philosophy of law", and as "one of the most important parts of Hume's philosophical justification for replacing traditional natural law with a secular and empirical conception of fundamental law" (Haakonssen, pp. 19–21). This is rather far-fetched. For we have seen that Hume *could* account for self-love as the origin of justice, precisely because he had *freed himself* from the laborious task of discovering "fundamental law". It is indeed an innovation to explain justice as a social mechanism which plays an important role behind people's backs.[22] But this innovation could only be made on the basis of the concept of justice as an artificial virtue. Hume is clearly not referring to a sacred "higher" law, since he does not acknowledge the existence of these laws. And he can limit his discussion to the rules and laws within society, just because he is not aiming at justification. If this is Hume's innovation, it is not an innovation of natural-law theory.

An indication that Hume did not think of himself as an innovator in natural-law theory is that he himself did not consider his theory of justice as his lasting achievement. Examination of his later work, the second *Enquiry*, reveals a fundamental shift with respect to the theory of justice. As we have seen from the above quotation, in the *Treatise* Hume argues from self-love as the basis for justice. Self-love and only a low degree of rationality constitute the origins of justice. And in such a theory there indeed exists a "disparity between causes and effects" (Haakonssen, p. 19). But in the *Enquiry* he denies that self-love is the sole basis of justice. Instead, an important place is assigned to an opposite principle: that of fellow-feeling. It is this principle "which excites in our breast a sympathetic movement of pleasure or uneasiness" (E 221), and which causes us to approve of public interest: the main end of justice.

Hume even asserts here: "We have found instances, in which private interest was separate from public; in which it was even contrary: And yet we observed the moral sentiment to continue, notwithstanding this disjunction of interests" (E 219). Unfortunately, he does not provide us with an argument for the existence of this sentiment. He simply states in a footnote that "it is needless to push our researches so far as to ask, why we have humanity or a fellow-feeling with others". The principle is taken to be self-evident.

Of course, this new concept of fellow-feeling does not affect Hume's conventional and evolutionary view of justice. In the same *Enquiry*, Hume compares justice with language, and one might argue that it was his view that justice can originate out of human fellow-feeling just as language arises from the human capacity for speech. But it certainly does affect his theory of unintended consequences. The paradox between causes and effects has disappeared. For now justice is said to originate out of fellow-feeling and a regard for utility. And that is why Hume no longer tells us that justice was originally not intended by the inventors; rather, it arose out of "reason, forethought [and] design" (E 307n.). As Alasdair MacIntyre observed, in the Moral *Enquiry* the problem of how mankind could have developed morality, in spite of the fact that we are not naturally disposed to the public good, has disappeared.[23]

The fact that Hume was apparently no longer satisfied with his former account of the origins of justice – even if we consider the theory of the *Treatise* as a success – is significant. When we add to this the difficulty that already in the *Treatise* he does not work out a consistent theory of justice as an unintended effect, but slips into numerous inconsistencies by asserting repeatedly that the laws of justice are nevertheless "purposely contriv'd" (Haakonssen, pp. 24–5), we may suspect that Hume was himself uncomfortable with a theory of justice as an unintended consequence.

IX. SOCIAL CONTROL

So we see that in Hume's later work the paradox between people's intentions and the outcome of their actions is attenuated by the introduction of the concept of "fellow-feeling", and the idea that people naturally approve of public interest. This is significant. The persistent emphasis with which he advocated these ideas makes one think that they were crucial to Hume. But why? Has he returned to the business of justification, so that he has to provide human nature with more friendly features?

An answer to that question might be found if we turn back to the solemn announcement in the *Treatise* which I quoted above:

> We now proceed to examine two questions, viz. *concerning the manner, in which the rules of justice are established by the artifice of men*; and *concerning the reasons, which determine us to attribute to the observance or neglect of these rules a moral beauty and deformity.* (T 484)

This is his programme and it is twofold. First, he set himself the task of *explaining* the origins of justice as an artificial virtue. We saw how he carried out this part of the programme and we saw in what way his account differed from that of the natural lawyers. But the second part of the programme refers to what happens *after the establishment* of justice. He wondered what made people actually *follow* laws and rules.

His concern is similar to that of contemporary sociologists of law, who want to know the mechanisms by which rules or laws really function within society. Of course, natural-law theories did not supply an answer to that question. They were designed for a different purpose: they were trying to find justifications that could legitimize certain rules and laws.

It is therefore not surprising that it is exactly at this point that Hume attacked natural-law theory, as not suited to what were for him the most pressing problems of morality:

> The end of all moral speculations is to teach us our duty; and, by proper representations of the deformity of vice and beauty of virtue, beget correspondent habits, and engage us to avoid the one, and

embrace the other. But is this ever to be expected from inferences and conclusions of the understanding, which of themselves have no hold of the affections nor set in motion the powers of men? They discover truths: but where the truths which they discover are indifferent, and beget no desire or aversion, they can have no influence on conduct and behaviour. (E 172)

Time and again Hume criticizes reason for being "too inactive a principle". And indeed, reason provides no answer to Hume's questions. In order to understand the mechanisms by which people are induced to follow rules, it is not sufficient to assert that these rules are rational and legitimate. This may provide a motive for the virtuous behaviour of the rational Houyhnhnms in *Gulliver's travels*, but it does not explain the actions of ordinary human beings.

But neither is it sufficient to point to immediate self-interest. In this respect Hume was particularly bothered about the increasing complexity of society: "when society has become numerous, and has encreas'd to a tribe or a nation, this interest is more remote; nor do men so readily perceive that disorder and confusion follow upon every breach of these rules" (T 499). How is it possible that in a complex society, in which the effects of individual actions are not immediately felt, people still act according to justice?

Part of Hume's answer was that people always try to gain approval and avoid blame: "By our continual and earnest pursuit of a character, a name, a reputation in the world, we bring our own deportment and conduct frequently in review, and consider how they appear in the eyes of those who approach and regard us" (E 276). Anachronistically speaking, we might say that Hume's moral theory was meant as a theory of "social control".[24] Why are people following certain rules? Because their neighbours raise their eyebrows if they do not. This was the sort of wisdom Hume was after, and – like present-day sociologists of law – he thought that it was necessary to discover the mechanisms of social control in order to understand the effectiveness of the legal system at large.

Here again, one might be tempted to conceive of Hume's theory of approbation as a framework by which the moral actions of people can be justified. But as we have seen above, Hume treated human nature as an *explanans*, rather than as a justification or foundation of justice. The same applies here, for had he tried to develop a framework of justification by means of these feelings of moral approbation, he would have been compelled to ascribe those feelings to a neutral and disinterested observer. In fact he ascribes them to ordinary people with their passions and interests.

Having established that there is no motive for following the rules of justice (i.e. *after* its establishment), other than trying to receive the approval of others, he was anxious to find an answer to the question *why* people actually approve or disapprove of other people's actions. Again, natural law proved to be useless for his enquiries: reason is "not alone sufficient to produce any moral blame or approbation" (E 286). Instead, he asserted that sympathy with public interest is at the bottom of the moral distinctions people make.

The emphasis on natural feelings of sympathy with mankind is no slip; it is not just a relic from Hutcheson ill-suited to Hume's modern version of natural law.[25] These feelings play a vital role in understanding the mechanisms by which social control is exercised. That is why Hume was not fully satisfied with a theory of unintended consequences. It provided him with an adequate account of the origins of the rules of justice, but not with an adequate answer to the question why people actually follow these rules. And that is why, rather than asserting that private vices result in public benefits, Hume heroically struggled to connect public benefits to private virtues.

X. TRANSITIONS

We have seen that Hume's theory of justice as an artificial virtue, his account of the origins of this virtue and the way it functions after its establishment in a complex society, can all be regarded as answers to a problem that was very different from that of the natural lawyers. Hume did not want to justify laws, he did not want to sketch the boundaries of might and right, he was not trying to legitimize existing laws and practices. Instead, he was looking for an adequate description of how certain institutions are established and the roles they play in our lives.

The question arises: are we not stretching these differences too far? Is it not true that natural lawyers were equally interested in the ways laws function and the way people are socialized? Is it not true that natural lawyers were equally trying to answer the question why people follow rules?

A clue to answering these questions can be found in a crucial passage in Pufendorf, in which he refutes a well-known critique of the natural-law doctrine:

> It is no objection to our theory that most men do not know or understand the method whereby the commands of the law of nature are demonstrated, and that the majority of men usually learn this law and observe it as a matter of training or by following the general example of society; for we also daily see workmen do many things by imitation, or with tools whose method of use they cannot demonstrate, and yet such operations can nevertheless be called mathematical and based upon good reason. (II. iii, pp. 202–3).

Two levels are distinguished: on the one hand, one might analyse morality as the product of socialization; on the other hand, judgements might be formed as to the extent to which morality conforms to right reason. The first level describes what people actually do; the second evaluates these actions in the light of rational principles and reconstructs them as rational actions. In the previous section we saw that Hume was mainly interested in the first level: the manner in which people are "following the general example of society". Pufendorf, however, stressed the importance of the second level.

Pufendorf's two-level analysis is very similar to a well-known distinction among modern philosophers of science: that between the so-called "context of discovery" and the "context of justification". Although the actual process of scientific activity is messy and full of social constraints, its results can nevertheless be analysed *post hoc* as rational and in accordance with well-known rules of methodology.

When sociologists started to investigate the actual process of scientific discovery, philosophers at first regarded them with a mild eye, as it did not seem to undermine their own position. Whereas sociologists analysed the context of discovery, philosophers could focus on what really counted in their view: the context of justification. The underlying assumption of this position is obvious: although scientists appear to behave in a rather disorderly manner, their results can nevertheless be reconstructed as the outcome of a thoroughly rational process. Continuing sociological research, however, gradually undermined these arguments. Sociologists claimed that the idea of *post hoc* rationality itself was in fact no more than a product of the particular ideology of science. In their view the distinction between the two contexts is no more than a rhetorical device to elevate science above other social activities. In recent years the two levels of analysis have tended to be reduced to one.

It is just this shift from a two-level analysis towards a one-dimensional one, occurring now in modern philosophy of science, which took place some two hundred years ago in moral philosophy. What distinguishes Hume from natural-law theorists is not that he was the first to describe the social character of justice: Pufendorf also knew that morality arises within a specific social context, just as philosophers of science knew all the time that the actual process of science is bound by social constraints. But Hume was the first to leave out the level of justification. Whereas natural-law thinkers were mainly interested in the possibility of reconstructing morality and justice as rational, and focused on the context of justification, Hume concentrated on the context of discovery.

On the basis of this distinction we may assess the differences more clearly. It is certainly not true that natural lawyers were not interested in the way people follow rules, or how exactly positive laws had been created. They tried to be as realistic as possible in their description of these matters. But they thought that these issues were independent of what they conceived as their major task: to provide justifications. That is why they did not think that these questions undermined their search for justification. They thought it had little to do with the business they were engaged in.

They proved wrong in this belief. For their explanatory type of analyses did affect their justificatory activities. We have seen that the requirement of realism in describing human nature and the way primary institutions had been established was hard to reconcile with the demand for justification. Their success in describing the gradual process of civilization undermined their own purpose to such an extent that writers like Hume did not even recognize what this original purpose had been. In stark contrast to their success in these historical accounts stood their failure to provide for fixed standards by which to measure right and wrong or the justice and injustice of certain primary institutions.

So they unwillingly paved the way for Hume's criticism, a criticism which two centuries later was echoed by Feyerabend when he attacked the Popperian idea that there exists something like a "third world": a level of analysis independent of what people actually do or think.[26] Feyerabend's critique is comparable to Hume's critique of the inappropriateness of reason to regulate the behaviour of living human beings. It is just this kind of "third world" that Hume was criticizing by impugning the suggestion that there is "a real right or wrong; that is, a real distinction in morals, independent of these judgments" (T 460). Without the notion of such "real right and wrong" it is no longer possible to develop a moral methodology. And without such a methodology, a justification *post hoc* cannot be carried out.

XI. CONCLUSION

At the beginning of this essay I conjectured that Hume's use of certain concepts from the natural-law tradition might be compared to the way a contemporary social scientist uses Marxist concepts to address rather different problems from the problems these concepts were created to deal with. We now see more clearly that this is indeed what happened. We encounter topics like "the origin of government", "natural laws regarding property" or "the nature of promises", and, unaware of the shifting context, we are tempted to think that the writer is a devoted and conscious natural-law theorist, bent on contributing to that tradition and solving the same problems that the natural lawyers addressed.

And of course, if we adopt a very wide definition of 'natural law', we can still be right. If we think that natural law is characterized by a link between justice and human nature (*whatever* that link may be), if we think that natural law is marked by historical accounts of the development of some primary institutions (*whatever* the status of that account), then we can still say that Hume is a natural lawyer or filled the doctrine with a new content (Haakonssen, p. 12). But, in that case, our contemporary liberal social scientist who refers to "class structure" is a Marxist as well. The use of these labels is not only inflationary; it blocks an adequate understanding of the specific problems these theorists tried to cope with.

For there are numerous differences to be found if we contrast the two landscapes. Natural lawyers used the notion of human nature to find a fixed point of reference, descriptive and normative at the same time, from which laws of nature could be derived; but Hume used it to understand and explain the social world, the establishment of convention, and the way these conventions regulate our lives. Whereas in natural-law theory historical accounts of the development of civilization played a justificatory role, Hume used these accounts to understand how justice itself is established. But this move makes the whole purpose of natural law unrealizable.

What we have done has been to search for the *differences* between these two landscapes. This has shown us the sense in which Hume's philosophy can be understood as the culmination of a particular development that marked the seventeenth-century natural-law tradition. For already, in Grotius and Pufendorf, a shift towards explanation rather than justification can be traced. There were conflicting tendencies within the tradition that could not be solved or reconciled, and in this sense seventeenth-century natural-law doctrine paved the way for its own demise. The ambiguity between justification and explanation had to be resolved by choosing one or the other.[27] It is only in this respect that Hume's philosophy can be seen as a continuation of natural-law doctrine.

NOTES

1. D. Forbes, *Hume's philosophical politics* (Cambridge 1975).
2. K. Haakonssen, *The science of a legislator: The natural jurisprudence of David Hume and Adam Smith* (Cambridge 1981).
3. S. Buckle, *Natural law and the theory of property: Grotius to Hume* (Oxford 1991). See further my review of Buckle in *Grotiana* 11 (1990, publ. 1992), 43–50.
4. J. W. Moore, 'Natural law and the Pyrrhonian controversy', in *Philosophy and science in the Scottish Enlightenment*, ed. P. Jones (Edinburgh 1988), p. 31; see also Moore's contribution to the present volume.
5. I take this term from Forbes, p. 3 (title).
6. R. B. Sher, 'Professors of virtue', in *Studies in the philosophy of the Scottish Enlightenment*, ed. M. A. Stewart (Oxford 1990), pp. 93n., 101, 112. Another Edinburgh professor, William Scot, published a compendium of Grotius.
7. A beautiful description of such a development in medical science can be found in L. Fleck, *Entstehung und Entwicklung einer wissenschaftlichen Tatsache:*

Einführung in die Lehre vom Denkstil und Denkkollektiv (1935) (Frankfurt am Main 1980), pp. 146–65.

8. Thomas Aquinas, *Summa theologiæ*, qu. 91, art. 1; qu. 94, art. 2.
9. Hugo Grotius, *De jure belli ac pacis* (1646), ed. J. Brown Scott, trans. F. W. Kelsey (Oxford 1925), Prolegomena, par. 11.
10. Grotius, Prolegomena, par. 58; Samuel Pufendorf, *De jure naturæ et gentium libri octo* (1688), trans. C. H. and W. A. Oldfather (Oxford 1934), I. ii. 15, p. 23; John Locke, *Essays on the law of nature*, ed. W. von Leyden (Oxford 1954), p. 199. Locke's work was not known until the present century.
11. F. Palladini, 'Is the *socialitas* of Pufendorf really anti-Hobbesian?', paper presented to the Conference on 'Unsocial sociability', Max Planck-Institut, Göttingen, 1989.
12. B. de Spinoza, *Tractatus politicus* (1677), ch. 1, pars 1–2, in *The political works*, trans. A. G. Wernham (Oxford 1958).
13. A. O. Hirschman, *The passions and the interests: Political arguments for capitalism before its triumph* (Princeton 1977), pp. 14–20.
14. According to Forbes (ch. 1), the "experimental method" was part and parcel of the natural-law tradition, including Grotius and Pufendorf. As we have seen, it was not. They understood "science" as involving the ability to abstract from reality, not to investigate reality by an "experimental" or "empirical" method. The ambiguity of the term 'science' among natural lawyers has probably also led to the opposite misunderstanding, that Hume in his essay 'That politics may be reduced to a science' (Ess. 14–31) echoed the natural lawyers in his plea for a scientific approach to politics. He did not. In that essay he stresses empirical knowledge of how forms of government work in practice, not a demonstrable kind of knowledge such as the natural lawyers advocated.
15. Buckle is surely right in asserting that evolutionary theories play an important role in Grotius's account of the establishment of social institutions (Buckle, pp. 4–5). But this does not imply that people are wrong in attributing to Grotius the deductive method of a priori reasoning. The problem is precisely that, although Grotius wanted to give an a priori account of justice, he did not succeed in the task he set himself.
16. Moral entities "do not arise out of the intrinsic nature of the physical properties of things, but they are superadded, at the will of intelligent entities, to things already existent and physically complete . . . and come to their existence only by the determination of their authors" (*De jure naturæ et gentium*, I. i. 4).
17. Buckle does not seem to perceive the difference between "private property" and "justice". He therefore arrives at the erroneous conclusion that Hume's emphasis on the artificial character of justice is identical with Pufendorf's emphasis on the artificiality of the institution of private property (Buckle, pp. 88–9).
18. Hume's emphasis on the conventional, man-made character of justice has prompted Livingston to say that the concept of "convention" is the most important of Hume's philosophy: D. W. Livingston, *Hume's philosophy of common life* (Chicago 1984), p. 70.
19. Of course, Grotius also addresses the question "whether men in general possess any right over things which have already become the property of another" (II. vi. 1).
20. Grotius, unlike Pufendorf, however, is ambiguous on this point. Grotius's historical accounts are often accompanied by a certain flavour of nostalgia as well.

21. Hume himself was not aware of the enormous difference between his activity (explanation) and that of his forerunners (justification). That he perceived the natural lawyers as philosophers who were engaged in the same business may be gathered from his letter to Hutcheson, in which he writes that Grotius and Pufendorf "to be consistent" should have conceived of justice as an artificial virtue also (HL I, 33). It is not surprising that Hume was not aware of his innovation. The natural lawyers themselves thought that things could be justified *by explaining them.*

22. Although one might say that Hume merely extended the domain of the theory of unintended consequences, as it was familiar to Vico, Mandeville and Pascal. See Hirschman, pp. 14–20.

23. A. C. MacIntyre, Introduction to *Hume's ethical writings* (New York 1965), p. 15.

24. I use this term because it figures prominently in modern sociology of law.

25. For a similar discussion of whether Hutcheson's philosophy is a continuation of natural-law tradition, see J. W. Moore, 'The two systems of Francis Hutcheson', and K. Haakonssen, 'Natural law and moral realism', both in Stewart, *Studies.*

26. P. Feyerabend, 'Consolations for the specialist' in *Criticism and the growth of knowledge,* ed. I. Lakatos and A. Musgrave (Cambridge 1970), pp. 218–19.

27. Continental philosophers like Leibniz and Kant opted for the opposite resolution: according to Kant, it is pure reason alone, not sociological explanations, that can provide true criteria of justice.

5

Butler and Hume on habit and moral character

JOHN P. WRIGHT

Readers of Hume's philosophy are familiar with the central role which the principle of custom or habit plays in his theory of the understanding. For Hume, this principle leads us to our belief in causation and the existence of things not immediately present to our senses. However, in Book I of his *Treatise of human nature,* he suggested that the principle has direct importance not only in our cognitive life, but also in our emotions and our actions in relation to others. He wrote that "the far greatest part of our reasonings, with all our actions and passions, can be deriv'd from nothing but custom and habit" (T 118). Yet there is little explicit discussion of this principle either in Hume's writings on the passions or in his account of morals. The question then arises as to what role custom and habit play in his theory of the passions and in his moral theory.

I shall argue that a clue is to be found in Book II, Part III, of the *Treatise,* where, in discussing the influence of custom on the will, Hume refers to the views of a "late eminent philosopher":

> But custom not only gives a facility to perform any action, but likewise an inclination and tendency towards it, where it is not entirely disagreeable, and can never be the object of inclination. And this is the reason why custom encreases all *active* habits, but diminishes *passive,* according to the observation of a late eminent philosopher. The facility takes off from the force of the passive habits by rendering the motion of the spirits faint and languid. (T 424)

This theory plays a central role in Hume's account of what he calls a "calm" passion – a notion which plays an important role in his moral theory.

Two possibilities have been suggested as referents of Hume's phrase 'late eminent philosopher' – Francis Hutcheson and Joseph Butler. Both were alive at the time Hume was writing, but this is consistent with the fact that he used the word 'late' where we should use 'recent'. David Yalden-Thomson has suggested that Hume had in mind a passage in Hutcheson's *System of moral philosophy.* However, this identification seems implausible on straightforwardly chronological grounds.[1] A far more plausible candidate is Butler. In their nineteenth-century edition of Hume's *Philosophical works,* Green and Grose claimed that Hume's comment referred to Part I, chapter 5 of Butler's *Analogy of religion, natural and revealed, to the constitution and course of nature.*[2] This was published in 1736, three years before the first two Books of Hume's *Treatise.* The passage in Butler was probably the source for both Hume's and Hutcheson's discussion of active and passive habits.[3]

Hume returned from France the year after the publication of the *Analogy,* and soon thereafter compared notes with Henry Home on their respective assessments of Butler's philosophy (HL I, 24–5). Hume was to praise Butler in the *Treatise,* as a proponent of the application of the experimental philosophy to the science of man (T xvii). He would have found Butler's exposition and defence of the use of "Probable Evidence" in the Introduction to the *Analogy* congenial, and would have recognized the necessity to soften or remove the critique of natural and revealed religion contained in the draft of his *Treatise* if he was to win Butler's support for his own work. It is therefore reasonable to conclude that Hume was looking at Butler's latest work in 1737.[4] In the particular chapter identified by Green and Grose, Butler discussed the way we are led by analogy to conclude that we can improve ourselves for a future state through our own actions. While Hume would not have approved of Butler's theological conclusion, he did accept its chief premise, that through the repetition of our actions in this life we are able to develop our moral character. Butler wrote that we are capable of "getting a new Facility in any Kind of Action, and of settled Alterations in our Temper or Character" (pp. 119–20; Halifax, p. 87). Both authors employ the same term, 'facility'; and Butler's explanation of the way that this facility comes about is based on the distinction to which Hume refers, a distinction between the effects of passive and active habits.

I. BUTLER ON CUSTOM AND MORAL CHARACTER

In stressing the centrality of repeated activity in the formation of moral character, Butler was adapting an account of virtue which goes back to Book II of Aristotle's *Nicomachean ethics.* Aristotle wrote that "moral or ethical virtue is the product of habit (*ethos*)" and that "our moral dispositions are formed as a result of the corresponding activities".[5] Butler wrote that,

> in like manner as Habits belonging to the Body, are produced by external Acts: so Habits of the Mind are produced by the Exertion of inward practical Principles, *i. e.* by carrying them into Act, or acting upon them; the Principles of Obedience, of Veracity, Justice and Charity.

He stressed that the production of such habits requires more than just thinking or talking about virtue; indeed he argued that this would make us insensible to moral distinctions. He concluded that "practical Habits are formed and strengthned by repeated Acts" (pp. 121–2; Halifax, pp. 88–9).

What seems original in Butler's account is his view of the effect which repetition has on any form of passive response of the mind – whether it be thought or feeling. Thoughts, he wrote, "by often passing through the Mind, are felt less sensibly" (p. 122; Halifax, p. 89). Butler noted that through habit we become insensible of the effects of associations of ideas, including those involved "in correcting the Impressions of our Sight concerning Magnitudes and Distances, so as to substitute Judgment in the Room of Sensation imperceptibly to ourselves" (p. 120; Halifax, p. 87). This example, as we shall see, has particular relevance in Hume's account of the development of our moral judgements. But what is central for Butler's own account of the formation of moral character concerns the effect of repetition on *feelings*. He wrote that "from our very Faculty of Habits, passive Impressions, by being repeated, grow weaker" (p. 122; Halifax, pp. 88–9). He mentioned in particular fear (including fear of death) and pity for others. By constantly experiencing such emotions we become less and less affected by them.

Such feelings are the original motives for our actions, and it is through the different psychological effects of habit on our motives and actions that our moral dispositions are formed.

[A]ctive Habits may be gradually forming and strengthening, by a Course of acting upon such and such Motives and Excitements, whilst these Motives and Excitements themselves are, by proportionable Degrees, growing less sensible, *i. e.* are continually less and less sensibly felt, even as the active Habits strengthen. (p. 123; Halifax, p. 89)

Thus, as we gain a stronger inclination to act in a certain way, the actual motives which originally induced us to act in that way come to affect us less and less. The importance of this observation in the formation of moral dispositions is clear from examples Butler gives of courage and benevolence. The apprehension of danger causes the passive impression of fear and the action to defend ourselves. But as we constantly confront such situations and become habituated to defending ourselves, our feeling of fear becomes less and less; we are more and more capable of defending ourselves. Similarly, when we see others in distress, we feel pity and are inclined to relieve their distress.

But let a man set himself to attend to, inquire out, and relieve distressed Persons, and he cannot but grow less and less sensibly affected with the various Miseries of Life, with which he must become acquainted; when yet, at the same time, Benevolence, considered not as a Passion, but as a practical Principle of Action, will strengthen: and whilst he passively compassionates the distressed less, he will acquire a greater Aptitude actively to assist and befriend them. (pp. 122–3; Halifax, p. 89–90)

The lessening of feeling is important in the development of moral character, in so far as a strong sensitivity to the sufferings of others can repel us, as well as inclining us to perform a benevolent action. Indeed, habit tends to lessen the unpleasant feelings which originally motivated us, as well as giving us a new pleasure in the performance of the activity itself. According to Butler,

> by accustoming ourselves to any Course of Action, we get an Aptness to go on, a Facility, Readiness, and often Pleasure, in it. The Inclinations which rendered us averse to it, grow weaker: the Difficulties in it, not only imaginary but real ones, lessen: the Reasons for it, offer themselves of course to our Thoughts upon all Occasions: and the least Glimpse of them is sufficient to make us go on, in a Course of Action, to which we have been accustomed. (p. 125; Halifax, p. 91)

Thus, when we become accustomed to any action, we no longer need any strong feeling to require us to perform it, and are inclined to perform it whenever we apprehend that we are in an appropriate situation. We are then in a position to consider what Butler calls the "Reasons" for the action.

II. HUME ON CUSTOM AND CALM PASSION

In Book II, Part III, Section V of the *Treatise*, where Hume refers to Butler's doctrine, he is concerned with the general effects of custom on the will, not specifically on the development of moral character. He opens by claiming that "nothing has a greater effect both to encrease and diminish our passions, to convert pleasure into pain, and pain into pleasure, than custom and repetition" (T 422). The "*original* effects" of custom are twofold: first, on the development of "a *facility* in the performance of any action or the conception of any object; and afterwards a *tendency or inclination* towards it". It is in his discussion of the effect of custom on our inclination or disposition to act that Hume explicitly refers to the principle of the "late eminent philosopher". He notes that the "facility" which arises from the repetition reduces "the force of the passive habits" and reinforces the force of the active ones.[6] In this section he does not elaborate on the principle or give any hint as to its relevance for his own moral philosophy.

However, in the two previous sections, in his elaboration of the notion of what he calls a "calm" passion, Hume makes significant claims concerning the effects of custom on the development of a person's character.

Butler's principle is fundamental to the account of "calm passion" which Hume gives in Sections III and IV.

In Section III, Hume discussed the common claim that there is a combat between reason and passion and that "men are only so far virtuous" as they act in conformity with reason (T 413). Hume himself argued that reason itself can never be opposed to a passion, and that what is commonly called "reason" in this context is really nothing but a calm passion. He wrote that "every action of the mind, which operates with the same calmness and tranquillity, is confounded with reason" (T 417). The combat, as Hume goes on to describe it, is between "calm" passions and "violent" ones. Which prevails depends on the "*general* character or *present* disposition of the person" (T 418). The general state of character in which the calm passions win out over violent ones is called "strength of mind".

How exactly are we to understand what Hume calls a calm passion? How is it possible that such a passion can overcome a violent one? In his later *Dissertation on the passions* (1757), Hume characterized a calm passion as one which "takes a comprehensive and a distant view of its object, and actuates the will, without exciting any sensible emotion" (GG IV, 161). He gave as examples a person who pursues his profession with diligence because of "a calm desire of riches and a fortune" and one who "adheres to justice . . . from a calm regard to public good, or to a character with himself and others". We may assume that the first person will not be swayed by temptations of sensual pleasures and the latter will not be overcome by a desire to gain by cheating others. But what happens when such temptations and desires become violent? How can the calm passions ever win out over the violent ones?

On current interpretations, this is very puzzling. Páll Árdal has argued that the factor which is "decisive" in Hume's characterization of the calm passions is "low emotional intensity".[7] Following this analysis, Annette Baier has recently argued that "a typically calm passion counteracts a typically violent one by becoming briefly violent during the time of opposition".[8] But as far as I can see, there is no textual evidence for this interpretation, and it disregards the connexion which Hume draws between a person's character and their possession of a calm passion. To understand this, we need to recognize the fundamental role which custom in general and Butler's principle in particular play in Hume's account of calm passions.

At the beginning of Section IV, Hume writes:

'Tis evident passions influence not the will in proportion to their violence, or the disorder they occasion in the temper; but on the contrary, that when a passion has once become a settled principle of action, and is the predominant inclination of the soul, it no longer

produces any sensible agitation. As repeated custom and its own
force have made every thing yield to it, it directs the actions and
conduct without that opposition and emotion, which so naturally
attend every momentary gust of passion. We must, therefore, distinguish betwixt a calm and a weak passion; betwixt a violent and a
strong one. (T 418–19)

In this passage Hume implicitly divides what he calls a "passion" into an
active and a feeling component; the feeling component is called an "emotion". A passion is calm in so far as the feeling or emotive component is
diminished. But what Hume calls its strength or weakness is determined
by its influence on the will – that is, on action. Note his reference to
"repeated custom". A passion to which we have become *accustomed* forms
"a settled principle of action"; but, as Butler has taught, it "no longer
produces any sensible agitation" and "it directs the actions without . . .
opposition and emotion". Thus custom can bring about a passion which
is both calm and produces a strong effect on the will. Such a calm strong
passion can prevail over a violent one.

   Unlike a violent passion, a calm one can be stimulated by a "remote"
good (T 419). The example which Hume gave at the end of Section III
makes this clear. He noted that "[m]en often counter-act a violent passion
in prosecution of their interests and designs". Thus it is clear that, when
we act through our own long-range self-interest, we are able to act independently of what Hume calls "present uneasiness" (T 418). We are able
to distance ourselves from the pain of the present moment and are affected
by a pleasure or good which is distant from us. When we come to
examine Hume's account of the origin of justice, we shall see that he
thinks that this ability arises through repeated action – that is, through
custom and habit.

III. HUME VS HUTCHESON ON CALM PASSION

It is important to distinguish Hume's account of the distinction between
so-called "reason" and passion from that of Hutcheson. At first glance,
Hume appears to follow very closely the account which Hutcheson gave
in his *Essay on the nature and conduct of the passions*, first published in
1728. In this work Hutcheson called his readers' attention to the distinction
between "the *calm Desire* of Good, and Aversion to Evil, either selfish or
publick, as it appears to our *Reason* or *Reflection*; and the *particular
Passions* towards Objects immediately presented to some Sense".[9] He
went on to distinguish both the calm desire for one's own good from
"particular *selfish Passions*" such as ambition, lust, etc.; and the calm
desire for the happiness of others from particular other-directed passions
such as love, compassion and natural affection.

   The fundamental contrast in both cases is between desire and passion, where the object of the latter is present to the senses and the object of the former appears to *"Reason* or *Reflection"*. Habit plays a role in Hutcheson's account, not in constituting the calm desires as such, but rather in strengthening them: "We obtain *Command* over the *particular Passions*, principally by strengthning the *general Desires* thro' frequent Reflection, and making them *habitual*, so as to obtain Strength superior to the *particular Passions"* (*Essay*, p. 30). The strengthening of "calm universal benevolence" so that it prevails over all particular passions, including altruistic ones, is the surest way for us to feel "constant *Self-Approbation"* (p. 31).

While it is clear that Hume was influenced in his discussion of these topics by Hutcheson, there is a fundamental difference in the two accounts. When he introduced the notion of "calm desires and tendencies" in the *Treatise*, Hume insisted that they are "real passions". For him, calm influences on the will include not only desires for some good, but also "certain instincts originally implanted in our natures, such as benevolence and resentment, the love of life, and kindness to children". He noted that there are violent emotions "of the same kind" as these calm passions. For example, in both cases "resentment" involves my desire of "evil and punishment" to another person who has harmed me, without considerations of my own interest (T 417–18). Unlike Hutcheson, Hume held that there can be calm passions which do not lead us to seek some good either for ourselves or others.

Hume directly criticized Hutcheson's distinction between calm desires and passions in a letter of January 1743, in which he was commenting on Hutcheson's newly published *Philosophiæ moralis institutio compendiaria*. Here Hutcheson had contrasted the "calm desire of happiness" with violent passions such as "lust, ambition, anger, hatred, envy, love, pity, or fear".[10] Hume criticized Hutcheson's view that these latter passions are always violent, noting in particular that "There is a calm Ambition, a calm Anger or Hatred, which tho' calm, may likewise be very strong, & have the absolute Command over the Mind." This is particularly interesting in the light of the remarks he had made in the *Treatise* about resentment. For what we normally call "resentment" is nothing but calm anger. Making implicit use of Butler's principle, Hume argued that "the more absolute" passions are, the more "we find them to be calmer". Conversely, "Self-love may likewise become impetuous & disturb'd, especially where any great Pain or Pleasure approaches" (HL I, 46). For Hume, unlike Hutcheson, even the desire for good for ourselves can be violent.

James Moore and M. A. Stewart have recently argued that Hutcheson's philosophy should be seen as an example of a kind of "Christian Stoicism" which was prevalent in Scotland in the eighteenth century.[11] Stewart points out that Hutcheson, unlike Hume, believed that a philosophical study of the nature of virtue "will enhance our powers of self-control, an essentially rational function, and thereby promote better order in the individual and in society". In the light of this claim it is interesting to note that in his essay 'The sceptic', which was published in 1742, Hume's disagreements are largely with the Stoic methods of attaining happiness.[12] Hume's Sceptic attacks the "*artificial* arguments of a SENECA or an EPIC- TETUS" which attempt to make us indifferent to the evils of human life through "refined reflections" (Ess. 172–3).

In contrast to the Stoic, the Sceptic holds that philosophy "insensibly refines the temper, and it points out to us those dispositions which we should endeavour to attain, by a constant *bent* of mind, and by repeated *habit*" (Ess. 171). Hume stresses that habit provides a "powerful means of reforming the mind, and implanting in it good dispositions and inclina- tions" (Ess. 170–71). To see how it does this we need carefully to consider key facets of Hume's moral theory as it is developed in his *Treatise of human nature*.

For Hutcheson and Hume, a calm desire is one which takes a distant view of its object. What I want to claim is that Hume draws from Butler the idea that there is a process by which this distancing takes place. Custom and experience have a fundamental role in this process. The process itself seems to me to play a central role in Hume's discussions of the origin of justice and in his account of our moral judgements. I shall argue that in both cases the effect of custom, though only implicit, is fundamental. In the first discussion, Hume describes the way long-range self-interest overcomes the interests of the present moment. In the second, he describes the way we come to a common standard of morality through our sympathy with the feeling of others.

IV. CUSTOM AND THE ORIGIN OF JUSTICE

When Hume introduced the notion of "reason" as "calm passion" in Book II of the *Treatise*, he discussed the conflict between violent passions on the one hand and interest on the other:

> Men often act knowingly against their interest: For which reason the view of the greatest possible good does not always influence them. Men often counter-act a violent passion in prosecution of their interests and designs. (T 418)

This passage may appear to suggest that Hume was following the eight- eenth-century tradition identified by Albert Hirschman, which maintains that interest, or (what Hume also calls) "love of gain" (see T 492), is a means of controlling people's violent passions and so civilizing them.[13] In fact, as we have clearly seen, in Hume's account any passion, including interest, can be calm or violent.

In Book III, in his discussion of the origin of justice, Hume claims that interest itself begins as a violent passion:

> All the other passions, beside this of interest, are either easily re-
> strain'd, or are not of such pernicious consequence, when indulg'd.
> ... This avidity alone, of acquiring goods and possessions for ourselves
> and our nearest friends, is insatiable, perpetual, universal, and directly
> destructive of society. (T 491–2)

In contrast to those thinkers who stand at the centre of Hirschman's
account, Hume goes on to describe how the other passions "inflame this
avidity". Like Hobbes,[14] Hume thought that there is a natural greed
(and, he added, a confined "generosity": T 487) which, unchecked,
would lead to the destruction of society. Hume wrote that unchecked
self-interest would lead to "violence and an universal licence", and from
thence to the "solitary and forlorn condition" (T 492) of the Hobbesian
state of nature.

Hume also followed Hobbes in maintaining that the only solution to
the problems which arise from our passion for acquiring possessions
arises from that passion itself. For Hume, it is through a kind of self-
regulation and self-restraint that the passion of interest becomes calm:

> There is no passion, therefore, capable of controlling the interested
> affection, but the very affection itself, by an alteration of its direction.
> Now this alteration must necessarily take place upon the least reflec-
> tion; since 'tis evident, that the passion is much better satisfy'd by
> its restraint, than by its liberty, and that by preserving society, we
> make much greater advances in the acquiring possessions. (T 492)

Hume's use of the term 'reflection' in this passage should not lead us to
think he is describing a self-conscious process, of the kind described by
Hobbes and Locke, in which persons join together to promise to respect
the possessions of others and set up rules for the ownership and transfer
of property. Hume held that the establishment of justice results from a
kind of "convention or agreement" among people, but he rejected all
notions of a formal social contract which results from promises which
they make to one another (T 490). Like Grotius, Hume denied that this
agreement between human beings arises "through a mere act of will".[15]

Hume claimed that we originally come to agree to respect the possessions
of others through a natural "progress of the sentiments" (T 500):

> Two men, who pull the oars of a boat, do it by an agreement or
> convention, tho' they have never given promises to each other. Nor
> is the rule concerning the stability of possession the less deriv'd
> from human conventions, that it arises gradually, and acquires force
> by a slow progression, and by our repeated experience of the incon-
> veniences of transgressing it. (T 490)

Hume's use of the expression 'repeated experience' suggests that the
principle which operates in this process of trial and error is custom and
habit. The natural principles of reasoning which he described in Book I,

Part III of the *Treatise* (see especially T 102–3) come into play here. Through experience of the "inconveniences" which result when we take the possessions of others, we learn that it is not in our interest to do so. Moreover, experience convinces us that "the sense of interest has become common to all our fellows, and gives us a confidence of the future regularity of their conduct: And 'tis only on the expectation of this, that our moderation and abstinence are founded" (T 490). There is in Hume's account a progression from a pure self-interest to a self-interest which is limited through the recognition of the interests of others – from an object which is immediate to one which is more remote.

As in Butler's examples, the action associated with a certain passion – in this case the acquiring of goods – becomes more successful as the motive which leads us to perform it is tamed: by developing a convention whereby each person enjoys "what he may acquire by his fortune and industry", the passions "are restrain'd in their partial and contradictory motions" (T 489).

For Butler, as I come to act in courageous ways my emotion of fear is calmed, and I overcome my inability to deal with the situation. Similarly, for Hume, as I come to act justly my desire to acquire goods becomes calm and my actions cease to be self-defeating, at least for the most part. Hume stresses that while our interest in justice becomes "so strong a passion", nevertheless it is frequently overwhelmed by present interest. It is this which accounts for our need for government (T 534).

The person who has acquired the habit of seeking his own possessions while at the same time respecting the possessions of others, who has acquired calm self-interest, is a just person according to Hume. It is such a character who, on Hume's account of moral sense, receives our moral approval. However, it is important to note that what we approve of in this case is a character who follows self-interest; or, more accurately, one who is still following his passion to acquire goods for himself and his family – albeit while respecting the possessions of others. This account of moral character contrasts with that of Hutcheson, who thought that the moral sense leads us to approve only of a character who possesses benevolence, or the calm desire to promote the happiness of others.[16] Hume asked himself why we approve of such a character whose respect for the rules of justice is "at first mov'd only by a regard to interest" (T 499). Unlike Hutcheson, he does not require that we morally approve of the person because they are motivated by a desire to do good to others. Rather we approve of such a character because of the "disorder and confusion" which a lack of respect for the rules of justice tends to cause in human society. It is our sympathy with others who are affected by the agent – not our approval of other-directed motives of the agent – which causes us to approve of a just character and disapprove of an unjust one.

We saw earlier that Butler treated associations of ideas as passive habits, noting in particular those associations which result in our judging insensibly that an object in our visual field has a uniform size. Like Butler, Hume recognized that the associations which are formed through repeated experience become insensible. This is clear from his *Enquiry concerning human understanding*, where he sought to explain why we fail to recognize the source of our judgements concerning matters of fact: "Such is the influence of custom, that, where it is strongest, it not only covers our natural ignorance, but even conceals itself, and seems not to take place, merely because it is found in the highest degree" (E 28–9).

Similarly, we are not able to recognize the basis for our judgements concerning the moral disapproval of an unjust person or approval of a just person. This judgement is based on the pernicious or beneficial consequences which result to those affected by such a character. In his *Enquiry concerning the principles of morals* Hume wrote of

> the influence of education and acquired habits, by which we are so accustomed to blame injustice, that we are not, in every instance, conscious of any immediate reflection on the pernicious consequences of it. The views the most familiar to us are apt, for that very reason, to escape us; . . . The convenience, or rather necessity, which leads to justice is so universal, and everywhere points so much to the same rules, that the habit takes place in all societies; and it is not without some scrutiny, that we are able to ascertain its true origin. (E 203)

Through habit we become unconscious of the utility which lies at the root of our approval of artificial virtues such as justice.

V. THE DEVELOPMENT OF A COMMON STANDARD OF MORAL JUDGEMENT

In the *Treatise*, in his explanation of what he calls "our calm judgments concerning the characters of men" (T 603; cf. 583–4), Hume uses as an analogy that same example from optics which Butler used to explain the way we become insensible of passive associations. Hume seeks to explain how we maintain a single moral point of view, in spite of the fact that the "advantage or harm" of the persons we must sympathize with is "often very remote from ourselves, yet sometimes 'tis very near us, and interests us strongly by sympathy". In the case of sight,

> All objects seem to diminish by their distance: But tho' the appearance of objects to our senses be the original standard, by which we judge of them, yet we do not say, that they actually diminish by the distance; but correcting the appearance by reflexion, arrive at a more constant and establish'd judgment concerning them.

The "reflexion" to which Hume refers is clearly one of which we become insensible. Through experience we come to see the object as of constant size by substituting judgement in the place of sensation. Similarly,

> tho' sympathy be much fainter than our concern for ourselves, and a sympathy with persons remote from us much fainter than that with persons near and contiguous; yet we neglect all these differences in our calm judgments concerning the characters of men.

Hume notes that it is especially our constant conversation with other persons which causes us to "form some general inalterable standard, by which we may approve or disapprove of characters and manners" (T 603; cf. 583). As in the case of sight, Hume holds that it is through *experience* that we arrive at this calm judgement concerning human character:

> But these variations we regard not in our general decisions, but still apply the terms expressive of our liking or dislike, in the same manner, as if we remain'd in one point of view. Experience soon teaches us this method of correcting our sentiments. (T 582)

But how does experience operate? Certainly not in any self-conscious way. Both in the case of sight and in the case of morals, the common point of view is reached through the insensible effects of custom. The weakening of the strong effect of self-interest and sympathy with those close to us comes about through this experience, but not through any kind of explicit reflective process. We have a natural tendency to blame morally a person whose actions have resulted in a great loss to ourselves or our close friends; however, it is by constantly exposing our feelings to the feelings of others, and by hearing their judgements even in those cases which directly concern us, that we reach an impartial moral point of view. This development in our moral judgements is a constant process, which takes place throughout our lives.

It may be objected that the parallel with Butler's account of the influence of habit breaks down here. For Butler is concerned with the development of moral character, not moral judgement. However, one might very well regard the very making of moral judgements as an action which builds moral character. Our feelings of sympathy become calm and consistent when we constantly make moral judgements in the presence of others who have different points of view. In this process we become better judges both of ourselves and of others, and so develop our moral characters in the most general way.

VI. CONCLUSION

These reflections take us to the heart of Hume's moral theory. No less than our judgements of causality, our moral judgements are the result of a progressive development of the human mind. In his first *Enquiry*, Hume characterized "Custom or Habit" as follows:

> wherever the repetition of any particular act or operation produces a

propensity to renew the same act or operation, without being impelled by any reasoning or process of the understanding, we always say, that this propensity is the effect of *Custom*. (E 43; cf. T 102)

Following Butler, Hume held that the effect of such repetition on the passions is to increase our tendency to perform the corresponding action while, at the same time, lessening the passive feeling. We have seen that it is the repeated pursuit of self-interest which leads to the development of the cool virtue of justice; also, that the development of ourselves as moral beings capable of impartial judgements results from our repeated experience of the sentiments of others on ourselves. It is true that this account of the moral point of view takes us far from the God's-eye point of view supplied by Butler's "conscience".[17] The moral point of view for Hume is a very human-centred view. Nevertheless, what I hope to have shown is that Hume adopted the principles Butler used in his account of the development of moral character in reaching his own account of the development of that calm passion which constitutes our judgements of both our own actions and those of others.

NOTES

1. D. C. Yalden-Thomson, 'An index of Hume's references in *A treatise of human nature*', *Hume studies* 3 (1977), 53–6. The relevant passage is to be found on pp. 31–3 of Hutcheson's posthumously published *System of moral philosophy* (1755). Yalden-Thomson claimed in support of this conjecture that Hutcheson's work circulated in Scotland in manuscript for many years prior to publication. But in fact it was not completed until 1737, having been begun three or four years previously (W. R. Scott, *Francis Hutcheson* (Cambridge 1900), p. 113). There is no reason to think that Hume, who left Scotland in 1734 and lived in France and England until the first two Books of the *Treatise* were published in early 1739, would have had access to, or even any knowledge of, this manuscript.

2. GG II, 202. My quotations are from the second edition of the *Analogy* (1736), with page references also to the edition by S. Halifax in volume I of Butler's *Works* (Oxford 1874). For a general view of the relationship between Hume's moral philosophy and that of Butler, see T. M. Penelhum, 'Butler and Hume', *Hume studies* 14 (1988), 251–76.

3. On the probable influence of Butler's *Analogy* on Hutcheson's *System*, see Scott, pp. 200–211.

4. The same inference is drawn from Hume's correspondence by R. M. Burns, *The great debate on miracles* (Lewisburg, PA 1981), p. 111; and by D. Wootton, 'Hume's "Of miracles"', in *Studies in the philosophy of the Scottish Enlightenment*, ed. M. A. Stewart (Oxford 1990), p. 195, n. 10. This is not to dispute that Hume was also familiar with Butler's *Sermons* (HL I, 47).

5. Aristotle, *Nicomachean ethics*, tr. H. Rackham (London 1968), pp. 71, 75.

6. T 224. In discussing the facility of the mind, Hume also refers to the effects of custom on feeling. He notes that, when we first perform an action, the novelty causes an agitation which is painful as well as pleasurable (T 422–3).

However, echoing Butler, he adds that "By degrees the repetition produces a facility, which is another very powerful principle of the human mind, and an infallible source of pleasure, where the facility goes not beyond a certain degree." Hume stresses that the "facility", if it becomes too great, can also cause a disagreeable sensation (T 424).

7. P. S. Árdal, *Passion and value in Hume's Treatise* (Edinburgh 1966), p. 97.
8. A. C. Baier, *A progress of sentiments* (Cambridge, MA 1991), p. 168.
9. Francis Hutcheson, *An essay on the nature and conduct of the passions and affections* (1728), p. 29.
10. See the translation, *A short introduction to moral philosophy* (1747), p. 9.
11. See Moore's essay in this volume, and M. A. Stewart, 'The Stoic legacy in the early Scottish Enlightenment', in *Atoms, pneuma, and tranquillity*, ed. M. J. Osler (Cambridge 1991), p. 290.
12. Ess. 159–89. Note Hume's summary of the *virtuous* disposition of mind, p. 168. What he says here corresponds with many of the positive features of happiness identified in his essay 'The Stoic' (Ess. 146–54).
13. A. O. Hirschman, *The passions and the interests* (Princeton 1977). Montesquieu and Sir James Steuart play a key role in Hirschman's story.
14. See Thomas Hobbes, *Leviathan* (1651), I. xiii. In fact Hume's account is far more unequivocal than that of Hobbes. Hobbes lists "Competition" or love of "Gain" as only one among three causes of the war "of every man, against every man"; the others are fear of others and "Glory". Moreover, Hobbes states that "The Passions that encline men to Peace, are Feare of Death; Desire of such things as are necessary to commodious living; and a Hope by their Industry to obtain them"; only the last two of these constitute what Hume calls the "interested affection". See the edition of C. B. Macpherson (Harmondsworth 1968), pp. 185, 188.
15. Hugo Grotius, *The law of war and peace* (1625), tr. F. W. Kelsey (Indianapolis 1925), II. ii. 5, p. 189. Hume refers to the original of this passage in his account of the origin of justice at E 307n.
16. See, for example, *An essay on the nature and conduct of the passions and affections*, pp. xvi–xvii. Butler had criticized Hutcheson's attempt to reduce all virtues to benevolence in the 'Dissertation upon the nature of virtue', appended to the second edition of his *Analogy*.
17. For a good discussion of this notion in Butler's moral theory, see T. M. Penelhum, *Butler* (London 1985), ch. 3.

6

Hume, Reid and the science of the mind

P. B. WOOD

Given the wide-ranging and seemingly endless philosophical debates aroused by Thomas Kuhn's *The structure of scientific revolutions* since its publication in 1962, it may seem whimsical to claim that there are important themes in the book which have not received the critical attention they deserve. Yet it is arguable that scholars have largely ignored the historical implications of his analysis of the nature and function of disciplinary matrices, which for Kuhn were embodied in paradigmatic works such as Newton's *Principia* and in what he called "exemplars", that is, those concrete solutions to specific technical problems found in textbooks and journal articles which serve to shape the individual scientist's perception of his or her field.[1] Kuhn's remarks on the role of disciplinary matrices, paradigms, and exemplars in the learning and doing of science are highly suggestive, and they serve to underline the significant ways in which paradigmatic texts implicitly define the content, scope, heuristic techniques and methodological ideals of a scientific discipline or sub-discipline.

But what has Kuhn's discussion of disciplinary matrices, paradigmatic scientific texts and exemplars to do with the history of philosophy? I shall try to illustrate at least some of the ways in which I believe Kuhn's approach to the history of science can be used fruitfully by historians of philosophy. Even though the intellectual and social parallels between what we now call "philosophy" and "science" are far from exact, I would insist that when writing the history of philosophy we need to follow Kuhn's lead, and explore the ways in which what I shall call "canonical" texts have both implicitly and explicitly defined the scope and method of the philosophical enterprise. Such concerns are of special relevance to the study of the seventeenth and eighteenth centuries, when the map of human knowledge was redrawn and the very nature of philosophy was transformed. In particular, Kuhn's ideas can be turned to account when trying to reconstruct the disciplinary parameters of one of the central intellectual endeavours of the Enlightenment, the science of the mind. David Hume and Thomas Reid were instrumental in the construction of that science in eighteenth-century Scotland, and in this essay I want to draw on Kuhn's insights into the functions of paradigmatic or canonical texts in order to discuss the formation and elaboration of Hume's and Reid's conception of the true scope and proper method of the practice they referred to as "the anatomy of the mind".[2] Specifically, I want to investigate two related themes, namely Hume's and Reid's indebtedness to natural-historical approaches to the study of human nature, and their respective definitions of the scope of the science of the mind.

I

Let me begin by identifying those authors whose texts were regarded as canonical by Hume. In a well-known passage in the Introduction to *A treatise of human nature*, Hume referred explicitly to the writers he celebrated as having applied the "experimental philosophy to moral subjects", namely "Mr. *Locke*, my Lord *Shaftesbury*, Dr. *Mandeville*, Mr. *Hutchinson*, Dr. *Butler*, &c." (T xviin.). Although Hume was schooled in the writings of natural philosophers like Boyle and Newton, it is clear from this passage that his conception of the "experimental philosophy" and its use in the science of human nature was formed largely on the basis of his reading of Bacon and the moralists he cited here, whose works can be said to have served as paradigms for Hume's own projected methodological reform of the moral sciences. Hume does refer explicitly to Newton's Rules of Philosophizing in the second *Enquiry* (E 204),[3] but we should not infer from this that his science of morals can be straightforwardly reconstructed along Newtonian lines. Rather, we need to look more closely at the methods recommended and/or exemplified in the texts of the moralists in order to understand Hume's methodological strategies.

From the apologetics of such early Fellows of the Royal Society as Joseph Glanvill, Abraham Cowley and Thomas Sprat onwards, Francis Bacon was portrayed as the father of the experimental method.[4] The Introduction to Hume's *Treatise* and other passages in his writings demonstrate that he too saw Bacon as "the father of experimental physicks", and he undoubtedly derived from Lord Verulam's works the message that philosophers must proceed according to the canons of the inductive method expounded in the *Novum organum* of 1620 (T xvi–xvii, 646; cf. E 174).[5] But what commentators often downplay when discussing Bacon's methodological directives is that he believed that copious natural histories documenting the phenomena of God's creation had first to be compiled before this method could be successfully applied.

Significantly, Bacon did not exempt the human mind from his natural-historical programme. In the tract entitled 'Preparative towards a natural and experimental history' which he appended to the *Novum organum*, he itemized the various histories required for a solid foundation for the true system of inductive philosophy, and among those listed he included histories of the human senses, the passions and the intellectual faculties of the mind. Moreover, in *The advancement of learning* (1605) and *De augmentis scientiarum* (1623), Bacon sketched a projected branch of learning he called "the culture of the mind", which he thought would encompass what was, in effect, a natural history of human character types.[6] Thus Bacon can be seen to have initiated a move towards the natural history of the human mind which subsequently bore fruit in the major writings of the authors whom Hume mentioned in the Introduction to his *Treatise*.[7]

At the beginning of Book I of his *Essay concerning human understanding*, John Locke announced that he had employed a "Historical, plain Method" in dealing with "the discerning Faculties of a Man", and in Book II he claimed that he had "given a short, and, I think, true *History of the first beginnings of Humane Knowledge*". Locke was primarily concerned with the classification and description of our ideas and the powers of the mind, as well as with the temporal history of the human mind, in so far as he endeavoured to chronicle the genesis of our ideas and the progressive development of our intellectual faculties.[8]

In his published sermons, Joseph Butler was similarly interested in cataloguing the various principles of action in human beings, and he invoked the practice of the natural historian when criticizing Hobbes's reduction of benevolence to a species of the love of power. Butler argued that Hobbes "had a general hypothesis, to which the appearance of good-will could not otherwise be reconciled", and he insisted that the existence of benevolence as an independent principle of action could be demonstrated by experimental or natural-historical means:

> [L]et it be observed, that *whether man be thus or otherwise constituted, what is the inward frame in this particular*, is a mere question of fact or natural history, not proveable immediately by reason. It is therefore to be judged of and determined in the same way other facts or matters of natural history are: by appealing to the external senses, or inward perceptions . . . by arguing from acknowledged facts and actions . . . and lastly, by the testimony of mankind.[9]

Hence Butler apparently thought his sketch of the components of human nature in his sermons constituted a natural history of man *qua* moral agent. Both Locke and Butler, therefore, engaged in the classification and description of our intellectual and active powers and of our ideas and passions, and hence their works exemplified a natural-historical approach to the science of the mind.

Although there is no overt comment on the natural history of the mind in Hume's methodological preamble to the *Treatise,* his classification of our perceptions into impressions and ideas, and into the categories of simple and complex, which gave, in Hume's words, "an order and arrangement" to the mental objects under scrutiny, reflects his indebtedness to the natural-historical approach championed in the canonical texts of Bacon, Locke and Butler (T 2; cf. E 18). Moreover, as part of his natural history of the human mind, Locke compared our mental functions to those of animals, and Hume followed suit in the *Treatise*. According to Hume, it was manifestly true that animals have "thought and reason", and he insisted that any theory of the mind had to be tested against evidence drawn not only from the observation of "persons of the most accomplish'd genius and understanding", but also from the study of the mental capacities of "animals . . . children, and the common people in our own species". Then, having emphasized the relevance of such comparative evidence, he proceeded to claim that the form of reasoning found in animals provided "an invincible proof of my system", because it illustrated perfectly how habit and custom govern the operations of the mind.[10]

A clearer indication of his methodological debt to Locke and Butler comes in the first section of the *Enquiry concerning human understanding*, where Hume returned to the seemingly irresolvable problem facing the introspective method which he had posed in the *Treatise*, namely, that the use of introspection disrupts the natural operations of the mind. While Hume could offer no definitive solution to this problem, his response to it was, in part, a pragmatic, natural-historical one:

> It becomes, therefore, no inconsiderable part of science barely to know the different operations of the mind, to separate them from each other, to class them under their proper heads, and to correct all that seeming disorder, in which they lie involved, when made the object of reflexion and enquiry. This task of ordering and distinguish- ing, which has no merit, when performed with regard to external bodies, the objects of our senses, rises in its value, when directed towards the operations of the mind . . . And if we can go no farther than this mental geography, or delineation of the distinct parts and powers of the mind, it is at least a satisfaction to go so far.[11]

Although one might initially regard this passage as signalling a new methodological direction in the *Enquiry*, such an interpretation would be misguided, for Hume was here making explicit the principles guiding his classification of our perceptions in the *Treatise*. Moreover, it should be noted that in the *Enquiries* Hume did not entirely renounce the search for the general principles governing the phenomena of the mind which he had undertaken in the *Treatise*. Hume was certainly prepared to accept the limited knowledge available in the geography of the mind, but he did hold out the hope that it might be possible to discover "at least in some degree, the secret springs and principles, by which the human mind is actuated in its operations".[12] Methodologically, therefore, the *Treatise* and the *Enquiries* seem to be of a piece, because in these works Hume sought to discover the mechanisms of the mind through the use of induction and the classificatory and descriptive methods of the natural historian.

In recent years, Hume scholars have begun to investigate the possible connexions between Hume's speculations in the science of the mind and his historical researches, and some have now begun to speak of Hume as a "natural historian of man".[13] While this interpretative turn is to be welcomed, more precision is needed in specifying the sense(s) in which Hume can be considered as a "natural historian", as opposed to simply an (albeit highly philosophical) "historian" of humankind. There is little doubt that Hume thought that the anatomist of the mind could combat the limitations of the introspective method through the study of the historical record:

> We must therefore glean up our experiments in this science from a cautious observation of human life, and take them as they appear in the common course of the world, by men's behaviour in company, in affairs, and in their pleasures.[14]

History could thus provide Hume with a fund of "experiments" which could be utilized to elucidate or illustrate the operations of the governing principles of the human mind, and his 'Historical essay on chivalry and modern honour' shows Hume using historical evidence in this way at a formative stage of his career.[15]

Later, in the first *Enquiry*, Hume made explicit the methodological connexion he saw between history and the science of the mind when he wrote that the "chief use" of history

> is only to discover the constant and universal principles of human nature, by showing men in all varieties of circumstances and situations, and furnishing us with materials from which we may form our observations and become acquainted with the regular springs of human action and behaviour. (E 83)

Consequently, Hume regarded the "records of wars, intrigues, factions, and revolutions" which made up the annals of history as "so many collections of experiments, by which the politician or moral philosopher fixes the principles of his science".[16] But Hume's use of history does not in and of itself make him a natural historian; why, then, call him such?

Part of the answer lies in Bacon's map of human knowledge, for Bacon there classed together natural and civil history on the ground that both were founded in the faculty of memory. Bacon also recognized the existence of what he called "mixed histories", which blended together information from the natural and the civil domains, so that he envisaged both a deep structural connexion between the two branches of history, and an intersection between them in terms of their objects of study (*Philosophical works*, pp. 426–39). As I have argued elsewhere, Bacon's conception of the links between natural and civil history was highly influential in the Scottish

Enlightenment. Scottish virtuosi such as Sir Robert Sibbald collected both antiquities and natural specimens, and in the universities the curricula embodied Bacon's scheme of human knowledge. It was thus possible for Scottish men of letters like Lord Kames and Lord Monboddo to see themselves as natural historians of human society because of the tendency to elide natural and civil history, and it may well be that Hume too regarded himself in this light, especially given his methodological debt in the science of the mind to the paradigmatic texts of Bacon, Locke and Butler.[17]

Yet we should exercise some care in attempting to characterize Hume's brand of natural history, since it is arguable that he cultivated a style which differed in important respects from that of many of his Scottish contemporaries. One of the central themes of Hume's *Natural history of religion* is that in the development of religious ideas and practices polytheism precedes the emergence of monotheism. Hume did appeal to the historical record and to "our present experience concerning the principles and opinions of barbarous nations" in order to substantiate his argument; but it is significant that he also insisted that

> according to the natural progress of human thought, the ignorant multitude must first entertain some groveling and familiar notion of superior powers, before they stretch their conception to that perfect Being, who bestowed order on the whole frame of nature.[18]

To clinch his argument, Hume thus invoked the "natural progress of human thought", by which in this context he meant the propensity of the mind to rise "gradually, from inferior to superior", by "abstracting from what is imperfect" until it forms an idea of perfection.[19] But how are we to understand the phrase 'natural progress'? Hume might be taken here to mean simply that, in the ordinary course of things, it is an empirical fact that the mind always begins with concrete ideas and arrives at an idea of perfection through a process of abstraction. Such an interpretation would of course be entirely compatible with Hume's own view of the contingent nature of the laws governing the mind and the behaviour of people in society. Yet Hume seems to be after something stronger in this section of the *Natural history*, since he claims that "polytheism or idolatry was, and must necessarily have been, the first and most ancient religion of mankind" (NHR 310). Hume implies, therefore, that, in its "natural progress", the mind necessarily evolves according to a set pattern, and hence that the improvement of humankind follows an inevitable course in its initial stages. Consequently, the kind of necessity involved in this process seems to be rather different from that typically ascribed to Hume by his critics and commentators.[20]

A related ambiguity in the use of the term 'natural' can be found in the works of another Scot who understood Hume well, namely Adam Smith.

In the third book of *The wealth of nations* (1776), Smith described the "natural" course of economic development, from the first rudiments of agriculture to the culminating stage of foreign trade; but he was forced to admit that "though this natural order of things must have taken place in some degree in every such society, it has, in all the modern states of Europe, been, in many respects, entirely inverted".[21] The "natural order" of economic growth had not been straightforwardly instantiated in the history of Europe, he said, because of the perturbations caused by human institutions such as manners and customs. Hence in Smith's view, history did not conform to the "natural" or logical sequence of economic development specified by his theory, which resulted in the curious gap he saw between the "natural" and the actual historical record.

This gap between the "natural" and the actual was even more dramatically highlighted in Dugald Stewart's discussion of conjectural history in his *Account of the life and writings of Adam Smith* (1794). Having surveyed the contributions of Hume, Smith, Montesquieu, Montucla, Kames and Millar to this genre of history, Stewart claimed that, even if differing accounts were given of "the progress of the human mind in any one line of exertion", they were not to be thought of as being contradictory:

> If the progress delineated in all of them be plausible, it is possible at least, that they may all have been realized; for human affairs never exhibit, in any two instances, a perfect uniformity. But whether they have been realized or no, is often a question of little consequence. In most cases, it is of more importance to ascertain the progress that is most simple, than the progress that is most agreeable to fact; for, paradoxical as the proposition may appear, it is certainly true, that the real progress is not always the most natural.[22]

For Stewart (as for Smith) the course of history often deviates from the "natural" progress of humankind because of contingent factors which check the realization of what Stewart called the "general provision which nature has made for the improvement of the race" (p. 296). Consequently, to write a natural history of our species, in the sense of the term 'natural' used by Smith and Stewart, and perhaps by Hume, was not necessarily the same task as that envisaged by other natural historians of humankind in the Scottish Enlightenment. Hume considered himself, in part, as a natural historian of the mind, and there are good reasons to think that he likewise regarded himself as a natural historian of human societies. However, given the ambiguities of the word 'natural', we need to ask ourselves about Hume's style of natural history, and how it related to those practised by his contemporaries.[23]

One Scottish contemporary who also employed the techniques of the natural historian in the science of the mind was Reid. Reid is typically seen as being the most rigorous proponent of the Newtonian method in the Scottish Enlightenment, yet such an interpretation of his methodological outlook is a highly selective one.[24] In general terms, Reid regarded Descartes's reliance on introspection as initiating a methodological revolution in the science of the mind, which was then consolidated by Malebranche, Locke, Berkeley and Hume; for Reid, their works thus served as canonical texts (*Inquiry*, pp. 458, 463–6, 473–4). But, like Hume, Reid was especially indebted methodologically to the writings of Bacon, Locke and Butler, and he assimilated their natural-historical approach to the study of the mind.[25]

Reid apparently assumed the role of the natural historian in his pneumatology course given from 1752 to 1764 at King's College, Aberdeen, for in an outline of his philosophy course drawn up in 1752 he noted that these lectures detailed "the History of the Human Mind and its Operations & Powers", which encompassed both the enumeration of the different faculties of the mind and, following Locke, their temporal evolution.[26] Reid too seems to have written the third of his *Essays on the active powers of man* in a natural-historical and classificatory mode, since he there catalogued the various "principles of action" of the human mind in a manner highly reminiscent of Butler's discussion of these principles in his Rolls Chapel sermons.[27] We can see, then, that Reid followed the methodological example set in the works of Bacon, Locke and Butler, and employed the techniques of the natural historian in his "anatomy of the mind". Moreover, there is little doubt that the methodological message of their works was reinforced by Reid's own predilection for natural history, a science which he pursued informally for most of his career and which he lectured on as a regent at King's following the sweeping curriculum reforms there in 1753.[28]

Although Reid used the classificatory and descriptive methods of the natural historian in the science of the mind, he was also clearly aware of the limits of those methods when trying to discover the principles and powers of the human mind. In the Introduction to his *Inquiry into the human mind*, Reid argued that mere introspection could not discern the original powers, perceptions and notions of the mind, because "before we are capable of reflection, they are so mixed, compounded and decompounded, by habits, associations, and abstractions, that it is hard to know what they were originally". To solve this problem, Reid maintained that the anatomist must analyse the contents and powers of his own mind in order to "unravel his notions and opinions, till he finds out the simple and original principles of his constitution, of which no account can be given but the will of our Maker". Having discovered these principles, the mental anatomist can then go on to develop a "system" which will enumerate "the original powers and laws of our constitution" and explain "the various phænomena of human nature".[29] Hence Reid saw that the method

of the anatomist had to be a fusion of the techniques of the natural
historian with Newton's highly successful form of analysis; and while
these two elements of his methodology may strike us as incompatible, for
Reid such a fusion was possible because he maintained that the method
of analysis uncovered natural laws or "general facts" rather than efficient
causes (pp. 283–4). By renouncing the search for such causes, he broke
with Bacon's notion of induction, and in so doing facilitated the combination of the methods of the natural historian, who sought to establish
particular facts, and those of the natural philosopher, who sought general
ones.[30]

Reid's method in the anatomy of the mind was thus a blend of elements
drawn from the writings of Bacon, Locke, Butler and Newton. Yet there
is little doubt that the works of Newton took on a special symbolic
significance for Reid, and that he regarded Newton's *Opticks*, and especially
the *Principia*, as exemplary texts for the practice of philosophy. Like the
majority of his contemporaries, Reid recognized Newton's positive achievements, and wished to emulate in the moral realm the methods Newton
had ostensibly followed in the natural one. But it should be emphasized
that Newton's method (or at least Reid's interpretation of it) served a
largely critical, rather than a constructive, function in Reid's *oeuvre*. For
example, his earliest extant critique of the theory of ideas in his King's
College graduation orations for 1759 and 1762 turns, in part, on his use
of methodological themes drawn from Newton. Reid sharpened these
criticisms in the *Inquiry*, and there deployed Newton's strictures on the
use of hypotheses against the proponents of that theory, as well as the
Newtonian strategy of invoking an *experimentum crucis* (*Inquiry*, pp. 41,
136–7, 143–51). After his move in 1764 to the Glasgow chair of moral
philosophy, Reid refined his interpretation of Newton's first Rule of
Philosophizing in his lectures in the context of his critical review of the
dominant physiological theories of perception, and he subsequently turned
his reading of Newton to good account when attacking the ideas of David
Hartley and Joseph Priestley.[31] Consequently, we should recognize that
Reid's use of Newton was conditioned by the fact that he regarded
Newton's methodological dicta as providing the ideal weapon with which
to do battle with his philosophical adversaries. Indeed, given Hume's
occasional use of these same dicta, it may be that Reid was initially
prompted to articulate his own view of the Newtonian method and its
application to the science of the mind at least in part by Hume's appeals.

II

Let me now turn to the question of how Hume and Reid defined the
scope of the science of the mind in the light of the canonical works of
Descartes, Malebranche and Locke. In drawing the limits of their science,

both thinkers looked to a common canonical text, namely Locke's *Essay*, wherein Locke announced that his purpose was to "enquire into the Original, Certainty, and Extent of humane Knowledge; together, with the Grounds and Degrees of Belief, Opinion, and Assent", and that consequently he would

> not at present meddle with the Physical Consideration of the Mind; or trouble my self to examine, wherein its Essence consists, or by what Motions of our Spirits, or Alterations of our Bodies, we come to have any Sensation by our Organs, or any *Ideas* in our Understandings; and whether those *Ideas* do in their Formation, any, or all of them, depend on Matter, or no. These are Speculations, which, however curious and entertaining, I shall decline, as lying out of my Way, in the Design I am now upon. (*Essay*, I. i. 2)

Locke thus professed to restrict himself in the *Essay* to the determination of the levels of certainty possible in the different branches of human knowledge, and to the analysis of our ideas, which he considered solely as objects of the mind, thereby excluding any discussion of the physiological processes underlying the operation of our mental faculties. Hume followed suit, in principle if not in practice, and specifically eschewed any comment on the nature of our sensations, writing in the *Treatise* that the "examination of our sensations belongs more to anatomists and natural philosophers than to moral; and therefore shall not at present be enter'd upon". Hume too was careful in his use of the term 'impression', explaining in a footnote that he "would not be understood to express the manner, in which our lively perceptions are produced in the soul, but merely the perceptions themselves", and he similarly avoided any reference to causal mechanisms when he came to discuss the association of our ideas. Comparing the "principles of union or cohesion among our simple ideas" to the power of attraction, Hume said of the "attractive principle" operative in the "mental world" that its "effects are every where conspicuous; but as to its causes, they are mostly unknown, and must be resolv'd into *original* qualities of human nature, which I pretend not to explain".[32] Hence, like Locke, Hume professed to exclude theorizing about the physical basis of mental phenomena from the science of the mind.

Yet Hume did in fact invoke, if only obliquely, physiological considerations when explaining the workings of belief, custom, ideas, the passions, and the faculties of imagination and memory. For as John Wright has argued, Hume's references to the behaviour of animals spirits and to the physical traces of ideas in the brain indicate his indebtedness to the physiological speculations concerning the physical processes underlying the various faculties of the mind of Descartes, Malebranche and, paradoxically, Locke.[33] For example, we find in the works of Descartes that his theory of the mind rested on a reasonably detailed account of the functions of the human nervous system, in which his theory of animal spirits figured prominently. According to Descartes, animal spirits played an important causal role in muscular motion, sensory perception, memory, the operations of the imagination, the arousal of the passions, and the general temperament of the individual. The details of Descartes's speculations on these topics need not concern us here, but one general point should be made. In his analysis of sensory perception in *L'Homme*, Descartes called the pattern of motions left by the animal spirits on the surface of the pineal gland "figures" or "ideas":

> [A]mong these figures, it is not those imprinted on the organs of external sense, or on the internal surface of the brain, but only those traced in spirits on the surface of [the pineal] gland . . . where the seat of imagination and common sense is, that should be taken to be ideas, that is to say, to be the forms or images that the rational soul will consider directly when, being united to this machine, it will imagine or will sense any object.[34]

For Descartes, then, ideas are (at least in part) *physical* entities which the soul "consider[s] directly"; indeed, it was because he conceived of ideas in this way that he located the seat of the soul in the pineal gland.[35] Descartes therefore regarded ideas as being as much physiological as mental objects, and his account of memory, the imagination and the passions likewise blended together physiology with what we would now call "philosophy". Physiological theory thus dovetailed with philosophical analysis, and hence Descartes's texts licensed the merger of the two within the scope of the science of the mind.[36]

A similar combination of physiological and philosophical considerations is to be found in the writings of Nicolas Malebranche. Like Descartes, Malebranche relied heavily on the theory of animal spirits, and in his *De la recherche de la vérité* (1674) he explained muscular motion, perception, the operations of the imagination, individual and national characters, habit and the passions, in terms of the behaviour of such spirits. Even though Malebranche denied that physiological processes were the efficient causes of mental events, he insisted none the less that the former occasioned the latter, and that their correlations were governed by "the general laws of the union of soul and body".[37] Consequently, physiology still played a central role in Malebranche's theory of the mind, despite his radical reconceptualization of the relations between mind and body.

Although Locke formally disavowed the kind of psychophysiological speculation found in the works of Descartes and Malebranche, there are a number of passages in the *Essay* which offer glimpses of the physiological theories to which he subscribed. Regarding our ideas of sensation, for example, Locke affirmed that all sensation is "produced in us, only by different degrees and modes of Motion in our animal Spirits, variously agitated by external Objects"; and if he did not specify the precise mechanisms involved in sensory perception, Locke did at least state in unambiguous terms that the seat of sensation was the brain, which he somewhat fancifully called the "mind's Presence-room" (II. viii. 4, iii. 1). When he came to add the highly influential chapter on the association of ideas to the fourth edition of the *Essay*, Locke borrowed from Malebranche's physiological account of habit in order to explain the customary connexions between our ideas, arguing that habitual modes of thought correspond to "Trains of Motion in the Animal Spirits, which once set a going continue on in the same steps they have been used to" (II. xxiii. 6). Locke was also indebted to Malebranche (as well as to Descartes) for his suggestion that physical traces in the brain are required for the faculty of memory to function properly. In a striking image, Locke compared the ideas stored in the memory to inscriptions on tombstones which deteriorate through time, suggesting that

> the Constitution of the Body does sometimes influence the Memory; since we oftentimes find a Disease quite strip the Mind of all its *Ideas*, and the flames of a Fever, in a few days, calcine all those Images to dust and confusion, which seem'd to be as lasting, as if graved in Marble.[38]

Elsewhere in the *Essay*, Locke drew attention to other instances of the effect of bodily states on our mental functions and ideas without analysing these correlations in any detail (II. xxix. 3; III. vi. 3). Consequently, Locke's *Essay* can be seen as exemplifying two competing styles of the science of the mind: one harking back to the writings of Descartes and Malebranche, in which physiological theory was routinely invoked to explain the operations of the human mind; and a second, effectively created by Locke himself, in which such theorizing was excluded from the investigation of our ideas.[39] Canonical texts can sometimes convey mixed methodological messages, and in the case of the *Essay* there was an unresolved tension between more traditional modes of philosophizing about the mind and Locke's new natural-historical approach, which in turn was reproduced to a lesser degree in Hume's *Treatise*.

Because he wanted to disentangle the skein of physiology and philosophy which he maintained had been spun by the proponents of the "ideal system", Reid drew attention to this tension in his critique of the theory of ideas.[40] Reid's criticisms addressed two major themes: (a) the largely conjectural nature of the mechanisms proposed by the supporters of that theory to explain perception and the other operations of the mind; and (b) the conflation by the advocates of the ideal system of physiological with (for want of a better term) "philosophical" issues. Regarding the first theme, Reid granted that in perception the objects perceived cause impressions in our sensory organs which are transmitted to the brain by the nerves, but he insisted that we do not know how those impressions produce sensations in the mind. Reid denied that impressions are the efficient causes of our sensations and perceptions (although he acknowledged that there was a correlation between them), and he dismissed out of hand the view he attributed to Locke that our ideas can be caused by a form of impulse action.[41]

Reid claimed, moreover, that philosophers had widely, and in his view mistakenly, assumed that "by the impressions made on the brain, images are formed of the object perceived; and that the mind, being seated in the brain as its chamber of presence, immediately perceives those images only, and has no perception of the external object but by them" (*Intellectual powers*, p. 98; cf. *Inquiry*, pp. 462, 484–5). Reid maintained that, on the contrary, there was no evidence which demonstrated conclusively that the mind was localized in the brain, and he was adamant that the assumption that there are images in the brain was incompatible with the findings of anatomical dissection. Furthermore, Reid thought that elementary anatomical facts contradicted the major physiological accounts of perception which had been proposed, and, more importantly, that these accounts all failed to resolve one fundamental issue, namely that "neither the motions of animal spirits, nor the vibrations of elastic chords, or of elastic æther, or of the infinitesimal particles of the nerves, can be supposed to resemble the objects by which they are excited" (*Intellectual powers*, p. 103; cf. *Inquiry*, pp. 353–7; AUL MS 2131/4/II/1 20–21). For both empirical and conceptual reasons, therefore, Reid concluded that the ideal system was theoretically bankrupt.

But apart from such criticisms, Reid was evidently disturbed by the conflation of physiology and philosophy in the (for him) canonical texts of Descartes, Malebranche and Locke. In Reid's view, the theory of ideas was embedded in a physiological account of perception tailored to suit its central tenets,[42] and thus part of his strategy in refuting that theory was to distinguish sharply between physiology and the philosophical analysis of perception. Consequently, he sought to enforce the boundaries between the two fields which had initially been drawn by Locke, and which Berkeley had endeavoured to reinforce in *The theory of vision vindicated and explained*. According to Berkeley, the theory of vision consisted of three parts: (a) the introspective analysis of our visual ideas and their relation to those of touch; (b) the geometrical representation of the behaviour of light; and (c) the anatomy and physiology of the eye and optic nerves, and the physical description of the nature of light. Berkeley thus saw what he called the "complete theory of optics" as being made up of physical, physiological and philosophical elements, but he was careful to distinguish between them, insisting that "To explain how the mind or soul of man simply sees . . . belongs to philosophy."[43]

Reid conceived of the science of optics in similar terms, as can be seen
in his lengthy treatment of the sense of sight in the *Inquiry* and in his
Essays on the intellectual powers of man, where he made a clear demarcation
between the physiology and philosophy of perception. In the *Essays,* he
wrote that

> In perception there are impressions upon the organs of sense, the
> nerves, and brain, which, by the laws of our nature, are followed by
> certain operations of mind. These two things are apt to be confounded;
> but ought most carefully to be distinguished. (*Intellectual powers,* p.
> 75)

Hence, as mentioned above, Reid attacked those who posited an efficient
causal connexion between impressions and our perceptions; he declared
that it was simply an inexplicable law of our nature established by God
that impressions on our sensory organs and nervous system were related
to our sensations.[44] By severing the causal link between impressions and
our ideas, and insisting on our nescience regarding the mechanisms linking
them, Reid was thus able to drive a wedge between physiology and
philosophy and to argue that the proponents of the theory of ideas had
illicitly confused them. Reid therefore turned Locke's explicit and restrict-
ive definition of the scope of the science of the mind into a weapon to be
deployed against the ideal system, and he added it to an already powerful
philosophical armoury which also featured the descriptive and classificatory
techniques of the natural historian and his austere formulation of Newton's
inductive method.

III

In a letter dating from March 1763, Reid told Hume that "I shall always
avow my self your Disciple in Metaphysicks".[45] Reid's comment may
initially seem disingenuous; but, as I have argued, through their reading
of a common set of canonical texts, both men came to share a commitment
to combining the use of inductive reasoning with the techniques of the
natural historian, and a definition of the scope of the anatomy of the
mind which excluded from its purview speculations concerning the physiological bases of mental functions.

From a methodological point of view, their adoption of a natural-
historical approach is significant for two reasons. First, the use made by
Hume and Reid of the descriptive and classificatory practices of natural
history suggests that the standard interpretation of the methodology of
eighteenth-century Scottish moralists needs to be reassessed. Most
historians continue to echo the view expressed by James M'Cosh that
"To the Scottish school belongs the merit of being the first, avowedly
and knowingly, to follow the inductive method, and to employ it systematically in psychological investigation."[46] The evidence reviewed above,

however, implies that the Scots' utilization of a natural-historical method in the science of man was equally novel, and that historians would do well to examine this hitherto largely unstudied topic.[47]

Secondly, the emulation of the practice of natural historians by Hume, Reid and their philosophical contemporaries illustrates the close connexions between natural and moral philosophy in the Scottish Enlightenment. In recent years, Nicholas Phillipson and Richard Sher have challenged received historical wisdom, and have argued that what made Scottish moral philosophy distinctive in this period was the highly didactic form of "moral preaching" perfected by Francis Hutcheson, Adam Ferguson and Dugald Stewart, rather than the application of the inductive method to the study of morals.[48] While their interpretation of the pedagogical functions of Scottish moral philosophy has much to recommend it, little is gained historically by ignoring or downplaying the interaction of natural and moral philosophy in eighteenth-century Scotland. It is undeniable that the ideology of scientism informed the outlook of men such as Hume and Reid; their programme for the methodological reform of morals was premised on the achievements of the savants and virtuosi who made the Scientific Revolution. Like other moralists of their time, Hume and Reid were also active participants in the culture of natural philosophy, which meant that in their works they addressed the problems and drew on the empirical information and theoretical resources they shared with their colleagues in the natural sciences. Moreover, we have seen in passages quoted above from Hume's writings that natural philosophy provided a language and a fund of analogies with which to describe mental and moral phenomena. It would be as idle, therefore, to deny the importance of the interplay between the two branches of philosophy, as it would be to dismiss as intellectually sterile or uninteresting the didactic dimension of Scottish moral thought described by Phillipson and Sher.[49]

The historical implications of the definition of the scope of the science of the mind advanced by Hume and Reid are similarly suggestive. In his *Perceptual acquaintance from Descartes to Reid*, John Yolton has contended that Reid's interpretation of the theory of ideas was fundamentally mistaken, in so far as Reid incorrectly claimed that for Descartes and Locke ideas were "special objects that could be viewed as intervening between objects and perceivers".[50] But if we examine Reid's interpretation in the context of how he thought the scope of the science of the mind had been defined in the canonical works of Descartes, Malebranche and Locke, his understanding of the term 'idea' becomes far more plausible. Given Reid's view that Descartes, Malebranche and Locke had all (illicitly) combined the philosophical analysis of our ideas with a physiological account of our mental functions, it is hardly surprising that he maintained that they believed that ideas were objects, especially after reading passages such as the one quoted above from Descartes's *L'Homme*.[51] Hence it is arguable that Reid's reconstruction of the theory of ideas reflects his belief that its proponents had conflated philosophy and physiology, although Reid's own scientific interests probably made him more attentive to the physiological dimension of the texts of Descartes or Locke than more narrowly "philosophical" readers.[52]

I hope to have shown that the notion of canonical texts can be used to advantage in the history of philosophy. Given the similarities in their philosophical education,[53] it is hardly surprising that Hume and Reid looked to many of the same works for methodological and theoretical guidance, and hence shared a common philosophical culture. In a sense, the identification of canonical texts amounts to little more than simply tracing "influences", the traditional analytical gambit of the intellectual historian. Yet Kuhn also encourages the historian to attend to the implicit features of such texts, be they argumentative strategies, methodological standards, or definitions of fields of study. I have tried to illustrate above how Hume and Reid extracted from the canonical works of Descartes, Malebranche, Locke and Butler such implicit messages. In terms of method, the approaches of both Hume and Reid owed much to the natural-historical features of the texts of Locke and Butler, as well as to the explicit methodological programme announced in the writings of Bacon. The two Scots thus engaged in the classification of what Reid called the "furniture of human understanding" (*Inquiry*, pp. 477–83), and they also investigated the similarities and differences between the mental capacities of animals and humankind, as well as the chronological development of our intellectual and active powers.

I would argue too that Hume and Reid also cultivated a similar philosophical style derived from their predecessors, namely that of the "anatomist of the mind", which Hume described so lucidly in the *Treatise* and in the first *Enquiry*.[54] As for their conception of the scope of the science of the mind, Hume and Reid received ambiguous signals from the works they regarded as canonical, because the precepts of Locke did not mesh with his own practice, nor that of Descartes and Malebranche. Hence Hume's philosophizing incorporated a vestigial physiological element, whereas Reid endeavoured to exorcise this element entirely from his analysis of perception because of his opposition to the theory of ideas. Consequently, Reid's response to the theory of ideas becomes intelligible only if we follow Kuhn and take into account the definition of the science of the mind implied by the canonical texts of Descartes, Malebranche and Locke.[55]

NOTES

1. T. S. Kuhn, *The structure of scientific revolutions*, 2nd edn (Chicago 1970). For his analysis of disciplinary matrices, paradigms and exemplars, see esp. pp. 176–204.
2. For Hume on the anatomy of the mind, see T 325–6, 620–21, 646, E 5–16; also HL I, 32–3. Reid discusses the anatomy of the mind in the opening section of *An inquiry into the human mind, on the principles of common sense* (all my quotations are from the 4th edition (1785), reissued Bristol 1990). Hume and Reid could have derived the phrase 'anatomy of the mind' from Shaftesbury: see his *Characteristicks*, 4th edn (1727), III, p. 189 (I owe this point to David Norton). See also Alexander Pope, 'The design', *An essay on man*, in *Poetical works*, ed. H. Davis (Oxford 1966), p. 239.
3. Discussions of Hume's familiarity with Newton are to be found in N. Capaldi, *David Hume: The Newtonian philosopher* (Boston 1975); J. Noxon, *Hume's philosophical development* (Oxford 1975), pp. 68–81; M. Barfoot, 'Hume and the culture of science in the early eighteenth century', in *Studies in the philosophy of the Scottish Enlightenment*, ed. M. A. Stewart (Oxford 1990), 151–90.
4. For early images of Bacon, see Thomas Sprat, *History of the Royal Society*, ed. J. I. Cope and H. W. Jones (London 1966), pp. Bv, B2v, 35–6; Joseph Glanvill, *Plus ultra* (1668), pp. 75, 86–8.
5. A less flattering view is expressed at H v, 153–4.
6. *The philosophical works of Francis Bacon*, ed. J. M. Robertson (London 1905), pp. 141–8, 410–11, 563, 571–8.
7. Apart from Locke and Butler, Shaftesbury is the only other figure in this group who explicitly alluded to "the natural History of Man", but he did not develop the idea in any detail (*Characteristicks*, II, pp. 186–7).
8. John Locke, *An essay concerning humane understanding* (1690), I. i. 2; II. i; II. xi. 15. Quotations are taken from the edition of P. H. Nidditch (Oxford 1975). For recent discussions of Locke as a natural historian of the mind see N. Wood, *The politics of Locke's philosophy* (Berkeley 1983), ch. 4; J. G. Buickerood, 'The natural history of the understanding: Locke and the rise of facultative logic in the eighteenth century', *History and philosophy of logic* 6 (1985), 157–90.
9. Joseph Butler, *Fifteen sermons preached at the Rolls Chapel and a Dissertation upon the nature of virtue*, ed. W. R. Matthews (London 1964), pp. 34–5n.
10. Locke, *Essay*, II. ix. 11–14, x. 10, xi. 5, 10; Butler, *Sermons*, pp. 12–14, 50, 54; T 176–9. See also T 325–8, 363, 397–8, 448, 467–8, where Hume draws comparisons between the workings of the mind in animals and in humankind. Hume restated his position in E 104–8, making the same points using less inflated language. While Locke and Hume were obviously responding to Descartes's characterization of animals as mere machines, this does not negate my claim that their comparisons between the mental functions of animals and of humankind were part and parcel of a natural-historical approach to the study of the mind. Indeed, one might argue that Descartes's theory of the "beast machine" was so controversial precisely because it brought into question standard assumptions derived from the domain of natural history about the relationship between humankind and the animal kingdom. In my view, Descartes's thesis was as much a natural-historical as it was a "philosophical" one.

11. E 13. Significantly, in the 1748 and 1750 editions of the first *Enquiry* Hume went on to discuss the classification of our passions, and praised Butler for having shown that there is no absolute distinction between the selfish and benevolent passions (GG III, 10–11).

    Hume may have evinced little sympathy for natural history in the first *Enquiry*, but he later (1765) purchased at least two volumes of Buffon's *Histoire naturelle* (1749–67), and met the author (HL II, 82).

12. E 14. On the search for general maxims in morals, see E 174–5.

13. N. T. Phillipson, *Hume* (London 1989), ch. 3. See also D. W. Livingston, *Hume's philosophy of common life* (Chicago 1984); *id.*, 'Hume on the natural history of philosophical consciousness', in *The 'science of man' in the Scottish Enlightenment*, ed. P. Jones (Edinburgh 1989), 68–84; C. Walton, 'Hume's *England* as a natural history of morals', in *Liberty in Hume's History of England*, ed. D. W. Livingston and N. Capaldi (Dordrecht 1990), 25–52.

14. T xix. Noxon, p. 192, misses the significance of this passage, and hence argues that "mid-way in his career, when writing *An enquiry concerning human understanding*, Hume decided that the student of human nature has more to learn from history than from the experimental method". Hume's texts do not, in my view, indicate such a shift.

15. E. C. Mossner, 'David Hume's "An historical essay on chivalry and modern honour"', *Modern philology* 45 (1947–8), p. 57. The essay is an early composition, although Mossner's dating of it to 1725–6 is now contested.

16. E 83–4. Hume also acknowledges here the value of "that experience, acquired by long life and a variety of business and company" (E 84) for the anatomist of the mind.

17. P. B. Wood, 'The natural history of man in the Scottish Enlightenment', *History of science* 28 (1990), 89–122.

18. NHR 311. As this section of the *Natural history* illustrates, Hume was, like Locke, interested in the temporal evolution of the human mind. However, Hume goes beyond Locke in suggesting that the historical development of a collective "mind" (be it of a social class or a whole society) mirrors the development of individual minds.

19. For another example of the use of the notion of the "natural" progress of the mind see Jean d'Alembert, *Preliminary discourse to the Encyclopedia of Diderot*, tr. R. N. Schwab and W. E. Rex (Indianapolis 1963), pp. 60–61.

20. Significantly, in the third book of the *Treatise* Hume traced the gradual association of our ideas of justice and virtue, and remarked that "this progress of the sentiments" is "natural, and even necessary" (T 500). For an analysis of Hume's view of necessity which is consistent with the thrust of these passages, see J. P. Wright, *Sceptical realism of David Hume* (Manchester 1983), ch. 4.

21. Adam Smith, *The wealth of nations*, ed. A. Skinner (Harmondsworth 1970), pp. 479–84 (p. 483).

22. Dugald Stewart, *Account of the life and writings of Adam Smith*, in Adam Smith, *Essays on philosophical subjects*, ed. W. P. D. Wightman and others (Oxford 1980), p. 296.

23. Compare here Wood, 'Natural history of man', pp. 113–14. For his part, Hume was acutely aware of the ambiguities of the term 'natural': see T 473–5.

24. The standard modern exposition of this view is L. L. Laudan, 'Thomas Reid and the Newtonian turn of British methodological thought', in *The methodolo-*

gical heritage of Newton, ed. R. E. Butts and J. W. Davis (Oxford 1970), 103–31. Laudan here seriously underestimates the use Reid made of Bacon's writings.

25. For one expression of Reid's assessment of Bacon see *Philosophical orations of Thomas Reid*, ed. D. D. Todd, tr. S. D. Sullivan (Carbondale, IL 1989), p. 38, where he states that Bacon led Newton "by the hand". In his first oration, Reid cites Hippocrates, Socrates, Bacon, Montesquieu and Newton as the methodological exemplars for morals, politics, natural history and natural philosophy (p. 39). His own comments notwithstanding, Reid seems to have been a follower of Locke until his disillusionment with the theory of ideas, since in one of the few manuscripts which survive from the 1730s we find him defending Locke's account of abstract ideas against the criticisms of Berkeley and Peter Browne (AUL, MS 3061/10, fo. 2r–v). See also Reid's tribute to Locke in his *Essays on the intellectual powers of man* (1785), p. 144. Dugald Stewart first pointed out Reid's high regard for Butler in his *Account of the life and writings of Thomas Reid* (1803), pp. 188–9. Reid's meticulous reading notes taken in November 1738 from Butler's *Analogy of religion* survive (AUL, MS 3061/10, fos 3r–12v). Reid praised Butler publicly in the first of his graduation orations (*Philosophical orations*, p. 35).

26. AUL, MS 2131/8/V/1, fo. 2r; as we shall see below, Reid realized that the temporal development of the mind rendered the use of the introspective method problematic. Like Locke, he was also interested in how social circumstances affect the development of the faculties of the mind. See Locke, *Essay*, I. iv. 14–15; Reid, *Inquiry*, pp. 6–8, 449–50, and AUL, MS 2131/4/I/30.

27. Reid, *Essays on the active powers of man* (1788), pp. 98, 101–2; compare Butler, *Sermons*, pp. 12–14.

28. On Reid's natural-historical interests see P. B. Wood, 'Thomas Reid, natural philosopher', Ph.D. thesis, University of Leeds, 1984, ch. 5.

29. *Inquiry*, pp. 9, 11. Reid's doubts about the efficacy of introspection were thus subtly different from Hume's.

30. This is true, too, of Hume; for Hume on general and particular facts, see E 164–5.

31. On the development of Reid's attitude towards hypotheses, see my 'Reid on hypotheses and the ether: A reassessment', in *The philosophy of Thomas Reid*, ed. M. Dalgarno and H. E. Matthews (Dordrecht 1989), 433–46.

32. T 2, 8, 12–13; see also 84. The Newtonian rhetoric of the passage on T 12–13 would no doubt have caught Reid's eye, especially since he believed that proponents of the theory of ideas like Hume philosophized in precisely the manner which Hume condemns here: see Reid, *Philosophical orations*, pp. 59–61, and *Intellectual powers*, pp. 111, 224–5.

33. Wright, pp. 200–21. For a quite early sign of Hume's interest in psychophysiology, see E. C. Mossner, 'Hume's early memoranda, 1729–1740', *Journal of the history of ideas* 9 (1948), p. 502 (no. 38). Mossner suggests that this memorandum, as part of the group devoted to philosophy, may date from the period 1730–34, but his dating is now contested.

34. René Descartes, *Treatise of man*, tr. T. S. Hall (Cambridge, MA 1972), p. 86. Descartes's original was published posthumously in Latin in 1662 and in French in 1680.

35. Descartes, *Passions of the soul* (1649), art. XXXII; Reid later commented on this argument, in *Intellectual powers*, pp. 99–100.

36. For important discussions of Descartes's use of the term 'idea' see, *inter alia*,

N. Kemp Smith, *New studies in the philosophy of Descartes* (London 1952), pp. 146–60; J. J. MacIntosh, 'Perception and imagination in Descartes, Boyle and Hooke', *Canadian journal of philosophy* 13 (1983), 327–52; E. Michael and F. S. Michael, 'Corporeal ideas in seventeenth-century psychology', *Journal of the history of ideas* 50 (1989), 31–48. The Michaels argue that early in his career Descartes used the term 'idea' in a "corporeal" sense, but by the time he came to compose the *Meditations,* he used it in a very different, non-corporeal sense. But even if one accepts their argument, *The passions of the soul,* which was a late work written in 1645–6, contains precisely the kind of intermingling of philosophy and physiology which I have argued was characteristic of Descartes's writings.

37. Nicolas Malebranche, *The search after truth,* tr. T. M. Lennon and P. J. Olscamp (Columbus, OH 1980), p. 102. See further pp. 17, 49–50, 87–136, 140–41, 152–3, 162–8, 337–9, 402–3, 449–50, 502–9.

38. *Essay,* II. x. 5. Just before the quoted passage, Locke cites "the Constitution of our Bodies", "the make of our animal Spirits" and "the Temper of the Brain", as affecting the functioning of our memory. He also speaks of brain traces when commenting on the memory of animals at II. x. 10.

39. John Wright has recently drawn attention to Locke's indebtedness to the writings of his Oxford contemporary, the physician Thomas Willis, who combined the physiology and philosophy of mind in equal measure; see his 'Locke, Willis, and the seventeenth-century Epicurean soul', in *Atoms, pneuma, and tranquillity,* ed. M. J. Osler (Cambridge 1991), 239–58.

40. Reid believed (*Inquiry,* p. 29) that Malebranche, Locke, Berkeley and Hume had all proposed variants of the system of the mind founded by Descartes.

41. *Intellectual powers,* pp. 75–6, 79–82, 94–8, 104–5; *Inquiry,* pp. 384–90; P. Kivy, *Thomas Reid's lectures on the fine arts* (The Hague 1973), pp. 22–3, 28.

42. Reid also indicated that the theory of ideas had misled Briggs, Newton and Porterfield in their researches (*Inquiry,* pp. 352–62; *Intellectual powers,* p. 203).

43. George Berkeley, *The theory of vision vindicated and explained* (1733), sec. 43. Compare the definition of optics in Ephraim Chambers, *Cyclopædia* (1728), s.v. 'Optics'. A concrete example of the science of optics as envisaged by Berkeley and Chambers which Reid read closely was Robert Smith's *Compleat system of opticks* (1738). David Norton has pointed out to me that Hume also made an implicit distinction between the "metaphysical" and physical parts of optics (T 374–5).

44. It would seem that Reid's view of the relations between mind and body was derived from Malebranche and Locke. Like Malebranche, he stressed the importance of ascertaining the laws governing the union of mind and body, but he rejected Malebranche's theory of occasional causes (Kivy, *Reid's lectures,* p. 28). Reid's nescience regarding the mechanisms connecting mind and body replicates Locke's position (*Essay,* IV. iii. 28 – although, as Reid noted, Locke does suggest in this passage that our ideas are produced by impulse).

45. Reid to Hume, 18 March 1763: NLS, MS 23157, letter 3.

46. James M'Cosh, *The Scottish philosophy* (London 1875), p. 3.

47. For one of the earliest appreciations of the importance of natural history for the Scottish moralists see G. Bryson, *Man and society* (Princeton 1945), ch. 3; I have tried to develop her argument in my 'Natural history of man'.

48. N. T. Phillipson, 'The Scottish Enlightenment', in *The Enlightenment in national context,* ed. R. Porter and M. Teich (Cambridge 1981), 19–40; *id.,*

'Adam Smith as civic moralist', in *Wealth and virtue*, ed. I. Hont and M. Ignatieff (Cambridge 1983), 179–202; *id.*, 'The pursuit of virtue in Scottish university education: Dugald Stewart and Scottish moral philosophy in the Enlightenment', in *Universities, society and the future*, ed. N. T. Phillipson (Edinburgh 1983), 82–101; R. B. Sher, *Church and university in the Scottish Enlightenment* (Princeton 1985), ch. 5; *id.*, 'Professors of virtue', in Stewart, *Studies*, 87–126.

49. I have argued these points at greater length in my 'Natural history of man'; and in 'Science and the pursuit of virtue in the Aberdeen Enlightenment', in Stewart, *Studies*, 127–49. For a brilliant analysis of Hume's engagement with natural philosophy, see Barfoot, 'Hume and the culture of science'. Phillipson's *Hume* offers a more balanced treatment of these issues than is to be found in the essays cited in note 48.

50. J. W. Yolton, *Perceptual acquaintance from Descartes to Reid* (Minneapolis 1984), p. 15. Yolton's challenge to standard readings of seventeenth-century theories of perception has found support in two recent studies: S. M. Nadler, *Arnauld and the Cartesian philosophy of ideas* (Manchester 1989), and N. Jolley, *The light of the soul* (Oxford 1990).

51. As his discussion in the *Intellectual powers* indicates, Reid thought that Descartes and Locke offered much the same physiological account of perception; see pp. 95–6, 99–101, 125–6, 137–9, 145.

52. Reid's interest in optics may have prompted him to read Robert Hooke's *Posthumous works* (1705), to which he refers in the *Intellectual powers*, pp. 146–7. Hooke provided Reid with a clear example of someone who believed that ideas were physical entities.

53. Reid's regent at Marischal College, Aberdeen, in the 1720s was George Turnbull, who trained in Edinburgh. Turnbull's advocacy of the use of Newton's method in the study of morals may have owed something to Robert Steuart, who was nominally responsible for lectures on both ethics and natural philosophy at Edinburgh following the introduction of the professorial system in 1707. It is significant that Hume, whose scientism was like that of Turnbull's, was also a student of Steuart.

54. I have dealt with the question of a common style in 'Science and the pursuit of virtue'. I should note here, however, that in his graduation oration for 1753, Reid claimed that the moralist should speak to the hearts of men (*Philosophical orations*, p. 34). Yet in his own lectures, Reid rarely indulged in the kind of morally uplifting rhetoric popularized by Hutcheson among others.

55. I would like to thank the Advisory Research Committee of Queen's University and the Social Sciences and Humanities Research Council of Canada for their financial support, and the Librarian of Aberdeen University along with the Trustees of the National Library of Scotland for permission to use manuscripts in their care.

7

Hume's doubts about probable reasoning: was Locke the target?

DAVID OWEN

I. INTRODUCTION

What has come to be called "Hume's problem of induction" is special in many ways. It is arguably his most important and influential argument, especially when seen in the context of his more general discussion of causality. It has come to be one of the great "standard problems" of philosophy and yet is, by most accounts, almost unique in having no ancient precursor. Interestingly, the argument is frequently presented in terms that the author never used – in terms of the contrast between deductive and inductive reasoning. Hume's own contrast is between demonstrative and probable (or moral) reasoning. He used the word 'induction' twice in the *Treatise* (T 27, 628), but in neither case is it clear that it is used to report a piece of probable reasoning. One of the few occurrences of 'deduce' or 'deducing' occurs in the second *Enquiry*, where he writes of "following the experimental method, and deducing general maxims from a comparison of particular instances"[1] – hardly a paradigm of what we would call deductive reasoning. There are studies of Hume's problem about probable reasoning which pay attention to what he meant by demonstration and probability; however, these are basically ahistorical, treating Hume's texts as though they were contemporary.[2]

I believe that it is difficult to make sense of his problem without taking into account the eighteenth-century conceptions of demonstrative and probable reason. Part of the difficulty is the failure to identify Hume's target in his negative argument about probable reasoning (vague and unsubstantiated reference is sometimes made to the "rationalists"); part is in identifying the role that the uniformity principle plays in his argument. I shall maintain that a careful look at Locke's *Essay concerning human understanding* (1690) helps us overcome these difficulties: Locke has a well-developed view of demonstrative and probable reasoning; his confidence in "conformity" as a ground of probability is a likely target of Hume's criticism, and his account sheds much light on what role the principle of uniformity might play in Hume's account.

I take it as uncontroversial that Locke, following Descartes, rejected a formal, logical account of demonstrative reasoning. Instead of using a formal, syllogistic account of how two propositions can entail a third, he concentrated on the relation two ideas bear one to another.[3] A demonstration gets its force, not from what we would call a deductive relation between one set of propositions (the premises) and another proposition (the conclusion), but rather from the relation one idea bears to another, either directly, or via a chain of intermediate ideas. Locke's account of probable reasoning is analogous to his account of demonstrative reasoning: in the latter case, the ideas are related intuitively or certainly; in the former, the ideas are related only "for the most part" (*Essay*, IV. xv. 1).

It is true that Locke writes of inferring one proposition from another, but this is always cashed out in terms of relations of ideas via a chain of intermediate ideas.[4] It is also true that he occasionally uses the terms 'deduce' and 'deduction'. But these are never used in our sense that has to do with formal deductive validity. Rather, they are used in the informal sense of 'argue' or 'infer', and 'argument' or 'inference', as has been noted by Yolton. In the rest of this essay, I will explicitly flag the use of 'deduction' and its cognates if I wish to use them in Locke's or Hume's senses.

Hume was justifiably proud of his grasp of the concept of probability. His argument about miracles is arguably a landmark in its development. In the *Abstract* (1740) he describes a main theme of the *Treatise* in the following way:

> The celebrated *Monsieur Leibnitz* has observed it to be a defect in the common systems of logic, that they are very copious when they explain the operations of the understanding in the forming of demonstrations, but are too concise when they treat of probabilities, and those other measures of evidence on which life and action intirely depend, and which are our guides even in most of our philosophical speculations. In this censure, he comprehends *the essay on human understanding, le recherche de la verité*, and *l'art de penser*. The author of the *treatise of human nature* seems to have been sensible of this defect in these philosophers, and has endeavoured, as much as he can, to supply it. (T 646–7)

The reference to Locke here is intriguing. Even though it is, in fact, Leibniz's reference, and alludes to Locke's failure to pay enough attention to probable reasoning, it is some indication that a close look at Locke (not to mention Malebranche and Arnauld) on probable reasoning will help us understand Hume's argument. As far as I can tell, Hume's argument about probable reasoning has never previously been presented in terms of the Lockean background of a non-formal account of demonstrative and probable reasoning. Hume shared Locke's non-formal account of probable reasoning. To understand his sceptical argument, we need to understand where they parted company.[5]

Part III of Book I of *A treatise of human nature* is called 'Of knowledge and probability'. It soon emerges, in Section I, that Hume is using 'knowledge' in the traditional sense of *scientia*, the term reserved for that which is intuitively or demonstratively certain. It is opposed to probable belief or opinion. In the *Treatise*, the contrast is presented in terms of the difference between two classes of the seven philosophical relations which Hume identifies. These relations are supposed to exhaust the way the mind can compare ideas and thus provide a complete taxonomy of the objects of knowledge or belief. The two classes are distinguished as those that "depend entirely on the ideas, which we compare together, and such as may be chang'd without any change in the ideas" (T 69). The former class includes resemblance, contrariety, degrees in quality, and proportions in quantity and number. The latter class of relations is such that any given relation between objects or ideas may be changed "without any change on the objects themselves or on their ideas". This class contains identity, causation and relations of time and place.

This way of making the distinction between knowledge and belief is foreign to modern ears, because it is done in terms of properties of relations of ideas, rather than propositions. However, the distinction between properties of relations is important for understanding Hume's argument. He is distinguishing between those relations of the understanding which depend solely on the mind comparing ideas and those which depend on further experiential input. This is the forerunner of his better known distinction in the first *Enquiry* between "*Relations of Ideas*, and *Matters of Fact*" (E 25).

Hume goes on to claim that only those four relations that depend solely on our ideas can be "the objects of knowledge and certainty" (T 70). He distinguishes a part of this class that consists of three relations (resemblance, contrariety and degrees in quality) which "are discoverable at first sight, and fall more properly under the province of intuition than demonstration". The idea here is that those relations can be known immediately, simply by comparing the related ideas. Intuition requires no steps of reasoning: no intermediate idea need be found. Knowledge of relations of proportions of quantity or number, on the other hand, typically requires those mediate steps, as when we add up a column of figures.

In the next section, 'Of probability; and of the idea of cause and effect', Hume turns his attention to the remaining relations which comprise the objects of probability. Here too we find a division between relations of which we are immediately aware and a relation which requires intermediate steps of reasoning. The three relations are identity, situation in time and place, and causation. The objects of the first two are present to the senses (or memory: see T 82), and thus we have what is more properly called "perception rather than reasoning" (T 73). There is "a mere passive admission of the impressions thro' the organs of sensation".

> According to this way of thinking, we ought not to receive as reasoning any of the observations we make concerning *identity*, and the *relations* of *time* and *place*; since in none of them the mind can go beyond what is immediately present to the senses, either to discover the real existence or the relations of objects. 'Tis only *causation*, which produces such a connexion, as to give us assurance from the existence or action of one object, that 'twas follow'd or preceded by any other existence or action. (T 73–4)

The next hundred pages of the *Treatise* are devoted to examining this relation of causation and its related mode of reasoning.

In a very few pages Hume has come very near to the formulation of what has been called the problem of induction. In fact, all the pieces are there but one. He has divided the objects of the understanding into those that are known and those that are probable. Within each of these branches, there are relations of which we are immediately aware (through intuitive awareness on the one hand, and perceptual awareness on the other), and a relation which requires inference or reasoning (the demonstrative reasoning of algebra or arithmetic, and probable or causal reasoning). We can sum up this fourfold distinction in the following chart:

	Immediate	Inferential
Relations of ideas	Intuitive	Demonstrative
Matters of fact	Perception or Memory	Probable

In Section VI, where Hume formulates his problem, he begins by arguing that our inference from a sensed or remembered object to an object which has never been sensed cannot be demonstrative and prior to any experience of the objects going together. For the impression and idea are conceptually distinct and it is always possible to think one without the other (T 87). This is an argument he had laid out before in some detail, especially in Section III, 'Why a cause is always necessary', and is really just a further argument in favour of the original classification of the seven philosophical relations. Since the inference cannot be demonstrative, it must be based on experience, or be probable.

The circumstances of causal inferences involve contiguity, priority and constant conjunction. But, Hume thinks, this helps little in explaining the nature of the inference:

> For it implies no more than this, that like objects have always been plac'd in like relations of contiguity and succession; and it seems evident, at least at first sight, that by this means we can never discover any new idea. (T 88)

The worry is that, though we now know that experience, in certain circumstances, produces in us a new idea when we are confronted with a present impression, we have yet to show that it is by a process of reason or legitimate inference.

I submit that we can only understand this worry if we remember that probable inference, like demonstrative inference and unlike intuitive or perceptual awareness, requires some mediate step that stands between that which begins the inference and that which ends it; and, further, that the significant units in the inference are ideas, not propositions. The conception of reason that Hume is dealing with here involves becoming aware of how two ideas are related via the intervention of a further idea or ideas. This is necessary if the production of the new idea is to be the result of a process of reasoning and not of some other non-rational mental mechanism. So Hume asks

> Whether experience produces the idea by means of the understanding or of the imagination; whether we are determin'd by reason to make the transition, or by a certain association and relation of perceptions.

He goes on to say:

> If reason determin'd us, it wou'd proceed upon that principle, *that instances, of which we have had no experience, must resemble those, of which we have had experience, and that the course of nature continues always uniformly the same.* (T 88–9)

He proceeds to show that this uniformity principle is a matter neither of knowledge (it is not intuitively known, nor is it demonstrable), nor of probability (it is not a perceived relation, nor can probable or causal arguments be non-circularly advanced in its defence).

This famous argument has been the subject of much critical discussion. Two interpretations at apparently opposite ends of the spectrum are these, from Stove and from Beauchamp and Rosenberg respectively:[6] (a) Hume has shown that all probable or inductive arguments are deductively or logically invalid. But since only valid arguments are reasonable, he has shown that all probable arguments are unreasonable. (b) Hume has shown that inductive or probable reasoning cannot be conceived of in a particular rationalistic way as characterized by logical necessity. That conception of reasoning must be replaced by one that can account for the force of inductive or probable reasoning. The first position has Hume as an extreme sceptic about probable reasoning, while the second has Hume arguing against a certain outmoded rationalist conception of reason for the purpose of replacing it with his own more adequate account.

Though they appear radically different, they share three very important points.

Let us call the account of reasoning summed up by these three points 'R'. Then *the R account of reason* lays down that:

1. Demonstrative arguments are deductively valid arguments with necessarily true or self-evident a priori premises (Stove, p. 35; BR, p. 43).
2. The conception of probable argument being attacked in Hume's argument is that of a deductively valid argument with at least one contingent or empirical premise about the observed and a conclusion about the unobserved (Stove, pp. 36–8; BR, pp. 42–7).[7]
3. The role of the uniformity principle is to function as a premise in probable arguments. Without this premise, the arguments would be deductively invalid or lack the feature of logical necessity (Stove, pp. 42–4; BR, pp. 8, 49).

These three points hang together and seem plausible because they make sense of the text. The characterization of demonstrative reasoning (1) bears a resemblance to the scholastic view of demonstration derived from Aristotle, though I shall later argue that it needs to be couched in terms of relations of ideas rather than propositions. But even as it stands, it makes sense of Hume's argument that there can be no demonstrative arguments for the principle of uniformity.[8]

The characterization of the model of probable reasoning that Hume was attacking as a deductive model (2) has almost become orthodoxy,[9] replacing the older view that Hume's demonstrative/probable distinction is equivalent to the deductive/inductive distinction. The main reason for the prevalence of this view is that it appears to make sense of Hume's argument, in terms both of the role of the uniformity principle and of the charge of circularity made against any attempt to prove the principle by probable reason.

That is to say, points (2) and (3) hang together. An appealing way to interpret Hume's claim that, "if reason determin'd us, it wou'd proceed upon that principle" of uniformity, is to say that any probable argument has a deductive structure, but is invalid unless the principle is added as a premise.[10] Thus Stove claims (pp. 43–4) that the principle is required as a premise to turn an otherwise deductively invalid argument into a valid one. This is what Hume meant by saying that if reason determined us, it must proceed upon the principle of uniformity. And the charge of circularity is thus substantiated: if we attempt to prove the uniformity principle by probable arguments, those arguments, if valid, will have that very principle as a premise.[11]

The R account of reasoning, characterized by these three points, does not, of course, by itself determine an overall interpretation of Hume's famous argument. As we have seen, it is the basis for both the radically different interpretations (a) and (b) above. An interesting way to character-ize the difference between (a) and (b) is as follows.[12] Both (a) and (b) agree that Hume was concerned with the R account of reasoning. It holds that while there are two sorts of arguments, probable and demonstrat-ive, there is only one form of inference, deductive. According to R, the difference between probable and demonstrative arguments lies in the nature of the premises, not the mode of inference. Position (a) claims that Hume accepted the R account of reasoning, and thus concludes that probable arguments are unreasonable. Position (b) claims that R adequately characterizes both Hume's and his opponent's view of demonstrative reasoning (1), but that Hume's argument, which assumes a certain role for the uniformity principle (3), shows that his opponent's conception of probable reasoning (2) is flawed and needs to be replaced by a better account.

Contrary to both these positions, I want to argue that the R account of reasoning is incorrect, in each of its three points, as a characterization of either Hume's or his opponent's view. We have already noted that Hume's target cannot be those, if any, who thought probable arguments were demonstrative. Hume of course was concerned to distinguish probable or causal arguments from demonstrative arguments, and not reduce the former to the latter. But that task is already completed before the famous argument even starts. More importantly, Hume did not think that either demonstrative or probable arguments involved anything like what we would call deduction or deductive validity.[13]

Of course, others have rejected points (2) and (3). Stroud, for instance, has plausibly suggested that all Hume needs is the claim that a reasoner must believe the uniformity principle to be true in order for it to be reasonable to move from the present impression to the unobserved idea.[14] This claim is plausible without any undue restriction on what it is to be reasonable, such as "it is only reasonable to infer Q from P if P together with other premises known to be true deductively entails Q". For surely there is no sense in which it would be reasonable to infer Q from P on the basis of past experience if one did not think that past experience was relevant to future experience.

But to say that this is all Hume needs is only to suggest that there is a line of thought available to Hume; it is not to uncover his actual argument. Fogelin, while sympathetic to Stroud's account, thinks that the truth or falsity of points (2) and (3) "cannot be resolved because Hume's text is underdetermined on the matter" (Fogelin, p. 157). But I shall argue that not only are points (2) and (3) false, but so also is point (1). If we are to understand the conception of probable reasoning Hume is attacking, we must understand the contrast between demonstrative and probable reason-ing. And understanding that contrast requires rejecting the characterization of either type of reasoning as involving a deductive relationship between (sets of) propositions.

III. LOCKE ON DEMONSTRATIVE AND PROBABLE REASONING

Locke's account of intuitive and demonstrative knowledge is well known. For our purposes, it is important to emphasize, firstly, that the crucial relations in both sorts of knowledge are relations among ideas, not formal relations among propositions;[15] and secondly, that the intuitive knowledge is immediate, while demonstrative knowledge involves reasoning. If the crucial relations in knowledge are among ideas, not propositions, then it is fair to assume that, if we are to understand Locke on reasoning, we must look for structures of ideas, not formal structures of propositions. This in turn will help us understand probable reasoning, and we shall see that the notion of deductive validity has nothing to do with it.

Locke defines knowledge as "the perception of the connexion and agreement, or disagreement and repugnancy of any of our *Ideas*" (*Essay*, IV. i. 2). Intuitive knowledge is had when "the Mind perceives the Agreement or Disagreement of two *Ideas* immediately by themselves, without the intervention of any other" (IV. ii. 1). Moreover, intuition is the basis for all demonstrative knowledge: "Certainty depends so wholly on this Intuition, that in the next degree of *Knowledge*, which I call *Demonstrative*, this intuition is necessary in all the Connexions of the intermediate *Ideas*, without which we cannot attain Knowledge and Certainty."

Sometimes the mind cannot immediately apprehend the agreement or disagreement of two ideas because it "cannot so bring its *Ideas* together, as by their immediate Comparison, and as it were Juxta-position, or application one to another, to perceive their Agreement or Disagreement" (IV. ii. 2). In such a case, "it is fain, by the Intervention of other *Ideas* (one or more, as it happens) to discover the Agreement or Disagreement, which it searches; and this is that which we call *Reasoning*". Demonstrative reasoning is a means of apprehending the agreement or disagreement of two ideas by the intervention of other ideas. These intermediate ideas are called "proofs" (IV. ii. 3). Demonstrative reasoning, then, is a chain of ideas, not propositions, and the link between any two ideas in the chain is intuitive: "*in every step Reason makes in demonstrative Knowledge, there is an intuitive Knowledge* of that Agreement or Disagreement, it seeks, with the next intermediate *Idea*, which it uses as a Proof: For if it were not so, that yet would need a Proof", and "without the Perception of such Agreement or Disagreement, there is no Knowledge produced" (IV. ii. 7).

This conception of demonstrative reasoning, and indeed reasoni g in general, is foreign to both the scholastic/Aristotelian syllogistic reasoning that preceded it and the more modern notion of deductive reasoning that succeeded it. Although syllogistic reasoning is a logic of terms, each piece of syllogistic reasoning can be perspicuously rendered as a set of propositions. So too with deductive reasoning. This is because what makes either syllogistic or deductive reasoning good reasoning is formal validity, which depends on the structure of the propositions and the overall structure of the piece of reasoning. The content of the propositions is irrelevant: the goodness, i.e. validity, of the reasoning can be displayed in formal terms. Lockean reasoning is quite different. It is a chain of ideas such that the first idea in the chain is seen to be related to the last idea in the chain, not directly, but via intermediate ideas. The link between each adjacent idea is intuitive, and whether two ideas can be so related depends on the content of the ideas, not any formal structure.

Locke uses a geometric example to illustrate the nature of demonstration toward the beginning of Book IV (IV. ii. 2). One wants "to know the Agreement or Disagreement in bigness, between the three Angles of a Triangle, and two right ones" but one does not immediately perceive the relation. What is one to do?

> In this Case the Mind is fain to find out some other Angles, to which the three Angles of a Triangle have an Equality; and finding those equal to two right ones, comes to know their Equality to two right ones.

That is to say, one starts with the idea of the three angles of a triangle; one finds an idea of some other angles intuitively known to be equal to those three angles, and if those other angles are intuitively known to be equal to two right angles, one's demonstration is complete. Note that it makes little sense to cast this in terms of premises and a conclusion. The proposition to be demonstrated is that the three angles of a triangle are equal to two right angles. But one does not deduce this from premises. Rather, one starts with one idea that makes up part of this proposition (three angles of a triangle) and shows it to stand in the relation of equality to another idea (two right angles) by interposing the relevant intermediate ideas.

Locke's view of probable reasoning is strictly analogous to his view of demonstrative reasoning: it involves a chain of ideas in which the connexion between each link is not a matter of intuitive certainty but only appears to hold "for the most part":

> As Demonstration is the shewing the Agreement, or Disagreement of two *Ideas,* by the intervention of one or more Proofs, which have a constant, immutable, and visible connexion one with another: so *Probability* is nothing but the appearance of such an Agreement, or Disagreement, by the intervention of Proofs, whose connexion is not constant and immutable, or at least is not perceived to be so, but is, or appears for the most part to be so, and is enough to induce the

Mind to *judge* the Proposition to be true, or false, rather than the contrary. (IV. xv. 1)

In the title of the section from which this passage is taken, Locke announces that "Probability is the appearance of agreement upon fallible proofs", where "fallible proofs" are the relevant intermediate ideas.[16] Such ideas are also called "probable *Mediums*" (IV. xvii. 16). Probable reasoning results in belief or opinion, not knowledge; probability thus supplies "the defect of our Knowledge", and guides us where that fails (IV. xv. 3–4). One person can have demonstrative knowledge of the equality of the three angles of a triangle and two right angles, by perceiving "the certain immutable connexion there is of Equality, between the three Angles of a *Triangle*, and those intermediate ones, which are made use of to shew their Equality to two right ones"; while another "who never took the pains to observe the Demonstration" may have a probable belief on the basis of the testimony of a mathematician. In this case, the intermediate idea or proof is the veracity of the speaker (IV. xv. 1).

As one might expect, Locke as an early practitioner in probability is concerned to a large extent with testimony, as the example just given shows. But he was also concerned with probability whose ground was not testimony but "conformity of any thing with our own Knowledge, Observation, and Experience" (IV. xv. 4). Locke thought conformity with experience was a distinct ground of probability from testimony; Hume, of course, thought that probable reasoning based on testimony was just another instance of reasoning from experience, as he clearly states in his argument concerning miracles.

Locke thought conformity with "Knowledge, Observation, and Experience" could provide probable grounds for belief or opinion in unobserved matters of fact and was careful to point out that this did not constitute knowledge. He held that sensitive knowledge "*extends as far as the present Testimony of our Senses*, employ'd about particular Objects, that do then affect them, *and no farther*" (IV. xi. 9). Thus, if I see a man now, I have knowledge of his existence. But one minute later, if I am alone, that knowledge is replaced by probable belief, "since there is no necessary connexion of his Existence a minute since, with his Existence now: by a thousand ways he may cease to be, since I had the Testimony of my Senses for his Existence".

And therefore though it be highly probable, that Millions of Men do now exist, yet whilst I am alone writing this, I have not that Certainty of it, which we strictly call Knowledge; though the great likelihood of it puts me past doubt . . . : But this is but probability, not Knowledge. (IV. xi. 9)

Locke has much to say of interest to our current concerns in chapter XVII, 'Of reason'. Much of this chapter is devoted to arguments against syllogistic reasoning. Syllogistic reasoning was the only formal account of reasoning available to Locke, and his (and Hume's) rejection of it is further evidence that they had a non-formal account of reasoning. It is also of interest to note that Locke's commitment to probabilities as well as knowledge is one reason for his rejection of syllogism:

> But however it be in Knowledge, I think I may truly say, it is of *far* less, or *no use* at all *in Probabilities*. For the Assent there, being to be determined by the preponderancy, after a due weighing of all the Proofs, with all Circumstances on both sides, nothing is so unfit to assist the Mind in that, as Syllogism; which running away with one assumed Probability, or one topical Argument, pursues that till it has led the Mind quite out of sight of the thing under Consideration. (IV. xvii. 5)

In fairness to Aristotle, Locke admits that "all right reasoning may be reduced to his Forms of Syllogism" (IV. xvii. 4). The trouble is that the way we actually reason is not syllogistic, and trying to reason syllogistically may actually hamper us in the all-important task of discovering intermediate ideas. Once the intermediate ideas are discovered and their connexions perceived, we can then lay out the connexions syllogistically:

> Syllogism serves our Reason, but in one only of the forementioned parts of it; and that is, to shew the connexion of the Proofs in any one instance, and no more: but in this, it is of no great use, since the Mind can perceive such Connexion where it really is, as easily, nay, perhaps, better without it. (IV. xvii. 4)

In this chapter Locke speaks of reason and reasoning in general: it is the discovery of the intermediate ideas (sagacity) and the perception of the connexion between each idea and its adjacent idea in the chain (illation, also referred to as "inference"). If the perceived connexion is certain and immutable, knowledge results; if the perceived connexion is only probable or for the most part, we have opinion (IV. xvii. 2). There is a common structure to demonstration and probability, but it is not deductive validity.[17] It is the finding of intermediate ideas to link the first and last idea in the chain, and the perception or presumption of their agreement and disagreement. The following is Locke's clearest statement of the similarities and differences between demonstration and probability:

> There are other *Ideas*, whose Agreement, or Disagreement, can no otherwise be judged of, but by the intervention of others, which have not a certain Agreement with the Extremes, but an usual or likely one: And in these it is, that the *Judgment* is properly exercised, which is the acquiescing of the Mind, that any *Ideas* do agree, by comparing them with such probable *Mediums*. This, though it never amounts to Knowledge, no not to that which is the lowest degree of it: yet sometimes the intermediate *Ideas* tie the Extremes so firmly

together, and the Probability is so clear and strong, that Assent as necessarily follows it, as Knowledge does Demonstration. (IV. xvii. 16)

Throughout this chapter, Locke frequently writes of words and propositions, deductions, and even "deducing one Proposition from another, or making *Inferences in Words*" (IV. xvii. 18). But all this is not evidence that Locke had a concept of deductive validity and that reasoning proceeds as formal relations among propositions. On the contrary, it is just further evidence that 'deduction' is just a generic term for argument, either demonstrative or probable, though it is often confined to arguments that have been put into words. All reasoning with propositions is utterly dependent on the perceived connexion of ideas. Consider the passage quoted above in full:

Though the deducing one Proposition from another, or making *Inferences in Words*, be a great part of Reason, and that which it is usually employ'd about: yet the principal Act of Ratiocination is the finding the Agreement, or Disagreement of two *Ideas* one with another, by the intervention of a third.

Furthermore, concentrating on the inference of one proposition from another rather than on the real structure of ideas can lead to bad reasoning. This was one of the drawbacks of syllogism:

To infer is nothing but by virtue of one Proposition laid down as true, to draw in another as true, *i.e.* to see or suppose such a connexion of the two *Ideas*, of the inferr'd Proposition. . . . The Question now is to know, whether the Mind has made this Inference right or no; if it has made it by finding out the intermediate *Ideas*, and taking a view of the connexion of them, placed in a due order, it has proceeded rationally, and made a right Inference. If it has done it without such a View, it has not so much made an Inference that will hold, or an Inference of right Reason, as shewn a willingness to have it be, or be taken for such. (IV. xvii. 4)

We sometimes infer one proposition from another. But if we reason rightly, we will attempt to perceive the connexion of the two ideas of the inferred proposition in virtue of the intermediate idea(s) supplied by the proposition it is inferred from. Locke's example here is the inference from "Men shall be punished in another World" to "Men can determine themselves". If we reason rightly, we should start off with the idea 'men' and try to perceive its connexion with the idea 'can determine themselves' via a series of intermediate ideas.

Locke had a well-developed notion of probability. Like Hume, he thought that, apart from knowledge, which was very limited, attention must be paid to belief or opinion. Furthermore, like Hume, he thought that knowledge could be obtained either immediately by intuition or mediately by demonstrative reasoning, and that belief or opinion could be obtained mediately by probable reasoning. They differed in that Locke thought that what was obtained immediately by sense perception was sensitive knowledge, whereas Hume took that sort of cognitive awareness to be belief.[18] And, like Hume, he thought that (at least one) ground of probability was conformity with past experience.

IV. LOCKE AND HUME

Locke's claim that opinion and probability were needed as addenda to the more traditional categories of knowledge and demonstration was an important theme of the *Essay*. His was one of the earlier attempts to incorporate the relatively new notion of probability into what we now call epistemology. By the time Hume came to write the *Treatise*, Locke's *Essay* was arguably the most famous contemporary philosophical work in Britain and perhaps Europe. Hume shared with Locke an emphasis on ideas rather than words or propositions. Like Locke, indeed more so, he was concerned with belief and probable reasoning, not just knowledge and demonstrative reasoning.

In the section of the *Treatise* entitled 'Of probability; and of the idea of cause and effect', Hume claims that "All kinds of reasoning consist in nothing but a *comparison*, and a discovery of those relations, either constant or inconstant, which two or more objects bear to each other."[19] Since he is here concerned with belief and probability, rather than knowledge and demonstration, he goes on to distinguish the two cases of sense perception (and memory: T 82), or immediate awareness, and probable reasoning or inferential awareness. Probable reasoning takes place when only one, or neither, of the objects is present to the senses or memory. In these cases we have an inference from an impression to an idea, when one of the objects is present; or from an idea to another idea, when neither of the objects is present. The question of how such reasoning occurs is dealt with through most of Part III of Book I.

This is not to say that Hume's account of probable reasoning is just the same as Locke's. None the less, the similarity indicates that Hume had Locke, or a Lockean theory, very much in mind. And both Locke and Hume thought that conformity with past experience was a ground of probability. Indeed, much of the *Treatise* involves a sustained use of probable reasoning. But Locke thought that opinion based on probability was grounded in reason and the understanding every bit as much as demonstrative knowledge. Hume's argument concerning probable reasoning is an attack on this Lockean thought. Of course, Hume then goes on to give his own account of the nature and basis of probable reasoning, but the details of that account are beyond the scope of this essay.

The first paragraph in Section VI of Part III, entitled 'Of the inference from the impression to the idea', begins by repeating the argument that prior to experience the impression of one object can never carry the mind to the belief in the existence of another object. The idea or impression of the first object can never stand in the relevant relation to the idea of the second; there is no demonstrative connexion between them. This is Hume's rejoinder to those who thought we could have demonstrative knowledge of effects on the basis of causes, prior to the experience of their conjunction.

The main argument, which comes three paragraphs later, has a different target. Once we have past experience of the constant conjunction of two sorts of objects, we do indeed infer the existence of the second object. But now the question is, are we determined by reason to make the transition? On a Lockean view of probable reasoning, we are. We have an idea of the first object. Since we do not yet perceive the second, we can have no knowledge of its existence, any more than we can of the existence of the person who left the room a minute ago. But the conformity of the present object with our past experience of objects of that sort provides probable grounds for a reasonable inference to a belief in the existence of an unobserved object of the relevant kind. Such an idea is the medium via which we can reason. Analogously, the past experience of objects of the relevant sorts being conjoined provides probable grounds for – that is to say, provides the probable medium for – the inference from the perceived idea of the observed object to the idea of the existence of the unobserved object. As Locke had said (and note his use of the expression 'with reason'):

> This we call an Argument from the nature of Things themselves. For what our own and other Men's constant Observation has found always to be after the same manner, that we with reason conclude to be the Effects of steady and regular Causes. (*Essay*, IV. xvi. 6)

Constant observation, by ourselves and others, that "Fire warmed a Man", seems then to provide us with the probable medium that can take us from the idea of this fire to the idea that it has or will warm a man. Such constant experience puts us "past doubt, that a relation affirming any such thing to have been, or any predication that it will happen again in the same manner, is very true" (IV. xvi. 6). The probable medium here would be in accordance with one of the general grounds of probability, i.e. conformity to experience. So the first idea would be "this fire", the proof or intermediate idea would be "conforms to past experience with respect to warming", and the last idea would be "has warmed or will warm a man". But nowhere does Locke address the question of how constant experience or constant observation of a sort of thing's behaviour in the past can give rise to the idea that a current instance of that sort of thing conforms to that past experience.

Hume's insistence that if, after experience, reason determined us, it would proceed upon the uniformity principle, is his way of addressing this question. We have an impression of a fire. We have a constant experience of fires warming men. We come to have the idea of warming men that is suitably related to our impression of this fire. That is to say, we believe that this fire will warm a man. But there is a gap in the chain of ideas that constitutes this piece of probable reasoning, if it is a matter of reason determining us. As it stands, we cannot get from the idea of experienced warming to the idea of unexperienced warming, unless there is a further intermediate idea of conformity of unexperienced fires to past experienced fires in this respect of warming. The claim that "if reason determin'd us, it would proceed upon that principle" of uniformity is just the claim that if reason determined us, some such idea would always be available.

The appeal to a principle here can mislead us. For a principle sounds like some general proposition that might well function as a premise in a deductively valid argument. But Hume does not use the term in that way. Consider how he uses the notion of a principle, not in this negative argument about probable reasoning, but in his positive account of probable reasoning. Just a few pages later he writes:

> When the mind, therefore, passes from the idea or impression of one object to the idea or belief of another, it is not determin'd by reason, but by certain principles, which associate together the ideas of these objects, and unite them in the imagination. (T 92)

These principles are, of course, the three principles of association, as he makes clear in the next paragraph. No one, as far as I know, has suggested that when Hume appeals to the principles of association as an explanation for a certain sort of activity in our mental life, he is really presenting a deductively valid argument where one of those principles functions as a premise. The principles function as empirical generalizations that explain their instances by subsuming them. Similarly, if reason determined us, in probable reasoning, each instance of probable reasoning would contain, as an intermediate idea or "probable medium", some instance of the uniformity principle that would allow the transition from some past experience to some relevantly similar unobserved idea.

Hume argued for his principles of association earlier in the *Treatise* (T 10–13), and thus felt free to use them when explaining and defending his positive account of probable reasoning. But it is his negative account that chiefly concerns us. If reason determined us, in probable reasoning, then each such instance of probable reasoning would contain the relevant intermediate idea of conformity to past experience, that is to say, each piece of probable reasoning would proceed upon the uniformity principle. Thus to prove that reason does not determine us, i.e. that such intermediate ideas are not available to us, it suffices to show that the principle is not available to us.

We can look at the situation in the following way: since the principle is available to us neither by intuition nor sense perception, then if it is available at all, it must be as a result of demonstrative or probable reasoning. Suppose, contrary to what Hume argues, it is provable demonstratively. Then the situation would be as follows: we are trying to find a demonstrative argument "to prove, *that those instances, of which we have had no experience, resemble those, of which we have had experience*" (T 89). But no such argument is possible; it would start with the idea of experienced instances and then, via a chain of intermediate ideas each of which is necessarily related via resemblance to its adjacent ideas, end with the idea of resembling unexperienced instances. As a result, the first idea of experienced instances would be necessarily related to the last idea of unexperienced instances. But we know in advance that that is not possible: we can easily form an idea of unexperienced instances that do not resemble experienced instances. "To form a clear idea of any thing, is an undeniable argument for its possibility, and is alone a refutation of any pretended demonstration against it" (T 89).

Now suppose, again counterfactually, that the principle is believed as the result of probable arguments rather than known as the result of the demonstrative arguments. Then the situation would be as follows: we are trying to find a probable argument that will take us from the idea of experienced instances (or an actual impression of the senses or memory) to the idea of resembling unexperienced instances. But no such argument is possible: it would have to proceed from the former idea, via a chain of intermediate ideas, to the latter idea. But in a probable argument, such a chain of intermediate ideas would include a link that takes us from the idea of experienced instances to an idea of resembling unexperienced instances, and that is the very link we are trying to establish by this argument. "[P]robability is founded on the presumption of a resemblance betwixt those objects, of which we have had experience, and those, of which we have had none; and therefore 'tis impossible this presumption can arise from probability" (T 90).

Locke argued that conformity to experience was a ground of probability, and Hume concurred. But Hume showed that that ground was not based on reason, either demonstrative or probable. Hume's appeal to the principle of uniformity has nothing to do with the need for a premise to turn an otherwise deductively invalid argument into a valid one; rather it has to do with the lack of a suitable idea that would form the crucial connexion in the chain of ideas that constitutes a piece of probable reasoning. The relevant probable medium or fallible proof is just not available to us.

V. CONCLUSION

Hume argued against a certain conception of probable arguments as grounded in reason and the understanding. It has been my task to uncover what that conception actually was in order better to understand Hume's argument. That conception was non-formal, concerned at the most basic level with ideas rather than propositions. It involved showing that two ideas stood in a certain relation via showing that each idea was in turn related to an intermediate idea. In demonstrative reasoning, each link in the chain was certain while in probable reasoning each link was perceived to hold only "for the most part". Hume's argument about probable reasoning was thought by him to show that the requisite intermediate idea or ideas for probability were simply not available. Thus probability is not grounded in reason or the understanding, as Locke thought.

Hume goes on, in the next eighty pages of the *Treatise*, to give his own account of probability and probable reasoning. The details of that account are almost as controversial as the details concerning the more famous negative argument about probable reasoning, but I want to make one point here to avoid misunderstanding. In abandoning the notion of probability as grounded in reason and the understanding as traditionally conceived, Hume abandons the notion that reasoning always requires an intermediate idea to link the two ideas shown to be related. He makes this clear when he writes that the received view takes "reasoning to be the separating or uniting of different ideas by the interposition of others, which show the relation they bear to each other" (T 96n.). This view is faulty because, as he has shown,

> we may exert our reason without employing more than two ideas, and without having recourse to a third to serve as a medium betwixt them. We infer a cause immediately from its effect; and this inference is not only a true species of reasoning, but the strongest of all others, and more convincing than when we interpose another idea to connect the two extremes.

In these cases of probable reasoning from cause to effect a person reasons without reflecting on past experience and without recourse to the uniformity principle (T 103–4). Not all causal reasoning is like this, however. In those instances where we reason causally after only one experiment, we do indeed reflect on past experience and make use of something very like the uniformity principle (T 104–5). But the point remains. Hume has supplanted a view of reasoning which requires intermediate ideas with one that does not.

I began by noting that to understand Hume's sceptical argument we must resist the temptation to treat the demonstrative/probable distinction as the same as the deductive/inductive contrast. Much recent work has avoided that trap, but at the cost of treating both demonstrative and probable arguments as having a deductive structure. This strategy, though initially attractive, is equally flawed. Locke's neglected account of the nature of demonstrative and probable reasoning is the best starting point for understanding the conception of reasoning Hume was criticizing and, consequently, for understanding the account he put in its place.[20]

NOTES

1. E 174. A. C. MacIntyre has noted that Hume was unlikely to have meant by 'deduce' anything like what we would mean by that term. However, he still identified Hume's demonstrative arguments with our deductive arguments, and suggested that Hume maintained that all arguments are either deductive or defective. See 'Hume on "is" and "ought"', *Philosophical review* 68 (1959), 451–68.
2. T. L. Beauchamp and A. Rosenberg, in *Hume and the problem of causation* (Oxford 1981), hereafter BR, and D. C. Stove in *Probability and Hume's inductive scepticism* (Oxford 1973), transcend the simple error of mistaking Hume's demonstrative/probable contrast for the deductive/inductive one. However, as I shall show, they mislocate the target in Hume's negative argument about probable reasoning. Henceforth, I will speak of Hume's "argument concerning probable reasoning" rather than of his "argument about induction".
3. See J. A. Passmore, 'Descartes, the British empiricists, and formal logic', *Philosophical review* 62 (1953), 545–53; J. W. Yolton, *Locke and the compass of human understanding* (Cambridge 1970), pp. 91–5; M. D. Wilson, 'Leibniz and Locke on "first truths"', *Journal of the history of ideas* 28 (1967), 347–66.
4. A graphic example can be found in *Essay*, IV. xvii. 4 (p. 672, l. 25, to p. 673, l. 31, of the Nidditch edition (Oxford 1975)).
5. I do not mean to suggest that Hume's views on probable reasoning derive solely from, and in reaction to, Locke's, nor that Locke's views arose in a vacuum. The rise of the modern conception of probability in general, and Hume's conception of probable reasoning in particular, is a long, difficult and controversial story. Much of it is admirably presented in I. Hacking's *The emergence of probability* (Cambridge 1975), a book to which I am much indebted. My purpose here is not to tell that whole story. I have the much more limited aim of clarifying the structure of Hume's celebrated argument concerning induction in terms of his, and Locke's, views on the nature of demonstrative and probable reasoning.
6. Stove, ch. 2; BR, ch. 2.
7. In a few places, Beauchamp and Rosenberg seem to be maintaining the implausible thesis that the conception of probable reasoning that Hume is attacking is the claim "that at least some inductive arguments are demonstrative" (BR, pp. xviii, 41). This is implausible for the following reason: since they hold that demonstrative arguments have "self-evident a priori premises", it is clear that Hume had already shown that probable arguments could not be demonstrative by the beginning of Section VI, well before the main argument. So on this view, that famous argument is otiose! But later they make the weaker, more plausible claim that probable arguments share with demonstrative arguments, not the characteristic of having self-evident premises, but

only the feature of "logical necessity attending demonstrative arguments" (p. 43) or of "logical necessity that uniquely characterizes demonstrative reason" (p. 46).

8. As Stove, p. 35, correctly notes. He further notes (pp. 35–6) that it avoids saddling Hume with the view that there cannot be a deductively valid argument which has a contingent conclusion. This is more problematic, as will emerge later.

9. A. G. N. Flew, for instance, in *David Hume: Philosopher of moral science* (Oxford 1986), attributes this to Hume as a Cartesian assumption.

10. A. J. Jacobson, in her review of Flew in *Mind* 97 (1988), p. 296, though not agreeing with this tendency, realizes its near universal current acceptance: "Hume does also *appear* to assume that any good, rational argument for a matter of fact claim about the unobserved must include as a premiss that the future will resemble the past and exegesis of Hume has nearly universally assumed or argued that a particular conception of right reasoning or good argumentation is what gives rise to the requirement of the presence of this premiss."

11. In 'A defence of induction', in *Perception and identity*, ed. G. Macdonald (London 1979), pp. 115–16, J. L. Mackie accepts Stove's interpretation and adds the following consideration: if you interpret the model of probable reasoning that Hume is attacking as having a non-deductive structure so that experience made probable an inductive conclusion, then "Hume's claim that 'probability' would have to appeal, circularly, to the uniformity principle would be false". That is to say, points (2) and (3) above not only explain Hume's appeal to circularity; they are the only explanation of that circularity.

12. Here I am indebted to R. J. Fogelin, *Hume's skepticism in the Treatise of human nature* (London 1985), pp. 153–4.

13. It is worth mentioning one consequence of the R account of demonstrative reasoning. If a demonstrative argument is a deductively valid argument with necessarily true premises, then any set of three logically true propositions constitutes a demonstrative argument!

14. B. Stroud, *Hume* (London 1977), pp. 60–62.

15. Even in the chapter on truth (*Essay*, IV. v), where Locke most frequently talks about propositions, he reduces propositions, at least mental propositions, to ideas and their relations. I leave aside, for this essay, the complications raised by words and verbal propositions.

16. Realizing that 'proofs' means 'intermediate ideas' and 'arguments' means 'chains of intermediate ideas' is crucial for understanding Locke, as is his view that what holds ideas together in a chain is the content of the ideas and not some formal relationship. Though the basic thought is simple enough, the details are complex and controversial. See my 'Locke on reason, probable reasoning and opinion', *Locke newsletter* 24 (1993), 35–79.

17. There is a passage in IV. xvii. 2 that the unwary might take as evidence that Locke thought that both demonstrative and probable inferences were characterized by deductive validity: "*Illation* or *Inference* . . . consists in nothing but the Perception of the connexion there is between the *Ideas*, in each step of the deduction, whereby the Mind comes to see, either the certain Agreement or Disagreement of any two *Ideas*, as in Demonstration, in which it arrives at Knowledge; or their probable connexion, on which it gives or with-holds its Assent, as in Opinion." Here Locke talks of both demonstrative and probable arguments as 'deductions'. But both his general account of reasoning as non-

syllogistic, and his clear reference in this passage to the agreement or disagreement of ideas, indicate that here, as elsewhere, we must treat his use of 'deduction' as a synonym for 'argument'.

18. The comparison of intuition with sense perception is explicit twice in IV. xvii. 2, as is the comparison of demonstration with probability. And see T 86, where Hume says that "[t]o believe is in this case to feel an immediate impression of the senses".

19. T 73. 'Constant or inconstant' here is a clear echo of Locke, IV. xv. 1: where ideas in a chain have a constant relation, the reasoning is demonstrative; where not, the reasoning is probable.

20. This is a revised version of an essay first published under the title 'Hume and the Lockean background: Induction and the uniformity principle', *Hume studies* 18 (1992), 179–207.

8

An early fragment on evil

M. A. STEWART

In July 1993, the National Library of Scotland acquired a fragment of a
hitherto unknown Hume manuscript.[1] It came from 'The book of fame',
an autograph collection assembled by Martha, the sister of Hannah More,
the literary-evangelical bluestocking.[2] Hannah More came under the same
literary patronage, a generation later, that Hume had done in his time as
a clerk in Bristol. The connexion is the draper, John Peach, to whom
Hume reputedly sent some of his manuscripts for stylistic vetting even in
his mature years.[3] Whether Peach himself acquired, and passed to the
More sisters, one of Hume's manuscript cast-offs, we shall probably
never know; but there has to have been another supply route for a 1760
letter from Hume to John Roebuck, auctioned from the same collection.[4]

The fragment is a half sheet, folded once to create a four-sided unit;
the two leaves in their present state each measure approximately 18.7 by
22.9 cm. As usual with a Hume manuscript in its initial condition, the
pages are not individually numbered;[5] we do not know, therefore, how
much he had written of which this was the continuation. It is a narrative
work, not a dialogue, and appears to be Hume's own narrative, not a
transcription or translation, since it has on-line, interlinear, and marginal
corrections and additions. Hume had a general readership in view: he
wrote of what would "gain the Cause with most Readers".

It is from a work where Hume discussed what in the opening sentence
he calls "the System of Theism", and presented objections to it. It is
headed, tantalizingly, 'Sect. 7' and entitled 'Fourth Objection', so six
other sections and three earlier objections preceded it. But the headings
'Sect. 7' and 'Fourth Objection' were written at different times, in different
inks. When Hume sketched out his Fourth Objection he apparently did
not know where it would fall in a structure of numbered sections.[6]

He begins by sharply contrasting the intelligence and benevolence of
the Deity, then subsumes these under the broader categories of "natural"
and "moral" attributes. These qualities – the natural and moral – "are
totally distinct and separate". Their separation is founded in another
fundamental distinction, between reason and virtue, which have no neces-

sary connexion either in nature or in humankind. "A sound Understanding & a hard Heart are very compatible." We can only appeal to experience: does good predominate over evil, or vice versa? Translated into a question of happiness over misery, this appears to offer a clear decision procedure. Whichever predominates, then if the Author of Nature is intelligent, we may draw an appropriate inference.

The decisive test is to be carried out by weighing *degrees* against *frequency*. The distinction is marked for emphasis by Hume himself, and illustrated with a variety of examples. The pains of life outweigh its pleasures in degree; pleasures outweigh pains in frequency. Hume thinks, on balance, that evil predominates overall, and in this claims support from both the learned and the vulgar.[7] But he also has a psychological explanation of why we may think it. "What is Evil alarms us more, & makes more lasting Impression than what is agreeable; which we readily receive without Enquiry, & which we think Ourselves, in some measure, entitled to." The depiction of evil also affects the imagination more forcefully than the depiction of pleasures. But "I . . . shall not employ any Rhetoric in a philosophical Argument, where Reason alone ought to be hearken'd to".

An objective measure of the proportions is, then, unlikely, because we cannot attain the necessary distance. Hume thinks it would be like trying to settle the proportion of male to female births in the population by recalling our personal acquaintance, without the objective record of bills of mortality.[8] But some kind of probabilistic argument may still be possible. If the preponderance of evil over good is considerable, that will eliminate a benevolent supreme being. But if good prevails, it plainly does so by such a narrow margin that no theistic conclusion should be drawn.

The sentiments here are mainstream Hume. This needs to be stressed, since Sotheby's were at one time persuaded they had something very youthful on their hands.[9] There are strong links with Book I of the *Treatise,* in the sceptical use of the calculus of probability and a recognition of the influences on the imagination that may induce belief. The same factors were to have been at work in the abortive discussion of Miracles.[10] That *"Reason & Virtue* are not the same" suggests the discussion 'Of the influencing motives of the will' at II. iii. 3. The remarks on the unphilosophical impact of verbal painting on the imagination recall Hume's response to Hutcheson at III. iii. 6.[11] Elsewhere in Book III, he distinguishes between natural and moral attributes as applied to human beings, but there contends that the distinction – traced to the ancient moralists – is largely academic.[12] We esteem people nearly as much for their intellectual abilities as their moral character, and it is a mistake to think the one involuntary and the other not. While there is nothing in this inconsistent with the view that moral qualities cannot be deduced from natural, there is a certain discontinuity between Hume's official account of the virtues, as qualities variously useful and agreeable, and his discussions, at any period, of the moral attributes of divinity.[13]

When we turn to the relationship of the new piece to the argument of the *Dialogues*, the most striking thing is the lucidity and directness of its presentation compared with the diffuseness of Hume's writing on these themes by the 1750s. His target in the *Dialogues* will still be identified as "the System of Theism" (D 152, 165), and obviously there is still, underlying that whole work, the same exploration of, and contrast between, those divine attributes that bear some analogy to human intelligence and those analogous to human benevolence. The same concepts recur, but the rhetorical impact of the stark antithesis between intelligence and benevolence is somewhat dissipated in the more famous exposition.

The same is true of the generic distinction between natural and moral attributes, although that is explicit enough at three points in the *Dialogues*.[14] The phraseology is first assigned to Cleanthes, who comments that Philo's scepticism has found a worthy subject, "For to what purpose establish the natural attributes of the Deity, while the moral are still doubtful and uncertain?" (D 199). It is picked up by Philo, who remarks that

> when we argued concerning the natural attributes of intelligence and design, I needed all my sceptical and metaphysical subtilty to elude your grasp. . . . But there is no view of human life or of the condition of mankind, from which, without the greatest violence, we can infer the moral attributes, or learn that infinite benevolence, conjoined with infinite power and infinite wisdom, which we must discover by the eyes of faith alone. (D 202)

When Philo revives the distinction again in Part XII, it is to discredit human virtues in a way that defeats any attempt to establish divine analogues (D 219).

The contrast between degrees and frequencies of pain and pleasure survives in Part X of the *Dialogues*, in Philo's point that "if pain be less frequent than pleasure, it is infinitely more violent and durable. One hour of it is often able to outweigh a day, a week, a month of our common insipid enjoyments" (D 200). But the new fragment has the clearer analysis, abjuring the literary pathos that overtakes Philo and Demea in the other work. "Racks, Gravels, Infamy, Solitude, and Dungeons" reappear in the *Dialogues* as the "racking pains" that "arise from gouts, gravels, megrims, tooth-achs, rheumatisms", but with fewer compensating transient pleasures (D 199). The unfinished argument that, if good prevails, it does so by too small a margin to justify any inference, is in line with the conclusion of Part X: "allowing you, what never will be believed; at least, what you never possibly can prove, that animal, or at least, human happiness in this life exceeds its misery; you have yet done nothing: For this is not, by any means, what we expect from infinite power, infinite wisdom, and infinite goodness" (D 201). That will lead Philo into the Baylean refuge that recognition of our intellectual infirmity is the only answer to the Epicurean dilemma.[15]

If the new fragment thus serves as a kind of guide to Philo's argument in Part x, and reinforces Philo's role as Hume's spokesman, how far can we press the structural parallels between the two works? We no longer have the objections to the natural attributes of the Deity that preceded the present fragment. Nevertheless, the *Dialogues* conform to the same pattern of opening with an extended critique of the natural attributes. Can we find in this an equivalent three-stage analysis that might preserve the basic detail of Hume's lost narrative? My suggestions would be:

1. "That order, arrangement, or the adjustment of final causes is not, of itself, any proof of design, but only so far as it has been experienced to proceed from that principle" – which effectively summarizes the argument of Part II, and is not undermined by Cleanthes' come-back in Part III. Order and arrangement are natural features that form an inadequate basis for inference to any corresponding intellectual attribute.
2. We have no evidence in experience for the ultimate priority of mind over matter, and every reason to think the existence of mind needs to be and possibly can be explained in turn through natural causes – the underlying theme of Part IV, and Hume's version of the Stratonician hypothesis presented by Bayle.[16]
3. So far as experience goes, there are many different "springs and principles" to explain different kinds of order, not some single "principle of order throughout all nature" (Pt VII).

But there may be other candidates. Kemp Smith, writing long before this new discovery, had already reduced Philo's objections to three in his edition of the *Dialogues*, and only his third agrees fully with mine (D 99–100).

The new fragment belonged to an earlier work than the *Dialogues*. The hand is Hume's mature hand, the small, round, impeccably neat script evidenced by letters and other manuscripts from the late 1730s on. So this is not a remnant of the notebook on religion "wrote before I was twenty" that Hume burnt in later life, though the dialectical structure of that notebook may have left its mark on his subsequent writing.[17] But there is still one occasional archaic feature, a small 'f' which sometimes sweeps backwards in an open curve instead of coming down vertically to form a closed forward loop.[18] Isolated instances of this formation survive in single letters of 1739 and 1740 (HL I, 35, 38), and on the first page of Hume's undated 'Philosophy' memoranda.[19] The spelling is consistently archaic in line with his early to middle-period writing. The most striking archaism is 'outmost' for 'utmost'. However, Hume briefly revives that form in correspondence in the 1760s, so this detail cannot be trusted in isolation.

The paper is paper manufactured for the British market. The watermark consists in a horn and baldric mounted on a shield; above the shield is a crown, and below the shield the King's initials 'GR'. This crowned horn watermark occurs throughout the century, but the particular instance (the crown 9 mm. wider than the shield, the shield 4.5 cm. wide, and the whole watermark 9.5 cm. in length) occurs elsewhere in the Hume corpus in two letters of the early 1740s. One is the 1742 "Dung with Marle" letter to Henry Home, the other the charmingly whimsical note to William Mure where Hume threatens to return his useless quill to the goose.[20] The content of the latter establishes only that it postdates Hume's first acquaintance with Hutcheson and other friends of the Mure circle. The paper is not Hume's usual letter paper of the period and he was probably using up scraps.

Content can often be ambiguous. For example, there need be nothing topically autobiographical in the fragment's reference to "melancholy Views of things": the borderline between philosophy and melancholy is omnipresent in Hume's work (T 264, E 9, D 193, etc.). It is the formal features that determine the dating, and I see no chance that the fragment is pre-*Treatise*. The *Treatise* itself, moreover, is the only known and relevant work of Hume's that was ever written in "Sections". (The *Enquiry* was originally divided into Essays, the *Dialogues* into Parts; the Sections of *The natural history of religion* did not carry titles in the first edition and the present fragment has no obvious place in that work.) So we have to consider that what we have may be one of the "noble Parts" prudentially removed from the *Treatise* in 1739 to avoid offence, in company with an early discourse on Miracles and the essay on Immortality.[21] Since there is no present Section 6 to which this could be the sequel, we are trying to locate several missing sections together.

One possibility is that the present Part IV of Book I, 'Of the sceptical and other systems of philosophy', is a late expedient, combining four wide-ranging general sections (on scepticism with regard to reason and the senses, and the ancient and modern philosophies) with an awkward residue of two highly specific topical sections (on immateriality and identity) which hardly qualify as sceptical or other "systems". It makes sense to consider the latter as the residue of another self-standing Part (IV or V), tracing the applications of the preceding philosophy to the whole range of eighteenth-century pneumatology – the study of mind and Deity.[22] This would bring the structure of Book I more into line with that of the *Enquiry* which was in some way modelled on it.[23] It would also bring nearer to fulfilment Hume's promise in the Introduction to the *Treatise*, where he explains how his science of man, which was to embrace logic, morals, criticism and politics, was to feed back into the remoter sciences of mathematics, natural philosophy and natural religion. There is some feedback into mathematics and natural philosophy in Parts II and III of Book I, but virtually none, as the text now stands, to natural religion.

Alternatively, if what we have is truly a fragment of a hitherto unknown work, we would have to suppose that, with the *Treatise* out of the way, Hume immediately turned, not only to his new literary genre – the light essay – but also, contrary to all previous evidence and probability, to a second narrative work in the treatise or dissertation mould; or at least, that he was already working on such a work until the ill success of the *Treatise* caused him to abandon both the work and the genre, to concentrate single-mindedly on his essay interests. In the absence of positive evidence for this, and given the chronological constraints imposed by the formal features of the manuscript, the other hypothesis is the more economical, though still necessarily provisional.

At all events, we now see that a significant part of Hume's mature philosophy of religion was fully worked out by around the time of the *Treatise*, and more directly indebted to its logical and psychological doctrine than was previously appreciated. The possibility that Hume may already have applied to his own work the distinction between philosophical argument and rhetoric, before his run-in with Hutcheson, is also striking.[24]

The following transcription, and the accompanying photographic reproduction, are published by permission of the Trustees of the National Library of Scotland.[25] In the textual notes, wording deleted by Hume is enclosed within square brackets [. . .]. Wording added interlinearly or in the margin after the initial writing is enclosed within slashes \. . ./. Braces {. . .} are used to enclose undeleted matter that needs deletion. A few characters now masked by mounting paper in the margins of page 4 are still legible under cold light.

SECT. 7

FOURTH OBJECTION

The *fourth* Objection is not levell'd against the Intelligence of the Deity, but against his moral Attributes, which are equally essential to the System of Theism.

The Attempt to prove the moral Attributes from the natural, Benevolence from Intelligence, must appear vain, when we consider, that these Qualities are totally distinct & separate. *Reason* & *Virtue* are not the same; nor do they appear to have any immediate Connexion, in the Nature of things. Even in Man, any degree of the one affords no presumption for an equal degree of the other. A sound Understanding & a hard

Heart are very compatible. Allowing, therefore, the Intelligence of the Deity to be prov'd by [a]Phænomena, ever so clear & decisive; we can draw no Inference concerning his Benevolence, without a new Set of Phænomena, equally clear & decisive.

Whether the Author of Nature be benevolent or not can only be prov'd by the Effects, & by the Predominancy either of Good or Evil, of Happiness or Misery, in the Universe. If Good prevail much above Evil, we [b]may, perhaps, presume, that the Author of the Universe, if an intelligent, is also a benevolent Principle. If Evil prevail much above Good, we may draw a contrary Inference. This is a [c]Standard, by which we may decide such a Question, with some Appearance of Certainty; but when the Question is brought to that Standard, [d]& we wou'd willingly determine the Facts, upon which we must proceed in our Reasoning; we find that 'tis very difficult, if not absolutely impossible, ever (*p. 2*) to ascertain them. For who is able to form an exact Computation of all the Happiness and Misery, that are in the World, & to compare them exactly with each other? I know it is the common Opinion, that Evil prevails very much above Good, even [e]amongst [f]Mankind, who are the most favour'd by Nature of all sensible Creatures: But still some think, they have Reason to dispute [g]this popular Opinion. What one may safely pronounce on this head, is, that if we compare Pains & Pleasures in their *Degrees*, the former are infinitely Superior; there being many Pains, & even durable ones, extremely acute; & no Pleasure, that is at the same time very intense & very durable. Love betwixt the Sexes is, I believe, the only one, that has any Pretensions to the Character of an exquisite & intense Pleasure, whether we consider the bodily Enjoyment [h]which it affords, or the Tenderness & Elegance of that Friendship, which it inspires. Perhaps Men of strong Genius may find as high Pleasures in Study & Contemplation. But what is all this in Comparison of those many cruel Distempers & violent Sorrows, to which human Life is subject? In this View, therefore, Pains & Pleasures are not to be put into the Ballance with each other. On the other hand, if we compare the *Frequency* of Pains with that of Pleasures, we shall find, that the latter have the Advantage, and that small Pleasures, to the greatest Part of Mankind, return oftener, (*p. 3*) than Pain or Uneasyness. When a Man is in good Health & in good Humour, every common Incident of Life affords him Satisfaction; to go to bed; to rise again; to eat; to drink; to converse;

---

[a] [ever so certain] Phænomena, \ever so clear & decisive;/

[b] may\, perhaps,/

[c] [certain] Standard, by which we may decide such a Question[;]\, with some Appearance of Certainty;/

[d] \& we wou'd willingly [ascertain] \determine/ the Facts, upon which we must proceed in our Reasoning; we find that/ 'tis very difficult, if not absolutely impossible, ever to [decide it] \ascertain them/

[e] among\st/

[f] [Men] \Mankind/

[g] [the] \this/ popular Opinion [in this particular]

[h] \which/

Sect. 7

David Hume

Fourth Objection

The fourth Objection is not levell'd against the Intelligence of the Deity, but against his moral Attributes, which are equally essential to the System of Theism.

The Attempt to prove the moral Attributes from the natural, Benevolence from Intelligence, must appear vain, when we consider, that these Qualities are totally distinct & separate. Reason & Virtue are not the same; nor do they appear to have any immediate Connexion, in the Nature of things. Even in Man, any degree of the one affords no presumption for an equal degree of the other. A sound Understanding & a hard Heart are very compatible. Allowing, therefore, the Intelligence of the Deity to be prov'd by ~~any certain~~ ever so clear & decisive, Phænomena, we can draw no Inference concerning his Benevolence, without a new Set of Phænomena, equally clear & decisive.

Whether the Author of Nature be benevolent or not can only be prov'd by the Effects, & by the Predominancy either of Good or Evil, of Happiness or Misery, in the Universe. If Good prevail much above Evil, we may perhaps, presume, that the Author of the Universe, if an intelligent, is also a benevolent Principle. If Evil prevail much above Good, we may draw a contrary Inference. This is a ~~certain~~ with some Appearance of Certainty; Standard, by which we may decide such a Question; but when the Question is ~~& we would willingly ascertain~~ deter mine the Facts, upon which we must proceed in our Reasoning; we find that brought to that Standard, 'tis very difficult, if not absolutely impossible, ever

to

ascertain them

to ~~determine~~. For who is able to form an exact Computation of all the Happiness and Misery, that are in the World, & to compare them exactly with each other? I know it is the common Opinion, that Evil prevails very much above Good, even amongst ~~them~~ ^{Mankind}, who are the most favour'd by Nature of all sensible Creatures: But still some think, they have Reason to dispute ~~the~~ ^{this} popular Opinion ~~in this particular~~. What one may safely pronounce on this head, is, that if we compare Pains & Pleasures in their Degrees, the former are infinitely superior; there being many Pains, & even durable ones, extremely acute; & no Pleasure, that is at the same time very intense & very durable. Love betwixt the Sexes is, I believe, the only one, that has any Pretensions to the Character of an exquisite & intense Pleasure, whether we consider the bodily Enjoyment ^{which} it affords, or the Tenderness & Elegance of that Friendship, which it inspires. Perhaps Men of strong Genius may find as high Pleasures in Study & Contemplation. But what is all this in Comparison of those many cruel Distempers & violent Sorrows, to which human Life is subject? In this View, therefore, Pains & Pleasures are not to be put into the Ballance with each other. On the other hand, if we compare the Frequency of Pains with that of Pleasures, we shall find, that the latter have the Advantage, and that small Pleasures, to the greatest Part of Mankind, return oftener

than

than Pain or Uneasyness. When a Man is in good Health & in good Humour, every common Incident of Life affords him Satisfaction; to go to bed; to rise again; to eat; to drink; to converse; to enjoy the Weather; to perform his Business; to hear News; to retail them. These Incidents compose the Lives of most Men; & these are not without Enjoyment. But whether those Pleasures, by their Frequency, are able to compensate the Acuteness of our Pains, I must confess I am not able to determine with any Certainty. When I consider the Subject with the outmost Impartiality, & take the most comprehensive View of it, I find myself more inclind to think, that Evil predominates in the World, & am apt to regard human Life as a Scene of Misery, according to the as well as of the Generality of Mankind, from the Beginning of the World to this Day, Sentiments of the greatest Sages! I am sensible, however, that there are many Circumstances, which are apt to pervert my Judgement in this particular, & make me entertain melancholy Views of things. What is Evil alarms us more, & makes more lasting Impression than what is agreeable; which we readily receive without Enquiry, & which we think Ourselves, in some measure, entitled to. Besides, the greater Intenseness of our Pains has a much more powerful Influence on the Imagination than the super- :ior Frequency of our Pleasures; & tis almost impossible for us to make a just Compensation betwixt them. Shoud I enumerate all the

Evils

Evils, ~~to which~~ ^incident to^ human Life, ~~is subject~~, and display them, with Elo:quence, in their proper Colours, I shou'd certainly gain the Cause with most Readers, who wou'd be apt to despise, as frivolous, all the Pleasures, which cou'd be plaid in Opposition to them. Victuals, Wine, a Fiddle, a warm Bed, a Coffee-house Conversation make a pitiful Figure, when compar'd with Racks, Gravels, Infamy, Solitude, and Dungeons. But I take no Advantage of this Circumstance, & shall not employ any Rhetoric in a philosophical Argument, where Reason alone ought to be hearkend to. ^

But tho' it be difficult to decide this Question, whether there be more Good or Evil in the Universe, we may perhaps, find Means independent of it, to decide ^in some tolerable manner,^ that other Question concerning the Benevolence of the Deity. Were Evil predominant in the World, there wou'd evidently remain no Proofs of Benevolence in the supreme Being. But even if Good be predominant; since it prevails in so small a Degree, and is counter ballanc'd by so many Ills; it can never afford any Proof of that Attribute. Pains & Pleasures seem to be scatterd indifferently thro Life as Heat & Cold, Moist & Dry are dispers't thro the Universe; & if the one prevails a little above the other, this is what ~~must necessarily~~ ^will naturally^ happen in any Mixture of Principles, where an exact Equality is not expressly intended. On every Occasion, Nature seems to employ either.

[left margin:]

I shall only ^infer from the whole^ ~~conclude~~, that the Facts are here so complicated & dubious ^or so certain^, ~~that the~~ ^that a^ Conclusion can ~~ever~~ ^now^ be form'd from them, & that no ^single^ Con: clusion will ever be made by any Dis: putes upon this subject; but that ~~the~~ each Disputant will ^still^ ~~not~~ go off from the Field with a stronger Con: firmation of those Opinions & Prejudices, which he brought to it.

into a Controversy even whether more Males or Females are born; and this Question were to decided merely by our running over all the Families of our Acquaintance, without the Assistance of any Bills of Mortality, which bring the Matter to a Certainty.

to enjoy the Weather; to perform his Business; to hear News; to retail them. These Incidents compose the Lives of most Men; & these are not without Enjoyment. But whether those Pleasures, by their Frequency, are able to compensate the Acuteness of our Pains, I must confess I am not able to determine with any Certainty. When I consider the Subject with the outmost Impartiality, & take the most comprehensive View of it, I find myself more inclin'd to think, that Evil predominates in the World, & am apt to regard human Life as a ⁱScene of Misery, according to the Sentiments of the greatest Sages ʲas well as of the Generality of Mankind, from the Beginning of the World to this Day. I am sensible, however, that there are ᵏmany Circumstances, which are apt to pervert my Judgement in this particular, & make me entertain melancholy Views of things. What is Evil alarms us more, & makes more lasting Impression than what is agreeable; which we readily receive without Enquiry, & which we think Ourselves, in some measure, entitled to. Besides, the greater Intenseness of our Pains has a much more powerful Influence on the Imagination than the superior Frequency of our Pleasures; & 'tis almost impossible for us to make a just Compensation betwixt them. Shou'd I enumerate all the (*p. 4*) Evils, ˡincident to human Life, and display them, with Eloquence, in their proper Colours, I shou'd certainly gain the Cause with most Readers, who wou'd be apt to despise, as frivolous, all the Pleasures, which cou'd be plac'd in Opposition to them. Victuals, Wine, a Fiddle, a warm Bed, a Coffee-house Conversation make a pitiful Figure, when compar'd with Racks, Gravels, Infamy, Solitude, and Dungeons. But I take no Advantage of this Circumstance, & shall not employ any Rhetoric in a philosophical Argument, where Reason alone ought to be hearken'd to. ᵐI shall only infer, from the whole, that the Facts are here so complicated & disperst, that a certain Conclusion can never be form'd from them, & that no single Convert will ever be made by any Disputes upon this Subject; but each Disputant will still go off the Field with a stronger Confirmation of those Opinions & Prejudices, which he brought to it. Did a Controversy arise whether more Males or Females are born; cou'd this Question ever be decided merely by our running over all the Families of our Acquaintance; without the Assistance of any Bills of Mortality, which bring the Matter to a Certainty?

ⁱ Scen{c}e
ʲ \as well as of the Generality of Mankind, from the Beginning of the World to this Day/
ᵏ \many/
ˡ [to which] \incident to/ human Life\,/ [is subject,]
ᵐ \I shall only [conclude] \infer,/ \from the whole,/ that the Facts are here so complicated & disperst, that [no] \a [ ]/ \certain/ Conclusion can [ever] \never/ be form'd from them, & that no \single/ Convert will ever be made by any Disputes upon this Subject; but [that] each Disput[e]\ant/ will \still/ go off [from] the Field with a stronger Confirmation of those Opinions & Prejudices, which he brought to it. Did a Controversy arise whether more Males or Females are born; cou'd this Question ever be decided merely by our running over all the Families of our Acquaintance; without the Assistance of any Bills of Mortality, which bring the Matter to a Certainty?/ (*added in margin*)

But tho' it be difficult to decide this Question, whether there be more Good or Evil in the Universe, we may, perhaps, find Means, independent of it, to ⁿdecide, in some tolerable manner, that other Question concerning the Benevolence of the Deity. Were Evil predominant in the World, there wou'd evidently remain no Proofs of Benevolence in the supreme Being. But even if Good be predominant; since it prevails in so small a Degree, and is counter ballanc'd by so many Ills; it can never afford any Proof of that Attribute. Pains & Pleasures seem to be scatter'd indifferently thro Life, as Heat & Cold, Moist & Dry are disperst thro the Universe; & if the one prevails a little above the other, this is what ᵒwill naturally happen in any Mixture of Principles, where an exact Equality is not expressly intended. On every Occasion, Nature seems to employ ᴾeither.

ⁿ decide\,in some [ma] tolerable manner,/
ᵒ [must necessarily] \will naturally/
ᴾ either. (*catchword: punctuation uncertain*)

NOTES

1. Accession 10805; Sotheby's sale catalogue, 'English literature, history & illustration', 19 July 1993, lot 170. No other portions remain in the vendor's possession.
2. Hume's name on the manuscript is in Martha More's hand. Cf. Bodleian Library, MS Wilberforce c. 48, fo. 56.
3. W. Roberts, *Memoirs of the life and correspondence of Mrs. Hannah More* (London 1834), I, pp. 16–17; J. Latimer, *Annals of Bristol in the eighteenth century* (Bristol 1893), pp. 189–90.
4. Lot 171. Hume's nephew in later life sometimes gave away samples to collectors, and Hannah More herself moved into national literary circles where contacts with Scots literati would have been a possibility.
5. See NLS, MSS 23160–62 (*History, Dialogues*), where the page numbering is demonstrably late. A faintly pencilled figure in the top left corner of the new fragment is not a page count. Related markings occurred on other items, not by Hume, from the same collection (lots 162–3).
6. The centred heading 'Sect. 7' counts against our having here the fourth division of a single section. Hume elsewhere wrote his running heads in the left margins. It is, however, possible that the preceding Section 6 was thus divided, and that the decision to turn the Fourth Objection into an independent section was taken later because of its distinctive content.
7. Hume does not recognize Butler's point (*Analogy of religion* (1736), Pt I, chs 2–3) that the test of the moral attributes is not the existence of pleasure or pain, but whether its distribution is just.
8. Bills of mortality (monthly burial records) for Edinburgh in Hume's day show consistently more female than male adult deaths but do not differentiate the sex of children. He is referring to the practice instituted by the town council in 1695 of appending christening records to mortality records (M. Flinn and others, *Scottish population history from the 17th century to the 1930s* (Cambridge 1977), pp. 73–4).
9. Remnants of this view have survived at two points in the sale catalogue, where they claim, rather incautiously, that this may be "Hume's first known attempt to apply . . . the 'Experimental Method of reasoning' to a philosophical

question", and that the distinction here between reason and virtue "is Hume's famous distinction between 'is' and 'ought', which may well have been first developed in the context of this particular argument". If anything, it is because these parts of his philosophy are already in place that Hume is able to handle the problem of evil so expeditiously. The 'is-ought' distinction – between two kinds of "relation or affirmation" – comes as a logical addendum to *Treatise* III. i. 1. But the point at issue in the new piece is not the logical point that moral judgement does not derive from reason, but the substantive point that moral activity does not.

10. See M. A. Stewart, 'Hume's historical view of miracles' (this volume).
11. Cf. HL I, 32–3.
12. III. iii. 4. Cf. HL I, 33; E 312–23.
13. Some of Hume's qualms come to the surface in a letter to Hutcheson (HL I, 40).
14. The division between natural and moral attributes is found in Samuel Clarke, *Demonstration of the being and attributes of God* (1705), pp. 245–7. It is more fully explained by the neo-Clarkean Samuel Colliber, who treats it as commonplace in his *Impartial enquiry into the existence and nature of God* (1718), pp. 28–30. Colliber's account forms the basis for Edmund Law's influential annotations to the English translation of William King's *Origin of evil* (note 18, pp. 45–50, in the 1731 edition), annotations partly directed against Bayle. The natural attributes are judged to be deducible from the notion of a self-sufficient being: they include self-determination, intelligence, immutability, omnipotence and omniscience. The moral attributes stem from God's freely chosen relationship with the sentient creation. Law had held that they might still be "deduced", albeit not "demonstrated", from the natural attributes.
15. The suggestion that pleasures and pains balance out had been used by Bayle, in the *Dictionary* article 'Paulicians', to show that, without recourse to revelation, the Manichaeans have the best of the argument (*Dictionnaire historique et critique*, 2nd edn 1702; English translation by Pierre Desmaizeaux, 1734–8). That the balance is one of degree versus frequency was also maintained, if not in this terminology, in the article 'Xenophanes'.
16. Pierre Bayle, *Continuation des pensées diverses* (1705), CVI. Bayle's debate between Stratonicians and Stoics before the Athenian public was clearly Hume's model for *Enquiry* XI.
17. HL I, 154. Hume's letters to Michael Ramsay from 1727 to 1732 (HL I, 9–12; II, 336–7) are in a recognizably immature hand; the hand in a 1734 letter, and in the letter to a physician (HL I, 12–21), is transitional (NLS, MSS 23151–2). The change was apparently perfected during Hume's period of intensive writing in France. His letter hand and literary hand are not distinguishable.
18. The older formation continues to survive in the second 'f' of double 'ff'. The fragment does not have the immature 'ff' with stunted second 'f' found in Hume's writing up to the early 1730s.
19. NLS, MSS 23151, 23159 (14). E. C. Mossner's dating of Hume's reading notes to the period 1730–34 is almost certainly too early ('Hume's early memoranda, 1729–1740', *Journal of the history of ideas* 9 (1948), 492–512).
20. NHL 7; HL I, 52. The originals are in SRO and NLS.
21. NHL 2–3. Unfulfilled hints of treatments of these other topics have been identified by David Norton and John Gaskin at T 120, 250. In the latter context Hume also briefly raises Baylean questions about divine causation that bear on the problem of evil.

22. Or, if Part IV was always intended to have its hybrid character, we should probably assume that Sections 5–7 were initially taken up with natural religion, to be followed by other topics in pneumatology.

23. It is less clear how the discussion could have been worked into, and deleted from, Book III, despite evidence that Hume was reworking that up to the last minute as part of a continuing adjustment to Hutcheson's criticism.

24. But cf. T xiv, 123, 412, 426. For the mannerism of starting off in incipient rhetorical mode and then drawing back, cf. E 177.

25. The transcription was prepared with the assistance of Miss Ruth Savage.

9

Hume's historical view of miracles

M. A. STEWART

Hume's critique of the foundations of revealed religion in Section X of the first *Enquiry*, like that of natural religion in Section XI, combines philosophical with literary artifice. In addressing the former topic, he is mainly concerned with the weight to be attached to the testamentary evidence for miracles; his interest in conceptual or ontological issues is subordinate to this primary epistemological concern. But the sceptic who would disclaim knowledge need not disclaim his beliefs; and even in print, Hume scarcely disguises the conviction he avowed in private, that, however complete the proof, "all the testimony which ever was really given for any miracle, or ever will be given, is a subject of derision" (HL I, 349). Rhetoric and example are combined in a way that defeats the pretence that orthodox Christianity has been insulated from attack. Hume refers to Old Testament stories and to those of latter-day Catholicism; he looks at those of other religions and of none; and he even invents his own. His silence on the New Testament narratives, the primary concern of his original readers, is striking. But he has been building up a repertoire of analogies and parodies whose intention and effect are to undermine the stories he fails to address.

Hume prepared his discussion originally for the *Treatise*. It underwent some revision before he published it in the *Enquiry*.[1] How far any continuing revisions were in response to other literature appearing around the 1740s is still underresearched.[2] But even if the text was revised, the philosophy that underlies it is plainly present in the earlier work – and, I shall argue, in sources earlier than Hume.

Few Protestants in Hume's day shared the Cartesian conviction that the foundations of religion lie in strict demonstration. Belief was attended with as much certainty as our condition requires – "moral" certainty – but liberal thinkers increasingly preferred the broad precepts and social values of natural religion to the minutiae of dogmatic theology. The roots of this epistemology lie in English episcopal writers of the previous century like

Chillingworth, Wilkins and Tillotson. Locke had introduced a layman's caution in stressing the relationship of faith to belief rather than knowledge, and to probability rather than certainty; but he still defended a view of religious belief as both reasonable and reasoned.[3] Hume recognized Locke's role in this tradition (D 138).

At a time when representatives of the corresponding tradition in Scotland had risen to positions of power and patronage, Hume challenged the foundations in reason of this new tendency. The *Enquiry* was first presented as a slightly contrived set of *Philosophical essays,* with forays into religion and morals, and into history and aesthetics, as well as psychology and metaphysics. Hume compiled it, in part, on the rebound from his defeat for the Edinburgh chair of moral philosophy in 1745. He incorporated into Sections v and xi a criticism of the neo-Stoic philosophy which had become established among the liberal clerics who had helped spike his chances, responding to them with a spirited defence of scepticism as the enemy only of vested interests.[4] Scepticism is the one philosophy consistent with a true knowledge of the human mind, but its effect is more intellectual than practical. It may moderate our enthusiasm, if we see that religion and morality are beyond the scope of reason except so far as either of them is dependent on causal reasoning; but it cannot change our living (cf. T 250–51).

This unseating of rational theology or natural religion forces the believer back towards revealed religion, where the new-light divines were not entirely comfortable. That is hardly surprising. For whereas natural religion saw God's power manifested in nature's regularity, revealed religion appeared to run counter to this, recognizing it in irregular intervention in the regularity.[5] Personal revelation had been a respectable element in traditional thought, but its credentials had been dented by Locke's analysis of faith and enthusiasm, of which there are significant echoes in Hume.[6] Religious experience does not carry its authenticity on its face and needs rational tests to verify its origin. Natural religion thus has to come to the rescue of revealed; if it has inherent problems of its own, there will not be much of a rescue.

The believer's remaining refuge was the public revelation of the written, and ultimately spoken, word of the Scriptures. Here evangelical and liberal alike could defend Protestantism as the restoration of a religion securely rooted in its biblical origins without the corrupting traditions of the papacy. All the main Christian traditions still accepted a literal reading of the biblical narratives, though there was growing evidence that the received text was unsafe.[7] But here the danger Locke had seen in the appeal to religious experience only repeats itself. Protestants did not accept Catholic reports of confirming miracles in the post-apostolic period, and therefore needed an adequate test which would distinguish real from counterfeit; and Catholics could not see the legitimacy in a Reformation unsupported by miracles. Both parties faced embarrassment from Jewish scholars, whose rationalizing away of the foundation myths of their own religion undermined the Christian rationale for something bigger and better of the same kind.[8]

The distinction between real and counterfeited past events is one we are all familiar with. It requires us to distinguish sound from unsound historical narration. To the eighteenth-century Christian, the Bible constituted a record of past utterances, actions and events which, taken as a totality, had an overall credibility. The theoretical problem was to bridge the gap between the premise that certain doctrines had been delivered and the conclusion that they were true, and do it without circularity. The bridge lay in the credibility of the actions reported to have accompanied the doctrinal utterances. So biblical doctrine was proved authentic by the accuracy of the record of the wonders worked by those who inculcated it.[9]

What Hume thought he could show, in common with some deist writers,[10] was that the same philosophy which forced the believer back on to this defence also undermined it. To expose this would be the final triumph of scepticism. It would destroy the whole strategy of Protestant apologetics, if Tillotson's famous argument against the Catholic cause turned out to be of a kind which must in the end defeat the Protestant alternative. As Hume saw well enough, Tillotson's attack on transubstantiation had been intimately bound up with the vindication of traditional miracle stories (E 109).

II

The key concepts that run through the debate on miracles are those of *probability* and *testimony*.[11] To understand Hume's contribution is to understand his place in the development and application of these concepts in relation to each other. Issues of probability arise where there is discrepancy in the evidence. Things usually go one way, but at least once they seem to have gone another way, whether we are talking about natural phenomena, or the reliability of particular witnesses, or about the one relative to the other; and we have to assess instances in relation to circumstances. Though not yet highly mathematized, probability is tied in with concepts of quantity, of weighing and outweighing, and their mental analogues in terms of (loosely conceived) degrees of belief.

Testimony enters the picture because it takes us beyond our own present experience and memory to the experience and memory of others. It is the means by which we can be aware of contingent events distant from us in space or time. It is therefore our primary resource for any knowledge of history: we are dependent on the surviving testimony of witnesses of the past.[12] Antiquaries – those who studied the artefacts, and occasionally the fossils, of the past – were not unknown at this time, but their work was not systematically integrated into historical studies; and though there had been significant works written on the recent past, history as an educational discipline was still a synthesis of biblical and Graeco-Roman sources. It is a commonplace that Hume discusses miracles exclusively as a topic of derived reports, with only a dismissive glance at the experience that is the subject of the reports. In the Protestant culture in which he lived, it was taken for granted that no one then living had experienced or would experience a miracle of the biblical kind. Miracles belonged to the age of Moses and of his successor, Christ; once they had validated their respective revelations, their job was done.[13] Hume's pious fellow-countryman, Robert Wodrow, was as critical as Hume of what he called "the stupide bigotry and superstition of the Papists", in expecting continuing manifestations in support of truths that had been already verified.[14]

This may be hard to square, at a deeper theoretical level, with a continuing belief in the efficacy of prayer (with its assumption of particular providence), or with the orthodoxy gently satirized by Hume in the conclusion to the essay, that faith is founded in the gift of grace (i.e. God's working a separate effect in the heart of each believer); and any good Calvinist of the period knew in his or her heart that the Protestant Succession had survived the political crises of 1689 and 1714 through providential fixing. But these were not perceived as contrary to any laws of nature: they were manifestations of nature's working itself out to the benefit of those whose deserts were identified in the divine plan. The question of the authenticity of miracles could still be isolated as a strictly historical one about the foundation of some of the great monotheistic religions. Going outside the experience of any living person, it had to appeal to the experience of now non-living persons, and constituted a test case for any consistent and reliable set of historical principles. The notion of "testimony of witnesses" has, however, more than historical associations: it also has legal overtones.[15] The historian's desire to subject his witnesses to "cross-examination" in order to eliminate fabulous stories, implying the ostensible superiority of oral over written evidence, is as old as Thucydides,[16] and the idea of "trying" those who had been witnesses to miracles surfaces in a few writers.

The first major author in the English-language tradition to embody the conviction that the philosophical problems about miracles are problems of historical credibility seems to have been Henry More, in Book III of *An antidote against atheism* (1652).[17] Everyone knows of bogus miracles, but they cannot be bogus unless there are true miracles that they simulate.[18] More laid down three conditions. It is "mere humour and sullenness", and the discounting of all history, to reject a miracle report if "what is recorded was avouched by such persons who had *no end* nor *interest* in avouching such things", if "there were many *Eye-witnesses* of the same Matter", and if "these things which are so strange and miraculous leave any sensible *effect* behind them". That this is too passive a set of criteria, and avoids any serious testing, is shown by Joseph Glanvill's application of the same standards in *Saducismus triumphatus* (1681) to vindicate the existence of witchcraft: "We have the *attestation* of thousands of eye and ear-witnesses, and those not of the easily-deceivable vulgar onely, but of wise and grave discerners; and that, when no interest could oblige them to agree together in a common *Lye.*"[19] But we do owe to Glanvill an early formulation of a principle that recurs down to Hume's time: "I *assent* where I see cause, and proportion the degree of my belief to that I have of evidence."[20]

More's heirs were the latitudinarian divines of the later seventeenth century. John Wilkins, in *The principles and duties of natural religion* (posthumous, 1675), acknowledged that miracle stories can be "fabulous and vain"; but to suggest they all are "were to subvert the Credit of all History" (p. 88). We rely on testimony for an account of persons or places at a distance, and this "depends upon the credit and authority of the Witnesses" who in favourable cases "may be so qualified as to their *ability* and *fidelity*, that a man must be a fantastical incredulous fool to make any doubt of them". So we all know there was such a person as Queen Elizabeth and is such a place as Spain. A second, lesser kind of assent, which "is called *Opinion* and *Probability*", arises "When though the proofs for a thing may preponderate any thing to be said against it, yet they are not so weighty and perspicuous as to exclude all reasonable doubt and fear of the contrary". Thirdly, there is "a *Hesitation* or suspension of Assent" when "the evidence of each side doth equiponderate" (pp. 4, 10–11). The dominant image is that of a balance tilting in favour of the "weight" of evidence.

Matters of history or geography differ from mathematics in the "*kind* or *degree* of Evidence as to us", but not in their truth or certainty. A certainty can be indubitable without being infallible, for example that this is a Roman coin and that an ancient gravestone – or that the sun will rise, and rise in the east, although "the contrary is not impossible, and doth not imply any contradiction" (pp. 22ff.).

> *When there is no such evident certainty, as to take away all kind of doubting; in such cases, a judgment that is equal and impartial must incline to the greater probabilities.* That is no just ballance, wherein the heaviest side will not preponderate. (p. 34)

And again:

> *If in any matter offered to Consideration, the probabilities on both sides*

be supposed to be equal: (In this case, though an impartial judgment cannot be obliged to incline to one side rather than to the other, because our *Assent* to things must by a Necessity of Nature, be proportioned to our *Evidence* for them; And where neither side doth preponderate, the ballance should hang even) *Yet even in this case, men may be obliged to order their Actions in favour of that side, which appears to be most safe and advantageous for their own interest.* (p. 37)

But Wilkins fails to explain what determines, or constitutes, "weight" in evidence.

The most philosophical of this group was Edward Stillingfleet. The seeds of Tillotson's argument against transubstantiation are also found in Stillingfleet's *Rational account of the grounds of Protestant religion* of 1665: "And if a Man may be bound to believe that to be false which his Sense judges to be true, what Assurance can be had of any *Miracles* which were wrought to confirm the *Christian Doctrine?*" (III. iii). In several works he defended the need for miraculous events in biblical times and sought to show how we can be confident of the historical record. No one disputes that the Bible reflects the imperfections of works created and transmitted by human hand, like any other works of history; but there is an inherent likelihood in its accounts of facts that are within human comprehension. Care was taken in checking the transmission, both in the lifetimes of the agents and later, because it was more than the informants' and transcribers' lives were worth to get it wrong. In *Origines sacræ* (1662), where these matters are extensively discussed, Stillingfleet treated of "the greatest evidence which can be given to a matter of fact" and "the difference of true Miracles from false" (II. ix-x; on the latter see also his Sermon XLVIII). The "greatest evidence" lies in eyewitness testimony where the matter was plainly visible, and where many disinterested witnesses agree, have the skill necessary to understand what they have seen, and give a clear and candid account with a consistency of corroborative detail. This is not to be overridden by the kind of preconceived theorizing we shall find in Hume, but only by better witnesses – those who "had greater knowledge of the things attested, and manifest greater fidelity in reporting them". Taking a leaf from Dante, and anticipating a rhetorical formula in Hume, Stillingfleet argued that the establishment of the Christian religion without miracles would have been a greater miracle than its establishment with miracles (II. x. 5).[21]

III

That believers are relying on testimony which, though fallible, is as secure as our condition requires is a commonplace of the period, and nowhere more so than in the most significant logic text in the century prior to Hume, the Port-Royal *Logic* of Arnauld and Nicole (1662). This adapted traditional logic to the psychology and epistemology of Cartesianism, but was heavily used on both sides of the sectarian divide. Written as a manual for Jansenist novitiates, it illustrates its logical and epistemological doctrines with examples congenial to this strand of Catholicism, which made it the subject of lively critical comment from Calvinist divines. A generation later, Locke's *Essay* carried to the limit the exclusion of traditional textbook logic and recast the new epistemology as a foundation for Protestant apologetics. Both works were landmarks in the study of testimony and probability in general and their relevance to miracles in particular, and brought probability into the mainstream of epistemological debate. I discuss briefly the Port-Royal view of these things, then Locke's. Hume acknowledges his acquaintance with both Port-Royal and Lockean accounts of probability in the *Abstract,* and with Locke's account in the *Enquiry* (T 647, E 56n.); but his greater debts are to Locke.[22]

Arnauld differentiated those matters which are an appropriate subject for belief or faith from those of which we have knowledge or science. Whereas knowledge is based on reason, belief is based on authority, human or divine. Where we give credit to human sources, these can be deceived. But where "so many" persons give a "uniform testimony", it becomes "morally impossible they could have conspired together to maintain [it] if it had not been true" (*Logic,* IV. xii). So there is security in numbers. It would be an absurdity to doubt the well-attested existence of the antipodes, or the famous personalities of ancient Rome.[23]

Faith in matters above reason still appeals to reason in detecting "miracles, and other extraordinary events" as proofs of God's authority for those truths we need to believe. But once established, it takes precedence over otherwise human reason and our senses – not that these, properly used, can conflict with what we believe on divine authority. Since the senses which perceive roundness and whiteness in the Eucharist do not tell us the nature of the substance causing the perceptions, they do not conflict with any true account of that substance; since reason shows us that the same body in its "natural condition" cannot be in two places at once, or two bodies in one place, whatever authorized mysteries of faith appear to challenge this are evidence of the finite mind's inability to comprehend the powers of the infinite (IV. xii). This notion of precedence is what was particularly contested by Protestant opponents, each party charging the other with arrogance.[24]

Although members of the Port-Royal community, including Pascal's niece, were thought to have been beneficiaries of contemporary miracles, there is no discussion of first-hand experience. Miracles are historically contingent phenomena, and in judging of any contingent matter two kinds of factors need to be distinguished and assessed. "Internal circumstances" pertain to "the fact itself", "external circumstances" to "the persons by whose testimony we are led to believe it".

> If all the circumstances are such that it never or rarely happens that the like circumstances are the concomitants of falsehood, our mind is led, naturally, to believe that it is true; and it is right to do so, especially in the conduct of life, which does not demand greater certainty than this moral certainty, and which must often rest satisfied in many circumstances with the greatest probability. And if, on the contrary, these circumstances are such as we very often find in connection with falsehood, reason determines, either that we remain in suspense, or that we consider as false what has been told us, when there is no appearance of its being true, although it may not be an utter impossibility. (IV. xiii)

The distinction between internal and external circumstances has to be gathered from examples, but it marks the beginnings of a later distinction between antecedent and consequent probability. Internal circumstances determine for Arnauld the "simple possibility" or impossibility of something, external circumstances its truer probability; and the latter relate to the sources of the report, both in themselves and in the context of their times. Arnauld considers the rival weight of the testimony of Eusebius and that of a notoriously "fabulous writer" to a certain event in early church history, and awards the contest to Eusebius (IV. xiii). His moves are typical of this rather lame debate: trace a story not to an eyewitness but to someone living a few years (or, for very ancient events, a generation or so) from the time of the actor principally involved; and argue the honourableness, rather than accuracy, of the source more from the evidence of motives and diligence than by (frequently missing) independent corroboration.

Arnauld expects the same attention – to the supposed facts and the "faithfulness and knowledge" of the source – to be given, case by case, in assessing miracle stories, to avoid the overreactions of credulousness and scepticism. Just as it is a bad argument that, because some miracle stories are well founded, every such tale must be taken on trust; so is it also a bad argument that, because rumours are promoted with greater elaboration and conviction the further we are from their source, everything which exceeds our narrow comprehension can be dismissed as equally idle. Some miracle stories are from demonstrably unreliable sources: these we properly discount. But even the Protestants know that Augustine, an author with particular significance for the Jansenists, was "a very intelligent and sincere man" and one of "the greatest friends of God". He is to be believed because "it is not probable that a wise man would have attempted to lie about things so public, in which he would have been convicted of falsehood by a multitude of witnesses, which would have brought disgrace on the Christian religion", particularly when he denounced the evil of fraudulently imposing on people (IV. xiv). Satisfy yourself of someone's character, then, and you satisfy yourself of the truth. This was important in vindicating against Protestants the Catholic practices of invoking saints and venerating relics which were the occasion of many of the purported miracles reported by Augustine. To impugn the practices was to undermine the reports and thereby contradict the agreed view of the saintly character.

Arnauld does not define a miracle (though he implies it is some form of supernatural intervention), or refer to laws of nature (which will be moral rather than metaphysical universals, in terms of the distinction drawn at II. xiii). He simply sees his exposition as instantiating a general principle of historical scholarship:

> It often happens that a fact which is scarcely probable in connection with a single circumstance which is commonly a mark of falsehood, must be reckoned certain in connection with other circumstances; and that, on the contrary, a fact which may appear to us true in connection with a given circumstance which is commonly a mark of truth, ought to be judged false in connection with others, which destroy this. (IV. xiv)

In effect, we accept whatever will achieve the greater coherence of the whole. There may be "common circumstances" in which "the greatest number of facts are found more often connected with truth than with falsehood": then, unless these are "counterbalanced by other particular circumstances, which weaken or destroy in our minds the motives of belief derived from these common circumstances", we should accept, as appropriate, either the moral certainty or the probability of the common circumstances holding again. But where there are countervailing circumstances, or other circumstances of a kind that "are very rarely unaccompanied with falsehood", the mind must, as appropriate, either suspend judgement or believe the alleged fact false, according to the "weight" of these circumstances. You will ordinarily take the word of two notaries, whose career interests are usually sufficient to keep them straight; but if they are known for corruption, have a personal interest in the falsification, or show other signs of roguery, you should neither believe them nor allow your disbelief to carry over to the word of the uncorrupt majority (IV. xv). Here we have finally coming out the idea of pitting evidence against evidence – the evidence of a common fact against the evidence of a contrary case – with the testimony of good witnesses counting as a common fact, and the onus on the contrary case, but not on a conforming case, to establish its credibility.

Locke's version of this methodology shows a deeper understanding of psychology and greater sensitivity to the risk of going in circles.[25] His caution extends even to what might otherwise seem to be the certainties of mathematics, where we accept these on the authority of a credible expert who is "not wont to affirm any thing contrary to, or besides his Knowledge, especially in matters of this kind" (*Essay*, IV. xv. 1).

In place of the Port-Royal account of internal circumstances, which seems to be concerned with little more than logical possibility, Locke discusses the substantive grounds of probability that lie in "the conformity of any thing with our own Knowledge, Observation, and Experience", illustrated by the standard example of the relativity of anyone's experience of ice. He distinguishes these from what Arnauld had called "external circumstances" – those that lie in the quality of the testimony – but deals with the latter more systematically than Arnauld did. They comprise, in semi-legal fashion, the number, integrity and skill of the witnesses, the design of the author where the source is written, the "Consistency of the Parts, and Circumstances of the Relation", and any adverse testimony. Locke differentiates beliefs based on the testimony of others from those based on the opinions of others: the latter, though common, are worthless (IV. xv. 4–6).

These "grounds of Probability" are, says Locke, "the measure whereby its several degrees are, or ought to be *regulated*" (IV. xvi. 1) – or, as he phrased it in his Index, Assent "ought to be proportioned to the proofs".[26] These "proofs" which, depending upon their strength, sway the judgement, are ideas that have an analogous role to the intuitive links which, in other contexts, can form a demonstrative chain.[27] The highest degree of probability attends particular matters of fact "when the general consent of all Men, in all Ages, as far as it can be known, concurrs with a Man's constant and never-failing Experience in like cases . . .: such are all the stated Constitutions and Properties of Bodies, and the regular proceedings of Causes and Effects in the ordinary course of Nature". Locke identifies this near-certainty with the uniform course of nature, and that in turn with the observed order of causes and effects, already anticipating Hume. "For what our own and other Men's constant Observation has found always to be after the same manner, that we with reason conclude to be the Effects of steady and regular Causes, though they come not within the reach of our Knowledge." The second highest degree of probability concerns particular matters of fact which conform to a generalization, borne out both by history and by our own experience, that things of this kind "are, for the most part, so" – e.g. that Tiberius was like most people in preferring private to public advantage. In both such cases, and in purely indifferent matters "when any particular matter of fact is vouched by the concurrent Testimony of unsuspected Witnesses", belief follows upon the testimony automatically (IV. xvi. 6–8).

But where testimonies conflict with "common Experience" and "the ordinary course of Nature", or with each other, our difficulty is "to proportion the *Assent* to the different Evidence and Probability of the thing". It is this scenario, where the ordinary course of nature (Locke, like Arnauld, avoids talking about "laws") is offset by alternative testamentary evidence, that Hume will go on to consider. There is room for so much variety in the circumstances of the reporters that, for Locke, the matter cannot be reduced to rules. "As the Arguments and Proofs, pro and con, upon due Examination, nicely weighing every particular Circumstance, shall to any one appear, upon the whole matter, in a greater or less degree, to preponderate on either side, so they are fitted to produce in the mind such different Entertainment, as we call Belief, Conjecture, Guess, Doubt, Wavering, Distrust, Disbelief, etc." Where the testimony is less than first-hand, the difficulties are compounded. "Passion, Interest, Inadvertency, Mistake of his Meaning, and a thousand odd Reasons, or Caprichio's, Men's Minds are acted by, (impossible to be discovered,) may make one Man quote another Man's Words or Meaning wrong."[28] And in matters beyond both observation and testimony, such as the existence of spirits or atoms, or the inner workings of nature, probability lies only in the formation of hypotheses by analogy (IV. xvi. 9–12).

Miracles are for Locke the one phenomenon "wherein the strangeness of the Fact lessens not the Assent to a fair Testimony given of it. For where such supernatural Events are suitable to ends aim'd at by him, who has the Power to change the course of Nature, there, under such Circumstances, they may be the fitter to procure Belief, by how much the more they are beyond, or contrary to ordinary Observation" (IV. xvi. 13). But although the testimony of God through revelation is infallible and overrides "the probable Conjectures of Reason", it cannot conflict with the clear (intuitive) "evidence of Reason" and is demonstrably spurious if it does.

Thus no alleged authority can render it credible that the same physical body is in more than one place at the same time, as would be required by simultaneous celebrations of the Mass: "the Evidence, *First,* That we deceive not our selves in ascribing it to GOD; *Secondly,* That we understand it right, can never be so great, as the Evidence of our own intuitive Knowledge, whereby we discern it impossible". Such beliefs, based on "Fancies" and "natural Superstition", are a source of "Follies" and "extravagant Practices in Religion" (IV. xviii. 5, 11). And to endorse others which, while not contrary to reason, nevertheless exceed the evidence, is the mark of enthusiasm. This is to *dis*proportion assent to evidence, when "all that surplusage of assurance is owing to some other Affection, and not to the Love of Truth". It is to indulge our "Passions or Interests", our "Temper and Inclination". The "Ease and Glory it is to be inspired and be above the common and natural ways of Knowledge" flatters our "Laziness, Ignorance, and Vanity".[29] Those who have had a true mission to communicate their revelation to the world, unlike modern enthusiasts, had it authenticated by a divine miracle (IV. xix. 1, 7, 15: a chapter added in 1700).

The point is reiterated in Locke's otherwise slight posthumous 'Discourse' on William Fleetwood's *Essay on miracles* of 1701, where he finally addresses the question of how we identify a miracle that corroborates a revelation. It is no longer a question of weighing contrary testimony against the consistency of nature; the testimony is taken at face value, and it is a matter of weighing the power needed to bring about a truly divine work against the inferior power to bring about other wonders. Rather than the number and variety of the witnesses, he emphasizes the "numbers, variety and greatness of the miracles" wrought in confirmation of the Christian doctrine.

That miracles are a special case was already a feature of Locke's account of probability in Draft A of 1671. Here a matter of fact "contrary to the ordinary course of things according to mine & the general observation of mankinde" may be found to be probable either by "the veracity of the witnesses" or by "the usefulnesse of such strange events to some end aimd at by him who had power to produce such irregularitys" (sec. 37). Locke intended to come back to miracles to be "more fully considerd" in their "due place", but never did so. By April 1681 he had gone through something of a sceptical crisis. "Not knowing how far the power of naturall causes doe extend them selves and what strange effects they may produce", we have a problem determining what is a miracle and what is not, let alone determining that it was done in confirmation of a revelation rather than (by an inferior spirit) in opposition to it.[30] The only thing we can be sure of is that no purported miracle can authenticate a doctrine which is "not conformable to reason".

> Twill always be as great a miracle that god should alter the course of naturall things to overturne the principles of knowledg and understanding in a man, by seting up any thing to be received by him as a truth which his reason cannot assent to, as the miracle it self and soe at best it will be but one miracle against an other, and the greater still on reasons side it being harder to beleive that god should alter and put out of its ordinary course some phænomenon of the great world for once, and make things out contrary to their ordinary rule, purposely that the minde of man might doe soe always afterwards then that this is some fallasy or naturall effect of which he knows not the cause let it looke never soe strange.[31]

A miracle could not render an incredible doctrine credible, but a credible doctrine could help validate a miracle; and in this Locke claims biblical support.

Thus inchoately for Port-Royal, explicitly for Locke, probability is –

in respect of every topic except miracles – proportional to the uniformity of history and of our own experience; and our experience both of the type of fact involved and of the reliability of the informant are alike relevant in assessing the probability of a report. Where experience and report are out of step, we weigh the evidence and come down on the side of the stronger, being alive to the factors, like passion and interest, that can typically colour people's testimony. All this is echoed in Hume, down to the details of climatic variation as a stock example. So the basic epistemology of Hume's 'Of miracles' – the material which is expounded primarily in the first half of Part I of the essay – contains no original or distinctively Humean ideas. Hume's project, in effect, is to make Locke consistent.

Yet most of his readers, and Arnauld and Locke before them, did not sense any inconsistency in accepting the past occurrence of miracles and the reliability of carefully selected miracle reports. They had admitted enough natural theology elsewhere in their systems to be committed theists before considering the validity of miracle reports. Miracles helped establish a particular *system* of belief, whether it was the Catholic or the pre-Catholic tradition in the Church; but they did not form the basis for the initial theism.[32] To Arnauld and Locke it was natural, indeed essential, that a being in whom they already believed will have purposes for humankind that he will wish to communicate and must therefore have the effective means to do so. Both accepted a voluntarist theology that left God the discretion either to sustain or to supplement the established order on a given occasion;[33] and both saw the test of the reliability of any report that a miracle had occurred as lying in the impeccability of the witnesses and the moral worth of the doctrine it corroborated.

If they now seem curiously uncritical in their willingness to waive the rules in admitting (some) miracles, Hume's alternative use of the same epistemology to discredit their belief seems to beg questions on the other side: notably in his refusal to accept reports of anomalous events as part of the evidence of past history, while still accepting the testimony of others as contributory proof of the laws of nature.[34] Hume did see that the notion of miracle already assumes the notion of Deity, but contested the standard account of what miracles could be for. A miracle can "never be proved, so as to be the foundation of a system of religion". The sticking point was the witnesses, against whom there is both an a priori and an a posteriori presumption. For no matter how worthy the witnesses, they could not deliver what we need as proof of supernatural power in the face of competing reports (E 121, 129; HL I, 350–51).

IV

Hume borrows from Tillotson a strategy which must "silence the most arrogant bigotry and superstition" (E 109). It is one which, in Hume's hands, backfires on Tillotson himself, and on other Protestants who followed the Port-Royal tradition so far as to try to separate mysteries above reason from those contrary to reason. Hume's analogous argument will be "an everlasting check to all kinds of superstitious delusion" for as long as miracle stories persist – that is, for ever. He does not expect to eradicate the belief, any more than he expected on another occasion to eradicate the "superstitious" aversion to suicide (Ess. 577–80); he expects only to discredit it.

Tillotson's argument traded on the fact that the doctrine of transubstantiation was impervious to empirical confirmation, but derived its alleged authority from the Apostles, whose reports on the Last Supper necessarily carried less weight than their own observations of the activities of Jesus which gave credence to his words ("This is my body . . .") at that Supper. So our evidence that something contrary to sense has occurred depends on something which has assumed the reliability of the senses elsewhere in the tradition.[35]

Hume's source is the sermon, 'The hazard of being saved in the Church of *Rome*'. Only there does Tillotson make the point that those who accept the "credible relation" of the Apostles without having themselves seen the original miracles have *less* "evidence of the *truth of Christianity* than of the *falsehood* of *Transubstantiation*". This involves a distinction drawn more fully by Stillingfleet, between the "Physical Certainty" or "certainty by sense" that existed for the Apostles who were witnesses to Christ's miracles, and the "Moral Certainty" available to us now as well as to those of Christ's contemporaries who were not at the scene. The latter depends on "the credibility of the *Witnesses* who convey these things".[36] Locke adopted a similar strategy in arguing that the biblical revelation of the history of the Flood must carry less conviction for the reader than the event itself did for contemporary witnesses:

> [N]o Body, I think, will say, he has as certain and clear a Knowledge of the Flood, as *Noah* that saw it; or that he himself would have had, had he then been alive, and seen it. For he has no greater an assurance than that of his Senses, that it is writ in the Book supposed writ by *Moses* inspired: But he has not so great an assurance, that *Moses* writ that Book, as if he had seen *Moses* write it. So that the assurance of its being a Revelation, is less still than the assurance of his Senses. (*Essay*, IV. xviii. 4)

Applied to transubstantiation, the argument is that the only evidence we could have that the senses are wrong is the assurance that they are right.

We can avoid the air of contradiction by spelling out particulars of time and place, but the evidence for the exception is weaker in kind than that to which it is an exception, and is to that extent subverted by it.[37]

Both Tillotson and Hume assume a commonplace distinction between testimony and experience. Each gives a kind of priority to experience, albeit experience of different kinds, which makes miracle reports as impervious to confirmation for Hume as transubstantiation was for Tillotson. But that is not the main point. Parallel to the opposition between the senses being wrong in the particular case (in transubstantiation) and their being normally right (wherein lies the claim to authority of the alleged authors of the transubstantiation tradition) is an opposition between there being a departure from a law of nature (in a miracle) and there being a steady and uniform course of nature (to constitute the law from which the departure has occurred). The paradoxical formulation of this is that in order to recognize an exception to the order of nature we must have experience of an order to which there has been no exception. Again, we can avoid the contradiction by being more careful about circumstances; but again, the evidence for the exception is weaker in kind than the evidence for that to which it is an exception.

Throughout his discussion, however, and despite the superficial and perhaps deliberate appearance of contradiction, Hume's concept of miracle remains coherent. He shares an assumption of those he is criticizing, that the laws of nature must still hold now, if it is to be possible in principle to construe the purported miracles of the Old and New Testaments as miracles of those times. In its full definition, a miracle is "a transgression of a law of nature by a particular volition of the Deity, or by the interposition of some [other] invisible agent", though the first seven words create enough problems to occupy most of his attention.[38] Hume does not distinguish between a "transgression" of a law, a "violation" of it, and a supernatural event "contrary" to it (E 114–15); but he does distinguish contrariety from mere non-conformability. He omits, however, one condition in the traditional concept – that a miracle must be an observed phenomenon, since its role is to be the visible sign of superior agency, validating a doctrine or precept.[39] Since the laws are what operate in the absence of such signs, the concepts of law of nature and miracle are complementary rather than antagonistic, but they are not equally susceptible of practical application. There is no reason in principle why a Deity that can intervene once cannot intervene in the same way a second time, and the law that operates in the absence of any intervention will remain intact; but unless we know how to detect intervention without circularity of argument, the notion is academic.

The true dilemma in the case arises from setting proof against proof in precisely the way Locke had prescribed for problematic phenomena.[40] It is to set proof from the normal course of nature against that from testimony, and thus the evidence for the inherent unlikelihood of the phenomenon against the quality of the contrary witnesses.[41] It is true that Hume claims in Part I to have a "*proof* . . . against the existence of any miracle" (E 115, cf. 127); but it is the possibility of another, incompatible proof that gives the subject its sceptical interest. Hume's use of the legalistic term 'proof' is to be understood in the light of his tripartite distinction between demonstration, proof and probability, "by proofs meaning such arguments from experience as leave no room for doubt or opposition" (E 56n.). We have a proof that the sun will rise tomorrow from the uniformity of human experience, yet there is no logical absurdity in the suggestion that it will not; and we must have a comparable proof of any law of nature from a comparable natural uniformity, though there is no logical absurdity in the suggestion of a supernatural exception. Hume wrote to Hugh Blair:

> I find no difficulty to explain my meaning, and yet shall not probably do it in any future edition. The proof against a miracle, as it is founded on invariable experience, is of that *species* or *kind* of proof, which is full and certain when taken alone, because it implies no doubt, as is the case with all probabilities; but there are degrees of this species, and when a weaker proof is opposed to a stronger, it is overcome. (HL I, 350)

If, in the case of miracles, the weaker proof lies always on the side of the miracle, this is not because of the uniformity of nature considered in itself, but because – as Hume goes on to contend in Part II of the essay – there is no case in practice where uniform contrary evidence is of a standard that can offset the folly and knavery of the human race. We are obliged, he says,

> to compare the instances of the violation of truth in the testimony of men, with those of the violation of the laws of nature by miracles, in order to judge which of them is most likely and probable. As the violations of truth are more common in the testimony concerning religious miracles, than in that concerning any other matter of fact; this must diminish very much the authority of the former testimony, and make us form a general resolution, never to lend any attention to it, with whatever specious pretence it may be covered.

Although the contrary proof therefore remains hypothetical, we can, in principle, understand what it is that, taken in itself, would constitute proof that an exception to a uniformity had occurred. It is suggested not only by the pre-Humean tradition I have enunciated, but by the survival of that tradition in just those criteria on which in Part II of the essay Hume rejects particular reports as inadequate.

We would have an "entire proof" from testimony if we had a large number of mutually independent and impeccable witnesses, whose interests and passions were in no way engaged, and no contrary witnesses. They would have to be people who, on past evidence, never reported on matters beyond their competence, never misreported on matters within their competence. They must never have lied and must have no motive to throw over past habits simultaneously and independently on the new occasion. In such conditions, where credible testimony is offset by reliable experience, we would have proof of an event which transgressed the normal course of nature at the same time as we had proof against it in the uniform experience of the law it transgressed. And just as there is the bare possibility of such a proof, so is there the bare possibility of its outweighing the proof from past uniformity, if the weight of accredited witnesses outweighs the weight of other experiences, both sides admitting of no exceptions.

This is depicted by Hume as a simple outweighing in numbers, even though some of his criteria remain clearly qualitative (E 112). He himself despaired that the exercise could ever attain a legal rigour.

> I need not mention the difficulty of detecting a falsehood in any private or even public history, at the place, where it is said to happen; much more when the scene is removed to ever so small a distance. Even a court of judicature, with all the authority, accuracy, and judgment, which they can employ, find themselves often at a loss to distinguish between truth and falsehood in the most recent actions. But the matter never comes to any issue, if trusted to the common method of altercation and debate and flying rumours; especially when men's passions have taken part on either side. (E 126)

The contrary-miracles argument, on the other hand, does have some quasi-legal force. It "is not in reality different from the reasoning of a judge, who supposes, that the credit of two witnesses, maintaining a crime against any one, is destroyed by the testimony of two others, who affirm him to have been two hundred leagues distant, at the same instant when the crime is said to have been committed" (E 122).

In an attempt to make sense of the weighing of numbers, we might construct the following provisional scenario. In practice we will have had more than five thousand confirmations of every law of nature, but less would in normal circumstances be sufficient to convince us of any particular law; so it is hypothetically possible that we might have had five thousand credible witnesses to the miracle of the loaves and fishes, and fewer evidences – say, four thousand – of the naturally non-replicative powers of bread and fish if these were scarcer commodities than they are. Then our belief will somehow be swayed proportionately by the one quantity against the other: we will marginally favour the testimony of the witnesses, much as we would anticipate some future event for which the previous record had been five of one and four of another.

Few commentators have, however, taken on board that the only arith-
metical relation Hume discusses in this connexion is the strangely feeble
one of subtraction – as though, in the given case, we had a residual
thousand favourable witnesses and none against.[42] He cannot have meant
to transform a situation which involves a fair degree of counter-evidence
into one which completely discounts it, losing in the process the evidence
for the very law that has to be transgressed for the miracle to count; or to
turn a probability arising from a conflict of evidence into a certainty
arising from its being all on one side; or to make nonsense of the whole
image of the weighing scales which has been central to the tradition he is
coming from. The figure which results from the subtraction has to make
a proportional difference to quantities that would otherwise have balanced.

However we try to refine the crude formula, it has to be one that deals
in large figures. An imprecise argument of this type crops up periodically
in the apologetical literature, which would have been known to some in
Hume's day. This is the argument that the subsequent history of the
Christian church – the record of the millions through history whose
faith, founded in the New Testament narrative, has seemed to be subsequently validated by events in their own or other people's lives – is the
quantitative evidence that confirms the theistic interpretation of the original stories.[43] That, one might say, even if it cannot be sensibly quantified,
is a phenomenon on a scale to match the evidence for a law of nature.
But while it may prove something, perhaps about human nature, it is not
clear why it should prove what the believer wants it to prove; and it
cannot be reused as a counterweight every time to each different law of
nature challenged by miracle stories.

What is plain, however, is the fruitlessness, by Hume's standards, of
the commonest kind of attempt to counter his position by appeal to the
particular spectator. The few hints that Hume offers on eyewitness experience suggest that he thinks the individual was "deceived" (E 116). But if
we confine ourselves to his explicit argument, he appears to have no
reason to hold this, over and above reasons he has to discount the testimony;
and part of the effect of discounting the existence of miracles is undoubtedly
achieved by making out that no report of their occurrence could be made
credible. This has seemed to many readers unsatisfactory. Stick, if not
the post-apostolic Hume, then at least an earlier sceptical genius, in the
camp kitchen before the proliferating loaves and fishes, and he too, you
might think, would have to believe the evidence of his senses, even if he
could not convince posterity.

This misses the point. The Humean philosopher knows his senses and
judgement are as fallible as the next person's, and knows, at least intellectually, that his present isolated experience is qualitatively indistinguishable
from hallucination. He may, indeed, succumb; if he does, he has enough

psychological armoury to look back later on the features of the situation that influenced his belief and reflect that he is not free from the gullibility that infects his fellows. But to give a rational assent to the notion that he was himself witness to a miracle, he needs more than an overwhelming experience. Such experiences are, in their nature, almost impossible to assess – "in sleep, in a fever, in madness, or in any very violent emotions of soul, our ideas may approach to our impressions" (T 2). He needs evidence that his senses are trustworthy on this occasion based on evidence that they are always trustworthy in matters of this kind. With five thousand proven witnesses you stand a chance; with only yourself against the rest of the world the logistics are impossible. The only way the Humean philosopher could raise support for the evidence of his own senses is through the testimony of others, that they observed it too; but he would have to know from previous experience that they were equally impeccable, even to start to build up the proof against proof that is required.[44]

V

If we seek evidence from outside the essay on miracles for Hume's considered view on the matters there raised, there is occasional corroboration elsewhere in the *Enquiry*. In Section VI, he shows how belief in matters of fact is proportional to past experience, noting how "proof" is possible for uniform matters of fact. In Section VIII, he dismisses a potential traveller's tales of a community where everyone lives by principles of unalloyed altruism: we know enough of human nature, he suggests (though this itself is partly dependent on other testimony), to detect the fabrication, just as if the informant "had stuffed his narration with stories of centaurs and dragons, miracles and prodigies" (E 84). This harks back to Hume's account of the consistency of human action in Book II of the *Treatise*. Just as we would not believe a traveller who claimed to have observed "a climate in the fiftieth degree of northern latitude, where all the fruits ripen and come to perfection in the winter, and decay in the summer, after the same manner as in *England* they are produc'd and decay in the contrary seasons", neither would we if he reported a society like that of Plato's *Republic* or Hobbes's *Leviathan* (T 402). "There is a general course of nature in human actions, as well as in the operations of the sun and the climate."

> When any phænomena are constantly and invariably conjoin'd together, they acquire such a connexion in the imagination, that it passes from one to the other, without any doubt or hesitation. But below this there are many inferior degrees of evidence and probability, nor does one single contrariety of experiment entirely destroy all our reasoning. The mind ballances the contrary experiments, and deducting the inferior from the superior, proceeds with that degree of assurance or evidence, which remains. (T 403)

But the real source of this philosophy is in Book I, Part III, in those sections where Hume discusses most fully the progression from probability to proof. Belief, on Hume's view, is a phenomenon of the mind that can arise from any of the mechanisms of association, and he uses religious beliefs to illustrate all three of the relations of resemblance, contiguity and causation at work. Miracle stories are enlivened by the recollection of a visit to the Holy Land or Mecca (*contiguity*); Catholic belief is enhanced by the adoration of images (*resemblance*), while on the other hand disanalogies between our present and future state lessen belief in the latter; and superstitious people venerate objects that have descended from the physical possession of a holy person (*causation*) (T 99–101, 110, 115; cf. E 51, 53). In all such cases a present impression leads to an enlivened idea, and wherever customary connexions establish themselves in some degree, we have a "feeling concerning the superiority" of one evidence over another. "Credulity", which is a "too easy faith in the testimony of others", is based on a lethal combination of resemblance and causality (T 112–15); and a special and frequent case of it is to be found in "education", the habitual inculcation of second-hand opinion to the point where it blocks true learning from experience (T 116–17; cf. Locke, *Essay*, IV. xx). There is also an interaction between belief and passions in accepting the extravagances of "quacks and projectors":

> The first astonishment, which naturally attends their miraculous relations, spreads itself over the whole soul, and so vivifies and enlivens the idea, that it resembles the inferences we draw from experience. (T 120; cf. E 117–18).

Despite the lack of objective probability, then, miracle stories can and do affect us much as poetry can, and lead us to give credit to them as if they involve a degree of justification, or causal reasoning, which is actually missing (T 121–2).

The *Treatise* account of probability revolves round a distinction between philosophical and unphilosophical probability. Philosophical probability, which Hume also calls the probability of causes, can be assessed by rules, though in practice other factors may cloud our judgement. But unphilosophical probability, while in some sense contrary to reason, is not always to be resisted. Custom and habit can inflame the imagination and thereby distort our judgement, as well as direct us to the course of nature; but the non-rational forces of the mind can also serve as a corrective to the sceptical tendencies of unrestrained reason. Just as in Part IV, Section I, Hume exploits psychological mechanisms to block the regress argument against the credibility of reason, so in Part III, Section XIII, he blocks a similar argument about the diminishing credibility of the historical transmission of testimony. The credibility of a present report of past testimony is a different issue from the credibility of the original testimony, and

Hume is alive to the corruptions that can enter in and can in principle be compensated for. But he denies – against Locke, for example (*Essay*, IV. xvi. 10–11) – that there is anything seriously wrong in telescoping the causal sequence involved in the transmission of testimony and treating all repetitions of the same report as one and the same evidence.[45]

The same epistemology surfaces in Hume's *History*, in a discussion of the exploits of Joan of Arc, and in the essay on James Macpherson's Ossian forgeries.[46] In the former, Hume distinguishes the miraculous from the marvellous. The historian must reject the miraculous "in all narrations merely profane and human", and admit only so much of the marvellous as is "consistent with the known facts and circumstances", notwithstanding the quality of the testimony. Joan's pretensions to be inspired gave rise to the belief that she had assumed command of the French army. "But it is much more probable, that Dunois and the wiser commanders prompted her in all her measures, than that a country girl, without experience or education, could, on a sudden, become expert in a profession, which requires more genius and capacity, than any other active scene of life" (H II, 398, 403–4).

In 1760 Hume had succumbed to the national fervour to the extent of believing in the authenticity of Macpherson's *Fragments of ancient poetry* (HL I, 328–31). But after *Fingal* in 1761, Macpherson's increasing arrogance and the incisive criticism of the English critics raised Hume's suspicions. With no knowledge himself of oral traditions, he discreetly pressed Blair to find testamentary evidence for the work's oral ancestry.

> You think that the internal proofs in favour of the poems are very convincing; so they are; but there are also internal reasons against them, particularly from the manners, notwithstanding all the art, with which you have endeavoured to throw a varnish on that circumstance: and the preservation of such long, and such connected poems by oral tradition alone, during a course of fourteen centuries, is so much out of the ordinary course of human affairs, that it requires the strongest reasons to make us believe it. (HL I, 399)

The "internal reasons" here are of the kind that face both ways. They are more than considerations of content: they relate to the consistency or inconsistency of the new phenomenon with previous cultural phenomena, and in this respect are like the first kind of historical evidence prescribed by Locke. But because the internal evidence is inherently weak, Hume questions whether the second type of evidence, that of testimony, can establish a sufficient "proof". Whether he ever believed it could is unclear. The conclusion he thought provable was a more modest one than that the poems belonged to a distant Celtic past. It would diminish the case against outright forgery if they at least antedated Macpherson's reputed discovery of them. Macpherson had claimed there was an old manuscript in a Highland family: Blair must check it out. "Get that fact ascertained by more than one person of credit; let these persons be acquainted with the Galic; let them compare the original and the translation; and let them testify the fidelity of the latter." But then he must "get positive testimony from many different hands, that such poems are vulgarly recited in the Highlands, and have there been long the entertainment of the people". It is not enough – as Burke had lately discovered in Ireland – to find people who know some traditional poem or other involving some personalities named in the Ossian tales. Blair must write to all the Gaelic ministers, who must question every surviving bard, on every surviving phrase (HL I, 400; cf. 418). The appeal is to the numbers, independence and reliability of the witnesses, and the search must be comprehensive.

Blair aimed to comply with Hume's advice, and to supplement what he himself called the "internal evidence" with a record of recoverable testimony. This appeared in an Appendix to the second edition of *A critical dissertation on the poems of Ossian* in 1765. Hume remained sceptical of the true antiquity of the poems, but appeased Blair by saying he was "much satisfy'd with the Appendix" – perhaps as at least tending to exonerate Macpherson (HL I, 513, 516). The evidence was, however, more equivocal than Blair recognized,[47] and smacks very much of Arnauld's question-begging defence of the Church Fathers – circumstantial evidence of the transmitter's moral probity, and appeal to the silence of those who should have been first to convict him of fraud if their culture was misportrayed.

Privately, Hume became increasingly sure that Ossian was a forgery, and in a late letter to Gibbon he reinforced the scepticism of his fellow historian:

> It is, indeed, strange, that any men of Sense coud have imagin'd it possible, that above twenty thousand Verses, along with numberless historical Facts, could have been preservd by oral Tradition during fifty Generations, by the rudest, perhaps, of all European Nations; the most necessitous, the most turbulent, and the most unsettled. Where a Supposition is so contrary to common Sense, any positive Evidence of it ought never to be regarded. Men run with great Avidity to give their Evidence in favour of what flatters their Passions, and their national Prejudices. (HL II, 310–11)

This is the miracles strategy again: an alleged phenomenon can be so inherently implausible that one will sooner explain away the testimony than ever consider accepting it. So it is no surprise to find the parallel explicitly drawn in the essay on Ossian. Hume considers a number of internal circumstances "to show the utter Incredibility of the Fact", and indeed considers the argument too one-sided to merit the usual image: "let the following Considerations be weigh'd, or rather simply reflected on: For it seems ridiculous to weigh them" (p. 3). The "manners" of the Ossianic Celts he found particularly out of character.

We see nothing but the affected Generosity and Gallantry of Chivalry, which are quite unknown not only to all savage People but to every Nation not trained in these artificial Modes of thinking. . . .

But I derive a new Argument against the Antiquity of these Poems from the general Tenor of the Narrative. Where Manners are represented in them, probability or even possibility are totally disregarded: But in all other respects, the Events are within the Course of Nature, no Giants, no Monsters, no Magic, no incredible Feats of Strength or Activity. . . . I desire it may ⟨be⟩ observ'd, that Manners are the only Circumstances, which a rude People cannot falsify; because they have no Notion of any Manners beside their own: But it is easy for them to let loose their Imagination, and violate the Course of Nature in every other particular; and indeed they take no Pleasure in any other kind of Narrative. In Ossian Nature is violated, where alone she ought to have been preserv'd: Is preservd where alone she ought to have been violated. (pp. 5–8)

After exhausting the internal circumstances with more in this vein, and identifying reputed "violations" of nature with the inherently fabulous, Hume turns to "the external positive Evidence, which is brought by Dr Blair". "I own, that this Evidence, considerd in itself, is very respectable, and sufficient to support any Fact, that both lies within the bounds of Credibility, and has not become a Matter of Party." But this concession is a formality, since neither requirement is met. How then have so many worthy Highlanders "crowded to give Testimony" to a literature they knew nothing of till "yesterday"?

The same Names, that were to be found in their popular Ballads were carefully preserved in the new publication: Some Incidents too were perhaps transferr'd from the one to the other: Some Sentiments also might be copy'd: And on the whole they were willing to believe, and still more willing to perswade others, that the whole was genuine. On such Occasions, the greatest Cloud of Witnesses makes no manner of Evidence. What Jansenist was there in Paris, which contains several thousands, that would not have given Evidence for the Miracles of the Abbé Paris? The Miracle is greater, but not the Evidence, with regard to the Authenticity of Ossian.

The late President Forbes was a great Believer in the Second Sight; and I make no question, but he cou'd, on a month's warning, have overpowerd you with Evidence in its favour: But as finite added to finite never approaches a hair's breadth nearer to Infinite; so a fact, incredible in itself, acquires not the smallest Accession of Probability, by the Accumulation of Testimony. (pp. 17–18)

Hume's handling of probability concepts may not be identical with that of Arnauld or Locke; but it is recognizably in the same tradition, a tradition that he acknowledges is generally received (T 143). Philosophical probability enters the debate on the value of testimony, because the evidence alleged for a prodigy, whether religious or literary, necessarily challenges our experience. Already in the *Treatise*, where two "contrary views are incompatible with each other, and 'tis impossible the object can at once exist conformable to both of them, their influence becomes mutually destructive, and the mind is determin'd to the superior only with that force, which remains after substracting the inferior" (T 138). So when Hume comes to consider reports of unnatural phenomena, the same calculus is put to work, and used both in weighing the inherent credibility of the witnesses and in weighing their specific testimony against our other experience of nature.

The notion of ice to an Indian, and the reports of an eight-day darkness (E 114n., 127–8), are on a continuum of things which initially shock the person to whose experience they come as novelties, but which the mind eventually adjusts to as it finds analogies with things with which it is more familiar. The Indian remains ignorant of the cause of freezing even when he comes to find the idea intelligible; and the individual who indicates a willingness to search for the cause (whether natural or supernatural) of the eight-day darkness is certainly ignorant of it at the time that he comes to accept the fact. One has to accept the reality of the facts before considering whether they are just novelties or true miracles, before understanding their causation; though a critic might well think it is the understanding of causes that helps give credibility to the fact.

Ice is a novelty to someone of limited experience, but with greater experience can be seen to be a function of the laws of nature after all. What happens to water when it gets colder than anything the Indian[48] has experienced is something that is "not conformable" with his experience, but it is not "contrary" to it: contrariety would lie in its going solid at a tropical temperature. Unusual and dramatic cures cover too wide a range to be readily put as a class into either category, either the non-conformable or the contrary. So too, perhaps, do putative changes of substance to the scientifically immature. The eight-day darkness, with its apparent biblical precedent, is more intractable. It is posited as a one-off event, not unimaginable, and yet a clear challenge to our non-demonstrative assurance that the sun will rise tomorrow. It poses the question of whether we were right about the "law", and encourages us to search for one-off explanations that may either save, or lead us to redefine, the law. This is, at least for the time being, a case of contrariety to experience. It does not require an instant supernatural explanation; neither does it rule out any particular kind of explanation in the long term. "Reasonable men would only conclude from this fact, that the machine of the globe was disordered during the time" (HL I, 350).

The devotee of miracles might think Hume did not look very far to find at least remote analogies that would also justify him in entertaining the possibility of a resurrection, like recovery from drowning. His singling out of resurrection stories as beyond the pale of probability must have been a deliberate attempt to shock, since it takes the form of a blasphemous parody (E 128); but it is also a likely recognition that the credibility of Christ's resurrection had become the test issue in the controversy:[49] the orthodox theology of redemption depended on it, and if resurrection was possible, resistance to other miracles would crumble. Resurrection involves more than an extension of the complex processes of nature: it involves something close to a reversal of those processes, something to which Hume's strong term 'violation' is not unsuited. Other miracle stories, such as turning one substance into another, do not present the same shock to the system, the same undoing of the past, that resurrection stories do.[50] But they still provide sufficient disanalogies to previous experience to challenge the credence of those who are guided by that experience.

If we can think rationally about such alleged phenomena, we have two choices. We can reject the appearance and say it did not happen, or not as it appears to have done. Or we can leave our options, including that of a supernatural explanation, open. Hume does not deny the option – that would involve a degree of dogmatism that is not available to him. Rather, the defectiveness of our knowledge of causes in general and of the divine nature in particular is such that there is never sufficient evidence to make it our only recourse. Indeed, if there is not, by Hume's lights, sufficient evidence that a resurrection, the turning of a rod into a serpent, or any other event contrary to our experience of nature, has ever occurred, the question of what could have caused it does not arise.[51]

NOTES

1. John Gill has alerted me to something that must have been added as late as 1747: the reference to George Lyttelton's newly published *Observations on the conversion and apostleship of St Paul*, pp. 63–7, in a note to Part II in the first edition. Lyttelton juxtaposed a glowing portrait of Paul with Lucian's adverse account of the impostures of Alexander. Hume dropped this note in 1770, when two other first-edition notes were transferred to the body of the text (now at E 118–19, 127–9). Two major notes were added in the second edition of 1750 (now at E 114, with adjoining text also added, and 344–6: these remained notes through all future editions). So Hume continued revising, even writing, Part II for more than a decade after his abortive draft for the *Treatise*.

2. But see R. M. Burns, *The great debate on miracles* (Lewisburg, PA 1981), and D. Wootton, 'Hume's "Of miracles"', in *Studies in the philosophy of the Scottish Enlightenment*, ed. M. A. Stewart (Oxford 1990), 191–229. Hume's suggestion in the second edition that the miracles allegedly performed at the

   tomb of the abbé de Pâris were the best attested in history, yet still disputable,
   looks like an echo of Conyers Middleton's *Free inquiry* (1748), p. 224.
 3. This runs counter to Reformation thought, which founded religious faith not
   in human reason but in divine grace: A. Dulles, *A history of apologetics*
   (London 1971), pp. 113–16.
 4. M. A. Stewart, 'Academic freedom: Origins of an idea', *Bulletin of the Australian Society of Legal Philosophy*, 16:57 (1991–2), 1–31.
 5. Hume exploits the dilemma at NHR 328–9. Strictly, his view was that it
   took some generations for mankind to progress from an instinctive response
   to past and impending disasters, to a sense that nature is governed by stable
   laws. Only at the latter stage can theism arise, so there should be no prior
   sense of miracles, properly speaking. On the other hand, in the *Dialogues*,
   Hume saw the relentlessness of the laws of nature as an impediment to
   theistic belief. They entrap the helpless in pains that a benign Deity would
   intervene to avert (D 206).
 6. John Locke, *An essay concerning humane understanding* (1690; 4th edn 1700),
   IV. xviii. 2–5; xix. 5–15. See M. A. Stewart, 'Locke's "Observations" on
   Boyle', *Locke newsletter* 24 (1993), 21–34; C. Bernard, 'Hume and the madness
   of religion' (this volume); J. A. Passmore, 'Enthusiasm, fanaticism and David
   Hume', in *The science of man in the Scottish Enlightenment*, ed. P. Jones
   (Edinburgh 1989), 85–107. Quotations from Locke's *Essay* are from the
   Nidditch edition (Oxford 1975).
 7. C. G. Bolam and others, *The English Presbyterians* (London 1968), pp. 147–8.
 8. R. H. Popkin, 'The role of Jewish anti-Christian arguments in the rise of
   scepticism', in *New perspectives on Renaissance thought*, ed. J. Henry and S.
   Hutton (London 1990), 1–12. Edward Stillingfleet in *Origines sacræ* (1662),
   II. vi. 15, traced the tendency back to Maimonides, who had questioned
   whether the Mosaic dispensation was founded on miracles.
 9. Some writers accepted the possibility of false miracles, worked by diabolical
   agents. Then the prophetic power of the agents and their moral character
   were also relevant.
10. Burns, pp. 72–5.
11. This has been noted by Wootton; by P. Jones, *Hume's sentiments* (Edinburgh
   1982), ch. 2; and L. Daston, *Classical probability in the Enlightenment* (Princeton 1988), ch. 6. J. C. A. Gaskin, *Hume's philosophy of religion*, 2nd edn
   (London 1988), p. 135, suggests that the two topics "for the sake of clarity
   should perhaps be kept apart", but that is to obscure the source and
   substance of the debate.
12. T 82–4, E 45–6. Cf. R. G. Collingwood, *The idea of history* (Oxford 1946),
   pp. 73–85.
13. "Miracle-working was a Popish trick, and discarded [by Protestants] with the
   other parts of that religion" (HL I, 350). Some Huguenot communities,
   however, thought they had been blessed with the gift (Burns, p. 72), and
   Tillotson conceded that missionaries to a heathen people might still work
   miracles (Sermon CXXXIX). Other Protestants sometimes admitted miracles in
   the first centuries of the church, drawing the line at the (contested) point at
   which the Church of Rome established its Western ascendancy. But Locke in
   chapter 10 of *A third letter for toleration* (1692) challenged as muddle-headed
   any suggestion that miracles were necessary until Christianity was backed by
   political authority.
14. Wodrow tells a scatological tale of a Scotsman touring a Catholic country,

who took a quantity of laxative on a solemn day so as to be able to defecate over the altar at the high point in a mass. "He had his story ready for delivering, that for many dayes he had been under a violent constupation; that he belived nothing would releive him but this; that as soon as he came to the relict or hostee, by faith in it, this cure was wrought. And upon this, the Preists presently took it as a miracle, published it to the people, and he was happiest that could get some of the excrements." (*Analecta* (1843), III, p. 306, corrected.)

15. On the relevance of legal concepts to medieval and later debate on testimony, particularly in the Roman law tradition, see Daston, pp. 41–7, 192–6.

16. Thucydides I. 20–22; cf. Plato, *Phædrus* 274b ff. Thucydides treats with suspicion the hearsay of the past and ornamented accounts of the fabulous. He gives preference to his own experience over the reports of others. Even witnesses must be tested and checked, because they frequently do not agree. The same attitudes, and a need to avoid whatever smacks of the fabulous, were reiterated by Polybius, IV. 2, XII. 4b–d (cf. F. W. Walbank, *A historical commentary on Polybius* (Oxford 1957), I, pp. 6–16).

17. In the same year, Seth Ward discussed more at length than in depth the nature of "historical faith", both in general and in relation to the biblical narratives, in Part III of *A philosophical essay towards an eviction of the being and attributes of God*. We must consider the consistency of the historical claims with other knowledge; whether they are of a kind that could be known and whether the narrators were in a position to know them; and the character and competence of the narrators.

18. Cf. Origen, *Contra Celsum*, II. 51.

19. More shared Glanvill's belief, which was criticized by John Webster in *The displaying of supposed witchcraft* (1677). That most popular beliefs in miracles rested on similar principles to those in witchcraft, and that the latter could claim to have been sometimes tested in law, was recognized by Middleton, pp. 221–3.

20. *Scire/i tuum nihil est: or, The author's defence of The vanity of dogmatizing* (1665), p. 52.

21. Dante, *Paradiso*, XXIV. 106–8. Stillingfleet traces the argument to Chrysostom on I Corinthians. Cf. Augustine, *De civitate dei*, XXII. v; Aquinas, *Summa contra gentiles*, I. vi. 3; Hugo Grotius, *De veritate religionis Christianæ* (1627), II. xix. Other seventeenth-century exponents were Ralph Cudworth, *The true intellectual system of the universe* (1678), p. 709; Jacques-Bénigne Bossuet, *Discours sur l'histoire universelle*, II. xx.

22. I do not mean to discredit the work done by Wootton to show the likely influence on Hume of French libertine literature. But the line between that and progressive biblical criticism is a narrow one, and Locke's close study of the latter is one of the important neglected influences on the development of epistemology in the British context.

23. My quotations from the Port-Royal *Logic* follow the translation of T. S. Baynes, 8th edn (Edinburgh n.d.), which is more reliable than that of J. Dickoff and P. James (Indianapolis 1964). It is worth noting that there was a Gassendist tradition in logic as well as a Cartesian one. Gassendi's *Institutio logica* appeared four years before the Port-Royal text. It contains brief comments on "the authority of a narrator" (Pt I, canons 12–13).

24. These sections should be read beside the discussion of false judgement at III. xx. There the authors note the falsity of the proposition that what appears

bent to our senses is always bent, note the influence on our judgements of self-love, interest and passion, and stress the importance, when we depend on authorities, of attending only to those whose authority is above suspicion. We should not be persuaded by mere numbers, age, or social standing of witnesses; on the other hand, "piety, wisdom, moderation, are without doubt the most estimable qualities in the world, and they ought to give great authority to those who possess them in those things which depend on piety or sincerity".

25. Locke's account of probability is foreshadowed in Draft A of the *Essay* (1671). The Port-Royal *Logic* had appeared in 1662. Locke's methodology was redeployed for theological purposes in Isaac Watts's *Logick* (1724; 2nd edn 1726).

26. Locke is more overtly normative than others in this tradition. For Glanvill and Wilkins, and later Hume, the wise man does proportion his belief to the evidence, though both Wilkins and Hume see this proportioning as psychologically compulsive. Port-Royal had castigated "the blindness of the free-thinkers, who will believe nothing but what is proportionate to their reason" and fail to acknowledge truths above reason (*Logic*, IV. xiv).

27. See David Owen's contribution to this volume. My only disagreement with Owen is that I see Hume's representation of probabilistic inference more as a development of Locke's account than as an attack on it.

28. These factors had led Bayle to question the reliability of history altogether in his *Critique de l'histoire du calvinisme* (1682).

29. Hume condemns Stoicism in similar terms at E 40.

30. Scepticism on this point persists as late as the posthumous 'Discourse'. We cannot know what is objectively contrary to the "laws of cause and effect", but Locke is prepared to construe as a miracle whatever phenomenon is contrary to the spectator's own sense of nature, wherever it can be thought to serve divine ends.

31. Quoted from Locke's journals in *An early draft of Locke's Essay*, ed. R. I. Aaron and J. Gibb (Oxford 1936), p. 115. This material was unknown to Hume, but some of the argument survived at *Essay*, IV. xviii. 5.

32. Bacon in his *Essays* had argued that God did not work miracles to convince an atheist, who had to be convinced by the order of nature. Wilkins cites Bacon, adding that miracles are properly "for the confirmation of such doctrines as are not knowable by natural light" (*Natural religion*, pp. 91, 93). Cf. Stillingfleet, *Origines sacræ*, II. vi. 15; Robert Boyle, *Christian virtuoso*, Pt I (1690).

33. Note how Locke handles the Flood in section 192 of *Some thoughts concerning education*. God altered the centre of gravity for a time, causing it to "move round [the Earth] in a convenient space of time, whereby the Floud would become Universal" (3rd edn 1695). Although it was thereby the natural effect of supernatural intervention, it was "out of the ordinary course of Nature". Gravity is not, of itself, natural to matter as defined by its primary qualities; it is superadded, and its operation is therefore at any time due to God's activity; the ordinary course of nature follows from the normal form of this activity, while abnormal events are natural adjustments to any changes in it.

34. The argument, straightened out along Lockean lines, seems to be that we accept the testimony of others to the degree that we have previously found their testimony, or the testimony of others like them, reliable, in the sense of conformable to our own experience (E 109–10; HL I, 349).

35. For Hume's own verdict on transubstantiation, see NHR 343–4.
36. Stillingfleet, *Several conferences between a Romish priest, a fanatick-chaplain, and a divine of the church of England* (1697), p. 267. Tillotson gave simplified versions of the argument in *The rule of faith* (1666), III. ix. 9, in Sermons XXI and XXVI of the lifetime collection of his works, and in Sermons IX, LXXVII, CXLIV and CLXXVII of the posthumous Barker collection. W. R. Abbott demonstrated, at the Lancaster conference on 'Hume and Hume's connexions' in 1989, that although others of these are commonly cited as Hume's source, they are too simplified to serve the purpose.

    It is worth noting that Sermon XXI adopts the image of the scales which Hume himself picks up from elsewhere in the tradition, but it leaves Tillotson's argument more neutrally balanced than usual: "here ariseth a new Controversy, whether a Man should believe his Senses giving Testimony against the Doctrine of Transubstantiation, or bearing Testimony to the Miracle which is wrought to confirm that Doctrine: For there is just the same Evidence against the truth of the Doctrine, which there is for the truth of the Miracle. So that the Argument for Transubstantiation, and the Objection against it, do just ballance one another; and where the weights in both Scales are equal, it is impossible that the one should weigh down the other."
37. Locke gave a pleasant twist to the same argument in his journal for August 1676: "the question is not a matter of faith but of philosophy. . . . For the reality and essence of bread being in respect of us nothing but a collection of several simple ideas, which makes us know it, distinguish it from flesh, and call it bread, it is as impossible for a man, where he finds that complex idea, to know it to be flesh or receive it for such, as it is to believe himself a loaf" (quoted in *Essays on the law of nature*, ed. W. von Leyden (Oxford 1954), p. 278). Belief in transubstantiation must "destroy the testimony of our senses, overturn all our knowledge, and confound all measures of faith and reason" – an echo of Stillingfleet and Tillotson.
38. We may be missing clues by not knowing the source of this definition. Samuel Clarke wrote in his second series of Boyle Lectures (1706): "if by the *Course of Nature*, be meant only (as it truly signifies) the *constant and uniform manner* of Gods acting either immediately or mediately in preserving and continuing the Order of the World; then, in that Sense, indeed a Miracle may be rightly defined to be an effect produced contrary to the usual Course or Order of Nature, by the unusual Interposition of some Intelligent Being Superiour to Men" (pp. 356–7). Later, he referred to "the interposition either of God himself, or of some Intelligent Agent superiour to Man, for the Proof or Evidence of some particular Doctrine, or in attestation to the Authority of some particular Person" (p. 367). Wilkins, p. 402, had scorned the idea that "the universal Laws of Nature" should "frequently, or upon every little Occasion be violated or disordered". It is not clear if he would have used the language of 'violation' for those miracles he accepted.
39. So transubstantiation would not be a miracle, as Tillotson noted in *A discourse concerning transubstantiation* (1684) and in Sermon CLXXV.
40. Locke's usage differed from Hume's, but he allowed for proof in non-demonstrative cases (IV. ii. 3, xv. 3, xvi. 1, 9).
41. This is not just following out the received formula for weighing testimony against experience. It suits Hume's general sceptical strategy of constructing dilemmas on incompatible data: thus he gives elsewhere an argument from reason and experience that we do not perceive an external world, at the same

time as he shows on other grounds that the belief that we do not is not sustainable (E 151–2). Both the occurrence of supernatural events and the existence of the external world lie beyond the scope of our rational faculties, but for different kinds of reasons.

42. E 111, 113, 116. John Craig, in *Theologiæ christianæ principia mathematica* (1699), had suggested that, "given two opposed histories of the same thing", one computes relative probabilities and subtracts the lesser from the greater: "the remainder will be the total probability of the more probable history" (*History and theory*, Supplement 4 (1964), pp. 29–31). Craig turned a quasi-Lockean theory of probability into mathematical form, assigning values to the number of primary witnesses, the number of persons involved in the transmission of their testimony, the qualitative difference between oral and written transmission, and the degrees of time and space involved. Wootton suggests Hume may have known Craig's argument from French sources.

43. Origen, *Contra Celsum*, III. 33; Watts, *Logick*, II. v. 6 (6); Joseph Butler, *Analogy of religion* (1736; 2nd edn, 1736), II. vii.

44. The voice from heaven with which Cleanthes "embarrasses" Philo in Part III of the *Dialogues* might seem to be an illustration of a communally observable miracle. It is not beyond Hume to recognize unusual manifestations of intelligence and design (E 26–7), but the idea that there might be a single Pentecostal voice, speaking in one and the same utterance in every available dialect simultaneously, is surely ironic.

45. Cf. T 83. When Hume says that the utilization of testimony is founded in the relation of cause and effect, he has in mind the kind of causal chain that runs from the witness's original experience to our hearing or reading a report; so our receiving a holiday letter testifies to our friend's being abroad (T 196, E 26). The point is independent of any *analysis* of the causal relation, notwithstanding some recent commentary to the contrary.

46. H II, 397–410; 'Of the poems of Ossian': NLS, MS. 23159/17. On the former, see C. Bernard's contribution to this volume. Page references to the Ossian essay are to the manuscript, which dates from 1773 or later.

47. F. J. Stafford, *The sublime savage* (Edinburgh 1988), p. 169. Blair "had supplied Macpherson with his preconceived notions about what the poetry should be like, so it was hardly surprising that the published poems of Ossian should fulfil his expectations" (p. 173).

48. Hume's legend of the "Indian prince" who had not known ice (E 113) was added in the second edition. It has its antecedents, as Wootton has noted, in Locke, Sherlock, Butler and Skelton. But only Hume places the story in India. Locke placed it in Siam (*Essay*, IV. xv. 5). Hume may have conflated it in his memory with another Locke anecdote, about the "*Indian* Philosopher" who wondered what the world stood on (II. xiii. 19; xxiii. 2): both anecdotes involve elephants.

49. L. Stephen, *History of English thought in the eighteenth century*, 3rd edn, 2 vols (London 1902), I, pp. 228–53, traces this debate through Thomas Woolston, Zachary Pearce, Thomas Sherlock, Peter Annet, Samuel Chandler and Gilbert West. See also Watts, *Logick*, II. v. 5 (12).

50. Tillotson argued that the impossibility of God's causing "that that which hath been, should not have been" is comparable to the impossibility of transubstantiation (Sermon XCIX).

51. This essay was written while the author was a visiting fellow in the History of Ideas Program, Australian National University.

10

Hume and the art of dialogue

MICHEL MALHERBE

When philosophy becomes academic, it usually forgets that the search for truth requires a literary form, and that this form, rather than being something arbitrarily added, should be derived from the very nature of the enquiry. Sixteenth- and seventeenth-century authors were trained in the rhetorical tradition, and they were much more conscious that philosophy has its own language, which has to be determined according to its objects, methods and ends. And it is well known that for Hume and many eighteenth-century thinkers, if the easy philosophy appeals to all the resources of eloquence, precision, which is the virtue of the abstract and learned philosophy, governs both the way of reasoning and the way of writing.

With this general observation in mind, I want to provide some historical evidence that, throughout the eighteenth century, there was a debate about the nature and role of the art of dialogue in philosophical subjects, and that this art was held to be a true philosophical art. Hume was clearly aware of this view when he was writing his *Dialogues concerning natural religion,* as is shown by Pamphilus's introduction. And if we take seriously – i.e. literally – what is said in those two very carefully written pages, it will be clear that Hume's use of the dialogue form was not just a rhetorical device, to introduce more or less sophistication into the argument. Rather, he was employing exactly the kind of writing that is demanded by any philosophical enquiry into natural religion.

In this respect, the present study can be considered as a commentary on the beginning of the *Dialogues.* But this commentary will be achieved with the help of a contextual analysis of the eighteenth-century art of dialogue; for the *Dialogues,* using an unsystematic method of philosophizing, cannot be understood if the historical background is not examined. In the first section of this study, I shall be trying to make clear what could be meant in the eighteenth century by the claim that the art of dialogue is a true philosophical art, and I shall show that, as regards dialogue writing, the literary form cannot be severed from the definition of philosophical enquiry and its objects. In the second section, I shall be dealing with the justifications afforded for the dialogue form in moral philosophy, and, with the help of Shaftesbury, shall distinguish two opposite uses of this form: a rhetorical and a strictly philosophical use. In the third section, I shall examine how Hume takes this distinction into account, and shall offer a brief comparison between the two *Enquiries*, *The natural history of religion*, and the *Dialogues*, in respect of their form of writing.

Two preliminary remarks. First, when one relates Hume's text to other texts of the eighteenth century, it is not always possible to detect distinctive influences, or to delineate a single clear system which we can say is an exact representation of their general conception of dialogue writing. As a matter of fact, eighteenth-century philosophy, being communicative in intent, and anxious to be shared in "the world of man", is a kind of patchwork which cannot be synthesized without its characteristic genius being restricted. That is not to say that there would be no coherence, but it is a coherence that is more thematic than systematic. I shall assume that Hume is very sensitive to this complexity, and pays proper regard to it, even while he is reordering it in his own terms. Therefore the method of the first two sections of this study will be mostly contextual.

My second remark concerns the hackneyed problem of interpreting the *Dialogues*. I shall refrain from debating the questions usually raised under this topic. My ambition here is strictly limited: to give a content to Pamphilus's address to Hermippus on dialogue writing, from a study of its historical background and its implicit references, and then to offer an analysis of this text by a comparison with some other works of Hume. It will become apparent that, if the *Dialogues* are to be taken as philosophical dialogues, i.e. if they comply with the requirements of philosophy when applied to natural religion, they are *authorless*. Of course, such a conclusion is not entirely innocuous, since, if the *Dialogues* are authorless, they should not be interpreted by commentators on the author; but this general consequence will be kept for the conclusion.

I

Hume's *Dialogues* begin with the observation that the art of dialogue writing was mastered by the ancient philosophers, but "this method of composition has been little practised in later ages, and has seldom succeeded in the hands of those who have attempted it" (D 127).

This remark is a commonplace, which had been fully developed by Shaftesbury at the beginning of the century.[1] In his *Characteristicks* of 1711, Shaftesbury represented the dialogue form as a genuine art practised by Greek authors, an art even older than the systematic form of composition; it was so intimately bound up with philosophical enquiry that, far from being an artefact, a work of art, it was the *natural* way of philosophizing.[2] And in the introductory section of 'The moralists', Shaftesbury presented four main reasons to explain the Moderns' failure in this genre. These were:

1. the immuring of philosophy "in Colleges and Cells",[3] no longer producing statesmen or "any man of note in the Publick" (p. 24), but condemning the graver subjects to be dealt with with pedantry and dogmatism;
2. the correlative superficiality of conversations and dialogues, restricted to fashionable topics and corrupted by an exaggerated refinement and delicacy: "and surely no Writing or Discourse, of any great moment, can seem other than enervated, when neither strong reason, nor Antiquity, nor the records of Things, nor the natural History of man, nor any thing that can be call'd *Knowledg*, dares accompany it" (pp. 26–8);
3. worse – the disappearing of the originals, of nature itself, because of the dogmatic method which substitutes artificial representations for nature, and gives out a feigned wisdom for the truth of things: the Moderns are no longer able to draw or describe according to the genuine appearance of truth;
4. the ruin of free enquiry, the loss of the art of questioning and doubting, people hurrying to get hold of a hypothesis to which they cling with all their strength. "In short, there are good reasons, for our being thus superficial, and consequently thus dogmatic in Philosophy. We are too lazy and effeminate, and withal a little too cowardly, to dare *doubt*. The decisive way best becomes our Manners" – especially in religious matters (p. 32).

It is important to see, in the light of these comments of Shaftesbury's, that the issue of dialogue writing was a part of the general Ancient–Modern controversy; it was part of the reaction to scholastic or academic tradition, and reflected an attempt to define a modern philosophical writing in accordance with a new conception of philosophy, more open to "the world of man". The art of dialogue, and with it the genuine art of philosophy, should be restored, without servile imitation, for modern and undogmatic minds living in a free society.

Some fifty years later, in the preface to the third edition of his *Moral and political dialogues* (1765, first published anonymously in 1759), Richard Hurd comes back to the matter (with Shaftesbury in mind) and, at a time when the vogue for dialogue has affected nearly every subject,[4] renews the observation that dialogue writing has been neglected by the Moderns. But, like Shaftesbury, he is only concerned with philosophical dialogue, which he is endeavouring to distinguish from other forms of dialogue.[5] To do that, Hurd first sketches the history of philosophical dialogue in antiquity, from Plato to Lucian. He underlines the growth of scepticism in this form of philosophical writing (Plato, the Academy, and especially Cicero), and calls attention to the impossible attempt of Lucian to associate "two things, not naturally allied together, the severity of Philosophic Dialogue with the humour of the Comic" (p. 30); a comic dialogue usually has for its subject "not a question debated, but a tenet ridiculed or a character exposed" (p. 31). The Moderns have retained Lucian's model and emphasized the satirical or pleasant side. "But after all, the other species, the serious Philosophic Dialogue is the noblest and the best" (p. 32). As a result, taking into account the weight of scepticism and the risk of ridicule conveyed by the dialogue form in ancient philosophy, Hurd rules out religious topics. Not every subject is allowed to enter into modern dialogue, but "only such as are either in the strict sense of the word, *not important*, and yet afford an ingenuous pleasure in the discussion of them; or not so important as to exclude the sceptical unconclusive air, which the decorum of polite dialogue necessarily demands" (p. 10). Subjects must be serious, but not so important for human life as modern religious certainties.

On the other hand, however serious the subjects may be, literary rules must be set down in order to have the dialogue carried on in a natural way. And in this respect, according to Hurd, there are among recent writings only three philosophical dialogues: Shaftesbury's 'Moralists', Addison's *Dialogues upon the usefulness of ancient medals* (1726) and Berkeley's *Alciphron* (1732). But all three were wrong on a very important point: they represented imaginary and not real (historical) characters. Hurd's model is Cicero, and he opposes the strength of historical reality, even when artificially recreated, to the fictitious consistency of the characters that Shaftesbury demanded. When once historical characters have been introduced, one can "suppose them really conversing together", if the *decorum* (the formal apparatus and the rhetorical structure) is correctly managed; and then "the writer himself disappears" (p. 16).

Two lessons can be drawn from Hurd's self-justifying argument. First, whereas Shaftesbury insisted on the antiquity of dialogue writing and the *natural* congruity of this art of writing with philosophical enquiry, the only motive of true philosophy being precisely the spirit of free enquiry, Hurd, more sensitive to the history of philosophy and more conscious of the sceptical temptation which affects philosophical dialogue, introduces the distinction between speculative and practical matters, and denies that religion could be the object of a dialogue. A real dialogue cannot conclude dogmatically. But human life needs conclusions or decisions in practical matters; and religion is the most important practical affair for human life.

Secondly, while restricting the field of philosophical dialogue, Hurd and others enhance the role of the literary form: the form must agree with the object, and vice versa. In other words, a philosophical dialogue, however serious or important or rationally justified it may be, is endowed with a literary form which cannot be forgotten and which must be in accordance with the philosophical aims that are followed. Rules must be observed, for instance, relating to the definition and number of characters, their manners and the nature of the subjects; the presentation must be neither merely narrative nor merely didactic, and the dialogue must "be natural, easy and carried on with the unrestrained freedom of conversation".[6] All these rules, which are the conditions of a real dialogue, should be consonant with the conditions of true philosophy.

On the whole, there is in the eighteenth century a clear recognition that, because of the fetters of the dialogue form, even if this form is supposed to be more natural to the human mind, a justification must always accompany its use in philosophy; and this needs a preliminary agreement between author and reader, that the literary arrangement is in harmony with the philosophical end or object. In nearly all eighteenth-century dialogues, this occurs in the introductory section. But it will be noticed that, artlessly or quite speciously, this philosophical justification is often merged with the formal convention on which the whole frame of the dialogue is resting. Of course, there is no dialogue without a convention between author and reader; for, since the reader is also a spectator, and not one of the characters involved in the conversation, he must be introduced to the dialogue, as he would be in a theatre. And this is usually done by the supposed recital of some real and philosophical meeting, reported by one of those present for the benefit of some curious correspondent.[7] The "freer air" of the conversation, the apparent contingency of the talk, the loosening from exact reasoning, depend on this narrative disposition. As Shaftesbury says: "the Scene presents itself as by chance and undesign'd. You are not only left to judge coolly, and with indifference, of the Sense deliver'd; but of the Character, Genius, Elocution, and Manners of the Persons who deliver it" ('Advice to an author', p. 102). But all these literary features of dialogue are the condition of its being philosophical. The reader, being neither engaged on the stage nor involved in the action, can preserve his philosophical liberty as regards the arguments offered to him in the dialogue; and, more important, since he is called on to judge these arguments by himself, he remains free of any extraneous intellectual authority, even the author's.

II

It will be apparent, even at first reading, that Hume's *Dialogues*, which begin with Pamphilus's address to Hermippus, conform, by and large, to this widely received conception of the art of dialogue. We find in the exordium a general reflection on subjects that attract the dialogue form, the philosophical justification of religion being one such subject; a relationship is established between certain aims of philosophy and the form of dialogue, and the devices required by the literary convention are supplied: indications of time and place (a summer's day, Cleanthes' library), and a summary introduction to the characters. The characters are quickly identified, both by some particular trait and by their contrasting mental behaviour (the "accurate philosophical turn" of Cleanthes, the "careless scepticism" of Philo, the "rigid inflexible orthodoxy" of Demea). We shall see in section III below that while, contrary to Hurd, Hume presents dialogue as a legitimate medium for dealing with natural religion, he excludes its use in moral subjects.

But Hume's achievement must be considered more closely. From the literary side, it is notable that he satisfies the conventions with the greatest economy of means. The same restraint that we find in the introduction is to be found in the progress of the dialogue. The twelve Parts make up only one dialogue, without change of time or place, and with the same characters. Compare this, for instance, with Berkeley's *Alciphron*: Hume offers no dinner on a summer Sunday after church, to give rise to remarks on the behaviour of free-thinkers (Dialogue I); no walk on a beach, no shady rocks from which to escape the heat of the sun and get involved in the heat of a moral discussion (Dialogue II); etc. Cleanthes' library is enough to suggest the comfortable retirement of the company, far from the burden of civil business or the restlessness of the court or the city: this is a friendly controversy, giving free play to leisurely speculation.[8] Nothing happens from the outside; no surprise visit distorts the course of the dialogue; no second dialogue is developed inside the first (as in 'The moralists').

This economy can still be observed when Pamphilus presents the characters whose consistency regulates the logical progress of the conversation: he does not provide us with any other information about them except the one trait that concerns their philosophical turn of mind; and in the dialogue itself we learn nothing more about their personality: Philo's raillery is the mark of scepticism; Demea's indignations belong to all the religious orthodox; Cleanthes' coolness accompanies natural philosophy.[9] Thus the characters are changed into types: the carelessness of Philo is the carelessness of his scepticism;[10] the rigid orthodoxy of Demea is the inflexibility of a train of thought that can both debar discussion of God's existence and enforce the a priori argument. As for the rare events punctuating the dialogue, they are less real events than Pamphilus's intervening to stress certain points of nuance;[11] Demea's final retreat and the closure of the debate must be considered as the logical consequence of the discursive progress of the controversy.

By comparison with Cicero's clumsiness in *De natura deorum*, where characters are only names for philosophical systems which are didactically and alternately displayed, Hume's art of dialogue appears very clever and refined;[12] it is akin to the French *art classique,* for which the whole power of a drama springs from the progress of a dialogue where passions are rationally expressed and reason is the consistency of passions. Just as in *l'art classique* the machinery is blurred away at the very time when it appears that everything is conventional, so also, in Hume's *Dialogues,* the narration is reduced to its absolutely necessary formal minimum and gives way to the philosophical plot. The requirements of philosophy meet with the requirements of art.

So much for the literary form. But if the refinement of Hume's art is a pleasure for the reader, it is a difficulty for the commentator. I have said that the literary form should be taken together with the philosophical intention. But it is of the very essence of *l'art classique* that there cannot be in the text any manifest mark of the author himself. The dialogue develops by its own formal necessity. The same absence, therefore, must be the rule when we consider the philosophical purposes of the dialogue. This is unlike Section XI of the *Enquiry concerning human understanding,* and the Dialogue appended to the *Enquiry concerning the principles of morals,* where a certain *I,* who can be either the author or the narrator, or both at the same time, abruptly starts speaking and quickly introduces the other character, whose paradoxical or surprising conversation is said to be worth relating. Our text has no other means than Pamphilus's speech, to make clear the rationale of the dialogue, and offer general reflections (which one is supposed to share) about the dialogue art and its use in relation to natural religion. Of course, Pamphilus, quite explicitly, justifies the usefulness of a dialogue concerning natural religion. But there is no indication at all that the narrator should be identified with the author, for a part or for the whole of his discourse. In short, the meaning and import of Pamphilus's address have to be understood, if we want to appreciate its significance for Hume's philosophy. The difficulty is all the more complex, because, in the agreement tacitly concluded between Pamphilus and Hermippus about the adaptation of dialogue writing to natural religion – an agreement which is the condition of the progress of the dialogue – a double relationship is involved: one between the author and his dialogue, and one between the author and the reader.

The commentator has to be very careful, if not outright mistrustful, since the very first paragraph of the text is an abstract of the argument developed by Shaftesbury. Any eighteenth-century reader acquainted with Shaftesbury's *Characteristicks* could detect Hume's device.[13] Let us come back to Shaftesbury.

When an author wants to make clear his own intention and thereby dispel the obscurity that could derive from the dialogue form, he has a choice of methods. He can address the reader in an advertisement, dedicate the book to a prince or nobleman, comment on his intentions by way of an extended subtitle,[14] or expressly declare his intentions in a preliminary exposé.[15] Sometimes, he can achieve his purpose in a more allusive way; for instance, by an epistle of the narrator to his correspondent, with signals that the narrator is speaking in the name of the author.

The choice of the subject is usually considered justified by its importance, an importance on which both the author and the reader tacitly agree. But, this importance being granted, the author has to explain the reason why he has chosen the dialogue form. This is often developed as an excuse: the manifest nature of the truth under discussion would strictly require a more direct and proper form of writing, but the present corruption of morals, the spreading of atheism, and so on, demand that adversaries be put to confusion and, if possible, brought back on the right track. Of course, you take some risk when you give speech to atheists or materialists or wicked men; but you have to take the chance, if you want to teach them a lesson that could be exemplary for everybody. The risk taken, it is true, is inversely proportional to the degree of the author's involvement in his own dialogue. The more he intervenes in person or comments indirectly on what is going on, the more the force of the dialogue is his own force, and not the force of truth. Shaftesbury violently denounces these kinds of devices which, in his time, were mainly practised by divines.[16] Those "new orthodox dialogists", in their "theological dramas", not only speak through the hero's voice, but handle the characters (mainly the adversary) like inconsistent puppets. Dialogue is thus a mere "jocular method" instigated to make the heterodox laughable and to ensnare people's minds. Real dialogue, on the contrary, even in religious matters, requires that the adversary (e.g. atheists) should have their sense and wits like other persons, and the sceptic be allowed to demonstrate the full force of his criticisms.

Shaftesbury is doubtless very perceptive on the writings of his time. There are many examples of such unrefined dialogues, the purpose of which is not philosophical but popular, where the relationship between content and form is merely casual, the method being chosen for reasons irrelevant to the subject (the wish to convince, to castigate, . . . to make a name for oneself). But the critique is still effective against more learned and philosophical texts where dialogue writing is somewhat better employed. Take, for instance, Fénelon's well-known *Dialogues des morts*, addressed to the Duc de Bourgogne who was of a passionate and violent nature.[17] The reading of these dialogues was supposed by Fénelon to be a way for the young prince to discover himself, to train his own character and become conscious of the duties of a future king. The dialogic form is here chosen for its pedagogical quality, as a guide to the conscience, attractive enough to charm the attention of a young boy and tame a rebellious nature by insinuation.[18]

The same practical virtue of dialogue is involved in Mandeville's dialogues. *The virgin unmask'd: or Female dialogues betwixt an elderly maiden lady and her niece* (1709) already settled the method: thanks to a dialogue moving between fiction and admonition, the author's spokeswoman (Aunt Lucinda) practises the pleasant and soft medicine that youth, because of its inexperience, wants. The *Treatise of the hypochondriack and hysteric passions* (1711) is still more distinctive: on the one hand, Mandeville endeavours to discuss other doctrines that the dialogue allows to be displayed as so many adverse points of view; but on the other hand, the physician exerts his art on his two patients (one has studied medicine, but nevertheless needs to be cured), by having them participate in their own recovery.[19] Besides their theoretical role relating to psychological diseases, Mandeville's dialogues are performing a therapeutic function; and the cure of the characters is to be both the proof that the medical analysis and advice are reliable, and – why not? – a kind of relief of the reader himself. It is clear that, in such texts, even if the dialogue does not fall into a caricatural controversy (the author being able to give life to his characters and to have regard for adverse opinions), a pedagogical, moral or therapeutic intention comes in, and constantly reinforces the narrative and logical development of the dialogue itself. Either avowedly or in a more concealed way, the author has something to say or to do of his own, and the reader has to discover the ulterior purpose, if he wants to gauge the full meaning of the text.

But, however skilful the execution of the literary form may be, and however philosophical the intention, these dialogues are fundamentally flawed: the relationship between literary form and philosophical import, even if it is duly set down and justified, remains artificial. The matter could have been dealt with in another way. In Shaftesbury's words, the author acts like a scene-shifter; and the more skilful he is, the greater the illusion. But a philosophical dialogue should not deceive. And Shaftesbury plainly insists that the choice of the dialogue form should not proceed from some implicit purpose of the author, which a clever reader would be fitted, as in a game, to discover and interpret; on the contrary, it should respond to the very matter of the dialogue. It is the nature of the subject dealt with that prescribes the dialogue writing.

This requirement relating to dialogue writing results, in Shaftesbury's philosophy, from his classical conception of art as imitation. True art imitates nature; dialogue has to paint faithfully people's real life and the observable diversity of their opinions, sentiments and choices. When a particular side prevails, it is never without being balanced by some opposite reasons that have to be taken into account, even if they are not the strongest. This is true chiefly in regard to morals. People's manifold manners must not be condemned for their diversity; and morals have to express the truth, which cannot be done without a counterbalanced appraisal. Dialogue can do that, by representing each point of view, by giving each system of values its chance, and by proceeding carefully towards its end, that is to say, the decision that life requires. But dialogue does more than that. For, there being no moral life without the innermost bond between the particular and the universal, between circumstances and laws, between ends and values, dialogue provides the means to express the concreteness and diversity of manners with the universality of morals, through the mere fact of imitation or representation. The recital of people's lives in a dialogue, interrogating their doubts and their sentiments, delivers by itself, if the painting is faithful, the lesson which is to be understood. Shaftesbury's conception of dialogue retains more of fable or mime than it does of strict Platonic dialogue, where truth springs from the dialectical conflict of the characters by a progressive refining and elevation of their thoughts.[20] "The Philosophical Writings, to which our Poet in his *Art of Poetry* refers" – Horace was referring to the Socratic dialogues – "were in themselves a kind of Poetry, like the Mimes" ('Advice', p. 92).

Therefore dialogue writing allows the most important philosophical end to be achieved: "Know thyself". For the diversity of mankind is the diversity of your own mind; the opposition of opinions or manners in the outer world paints the inner conflict of your soul. "'Twas not enough that these Pieces treated fundamentally of *Morals,* and in consequence pointed out *real Characters* and *Manners*: they exhibited 'em *alive,* and set the Countenances and Complexions of Men plainly in view. And by this means, they not only taught us to know *Others*; but, what was principal and of highest virtue in 'em, they taught us to know *Ourselves*" ('Advice', p. 92). And by this relationship between the world of others and the intimate world, a path can be found towards moral knowledge of oneself and the knowledge of human nature. In the debate reproduced in a dialogue, there is often a distribution of the characters, a partition between some philosophical hero (Socrates in the Platonic dialogues, Theocles in 'The moralists'), the sceptic who urges the dialogue on, and the plain man who is our image. And when considering what is represented in the dialogue, the reader can trace his own doubts, and compare his plain humanity to actual wisdom. "In this, there were *Two* Faces which wou'd naturally present themselves to our View: *One* of them, like the commanding Genius, the Leader and Chief above-mention'd [Socrates]; the *other* like that rude undisciplin'd and headstrong Creature, whom we ourselves in our natural Capacity most exactly resembled" (p. 94). Dialogue, then, is our "pocket-mirrour". And we need not search any longer to understand why the Moderns are incapable of writing good dialogues: their literary impotence comes from the dread they have to look at themselves in the mirror, because the mirror cannot contrast their poor manners with a living model which, in some way, would be themselves. "Thus *Dialogue* is at an End. The Antients cou'd see their own Faces; but we can't" (p. 106).[21]

So, if dialogue is the original and natural way of philosophizing, and if it cannot be dealt with as a literary ornament, since beauty in writing and brilliancy of wit flow from knowledge,[22] it has an effect on philosophy itself: it prohibits intolerance and verbal violence, because life is tolerant and morals cannot be represented but in an inner questioning and public debate, leading to balanced decision and deliberate action. And tolerance prohibits dogmatism; dogmatism in moral matters would suppose the (pretended) wisdom of the one who is promulgating what is to be done, and entails the enslaving of the one who is ordered to carry out the law. Moral action requires a personal conversation with oneself, and this conversation can be induced only by the description of characters and by a model representation of various reasons or values motivating the moral sense.

This moral demand governs the relationship of the author with the reader and rules out any authoritarian proceeding. The author is not a master or tutor, and the reader is not a disciple or pupil.[23] It is not the master who teaches, but the scene of life and society, enhanced by the contrast of plain human nature in which one can recognize oneself, with heroic virtue in which one can project oneself forwards. The lack of dogmatism in philosophy thus implies that the author does not intervene in his own dialogue, and gives up the illusory advantage of being what he pleases or doing what he will in his creation. He should follow Homer's example, who, "instead of giving himself those dictating and masterly Airs of Wisdom, makes hardly any figure at all, and is scarce discoverable in his Poem. This is being truly a *Master*" ('Advice', p. 96). In short, in a dialogue "the Author is annihilated; and the Reader being no way apply'd to, stands for nobody" (pp. 100–102). The dialogue, if it is the faithful representation of people's manners and the exact dialogic reproduction of truth, stands by itself, as a painting hung on a wall, and lives its life according to its own necessity. A moral artist can imitate the action of the creator by knowing every part of the world he creates and preserves, and by committing the development of this world to the inner principle that is imprinted in its own foundation (p. 110). Correlatively, the reader should not search for the supposedly concealed purpose of the author, because what he has to discover is not the author, but himself; and he can find himself only in the dialogue of the moral world.

It has been worth reproducing Shaftesbury's whole argument, to make clear how a certain conception of moral philosophy was incorporated in an apparently literary debate. The discussion whether there is to be an artificial or an essential link between the content and the form of philosophical dialogue cannot be settled without thinking over the nature of philosophy. And it was useful to restore this philosophical issue as the background to Pamphilus's words, in order to understand that these first considerations are not just a preparatory airing of the subject, but relate to Hume's whole method of philosophizing about natural religion. To repeat, Pamphilus begins his address to Hermippus by summing up an argument which is well known and discussed by most of the authors of this time. But it could be said that the problem remains. If there is material evidence that Pamphilus is repeating Shaftesbury's argument, and thus assuming its argumentative arrangement, we are still at a loss to determine Hume's intention, there being no evidence that narrator and author should be identified. Nevertheless, it can be answered that we have no other information at our disposal than Pamphilus's words. And we cannot help feeling that these words are largely conventional. Pamphilus's discourse is so evidently permeated with the various conventional components of the discussion, that to credit Hume with some secret purpose is mere supposition. It is much easier to consider that *Hume is accepting the terms of the question*, that he is taking them as they are: the conventional elements of a conventional debate; and that convention precisely is the essential mark of any philosophical analysis of natural religion.

Consider Pamphilus's perfectly clear argument: If the subject requires a systematic manner, the didactic relationship of the author with the reader would be falsely lessened in dialogue, which then "conveys the image of *pedagogue* and *pupil*" (p. 127). And if, to avoid this rude behaviour, the author works his literary form and "carries on the dispute in the natural spirit of good company", then the success of the form is at the expense of the content; the delays and ornaments of dialogue weaken the force of the truth. And Pamphilus adds: "There are some subjects, however, to which dialogue-writing is peculiarly adapted, and where it is still preferable to the direct and simple method of composition" (*ibid.*). In regard to those subjects that are to be treated in an unsystematic manner, and that can be freed from the author–reader or the pedagogue–pupil relationship, i.e. without anybody (even the author of the dialogue) making use of his authority, the dialogue form will not be taken as a mere literary device, or the ornamental substitute for another method of composition that would be better suited to the subject;[24] it will be the required form of writing. There are two uses of dialogue writing: a rhetorical one and a methodical one. When applied to natural religion, dialogue writing is methodical. For certain subjects, convention can be the right method. In this case, the author does not intervene in the dialogue, nor does he try to influence the reader. Then the dialogue is authorless.

III

There is, nevertheless, a very important difference between Shaftesbury's and Hume's arguments; and this difference will help us to delineate Hume's own reinterpretation of Shaftesbury's scheme of reasoning. Hume does not think that dialogue could be a method to attain truth. Whereas Shaftesbury worked to renew the spirit of this ancient manner of writing, natural to philosophy, Hume vindicates the abandonment of dialogue writing by the Moderns.[25] From antiquity to modern times, the nature of philosophical enquiry has changed. In dialectical philosophy, truth was discovered through an exchange between several characters; this depended on a common sense that was gradually released through the debate. In modern philosophy, a new method has been fixed, more relevant to the requirements of science and the abstract virtues of exactness and regularity; and this method is the didactic one, which proceeds systematically, by laying down the point it wants to establish and deducing the proofs without interruption. "To deliver a SYSTEM in conversation scarcely appears natural" (D 127). The systematic manner is more natural to moral philosophy.

Its success in natural philosophy is a sufficient proof that we cannot simply reject it. "But 'tis at least worth while to try if the science of *man* will not admit of the same accuracy which several parts of natural philosophy are found susceptible of. There seems to be all the reason in the world to imagine that it may be carried to the greatest degree of exactness" (T 645–6). This comment by Hume himself in the *Abstract,* on the rationale of the *Treatise,* is still motivating Section I of the first *Enquiry.* Of course, "Moral philosophy, or the science of human nature, may be treated after two different manners; each of which has its peculiar merit, and may contribute to the entertainment, instruction, and reformation of mankind" (E 5). The easy philosophy "considers man chiefly as born for action"; with all the means of "poetry and eloquence" (and dialogue could be one of these means), it tries to influence his taste and sentiment, and appeals to the sense that nature has implanted in him and that cannot be perverted (if it can be misled) by the most erroneous reasonings. But there is room left for speculative philosophy, which appeals to man's reason, tries to distinguish truth from falsehood, and scrutinizes human nature "in order to find those principles which regulate our understanding, excite our sentiments, and make us approve or blame any particular object, action, or behaviour" (E 6). It must be observed that the more Hume builds up the merits of the easy philosophy written for a polite society or *l'honnête homme* – Shaftesbury's or Hutcheson's philosophy – the more he increases the need for the abstract study of the human mind: "How painful soever this inward search or enquiry may appear, it becomes, in some measure, requisite to those, who would describe with success the obvious and outward appearances of life and manners" (E 10). Moreover, and besides the pleasure of satisfying an innocent curiosity, true metaphysics must be cultivated "with some care, in order to destroy the false and adulterate", which breeds bigotry and superstition (E 12).

This text is well known, and very instructive, if we heed the balance that Hume is seeking to strike. It asserts the need and right of rational and systematic philosophy, to study not only the powers of human understanding, but also the principles of human life. There is no ambiguity on this point: the science of morals itself should be dealt with in a systematic manner.

There is a possible difficulty with this picture, posed by the second *Enquiry*. At first sight, Hume might seem, by contrast, to have chosen the easy philosophy in this work (and an easy style that emulates the spirit of dialogue writing), rather than the speculative philosophy. We might think, then, that he intended the operation of the speculative philosophy to be postponed until the appendices. Would Hume have lowered his ambitions in this way, and moved to this more modest conception of philosophy, one much nearer to Shaftesbury's specification? I think not. I should like to offer an argument which not only helps to determine the exact nature of the second *Enquiry*, but helps us too to understand the relationship between *The natural history of religion* and the *Dialogues*, and explains why the dialogue form essentially suits natural religion.

The key is to be found in the Introduction to *The natural history of religion*.[26] There, speculative philosophy, when it is applied to religion, has to pay attention to two distinct questions, "that concerning its foundation in reason, and that concerning its origin in human nature" (NHR 309). The former bears upon the foundation of religion in rational proofs; the latter, because it bears upon the general causes which generate religious sentiments and govern all religious phenomena, entails an enquiry according to the experimental method, which gathers the relevant matters into a natural history, classifies them, and by induction tries to find out and confirm more general principles.

Coming back to Section I of the second *Enquiry*, we find that there are two kinds of disputes: those actuated by stubbornness, or a spirit of opposition and a desire to show wit; and the others, more sincere, springing from a real difficulty which gives support to the dispute. Such is the controversy, and it is worth examining, "concerning the general foundation of Morals" (E 170). This debate is remarkable for the fact that, whereas the ancient philosophers, "though they often affirm, that virtue is nothing but conformity to reason, yet, in general, seem to consider morals as deriving their existence from taste and sentiment", our "modern en-quirers", on the contrary, "though they also talk much of the beauty of virtue and deformity of vice, yet have commonly endeavoured to account for these distinctions by metaphysical reasonings, and by deductions from the most abstract principles of the understanding" (*ibid.*). The equal authority of the ancients and the moderns, the crossed opposition between their reason and their sentiment, raise the question which will be answered at the end of the text. But this question about a rational foundation may be postponed. "Though this question, concerning the general principles of morals, be curious and important" – Pamphilus had used the same adjectives at D 127 (cf. 128) – "it is needless for us, at present, to employ farther care in our researches concerning it" (E 173). A more immediate study presents itself, more consonant with the method of experimental philosophy: the discovery of "the true origin of morals" (E 173). In this enquiry, "the only object of reasoning is to discover the circumstances on both sides" – the estimable and blameable – "which are common to these qualities; to observe that particular in which the estimable qualities agree on the one hand, and the blameable on the other; and thence to reach the foundation of ethics, and find those universal principles, from which all censure or approbation is ultimately derived. As this is a question of fact, not of abstract science, we can only expect success, by following the experimental method, and deducing general maxims from a comparison of particular instances" (E 174).

Thus the difference between the search for the rational foundation and the search for the scientific origin of moral phenomena is the difference between the a priori method, going from principles to consequences, and the experimental method, going from effects to causes. And, as in the *Treatise* (I. iii. 2ff.), the answer given to the question of the origin of morals will provide us with the solution to that relating to the foundation of morals.[27] This solution can be found in Appendix I, after we have been told in the Conclusion that, as a general principle, "Personal Merit consists altogether in the possession of mental qualities, *useful* or *agreeable* to the *person himself* or to *others*" (E 268). "If the foregoing hypothesis be received, it will now be easy for us to determine the question first started, concerning the general principles of morals" (E 285). The preceding enquiry tells in favour of a foundation of moral distinctions in a moral sense, reason being given the role of enlightening this sense.

This positive answer explains the nature and the function of the conclud-ing 'Dialogue'. The controversy has come to an end, thanks to the scientific method; and this dialogue cannot let the dispute start again. In fact, it recapitulates the whole development of the text, by discussing a topic which, if it were kept open, would call in question Hume's whole theory:

does the meaning of moral terms vary with places and times? The idea is propounded by Palamedes, "who is as great a rambler in his principles as in his person, and who has run over, by study and travel, almost every region of the intellectual and material world" (E 324). *I* gives the answer.[28] And *I* turns out to be both the narrator and Hume, because there is no other way of concluding than to assert that there is the same, universal sense of praise and blame attached to human nature, but that manners are to be estimated according to rules known among the persons themselves. The dialogue form is here a literary device for which Hume gives no justification, but which allows the author to elaborate this rather complex matter, and to manage a final retort (on the bad influence of religion on morals!), which is *la chute du texte*. Thus there is no place in morals for a real dialogue, which would be motivated by the subject itself.[29] Since a conclusion can be reached, it is reached by the methodic way of philosophizing.

If we now turn to *The natural history of religion*, we can see the difference between morals and religion. As we noticed, the question of the foundation of religion is declared to be "the most important" and to admit of "the most obvious, at least, the clearest solution" (NHR 309). The solution is not produced, nor can it be derived from the study of the origin of religion. And the general corollary, at the end of the text, seems rather confusing: it actually gives the origin of the design argument (the contemplation by a learned mind of "the uniform maxims, which prevail throughout the whole frame of the universe"), but cannot draw from it a true foundation. If the world by its ontological order inclines the mind to the belief in an intention, by its moral disorder it leads the same mind astray; and this mixture of good and evil, this contest between order and disorder, prevents any rational framing of assent. "The whole is a riddle, an ænigma, an inexplicable mystery" (NHR 362).

This sceptical ending has not prevented the text from displaying the causes of religion in a very positive way, and from judging quite categorically the relative merits and blemishes of the various forms of religion. But the question of the foundation of religion remains unsolved. The answer is to be found in the *Dialogues*;[30] and the answer is that the question cannot be answered. The foundation of religion is something that is prey to endless controversy and irreducible scepticism. Here, the subject itself demands the method of dialogue. Two kinds of subjects, Pamphilus says, are naturally associated with this manner of composition: "any point of doctrine, which is so *obvious*, that it scarcely admits of dispute, but at the same time so *important*, that it cannot be too often inculcated, seems to require some such method of handling it". "Any question of philosophy, on the other hand, which is so *obscure* and *uncertain*, that human reason can reach no fixed determination with regard to it; if it should be treated at all; seems to lead us naturally into the style of dialogue and conversation" (D 127–8).

Obvious is opposed to *obscure, important* to *uncertain*, but *curious*. The first qualities are those attributed to moral matters: they are important for human life, and they are obvious since they depend on the moral sense, which can govern even the plain man and always corrects philosophical reasonings when these go astray.[31] In this case, dialogue exerts a pedagogical function: the easy philosophy embellishes it with all the helps of poetry and eloquence, in order to inculcate duty and render virtue lovable (E 5–6). The second qualities belong to speculative matters, where exactness is cultivated and abstractness is the result, and where uncertainty is only compensated by the regularity of the method. But in this case, the systematic way of composition must be preferred to the art of dialogue, if the enquiry can be conducted methodically and attain a firm conclusion; that is, when philosophers are enquiring about causes and the origin of effects. But if uncertainty cannot be overcome, then "Reasonable men may be allowed to differ, where no one can reasonably be positive: Opposite sentiments, even without any decision, afford an agreeable amusement: And if the subject be curious and interesting, the book carries us, in a manner, into company; and unites the two greatest and purest pleasures of human life, study and society" (D 128). Such is the natural field of dialogue.

Pamphilus adds: "Happily, these circumstances are all to be found in the subject of NATURAL RELIGION." It is not so clear that this is a good thing, because, taken literally, this conjunction forbids any dialogue. It is not possible to join important (moral) matters and undecidable (cosmogonical and theological) topics, or to reconcile the pedagogical and rhetorical use of dialogue with the other use, the appropriate one; for in the first case, it is the author's intention which prevails over the content of the dialogue, whereas in the second it is the content which demands dialogue writing. To overcome this latent difficulty, Pamphilus explains the conjunction of these opposite circumstances by distinguishing the two questions of the existence and of the nature of God.[32] The divine existence is so *obvious* and so *important* for human life that the topic must be dealt with as a moral topic and the discussion considered as being rooted in human nature itself. (If this were so – but the *Dialogues* will show that the question of the divine existence is a speculative, not a moral one – eloquence would be needed to enforce the religious instinct against the insincere attacks of atheists.) On the other hand, the divine nature is so *obscure* that no certain determination will ever be reached, and so *uncertain* that there is no end to the controversy.[33] It is easy to see that Cleanthes' pupil is thus preparing Demea's argument that the existence of God is so beyond question that God's nature, being mysterious, is beyond controversy (D 141). We have to decide whether the religious question is practical or speculative. If it is practical, the controversy about the divine nature is governed by the evidence for the divine existence; and since we cannot understand God's infinite attributes, we must adore the profound mystery of his being: there is no room for a philosophical dialogue. But if the question is speculative, it has no importance for human life, nor does it create any trouble in human society; and philosophical dialogue can extend the debate from the nature of God to his existence. Either Demea or Philo is right; Cleanthes is wrong, when he tries to deal with the religious question according to the experimental, i.e. systematic, method. But Demea is wrong, since, thanks to Philo's scepticism, a philosophical dialogue may occur. When it relates to religion, philosophy cannot behave as it does with morals. Natural religion is a speculative topic, and can rightly be handed over to a sceptical dialogue.

IV

We may now sum up the whole argument by drawing together some of its consequences.

1. There are two kinds of dialogue: rhetorical (when the relationship between form and content is artificial) and philosophical (when the relationship is essential). And the art of dialogue is either ornamental or methodical.

2. Since Hume's *Dialogues* are philosophical dialogues (who can doubt it?), and since, being unsystematic, they are not governed by the author–reader structure, it is not the author, but the content itself, which regulates the controversy. Here Hume obeys Shaftesbury's prescription: the author and the reader stand for nothing in such philosophical subjects as natural religion.

3. Since no intention of the author enters into the controversy itself,[34] the *Dialogues* are to be read literally, but not interpreted. There is no hidden claim or tenet. The only purpose is the plain and explicit one, of faithfully relating a controversy on a supposedly obvious and important, but obscure and uncertain, topic, and of providing the reader with the twofold pleasure of study and society.[35]

4. The controversy is curious but, being endless, not important. It is definitely uncertain. Important topics are moral topics; and the science of morals can and must be dealt with philosophically, i.e. in a systematic manner.

5. The debate, then, is merely speculative. It is actuated by the contradictions between Demea, who wants to prevent any philosophical dialogue in favour of a merely rhetorical dialogue; Cleanthes, who wants to prescribe a systematic and truly scientific method by giving an experimental proof, and thus to put an end to the dialogue; and Philo, whose scepticism maintains the tension between the practical value of religion (which can

be studied in the experimental manner) and its simply speculative contents (which give way to endless controversy).

6. Since the dialogue submits to the logic of a rational and helpless enquiry into the foundation of religion – in a word, since we have to do with a text which is, through and through, a sceptical piece – we must conclude that no dogmatic teaching, positive or negative, can be derived from it with regard to the existence or nature of God.[36] We cannot come by means of it to a knowledge of Hume's own sentiments on religion, except to see that we cannot reach any conclusion. In that sense, the text is superficial. Of course, even if it makes no dogmatic pronouncement about religion, it provides a lot of critique.[37]

7. Since religion is for philosophy a curious, but not an important or certain matter – and philosophy is mainly concerned with important matters – the dialogue shows that we do not have to search for a Humean philosophy of religion, if by this we mean a philosophy which would reach any conclusion on theological subjects, or support any belief (whether rational or not) or any system of religion. So what is left? There remains an experimental philosophy of religious phenomena, mainly in *The natural history of religion;* and, in the *Dialogues*, a sceptical *deconstruction* of the rationality of religion.

NOTES

1. In his edition of the *Dialogues* (Oxford 1976), J. V. Price quotes, besides Shaftesbury, Matthew Tindal, *Christianity as old as the creation* (1731), p. iv, and Richard Hurd, *Moral and political dialogues* (1765), I, p. iv. Although Hurd's work appeared first in 1759, Hume would probably have written this part of his prologue before that date.

2. "I have formerly wondered why a *Manner,* which was familiarly us'd in Treatises upon most Subjects, with so much success among the Antients, shou'd be so insipid and of little esteem with us the Moderns" ('Advice to an author', I. i, p. 98). (I quote from the new standard edition by G. Hemmerich and W. Benda, Stuttgart 1981.) Cf. 'The moralists', II. i, p. 28.

3. The same words can be found in Hume's 'Of essay writing' (Ess. 534), an early essay withdrawn after the first edition in 1742. The first part of it is clearly influenced by the reading of Shaftesbury.

4. At the beginning of the century, Shaftesbury was mainly criticizing moral and religious dialogues in which preachers strove to fight a growing deism or indifference to religion. But the mode had since been extended to education, "moral" education (often aimed at marriageable young ladies), criticism, taste, etc. See James Forrester, *Dialogues on the passions, habits and affections peculiar to children* (1748); and, more importantly, David Fordyce's *Dialogues concerning education* (1745).

See also the vogue for "dialogues of the dead", imitated from Lucian and renewed by Fontenelle and Fénelon at the end of the seventeenth century. Among others, see William King (student of Christ Church), *Dialogue of the dead* (1699), on a critical topic; Matthew Prior, *Dialogue of the dead* (1714);

John Sheffield, 'Two dialogues of the dead', *Works*, II (1723); George Lyttelton, whose *Dialogues of the dead* (1760) were very influential and who referred to Lucian, Fontenelle and Fénelon; Sam. Pye, *Moses and Bolingbroke, a dialogue in the manner of the Right Honourable ***** author of Dialogues of the dead* (1765); the anonymous *Voltaire in the shades, or a dialogue on the deistical controversy* (1770); William Combe, *A dialogue in the shades between an unfortunate divine* [Wm Dodd] *and a Welch member of Parliament* [Chase Price] *lately deceased* (1777); and numberless dialogues published in magazines and periodicals. Hume himself was, after his death, one of the characters summoned to the Elysian Fields in the anonymous *Dialogue in the shades between General Wolfe, General Montgomery, David Hume, George Grenville and Charles Townsend* (1777) and *A philosophical and religious dialogue in the shades between Mr. Hume and Dr. Dodd* (1778). In dialogues 1 and 2 of Philip Parsons' *Dialogue of the dead with the living* (1779, but written before Hume's death, according to the author), Herbert of Cherbury appears to Hume in order to destroy the principles of deism which he himself had founded when he was living, and on which his successor had "endeavoured to build a firm and durable fabric"; behaving like the Commendatore, Herbert denounces Hume's arrogance and, at the end, leads him to repentance (in Pascalian terms)!

Lyttelton unwittingly emphasizes the reactionary nature of this literary form: "And sometimes a *new dress* may render an *old truth* more pleasing to those whom the mere love of novelty betrays into error, as it frequently does not only the *wits*, but the *sages* of these days" (Preface, 1765).

5. George Stubbes had tried to restore the Platonic manner, a manner "which enlivening Philosophy with the Charm of Poesy entertains at once the Understanding and the Imagination" (*A dialogue on beauty in the manner of Plato* (1731), p. iii; see also the same author's *Dialogue in the manner of Plato, on the superiority of the pleasures of the understanding to the pleasures of the senses* (1734), and Mandeville, *Fable of the bees*, Pt II (1729), Preface).

6. W. Gilpin, 'On dialogue writing', in *Dialogues on various subjects* (posthumous, 1807), p. 12. Whereas Shaftesbury had tried to catch again the spirit of ancient dialogue, Gilpin, a hundred years later, and rather dully, develops the various rules to be obeyed in dialogue writing.

7. We find a similar device in Henry More's *Dialogi divini* (1679), which begins with an epistle from one of the characters in the dialogue, writing to a distinguished friend who wants to know more of the conversation, and introducing the other characters, with some apology for the presence of the materialist and the mechanical philosopher. That there is an interesting comparison to be drawn between Hume's *Dialogues* and More's has been emphasized by Elmer Sprague in his 'Hume, Henry More and the design argument' (*Hume studies* 14 (1988), 305–27). See also Berkeley, *Alciphron*, I. 1, where the correspondent is not identified. The technique is a very old one: Cicero used it in *De natura deorum* to express his own views.

8. See the last paragraph of the address.

9. In this respect, Hume does not obey Shaftesbury's prescription, according to which dialogue has to paint enlivened characters.

10. See R. H. Hurlbutt, who, in 'The careless sceptic – the "Pamphilian" ironies in Hume's *Dialogues*', *Hume studies* 14 (1988), 207–10, rightly insists on the philosophical significance of this "carelessness". Whether this trait must be dealt with as irony is another story.

11. The narrator's signals are mainly comments on the behaviour of the characters:

Philo's raillery (an ordinary feature of the sceptic), D 132; his half-jesting vehemence, 150, and embarrassment, 155; again, Philo's air of triumph, 166, and his spirit of opposition, 213. Other comments identify Cleanthes' and Demea's changes of tone, e.g. 150, 169, 199, 212–13.

12. For an elaborate treatment of this point, see Hurlbutt, *Hume, Newton and the design argument*, rev. edn (Lincoln, NE 1985), pp. 214ff.

13. As early as 1726, Hume had acquired a copy of the third edition of the *Characteristicks* (E. C. Mossner, *Life of David Hume*, 2nd edn (Oxford 1970), p. 31). 'The moralists' had been to some extent parodied in the second part of *The fable of the bees* and *Alciphron*. In the latter work, Berkeley had attacked Shaftesbury directly for taking raillery or ridicule as a test of truth, a method congruent with the spirit of dialogue. The quarrel was still alive when in 1751 John Browne published his *Essays on the Characteristics of the earl of Shaftesbury*. For more details, see D. D. Eddy's introduction to his edition of this text (Hildesheim 1969), pp. vii ff.

14. See, respectively, Berkeley's *Alciphron* or Shaftesbury's 'Moralists', More's *Dialogi divini*, and again Berkeley's *Alciphron*.

15. See *De natura deorum*. Cicero begins with a philosophical exposé presenting the diversity of opinions about the gods, his choice in favour of the academic philosophy, and his reason for resorting to dialogue form as a means to free himself from ill-disposed critics (*ut omni invidia liberem*) (I. 6). For a general comparison between Cicero's text and the *Dialogues*, see J. V. Price, 'Sceptics in Cicero and Hume', *Journal of the history of ideas* 25 (1964), 97–106.

16. 'Miscellaneous reflections', in *Characteristicks*, ed. Robertson, pp. 337ff.

17. Fénelon's literary achievement was partly responsible for the success of this kind of moral and pedagogical writing.

18. Compare with Fontenelle's introductory epistle, addressed to Lucian: "Tous vos dialogues renferment leur morale, et j'ai fait moraliser tous mes morts; autrement ce n'eut pas été la peine de les faire parler; des vivants auraient suffi pour dire des choses inutiles."

19. See H. Good's introduction to his edition of *The virgin unmasked* (New York 1975), and P. Carrive, *La Philosophie des passions chez Bernard Mandeville* (Lille 1983), ch. 3.

20. Compare with the second part of Mandeville's *Fable of the bees*, the six dialogues of which conform to a dialectical pattern, truth rising from the progressive and mutual correction of tenets initially conflicting.

21. Consequently, Shaftesbury criticizes dialogues "fram'd after the manner of our antient Authors" (p. 102): "This is the plain *Dilemma* against that antient Manner of Writing, which we can neither well imitate, nor translate; whatever Pleasure or Profit we may find in reading those Originals" (p. 106).

22. "The Skill and Grace of Writings is founded, as our wise Poet [Horace] tells *us*, in Knowledg and Good Sense: And not barely in that Knowledg, which is to be learnt from common Authors, or the general Conversation of the World; but from those particular Rules of Art, which Philosophy alone exhibits" (pp. 91–2).

23. We have a good example of this authoritarian conception in the *Dialogue between a tutor and his pupil*, which is attributed to Herbert of Cherbury and was published in 1768. The pupil asks for advice and the tutor gives the answer. In fact, the pupil is consulting reason itself, which teaches through the tutor's voice. The dialogic form is a device to deal with the complexity of the question and to introduce a minimum credo in the struggle of religious sects and dogmas.

24. In his famous letter to Gilbert Elliot (10 March 1751), Hume also asks that the conditions of a real dialogue should be preserved: "I have often thought, that the best way of composing a Dialogue, wou'd be for two Persons that are of different Opinions about any Question of Importance, to write alternately the different Parts of the Discourse, & reply to each other" (HL I, 154). On the interpretation of this letter and Hume's avowal of his sceptical tendency, see the introduction to my translation of the *Dialogues* (Paris 1987), pp. 7–8.

25. "Most of the philosophers of antiquity, who treated of human nature, have shewn more of a delicacy of sentiment, a just sense of morals, or a greatness of soul, than a depth of reasoning and reflection. They content themselves with representing the common sense of mankind in the strongest lights, and with the best turn of thought and expression, without following out steadily a chain of propositions, or forming the several truths into a regular science" (T 645).

26. It is necessary to remember that the second *Enquiry* was published at a time when Hume was already working on *The natural history of religion* and the *Dialogues*.

27. The first editions were still more explicit on this tactical change.

28. Hume is quite explicit in a letter to an author who criticized his book: "I must only complain of you a little for ascribing to me the sentiments which I have put into the mouth of the Sceptic in the Dialogue. I have surely endeavoured to refute the Sceptic with all the force of which I am master; and my refutation must be allowed sincere, because drawn from the capital principles of my system. But you impute to me both the sentiments of the sceptic and the sentiments of his antagonist, which I can never admit of. In every Dialogue, no more than one person can be supposed to represent the author" (HL I, 173).

29. The same discursive structure occurs in Section XI of the first *Enquiry*. The friend who loves sceptical paradoxes, and *I*, equally agree on the same conclusion, the difference with the second *Enquiry* being that the conclusion is merely refutative, since the subject can be treated only in a speculative way. This dialogue, which contains a kind of second dialogue between Epicurus and religious philosophers in front of the Athenian people, is an artifice to represent a rather intricate argument, to soften somewhat its acuteness, and yet, analogously, in a final rebound, to strike the last blow which leaves no way out. In both texts, *I* says the last word.

30. For more details about the complementary character of the two texts, see the introduction to my translation of the *Dialogues*, pp. 13–20.

31. See, for instance, E 278.

32. This distinction is not new. Hume draws the elements of Pamphilus's argument to some extent from the introduction to Cicero's *De natura deorum*.

33. When he wants to close the controversy and put an end to the dialogue, Philo comes back to this distinction; but he stands on Cleanthes' side when considering the existence of God, since he admits some philosophical belief, prompted by a vague analogy, and on Demea's side when considering the nature of God, since he appeals to a revelation.

34. In this regard, all those commentaries on the supposed irony of Hume, which would proceed from the gap between what is said by the characters and the secret purpose of the author, fail to respect the nature of the text. Those commentators who have insisted on the fact that the dramatic structure of the text has a logic of its own have considered either that the rhetorical

form can stand by itself, and has no direct ties with the content (see for instance the suggestive but inaccurate paper of R. White, 'Hume's *Dialogues* and the comedy of religion', *Hume studies* 14 (1988), 390–407); or that it supports a meaning distinct from the literal one and is to be interpreted (see Hurlbutt, in the new chapter of the second edition of his book, where he considers the *Dialogues* as an artefact, the product of an implicit intentional act, which has to be restored). W. L. Sessions, in his recent paper, 'A dialogic interpretation of Hume's *Dialogues*' (*Hume studies* 17 (1991), 15–39), rightly claims that the literary form is essential to the philosophical message, but, prompted by dialogic hermeneutics, reads the *Dialogues* in a Shaftesburian way, i.e. as being supported by the spirit of agreement, and bearing on religious morals (piety).

35. There remains the problem of the long footnote in Part XII, initially added by Hume as a note, then deleted, and finally restored again as a note (D 219). (There is no manuscript evidence, or evidence in the content of the passage itself, for transferring this passage into the body of the text, as in Price's and some other recent editions.) The substance of this footnote is plainly to be attributed to the author of the *Dialogues*, i.e. to Hume himself, offering it by way of a commentary on the text: the dispute between sceptics and dogmatists is as unreal as that between atheists and theists. The device is quite sophisticated; but there is nothing to stop the author – like anyone else – from commenting on the argument as an outsider, while the text goes on according to its own internal logic. So the footnote, being a footnote, should not be understood as Hume's intervening in the progress of the dialogue – if anything, the reverse.

36. I have elsewhere tried to show that the whole content (ideas, arguments, discursive changes, etc.) is conventional and that Hume is repeating or parodying worn-out matter; see the introduction to my translation of the *Dialogues*.

37. In particular, it offers the most complete critique of finality ever made in the history of philosophy.

11

Hume and the madness of religion

CHRISTOPHER BERNARD

In *The natural history of religion*, Hume claims that there are societies without any religious beliefs. He draws the conclusion that "the first religious principles must be secondary", that they may be "perverted by various accidents and causes" (NHR 309–10). In this essay I shall examine Hume's account of some of these "accidents and causes" affecting religious belief, and argue that Hume's account of religion in his *Natural history*, his *Essays*, and his *History of England*, is based on principles of philosophical psychology which he originally developed in the *Treatise*.

I

Let me begin by calling attention to what Hume says in the *Treatise* about the faculty of imagination. He introduces this faculty by distinguishing it in two ways from memory. In the first place, the ideas of imagination are weaker than those of memory. When we remember any past event, "the idea of it flows in upon the mind in a forcible manner; whereas in the imagination the perception is faint and languid". Secondly, while the memory "preserves the original form in which its objects were presented" (T 9), fables and poems show us "the liberty of the imagination to transpose and change its ideas". When we read fables we find that "Nature there is totally confounded, and nothing mentioned but winged horses, fiery dragons, and monstrous giants" (T 10). However, says Hume, if we think more carefully about imagination, we shall see that it is not really any freer than memory. There are "universal principles" according to which it operates uniformly in all times and places. The imagination, he says, will naturally associate ideas through their qualities of resemblance, contiguity, and cause and effect.

The general importance of these principles for Hume's science of man can hardly be overestimated. With these seemingly trivial principles he attempts to provide a new foundation for the sciences. In introducing them, he stresses that it is their remarkable application, not the principles themselves, which should interest his reader: "Here is a kind of ATTRAC-TION, which in the mental world will be found to have as extraordinary effects as in the natural, and to shew itself in as many and as various forms" (T 12–13). The causes of these principles, which are "mostly unknown", he does not claim to explain.

Hume's views on the centrality of the imagination were not wholly original. Other writers had included in their studies of the mind principles which describe the connexions between ideas. In *The search after truth*, Nicolas Malebranche used the connexion of ideas in the imagination to explain how human beings are led into error. For example, he noted the deceptive role of resemblance. Because the apparent size of the moon "is not very different from that of an ordinary head at a certain distance", and because we so often look at faces, "we normally see a face in the moon".[1] Hume himself appears to have Malebranche's own psychophysiological explanation of this phenomenon in mind in Book I of the *Treatise* when he puts forward his own hypothesis about the causes of association (T 60–61); and he uses Malebranche's specific example of seeing a face in the moon in discussing the errors of resemblance in *The natural history of religion* (NHR 117).

In the chapter 'Of the association of ideas' added in 1700 to the fourth edition of *An essay concerning human understanding*, John Locke had written of how "some of our *Ideas* have a natural Correspondence and Connexion one with another"; on the other hand, "there is another Connexion of *Ideas* wholly owing to Chance or Custom; *Ideas* that in themselves are not at all of kin, come to be so united in some Mens Minds . . . and the one no sooner at any time comes into the Understanding but its Associate appears with it" (*Essay*, II. xxxiii. 5). Locke's interest here is in the origin of error, or the "Madness" that leads people to reject the "Evidence of Reason". It is plain that he considers the root of this "Madness", which is apparent even in "sober and rational Minds", to lie in the conjoining of ideas in the imagination (II. xxxiii. 3–4). He also draws the reader's attention to his earlier discussion of madness in chapter XI. Unlike *"Naturals"* who are "deprived of Reason", mad men "having joined together some *Ideas* very wrongly, . . . mistake them for Truths; and they err as Men do, that argue right from wrong Principles. For by the violence of their Imaginations, having taken their Fancies for Realities, they make right deductions from them" (II. xi. 13). So the unfortunate wretch who falsely believes he is king correctly infers that he has the right to demand respect and obedience.[2]

Locke held that doctrinal disputes result from such incorrect associations of ideas. For "such wrong and unnatural Combinations of *Ideas* will be found to establish the Irreconcilable opposition between different Sects of Philosophy and Religion" (II. xxxiii. 18). What happens is that "some independent *Ideas*, of no alliance to one another, are by Education, Custom, and the constant din of their Party, so coupled in their Minds, that they always appear there together, and they can no more separate them in their Thoughts, than if they were but one *Idea*, and they operate as if they were so". Locke comments that this "is the foundation of the greatest, I had almost said, of all the Errors in the World" (*ibid.*).

Hume's employment of the theory of association in his account of normal understanding marks an important departure from his predecessors. It is true that Locke implies that the association of the experience of touch with sight is necessary for the visual judgement of depth (*Essay*, II. ix. 8); and Malebranche's theory of "natural judgement" by association was used to explain a kind of natural correction of the errors of sight (*Search*, p. 34). But Hume's suggestion that imagination is responsible for all our correct judgements about matters of fact would have astonished his predecessors.

At the same time, in his writings on religion, Hume can be seen to be carrying on the tradition, begun by Malebranche and Locke, of showing how error and prejudice have their origin in the principle of the association of ideas. In so doing he was making use of a distinction which he drew in his *Treatise* between those principles of the imagination which are fundamental for human survival and those which "are observ'd only to take place in weak minds" (T 225).

II

I now turn to examine how Hume uses his account of the imagination to explain the way human beings arrive at religious belief. I shall begin with what he says about the first stirrings of polytheism and then turn to his account of the rise of Protestantism.

At the centre of his explanation of the origin of religion is an idea that is found throughout his work: that the mind "spreads itself" externally. This is to say that internal impressions, such as the impression of power, are associated with external impressions. The first instance we have of Hume using this doctrine is in Part III of Book I the *Treatise*, when he seeks to explain why it is so difficult not to believe that power does not lie in the objects: "'Tis a common observation, that the mind has a great propensity to spread itself on external objects, and to conjoin with them any internal impressions which they occasion" (T 167). He returns to the notion in Part IV when discussing secondary qualities (T 237). In Book III (T 469) and in the second *Enquiry*, projection is used in order to explain the genesis of our belief that virtue lies in the object itself. He writes of a "productive faculty" capable of "staining all natural objects, with the colours borrowed from an internal sentiment" (E 294). Hume's analysis of this projective disposition is founded on his view that certain relations facilitate the association of perceptions in the imagination.

Considering the comparatively wide audience Hume was writing for in

The natural history of religion, it is understandable that he does not discuss such an analysis in any great detail in that work. Nevertheless, he uses its results implicitly and faithfully in support of his thesis that the first manifestation of religion is polytheistic. He writes of how the projective tendencies of human beings lead them to transfer to external objects those qualities with which they are familiarly acquainted, and of which they are intimately conscious. "We find human faces in the moon, armies in the clouds; and by a natural propensity, if not corrected by experience and reflection, ascribe malice and good-will to every thing, that hurts or pleases us" (NHR 117). This "natural propensity" leads us to project our inner experience on to those objects which commonly engage our interest. We would not "see" faces in the moon unless we were drawn, as when we notice a great silvery glow, to look at it. Similarly, we project human power on to those objects on which our own well-being depends:

> We hang in perpetual suspence between life and death, health and sickness, plenty and want; which are distributed amongst the human species by secret and unknown causes, whose operation is oft unexpected, and always unaccountable.

As the "passions are kept in perpetual alarm by an anxious expectation" of these momentous events of our own lives, so the "imagination is equally employed in forming ideas of those powers, on which we have so entire a dependance" (NHR 316). Hume says of such powers that the "active imagination of men", which feels uneasy with abstractions, comes "to clothe them in shapes more suitable to its natural comprehension" (NHR 335). We associate these unknown powers with those human powers which commonly influence us.

Since human beings are dependent on the unknown powers, they ascribe to them the characteristics of those persons who have power over them. The imagination "represents them to be sensible, intelligent beings, like mankind; actuated by love and hatred, and flexible by gifts and entreaties, by prayers and sacrifices" (NHR 335). This is because religious belief reflects the primitive's assumptions about the political structure of his society.

This is made explicit in the *Natural history*, where Hume describes the transition from polytheism to theism. He speaks of the original "distribution of power and territory among the gods". A god may have "jurisdiction" in a particular nation. Sometimes, a particular god is represented "as the prince or supreme magistrate of the rest, who, though of the same nature, rules them with an authority, like that which an earthly sovereign exercises over his subjects and vassals". After a time, each nation builds up the "titles of his divinity", each seeking to outdo the others, "till at last they arrive at infinity itself" (NHR 330). And this is how polytheism gives way to theism.

It would seem to follow from the above that Hume believes that the progress of religion is consequent upon the development of society. It is only in societies that have progressed little beyond "brutes" that we find no religion (NHR 363). In such societies there would be no notion of dependence on a superior's decision which could be transferred or projected on to unknown causes; nor, where people live through familial affections and conventions, would there be an understanding of the wiles of entreaty and flattery.

Hume believes that there are also principles of the imagination which explain the expression and success of a particular set of theological principles, such as those which characterize Protestantism. In the essay 'Of superstition and enthusiasm', he writes that, though the human mind is subject to the terrors and anxiety that feed superstition, it is also prone to fits of "elevation and presumption".

> In such a state of mind, the imagination swells with great, but confused conceptions, to which no sublunary beauties or enjoyments can correspond. Every thing mortal and perishable vanishes as unworthy of attention. And a full range is given to the fancy in the invisible regions or world of spirits, where the soul is at liberty to indulge itself in every imagination, which may best suit its present taste and disposition. Hence arise raptures, transports, and surprising flights of fancy.

The enthusiast attributes such mental earthquakes to the operations of the Deity; just as he would attribute to the same extraterrestrial cause earthquakes of the non-metaphorical variety. And "in a little time, the inspired person comes to regard himself as a distinguished favourite of the Divinity" (Ess. 74).

However, this psychological process does not happen in a historical vacuum. If we turn to Hume's account of the beginnings of the Reformation in his *History of England*, we can begin to see in greater detail how he thought that various social forces operated in determining the peculiar nature of Protestant theology. I shall discuss the underlying psychological principles further in sections III and IV.

We can take up the story with Hume's report of how, in 1521, Bishop Arcemboldi of Genoa gave to the Dominicans the task of selling "general indulgences". This angered the Austin friars of Saxony, who had previously held the tender. The Dominicans subsequently praised the merits of general indulgences to a quite unprecedented degree. This was, Hume suggests, a robust attitude which stemmed, not from any belief as to the quality of the product, but from a desire of the Order of Preachers "to prove themselves worthy of the distinction conferred on them". However, their panegyrics scandalized the people, not because this indulgence was in itself more ridiculous than any other, but because the people were not yet accustomed to it. Furthermore, the scandal was intensified with sight-ings of Dominicans spending the monies collected from the devout in "taverns, gaming-houses, and places still more infamous" (H III, 138). All this helped to create the general sentiment upon which Luther was to build.

What at first animated Luther, Hume argues, were not beliefs about the institution of indulgences, or about the notion of a "general indul-gence"; they were not beliefs about the authority of the Pope, or indeed about any theological issue at all. Rather, what fired Luther was resentment against the "affront put upon his order". So his first harangues were not directed against the sale of indulgences, but against abuses which he claimed were committed by his order's rivals, the Dominicans. Soon, though, "being naturally of a fiery temper, and provoked by opposition, he proceeded even to decry indulgences themselves". Then, finding that the group opposing the interests of his own appealed to the authority of the Pope, he began to attack that authority too. And, "as he enlarged his reading, in order to support these tenets", he discovered some "new abuse or error in the church of Rome" (H III, 139).

Thus, according to Hume, the Reformation began as a fight within an institution between factions or religious orders that had their own interests. Its first stage ended in the founding of another institution with its own supporters and principles.

Luther was encouraged by the reception of his doctrine, and he soon found himself pursuing an object far more pleasing than the power to sell indulgences. He became quite incapable "either from promises of advance-ment, or terrors of severity, to relinquish a sect, of which he was himself the founder, and which brought him a glory, superior to all others, the glory of dictating the religious faith and principles of multitudes" (H III, 139).

According to Hume, the content of Protestantism was not established through revelation, but through its leaders' worldly desires.[3] In the same way as Luther had found "reasons" in order to justify the protection of his order's interests, so he and his followers arrived at theological prin-ciples, which, distinguishing them from Rome, served to unite them as a body. These monks discovered the intellectual foundations of Protestant-ism in their insults: they referred to the Pope as "antichrist", and to Rome as the "scarlet whore". About these peculiar expressions, Hume remarks that they "were better calculated to operate on the multitude than the most solid arguments" (H III, 141).

The "enthusiastic strain of devotion" arrived at by its leaders gave to the supporters a common identity through their opposition to the estab-lished religion. It therefore allowed the forces of sympathy to work. Just as Luther and his followers feverishly sought biblical quotations which would undermine the Roman church, so "in contradiction to the multiplied superstitions with which that communion was loaded, they adopted an enthusiastic strain of devotion, which admitted of no observances, rites, or ceremonies, but placed all merit in a mysterious species of faith, in inward vision, rapture and ecstasy" (H III, 141; see I, 350).

If the content of Protestantism was not established through revelation, then neither did reason bear "any considerable share, in opening men's eyes with regard to the impostures of the Romish Church". Philosophy, at this time, of all the branches of literature had "made the most inconsiderable progress"; and neither, Hume adds, is "there any instance that argument has ever been able to free the people from that enormous load of absurdity, with which superstition has every where overwhelmed them" (H III, 140).

In his accounts of the origin both of superstition and of the Reformation, Hume put considerable emphasis on the social nature of man. I will now consider some elements of his theory of belief that may make this emphasis more explicable.

III

Hume holds that religious belief is inherently weak and that, paradoxically, this accounts for much of the dangerous social consequences of religion. For religion comes to conceal the dominant passions. This idea was not original with Hume: it had been already explored by Bayle.[4] Hume's originality lies in his account of the way that groups function so as to support religious belief. It lies, also, in his account of the way that this support encourages religious hypocrisy and self-deception.

In the *Treatise*, Hume explains belief as a lively idea "related to, or associated with a present impression" (T 93). But there is little liveliness in a belief, say, about the afterlife, in comparison to the beliefs of common life (T 114; D 221). However, sympathy becomes a powerful force in sustaining what belief there is. The agreement of others plays an important role in sustaining not only political and speculative opinions, but also religious beliefs. Even "men of the greatest judgment and understanding" find it difficult to believe in opposition to their daily companions (T 316). This, Hume argues, is because the contiguity of their fellows, as well as all the resemblances between them, allows the "imagination" to "make the transition" between the idea of the other and "the idea of our person" (T 318). The result is that the lively idea I have of your belief enlivens my own.

Consider, for example, Hume's explanation of the fact that people die for religious beliefs. In the *History*, he remarked that "it is in vain for men to oppose the severest punishment to the united motives of religion and public applause". Thus, the belief of others in the glory of martyrdom inspires the one who is actually going to suffer. As the flames increase in their ferocity, the alleged heretic may begin to doubt the wisdom of his course; but when he catches sight of his fellow devotees, his faith is renewed. So courage, Hume remarks dryly, is "usual on these occasions" (H IV, 21). Since Hume holds that "the conviction of the religionists, in all ages, is more affected than real" (NHR 348), it is unsurprising that he believes that "public applause" is central in explaining martyrdom.

Hume's doubt about the sincerity of professions of religious belief makes its first appearance in the *Treatise*. Here, he seeks to explain how Catholics could deplore the massacre of the Protestants on St Bartholomew's Day, and nevertheless subscribe to a faith which condemns them to eternal punishment. "All we can really say in excuse for this inconsistency is, that they really do not believe what they affirm concerning a future state; nor is there any better proof of it than the very inconsistency" (T 115).

However, Hume thought that religious doubts are masked by a species of self-deception. In the *Natural history*, he wrote that:

the conviction of the religionists, in all ages, is more affected than real, and scarce ever approaches, in any degree, to that solid belief and persuasion, which governs us in the common affairs of life. Men dare not avow, even to their own hearts, the doubts, which they entertain on such subjects: They make a merit of implicit faith; and disguise to themselves their real infidelity, by the strongest asseverations and most positive bigotry. (NHR 348)

Discussing the Civil War in the sixth volume of the *History*, Hume remarked that religious hypocrisy "is of a peculiar nature; and being generally unknown to the person himself, though more dangerous, it implies less falsehood than any other species of insincerity" (H VI, 142).

To see what is involved in this scepticism, a form of scepticism generally ignored by commentators, I shall examine his discussions of Thomas à Becket and Joan of Arc. I shall argue that his understanding of belief and social psychology gives him a far more interesting, and perhaps pertinent, view of religious commitment than is generally ascribed to him.

In the *History*, Hume contrasts the character of Becket with that of Becket's opponent, Henry II. He presents Henry's actions towards the "haughty prelate" as motivated by his temporal interests. Henry sought to limit the power of the ecclesiastical authority and had made clear his intentions to Becket before he appointed him Archbishop of Canterbury (H I, 309). After the two quarrelled, Henry continued to seek a reconciliation because he feared excommunication. He dreaded this result, not out of fear for his soul, "but because it might make his subjects renounce their allegiance to him" (H I, 329; cf. 337).

While Becket was no less ambitious than Henry, his ambition and desire for fame were cloaked in piety. As Chancellor, he had exceeded any previous subject in the luxuriousness of his life (H I, 307); but once he was ensconced as Archbishop, his outward manner quickly changed, and he did everything "to acquire the character of sanctity". Yet, Hume notes, a penetrating observer would recognize that "the ambition and ostentation of his character had turned itself towards a new and more dangerous object". Becket's actions were designed to manipulate the opinion of others in his favour. Hume describes how he "wore sack-cloth next to his skin, which, by his affected care to conceal it, was necessarily the more remarked by all the world" (H I, 309–10). As Archbishop, he is described as engineering the "highest veneration of the public towards his person and his dignity" (H I, 331). His real motives, when he forced the final showdown between Henry and himself, have nothing to do with his desire to uphold the sanctity of his office. Becket was "instigated by revenge and animated by the present glory" (H I, 325).

Yet Hume does not consider Becket to be simply a hypocrite. All Becket's letters give evidence of "a most entire and absolute conviction of the reasons and piety" of his party (H I, 334). Nevertheless, there is deception. He was, says Hume, "able to cover, to the world and probably to himself, the enterprizes of pride and ambition, under the disguise of sanctity and of zeal for the interests of religion" (H I, 333). The deceived included himself.

Becket provides an example of a person who comes to disguise his own motives to himself, as a result of his desire to win the approval of others. In the *Essays*, Hume explains that, because religious feelings act only in fits and starts, the person may come to believe that religion is his animating principle because this is what others attribute to him. In order to carry out their duties, most clergy need "to maintain the appearance of fervour and seriousness, even when jaded with the exercises of their religion". This demeanour is required "to support the veneration paid them by the multitude". Like most men they are ambitious, but, Hume claims, the ambition of the clergy is served by "promoting ignorance and superstition and implicit faith and pious frauds". However, they become susceptible to "an overweaning conceit of themselves" when they are "regarded with such veneration, and are even deemed sacred, by the ignorant multitude" (Ess. 199–200). Thus, Becket led those around him to a belief in his own sanctity, by carefully presenting his character so as to satisfy their expectations as to how a pious ecclesiastic ought to behave. After a while he was fooled by his own act.

One reason why the opinion of others is so important for the religious believer is that there is no primary religious instinct or sentiment. This is why Hume lays such emphasis on the need for the religious believer to feign. Because fervour is often absent, a habit of dissimulation is by degrees contracted: And fraud and falsehood become the predominant principle. Hence the reason of that vulgar observation, that the highest zeal in religion and the deepest hypocrisy, so far from being inconsistent, are often or commonly united in the same individual character. (D 222)

Henry did not need to deceive himself in order to satisfy any ambition. But Becket had to act in a pious manner in order to satisfy his own desire for ecclesiastical power; he needed to disguise his own motives as directed towards an unworldly goal. In this way he expressed that ambition already discernible in his younger days.

In Hume's discussion of Joan of Arc, we have another instance of his attempt to display for the edification of his readers the forces that can lead to self-deception. While Hume argues that Becket was driven by ambition and love of glory, he presents Joan as animated by patriotism and compassion for the beleaguered, handsome and "amiable" Dauphin. Like Becket, the justifications Joan gave for her actions were religious; like Becket, she is held to have been sincere.

From the beginning, the phenomenon of sympathy had a powerful effect on Joan's actions: "inflamed by the general sentiment" that the Sovereign should be relieved of the distress caused by the English, her

unexperienced mind, working day and night on this favourite object, mistook the impulses of passion for heavenly inspirations; and she fancied, that she saw visions, and heard voices, exhorting her to re-establish the throne of France, and to expel the foreign invaders. (H II, 398)

Hume believes that sexual attraction (or romantic love) lay behind Joan's dreams. She belonged, after all, to that sex "whose generous minds know no bounds in their affections"; moreover, Charles was not only a Dauphin-in-distress, but a character "strongly inclined to friendship and the tender passions". It is no wonder, Hume remarks, that he became a "hero" for women (H II, 397).

Whilst the theme of Becket's sincerity was advanced through an artful contrast with Henry, that of Joan is developed through a contrast with the actions of Charles and his ministers. When Joan revealed to the French court her plan to raise the siege of Orléans, many in the court really believed in her divine credentials; nevertheless, enough care was taken to market Joan effectively, to suggest that they were not all prepared to put their trust in God and Joan alone. So "miraculous stories were spread abroad, in order to captivate the vulgar". A more romantic impression was created by tinkering with Joan's curriculum vitæ: before, she was a servant; now, she is a shepherdess. For good measure, they lopped nearly ten years off her age (H II, 399).

Certainly, Hume acknowledges that the dispirited French forces believed that Joan was divinely inspired. "A ray of hope began to break through that despair, in which the minds of all men were before enveloped. Heaven had now declared itself in favour of France, and had laid bare its outstretched arm to take vengeance on her invaders." Even "grave doctors and theologians" who examined Joan reached the conclusion that her claims were genuine. Hume, of course, did not see matters in quite this light; and not only because the French lost. His analysis is purely psychological. The conviction of the French was based on wishful thinking: "Few could distinguish between the impulse of inclination and the force of conviction; and none would submit to the trouble of so disagreeable a scrutiny" (H II, 399).

Thus it was hardly surprising that Joan, believed in by thousands of Frenchmen, not to mention the handsome Charles, should continue to see herself as a heavenly deliverer. Hume never doubts her sincerity. He writes of the "visionary dreams of inspiration, in which she had been buoyed up by the triumphs of success and the applauses of her own party" (H II, 409). In the end, the forces of interest, again under the guise of religion, led to her being burned as a heretic by the English. Hume sums up his own judgement of Joan by noting that "the more generous superstition of the ancients would have erected altars" to this "admirable heroine" (H II, 410).

I have chosen to examine Hume's narration of the historical episodes in this section in order to illustrate how Hume's understanding of religious belief is far more interesting than commonly thought. It is clear that his foundational work in the *Treatise* – for example, his understanding of the phenomena of belief, sympathy and the pressures of groups – informs his presentation of these episodes. Moreover, his theory of human nature allows him to go beyond the pronouncements of the parties to any controversy, and show how events were influenced by the prevailing attitudes of the age, especially those concerning religion. Knowledge of human nature makes historical knowledge possible; and history, in its turn, becomes a vehicle for greater knowledge of human nature.

IV

In my final section I shall show how a certain principle of the formation of the passions which Hume identifies in the *Treatise* – namely, the principle of opposition – plays a fundamental role in his analysis of the nature of Christianity.[5] The centrality of this principle in Hume's writings has been overlooked by previous commentators.

In Part III of Book II of the *Treatise*, Hume explains the principles by which, he thinks, a calm passion is converted into a violent one. He argues, for example, that a passion can become violent when it borrows "force from any attendant passion" (T 438). An important instance of this occurs when the two passions are opposed to each other. "'Tis observable", he writes,

> that an opposition of passions commonly causes a new emotion in the spirits, and produces more disorder, than the concurrence of any two affections of equal force. This new emotion is easily converted into the predominant passion, and encreases its violence, beyond the pitch it wou'd have arriv'd at had it met with no opposition (T 421).

His explanation is that "the efforts, which the mind makes to surmount the obstacle, excite the spirits and inliven the passion". In the *Treatise*, Hume uses this principle to account for very different kinds of phenomena; for example, that lovers become more passionately attached through "jealousies and quarrels",[6] and that the feeling of duty often feeds the passion to which it is opposed when it is unable to overcome it (T 420–21). In his *Essays*, he tacitly uses the same principle to explain the effects that political factions have on one another.[7] In his *History*, as we saw earlier, Hume argues that Luther was "provoked by opposition" to intensify his attack on the Catholic Church (H III, 139). And later, the reformers "carried matters much farther" because they were "excited by contest and persecution" (H III, 141). Similarly, what Hume called "the spirit of opposition" plays an important role in his explanation of martyrdom (H III, 443; IV, 21).

Hume uses this same principle of the passions to explain the nature of Christianity itself. According to Hume, Christianity represents a perversion of natural values. In the *Enquiry concerning the principles of morals*, he raises the question why philosophers have failed to recognize that the value of persons lies solely "in the possession of mental qualities, *useful* or *agreeable* to the *person himself* or to *others*". His answer is that "systems and hypotheses" which arise from Christianity have "perverted our natural understanding" (E 268). It is "superstition and false religion" which have led philosophers to value "celibacy, fasting, penance, mortification, self-denial, humility, silence, solitude and the whole train of monkish virtues" (E 270). Similarly, in his *Treatise*, Hume notes that Christians decry as "purely pagan and natural" all virtues, such as "a well-regulated pride" and ambition, that "have plainly a strong mixture of self-esteem in them" (T 600).

Hume places great emphasis for understanding the character of Christianity on the fact that in its early years it was a sect with principles "directly opposite" to those of "the polite part of the world". The Romans "despised the nation that first broached this novelty" (Ess. 61). It would seem that Christianity (as well as Islam) was formed by contradicting values of the classical pagan world. Writing on courage in *The natural history of religion*, Hume remarks that

> The heroes in paganism correspond exactly to the saints in popery,

and holy dervises in MAHOMETANISM. The place of HERCULES, THESEUS, HECTOR, ROMULUS, is now supplied by DOMINIC, FRANCIS, ANTHONY, and BENEDICT. Instead of the destruction of monsters, the subduing of tyrants, the defence of our native country; whippings and fastings, cowardice and humility, abject submission and slavish obedience, are become the means of obtaining celestial honours among mankind. (NHR 339–40)

Hume is suggesting that the Christian heroes held up for imitation by the priests slavishly submitted, rather than fighting against tyrants. They did not show courage and defend their lands. They sought to subdue themselves rather than those who oppressed them.

And yet Hume recognizes that the passions operate in complex ways, and that while Christians profess a slave morality, their actions are often rather different. In narrating the horrors of the Crusades, Hume exclaims: "So inconsistent is human nature with itself! And so easily does the most effeminate superstition ally, both with the most heroic courage, and with the fiercest barbarity!" (H I, 250). While Hume cites with approval the claim of Machiavelli that Christianity had prepared human beings "for slavery and subjection", he qualifies it by remarking that "there are many other circumstances in human society which controul the genius and character of a religion" (NHR 340). I have already noted a number of these circumstances: the influence of faction; ruling passions such as Becket's ambition and Joan's patriotism; and, in general, the way that passions are served by religion. The result is not a slavish mentality, though there will be extended exercises in "humility", especially amongst the clergy.

While Hume clearly thinks there is something perverse about Christian values, he also thinks they arise from universal principles of human nature. In the *Natural history*, he argues that, in general, sects will seek to please their gods, not by virtue, but by "frivolous observances, by intemperate zeal, by rapturous extasies, or by the belief of mysterious and absurd opinions" (NHR 357). The reason for this is that "a superstitious man" finds nothing in natural virtuous conduct which can be held to be performed for the sake of the Deity. Virtue is what we owe to society. So

> any practice, recommended to him, which either serves no purpose in life, or offers the strongest violence to his natural inclinations; that practice he will the more readily embrace, on account of those very circumstances, which should make him absolutely reject it (NHR 358).

Religion leads people to act against their "natural inclinations", including their moral ones.

Hume thinks that religion in general and Christianity in particular thrive on opposition. He held that the soul "seeks opposition", since opposition "supports and fills the passions" and is "agreeable to us" (T 434). This is "why we naturally desire what is forbid" (T 421), and why people come to value what is in "direct opposition to morality" or else to embrace "a new and frivolous species of merit" which distracts them from their duties (D 222). Thus, Christianity is attractive because we find it difficult to accept its values, which are unnatural to human beings. The Christian, Hume thought, is at war with himself. However, this is not the traditional Augustinian war against one's own evil desires, but rather a war against natural secular values.

I have been arguing that Hume tries to explain the inconsistency of Christianity through the natural mechanisms of the imagination and passions. He has adopted a radically different perspective on the subjugation of reason to the passions from that given by Calvin,[8] Malebranche[9] and Bayle,[10] who all saw this as a consequence of the Fall. Hume agrees that man is not guided by reason: but this is not on account of Original Sin. The temptation to reach for what is forbidden, which arises from the pleasure of enlivened passions rather than the Devil, is indeed deeply rooted in human nature. It makes us overstep the limits of reason and try to make virtues of what are, at best, morally insignificant acts, and, at worst, vices.

NOTES

1. Nicolas Malebranche, *The search after truth*, trans. T. M. Lennon and P. J. Olscamp (Columbus, OH 1980), p. 135.
2. A fuller discussion is provided by J. P. Wright, 'Association, madness, and the measures of probability in Locke and Hume', in *Psychology and literature in the eighteenth century*, ed. C. M. Fox (New York 1987), 103–27.
3. Compare Nietzsche's remark: "'Faith' has been at all times, with Luther for instance, only a cloak, a pretext, a screen, behind which the instincts played their game – a shrewd blindness to the dominance of certain instincts" (*The Anti-Christ*, tr. R. J. Hollingsworth (London 1968), p. 151).
4. Pierre Bayle, *Pensées diverses sur la comète* (1683).
5. For a more general discussion of Hume's views on the nature of Christianity, see J. C. A. Gaskin, *Hume's philosophy of religion*, 2nd edn (London 1988), chs 10–11.
6. Compare 'Of polygamy and divorces', where, in the 1742–8 editions, Hume wrote that the obstacles of "coldness", "disdain" and, in general, the "difficulties" of the courting period increase the amorous passion to rapture (Ess. 628).
7. For example, he argues that the "contradiction" between the accusations against and panegyrics for Walpole produced an "extraordinary ferment on both sides". Each faction grew fiercer and more extreme in its claims when it was violently opposed by the other (Ess. 28).
8. Following St Augustine, Calvin believed that, because Adam sinned, "man's

natural gifts were corrupted by sin, and his supernatural ones withdrawn".
What is left is a "residue of intelligence and judgement" which places us
above the beasts. However, what really controls us are our unworthy desires.
So though there is some appetite for truth "in the human mind", this "fades
out before it reaches the goal and then falls away into vanity". The human
mind is unfitted to search for the truth, and this is because we are under a
bondage; we are "enslaved" (*Institutes of the Christian religion*, ed. A. Lane
and H. Osbourne (London 1986), pp. 91–8; for Augustine, see *City of God*,
Bk XIV).

9. *Search after truth*, p. 120.
10. Bayle in the *Dictionnaire* (2nd edn 1702), s.v. 'Ovid', ascribes to Cicero the
notion of "*l'esclavage de la raison*", in a sentence which is rendered in the
English translation (1739): "reason had become the slave of the passions".
Peter Jones, in *Hume's sentiments* (Edinburgh 1982), p. 5, connects this with
a related passage in Bayle's *Pensées diverses*. Hume's examination of the
behaviour of the religious that I discuss in this essay provides some reason
for thinking that Bayle's comparable exercise in the *Pensées* was of greater
importance to Hume than is usually thought. In that wonderfully entertaining
book, Bayle argues that "man is not determin'd in his Actions by general
Notions, or views of his Understanding but by the present ruling passion of
his Heart" (*Reflections occasion'd by the comet* (1708), p. 279). The case is
argued through an examination of the actions of "idolaters" – that is, Catholics.
But besides its evident significance for understanding the development of
Hume's ideas on action, Bayle's thoroughgoing attack on Catholics seems to
have shown Hume the way to an attack on all Christians.

12

Kant's critique of Hume's theory of faith

MANFRED KUEHN

In a famous, or perhaps infamous, passage, Hume wrote:

> I am the better pleased with the method of reasoning here delivered, as I think it may serve to confound those dangerous friends or disguised enemies to the *Christian Religion*, who have undertaken to defend it by the principles of human reason. Our most holy religion is founded on *Faith*, not on reason; and it is a sure method of exposing it to put it to such a trial as it is, by no means, fitted to endure. (E 129–30)

Though this passage relates directly to his discussion of miracles, it can be argued that it is a succinct statement of his considered view on religious belief in general. Since Hume does not reject religious belief altogether, but is concerned to point out its non-rational or irrational character, his view appears to be compatible with that of proponents of Christian fideism. Indeed, he seems to be placing himself in this tradition when he states that "our most holy religion is founded on *Faith*, not on reason". Hume can be, and has been, taken to endorse the claim that, because religious beliefs are unjustifiable, they require something like a "leap of faith".[1] From the time of the publication of *Socratic memorabilia* in 1759 by Kant's critic and friend Johann Georg Hamann, Protestant fideist thinkers have employed Hume's critique of rationalist theology as a preparatory stage to authentic faith. A "Barthian Protestant" who believes that "there is no point of contact for arguments" between Christians and non-Christians, because faith is a "gift from God" which cannot be understood by Christians themselves, might even find some comfort in Hume's conclusions.[2]

While Hume clearly invited such a reaction, it would be wrong to conclude, on the basis of the passage quoted, that he found religious faith an attractive option, much less that he himself made such a leap of faith. Hume thought he had proved not only that the philosophical justification of religious belief is impossible, but also that anyone who accepts the kind of "evidence" available to the religious believer is irrational. He concluded his discussion of miracles with the statement that

> upon the whole, we may conclude, that the *Christian Religion* not only was at first attended with miracles, but even at this day cannot be believed by any reasonable person without one. Mere reason is insufficient to convince us of its veracity: And whoever is moved by *Faith* to assent to it, is conscious of a continued miracle in his own person, which subverts all the principles of his understanding, and gives him a determination to believe what is most contrary to custom and experience. (E 131)

Hume thought not merely that (a) Christian faith is not based upon reason ("mere reason is insufficient to convince us of its veracity"), but also that (b) it is inconsistent with a rational outlook (it "subverts" the understanding and gives the believer "a determination to believe what is most contrary to custom and experience"). I shall call (a) the doctrine of "insufficient reason in religion", (b) the doctrine of the "necessary contradiction of reason and religion", and shall refer to the combination of the two as "Hume's theory of irrational faith". As I understand it, this theory is entirely negative, implying the impossibility of any rational religious faith.[3]

In contrast to Hume, Immanuel Kant held that religious beliefs are fully rational. Though he argued that it is impossible for us to have genuine knowledge of religious truths, and claimed that he "found it necessary to deny *knowledge*, in order to make room for *faith*",[4] he also held that religious faith is essentially rational. He went so far as to argue that

> every belief, even one in historical matters, must indeed be rational, for the touchstone of truth is always reason. But a "rational belief" is one which is based on no other data than those contained in pure reason.

Moreover, "the concept of God and the conviction of His existence can be met with only in reason; they can come from reason alone, not from inspiration or any tidings, however great their authority".[5] Kant held not only that faith is not contradictory to reason, but also that its ultimate foundation could only be supplied by reason. Thus, he was opposed both to Hume's doctrine of insufficient reason in religion and to his doctrine of the necessary contradiction of reason and religion. Since Kant not only knew Hume's work well, but also took his ideas seriously, it is reasonable to suppose that he had a response to Hume's theory of irrational faith.

However, the relation between the views on religion of the two philosophers has received almost no attention from philosophical scholars. Although Kant's account of the importance of Hume's writings in his own philosophical development is well known,[6] his relation to Hume is usually discussed in terms of narrowly defined epistemological concerns. This is clearly a mistake. The epistemological problems at issue between the two derive their significance from broader religious or metaphysical concerns. This is clear from Kant's rejection of criticisms from Hume's British contemporaries of his analysis of causality:

> The question was not whether the concept of cause was right, useful, and even indispensable for our knowledge of nature, for this Hume had never doubted; but whether that concept could be thought by reason a priori, and consequently whether it possessed an inner truth, independent of all experience, implying a perhaps more extended use not restricted merely to objects of experience. (*Prolegomena*, pp. 6–7)

The "extended use" of causality (and other basic concepts) beyond "objects of experience" is largely a theological and religious use. When Kant chides Hume's critics further for having failed to look "very deeply into the nature of reason, so far as it is concerned with pure thinking", his point concerns precisely the data of pure reason which support rational belief. What Kant identified as Hume's problem concerning causality has a definite theological dimension; and his response to Hume must therefore be understood, at least in part, as a response to Hume's theological conclusions.

In this essay I shall investigate this theological dimension of Kant's conception of Hume's problem, to see how he thought he could answer Hume's criticism of religion. To this end, I shall first give a brief account of Hume's arguments for his theory of faith and take a look at its broader context. Secondly, I shall try to show how far Kant could agree with Hume. Thirdly, I shall sketch Kant's three different arguments for the rationality of religious faith, and finally offer some views about whether a Humean need be concerned about these arguments.

II

Hume was preoccupied with religion. Though he told Boswell a few weeks before his death that he "never had entertained any belief in Religion since he began to read Locke and Clarke",[7] his works are full of discussions concerned with what today is called the philosophy of religion. This preoccupation has sometimes been perceived as peculiar. However, given the importance of the subject in the eighteenth century and its momentous consequences for moral philosophy, it should not surprise us. Moreover, his discussions of religion come to negative, or at the very least sceptical, conclusions. While there are some scholars who believe they have discovered that Hume advocated a highly attenuated form of "theism",[8] the most straightforward reading of his texts favours an interpretation of them as arguments for agnosticism – perhaps the only fitting view for a genuine sceptic.

Hume offers essentially three different types of arguments against the reasonableness of theistic faith, namely (a) moral arguments, designed to show the evil consequences of theistic faith; (b) psychological explanations of its irrational causes; and (c) theoretical arguments, intended to undermine the "proofs" usually offered for articles of faith. Taking his writings as a whole, it is clear that the moral arguments are of central importance. He objects to religious faith mainly because he thinks it has harmful effects on morality.[9] I shall begin my discussion with these arguments.

According to Hume, religion is, by its very nature, opposed to morality. He divided popular religion into two kinds – enthusiastic and superstitious. Both lead to fanaticism, intolerance, hypocrisy, and other diseases of the commonwealth. Enthusiasm inspires "the deluded fanatic with the opinion of divine illuminations, and with a contempt for the common rules of reason, morality, and prudence". It "produces the most cruel disorder in human society" (Ess. 77). In his *Dialogues*, Hume wrote that "no morality can be forcible enough to bind the enthusiastic zealot. The sacredness of the cause sanctifies every measure which can be made use of to promote it" (D 222). However, history shows that the harmful effects of enthusiasm are only temporary. Though it promotes civil war or rebellion, in the long run it often leads to liberty and free thought (Ess. 78–9). Superstition, on the other hand, is "so virulent a poison" that it is more difficult to remedy (Ess. 578). It "renders men tame and abject, and fits them for slavery" (Ess. 78). It is superstition that Hume has primarily in mind in the final section of the second *Enquiry*, when he objects to the so-called "monkish virtues", like "celibacy, fasting, penance, mortification, self-denial, humility, silence, solitude". These practices "stupify the understanding and harden the heart, obscure the fancy and sour the temper" (E 270). Hume concludes that "religious virtues" are really moral vices.

In the *Dialogues*, Philo argues that, even if "superstition or enthusiasm should not put itself in direct opposition to morality", popular religion must "have the most pernicious consequences, and weaken extremely men's attachment to the natural motives of justice and humanity" (D 222). Religion substitutes for the rewards of morality itself those of a future life, and by doing so it diverts our attention from what should motivate us, and raises up "a new and frivolous species of merit". Moreover, the desire to please the Deity,

> not being any of the familiar motives of human conduct, acts only
> by intervals on the temper, and must be roused by continual efforts,
> in order to render the pious zealot satisfied with his own conduct,
> and make him fulfil his devotional task. Many religious exercises are
> entered into with seeming fervour, where the heart, at the time,
> feels cold and languid.

As a result, the practitioners of religion develop a "habit of dissimulation";

they perform religious practices without any religious feelings. Thus religion encourages "the deepest hypocrisy" and a form of self-deception which is opposed to moral consciousness (D 222).

Hume thinks that religious belief and practice have their real roots in irrational fears. However, as a form of self-deception, religion has a number of strategies for rationalization. In the *Dialogues*, Philo claims that while "terror is the primary principle of religion", its practitioners hold that religion is based on hope and reason.[10] In *The natural history of religion*, Hume argues that, while it would be a "noble privilege" of our reason "to infer so sublime a principle as its supreme Creator" from our experience of "the visible works of nature", an examination of the religious principles which have "prevailed in the world" will show that they are nothing but "sick men's dreams" (NHR 362). The sickness is not a mere accident of history; it is deeply rooted in "the mind, and springs from the essential and universal properties of human nature".[11] The only antidote is to be found in philosophy.[12]

Given Hume's views on the immoral consequences and irrational roots of religion, it is not surprising that much of his philosophy is designed to show the inadequacy of previous philosophical proofs of religious doctrines. Theological arguments constitute that "considerable part of metaphysics" which is "not properly a science" but "would penetrate into subjects utterly inaccessible to the understanding" (E 11). A careful study of the first *Enquiry* reveals that the principle that philosophy cannot go beyond experience is central in undermining "the foundations of abstruse philosophy, which seems to have hitherto served only as a shelter to superstition" (E 16). Because "we can go beyond the evidence of our memory and senses" only by means of the relation of cause and effect (E 26), and because this relation itself "arises entirely from experience" (E 27), all arguments that are "supposed to be the mere effects of reasoning and reflection . . . will be found to terminate, at last, in some general principle or conclusion, for which we can assign no reason but observation and experience" (E 44n.)

The constraints of experimental reasoning are clearly at work when, through the voice of Epicurus, Hume argues that any conclusions we attempt to form about the nature of the Deity are uncertain and morally irrelevant. Epicurus notes that "the experienced train of events is the great standard, by which we all regulate our conduct" (E 142). The uncertainty derives from the fact that "a particular intelligent cause" which brings about order in the universe lies "entirely beyond the reach of human experience". And because we can infer nothing about the cause but what we experience in the effects, there is no way that we can draw "new principles of conduct" from our speculations about the Deity. In this dialogue Epicurus's respondent agrees and endorses the principle that philosophy "will never carry us beyond the usual course of nature" (E 146). It is clear that this principle is shared by Hume himself, who condemns as "sophistry and illusion" everything that is neither abstract reasoning about the relations of ideas nor experimental reasoning about fact and existence (E 165). He thinks its adoption would liberate us from "religious fears and prejudices" (E 11), and help establish an accurate philosophy which would give us a more humane outlook on life.

It must be acknowledged that, in spite of his arguments against the rationality of theistic belief, Hume differentiated "true religion" from "vulgar superstitions" and allowed for a more positive evaluation of the former.[13] However, this "true religion" does not amount to much. Its only content seems to be a belief in "God as being the supreme *intelligent*, but not personal, source of order in the universe".[14] Because the universe exhibits regularity and some form of order, we are allowed to assume some quasi-intelligent source of this order. But this does not justify any formal institutions and cannot possibly give rise to religious duties. "Assent of the Understanding to the Proposition *that God exists*" seems to be all that can be asked for (NHL 13). In the *Dialogues*, Cleanthes argues that the role of true religion is "to regulate the heart of men, humanize their conduct, infuse the spirit of temperance, order, and obedience".[15] However, it is very doubtful that Hume really thought it had this result. Though he has Philo admit that Cleanthes' true religion has none of the common "pernicious consequences", the conclusion of the *Natural history* seems to be a more genuine expression of his own view:

> The whole is a riddle, an ænigma, an inexplicable mystery. Doubt, uncertainty, suspence of judgment appear the only result of our most accurate scrutiny, concerning this subject. But such is the frailty of human reason, and such the irresistible contagion of opinion, that even this deliberate doubt could scarcely be upheld; did we not enlarge our view, and opposing one species of superstition to another, set them a quarrelling; while we ourselves, during their fury and contention, happily make our escape into the calm, though obscure, regions of philosophy. (NHR 363)

Reason not only gives us no basis to accept any religious belief; it also allows us to escape from its domain.

III

Kant and Hume clearly agreed on many issues concerning religion. Like Hume, Kant resisted any attempt to found morality on religion.[16] Moreover, like Hume, he was opposed to organized religion with its internal and external duties, arguing that these were, for the most part, "artificial self-deceptions" (p. 188). Thus prayer "as an *inner formal* service of God and hence as a means of grace" was for him "a superstitious illusion" (pp. 182–3). Neither did he approve of church-going, claiming that devout "attestations of awe involve the danger of producing nothing but hypocritical veneration" (p. 186). And communion as a means of grace was, he said, "a religious illusion" (p. 188). I believe Hume would have liked a man, who, as the chancellor of his university, led the procession at commencement right up to the portals of the church and then made a sharp turn to go home and let the others enter without him. He claimed that he would not bend his knees for anybody, and that God would not ask him to do so.[17]

Kant also accepted one of the most important principles underlying Hume's philosophy of religion, the principle that we cannot have any knowledge beyond that of experience. In the *Prolegomena* he formulated "Hume's principle" as the principle that we should "not carry the use of reason dogmatically beyond the field of all possible experience" (p. 108). This principle is not far from what, a few pages later, he identifies as the "original proposition", which summarizes the whole of the *Critique of pure reason*: "reason by all its a priori principles never teaches us anything more than objects of possible experience, and even of these nothing more than can be known in experience" (p. 110). I have argued elsewhere that the Transcendental Analytic – especially the section called the Transcendental Deduction – is to a large extent a defence of Hume's principle.[18] The two philosophers are in substantial agreement in limiting human knowledge to experience.

It is true that, since Kant held that the intellect played a far more important role in experience than did Hume, he had to reformulate "Hume's principle" and defend it in a new way. In the *Critique of pure reason*, he argued that, even though we must assume a priori principles in order to account for ordinary experience and science, we cannot use these principles to assert anything that would go beyond experience. He argued that, as Hume had not paid enough attention to the a priori component in human knowledge, he had only "imagined" that he had "sufficiently disposed of" the pretensions of transcendent metaphysics (A760/B788). While Hume had set such subjects "outside the horizon of human reason", he had failed to define this horizon, because he was unable to "prescribe determinate limits to the activities whereby the understanding and pure reason extend themselves a priori" (A767/B795). According to Kant, Hume "merely *restricts* the understanding without defining its *limits*, and while creating a general mistrust fails to supply any determinate knowledge of the ignorance which for us is unavoidable". Hume's attempt to show our unavoidable ignorance by appeal to contingent facts is insufficient. According to Kant, our ignorance must be shown to be based on "principles which can constrain to a necessary renunciation of all right to dogmatic assertions". This is what differentiates the critical philosophy from the Humean sceptical method.

However, the result for theology appears the same. Kant argues not only that we cannot know anything beyond experience, but that we cannot even give empirical meaning to propositions in this realm.[19] In the Transcendental Dialectic, he argues that, for theoretical reason, the name 'God' does not refer us to anything that can be experienced in the world. It is a "mere idea" (A592/B620), that does not provide us with any clue "as to the *possibility* of any existence beyond that which is known in and through experience" (A602/B630). God "is in no wise given as a thinkable *object*" (A614/B642). God cannot even be thought as an actual object. The pure concept of the understanding in itself "has no significance" (*Prolegomena*, p. 103). Experience, for Kant, implies a relation to an object. However, for the ideas of reason no "corresponding intuition can be given and consequently no objective reality for them can be found in a theoretical way".[20] According to Kant, we cannot know anything about God; nor, it would appear, can we sensibly talk about God in theoretical contexts. Thus he appears to leave theology and faith in just as precarious a state as Hume.

IV

However, this was not Kant's final point of view. Contrary to Hume, he believed that theology is still possible, and that religion can not only coexist with a rational outlook but is actually required by it. He made three attempts to argue against Hume's theory of irrational faith. The first is to be found in his theoretical philosophy, especially the later parts of the *Critique of pure reason* and the *Prolegomena*. The second is made in the context of his practical philosophy, namely within the so-called Dialectic of Pure Practical Reason. The third argument is a pragmatic or political argument which Kant puts forward in one of his more popular essays.

The first argument takes its point of departure from Hume's criticisms of the Design argument in the *Dialogues*:

> Hume's objections to deism are weak, and affect only the proofs and not the deistic assertion itself. But as regards theism, which depends on a stricter determination of the concept of the Supreme Being, which in deism is merely transcendent, they are very strong and, as this concept is formed, in certain (in fact in all common) cases irrefutable. (*Prolegomena*, p. 104)

Kant did not think that Hume had undermined deism, which only represents God as "a thing containing all reality, without being able to determine any one reality in it". For this concept is vague, representing divine attributes as entirely different from human ones.[21] However, Kant believed that Hume had shown serious problems with theism. Hume thought that anthropomorphism is "inseparable from theism" and that this makes it "contradictory in itself" (p. 105). Kant agrees that, "if this anthropomorphism were really unavoidable", we would be left with a self-contradictory conception of the Supreme Being. However, he also believes that he can show that theism does not depend upon "dogmatic anthropomorphism". He argues that the difficulties for theism that Hume had presented could be removed, "by combining with Hume's principle, 'not to carry the use of reason dogmatically beyond the field of all possible experience,' this other principle which he quite overlooked, 'not to consider the field of experience as one which bounds itself in the eyes of our reason'" (*Prolegomena*, p. 108).

What Hume overlooked, according to Kant, is what may be called the "boundary principle", a principle which tells us not to expect too much from experience. Experience has boundaries, but those boundaries cannot be found within experience itself. This talk of boundaries is not easily understood. Nevertheless, it is very important because it goes to the heart of Kant's philosophy, having to do with the distinction between appearances and things in themselves. This much is clear: for him, boundaries (*Grenzen*) are different from limits (*Schranken*). He writes that "bounds (in extended beings) always presuppose a space existing outside a certain definite place and enclosing it; limits do not require this, but are mere negations which affect a quantity in so far as it is not absolutely complete" (p. 101). Kant believed that mathematics and natural philosophy allow of limits, but not of boundaries. While we may admit that there are things which are inaccessible to scientific study, this has no consequence for scientific enquiry *per se*. For we can never arrive at them as barriers to further enquiry. We can never say that scientific knowledge is complete, or that nothing new can be learned about nature. Science presupposes the principle of uniformity of nature and so allows of continuous progress. If a question can be properly formulated in science, it can in principle be answered. This is not so for metaphysics. Kant believes that metaphysics necessarily leads us towards boundaries. If we push our enquiries far enough, we shall arrive at questions which can – indeed must – be asked, but which cannot be answered (*Critique of pure reason*, Avii). Hume's "empiricism" may be a good strategy for science (at least, up to a point); but it is bad for metaphysics.

While Hume's principle simply tells us to refrain from doing something, the boundary principle commands us also to do something. It tells us to look beyond possible experience, so as to modify or restrict Hume's principle in those cases that have to do with boundaries of experience. We must admit that appearances do not exhaust all of reality. Appearances presuppose something which appears, which is "distinct from them (and totally heterogeneous)", namely a thing in itself (*Prolegomena,* p. 103). While we cannot *know* what is beyond experience, we can still *think* it. In fact, Kant claims that we must think such things, and that reason itself forces us to do so.

This leads to the crux of his first argument against Hume's theory of faith. Kant claims that, if we wish to understand the world as an ordered whole that can be rationally explained in its entirety, we must assume the existence of God as a designer:

> Without assuming an intelligent author, no comprehensible ground for the design and order can be stated without falling into patent absurdities. Although we cannot prove the impossibility of such design without an original intelligent author (for then we would have sufficient objective grounds for this assertion and would not need to appeal to subjective grounds), there yet remains, in spite of this lack of insight, a sufficient subjective ground for assuming such an author.[22]

Kant calls this "subjective ground" also a "need of reason". It does not require that we determine through an analogy with experience of our own intelligence what the Supreme Being is like. We merely postulate a rational cause of the order in the world, but recognize that we are completely unable to determine the nature of the cause as it is in itself. Thus our conception of this causality through reason is a positive concept which avoids Hume's charge of anthropomorphism (*Prolegomena,* p. 109). We must restrict Hume's principle which limits all our enquiries to experience, or rather, allow certain exceptions to it. Kant believes that these exceptions are not very numerous, being limited to certain definite needs of reason. The existence of God as a designer is one such need.

If his argument has succeeded, Kant will have proved both that reason is a sufficient basis for belief in the existence of God, and that there is no contradiction between reason and this belief. Reason, according to Kant, requires such a belief. We must believe in God, if we want to give a complete account of the world. However, as Kant realizes only too well, this so-called "need of reason" is "only conditional"; that is, "we must assume the existence of God when we wish to judge concerning the first causes of all contingent things, particularly in the organization of ends actually present in the world".[23] If someone, Hume for instance, were to reject such wishes as misguided, such a "need of reason" would also have to be rejected. Belief in the existence of God would amount to no more than wishful thinking. Accordingly, it would not be rational to believe in God.

However, this is not all Kant has to say on the subject. Nor does he believe that it is his most important argument. There is, he thinks, another need of reason, namely that of practical reason. And "here the need is unconditional", or so he believes he can show by means of an argument. This argument is to be found in the Dialectic of Pure Practical Reason of the second *Critique.*[24] There he argues that we must "postulate" or assume necessarily the existence of God, because of a *practical* need of reason. The argument proceeds as follows:

1. We are commanded by the moral law to work towards the highest good.
2. What is commanded as a duty must be possible.
3. The highest good is possible only under the condition that happiness and moral worth are proportional to each other.
4. Happiness for rational beings presupposes that nature is in harmony with the will of these rational beings.
5. There is not the slightest connexion between our rational will and nature.
6. Therefore, we must assume "a cause of the whole of nature, itself distinct from nature, which contains the ground of the exact coincidence of happiness with morality" (p. 228).
7. Such a cause must be the creator of the world, who acts through understanding and will.

This argument has puzzled many readers of the second *Critique*. Many have viewed it as an "objective" proof, or a demonstration of the existence of God. However, today it is commonly seen as a piece of practical thinking which expresses an existential predicament. It has been said that Kant's so-called proof "cannot even begin until some individual finds himself in the situation described".[25] On this view, Kant was only rationalizing something that is essentially non-rational.

I believe both of these approaches are wrong. Kant is attempting to defend a rational faith. He is arguing that we must bound Hume's principle because of definite and necessary needs of *practical* reason. The argument has to do with what we can reasonably or responsibly believe, not with what can be demonstrated.[26] It is meant to establish that theism is not nonsense, but rather itself gives sense to our moral discourse. Far from involving us in contradictions, as Hume thought, theism shows us how the needs of our practical reason can be satisfied.

If Kant's argument is successful, then morality not only allows us to believe, but actually leads us to belief. According to Kant, reason has a right "to an extension in its practical use which is not possible to it in its speculative use" (*Critique of practical reason*, p. 160). While this right does not afford us knowledge, it allows us to believe in God and maintain a rational outlook. "Morality thus leads ineluctably to religion."[27] Practical reason justifies the presupposition of the existence of God

> not merely as an allowable hypothesis but as a practical postulate. Granted that the pure moral law inexorably binds every man as a command (not as a rule of prudence), the righteous man may say: I will that there be a God . . . I stand by this and will not give up this belief, for this is the only case where my interest inevitably determines my judgment because I will not yield anything of this interest; I do so without any attention to sophistries, however little I may be able

to answer them or oppose them with others more plausible. (*Critique of practical reason*, p. 245)

Kant rejects Hume's theory of irrational faith, because he holds that reason and faith actually require each other. It is true that Kant agrees with Hume that reason alone cannot make us believe. But it can show us that we have the *right* to employ certain concepts in a certain way. Kant writes of a "faith of pure practical reason" (p. 247). While he does not think that this faith can be commanded, he thinks that reason guides us towards a decision to believe:

> As a voluntary decision of our judgment to assume [the existence of God] and to make it the foundation of further employment of reason, conducing to the moral (commanded) purpose and agreeing moreover with the theoretical need of reason, it is itself not commanded. It rather springs from the moral disposition itself. It can therefore often waver even in the well disposed but can never fall into unbelief. (*Critique of practical reason*, p. 247)

Kant believes that the postulates of pure practical reason follow inevitably. Their "possibility cannot be fathomed by human understanding, though no sophistry will ever wrest from the conviction of even the most ordinary man an admission that they are not true" (p. 236).

This last claim seems false. This may have been less apparent in the eighteenth century than it is now. But Kant himself knew about non-believers. In fact, in his popular essay 'What is orientation in thinking?', he himself addresses philosophers who have rejected the moral basis of religious belief. They have pursued what he calls the "maxim of the independence of reason from its own need", the "renunciation of rational belief", or "rational disbelief" (pp. 304–5). Kant thinks that this results in

> an unfortunate state of the human mind, which first takes from the moral laws all their effect on the heart as incentives, and then destroys all their authority, occasioning a turn of mind called "free-thinking," i.e., the principle of not acknowledging any duty.

He believes that this "free-thinking" will ultimately lead to oppression, because it will encourage those who wish to suppress all disorder "in civil affairs". Because they usually consider "the handiest but most energetic means" as the best, they will "completely destroy the freedom to think and subject it, like other pursuits, to the government. And so freedom in thought finally destroys itself when it wishes to proceed independently of the laws of reason." Accordingly, he appeals to the "friends of the human race and of that which is holiest to it", asking them to

> assume what appears most believable to you after careful and honest testing, whether it be facts or principles of reason; but do not wrest from reason that which makes it the highest good on earth, i.e. the

> prerogative of being the ultimate touchstone of truth. Otherwise you
> will become unworthy of this freedom and certainly lose it.

It is possible that this political argument was addressed to Hume. Kant
appears to be telling him that, even if he cannot accept religious belief on
theoretical grounds, he should accept it as necessary in the fight for
freedom. He is arguing that it is politically prudent to retain religious
belief.

In this context, it is interesting to note that, in his *Critique of pure
reason*, Kant does not limit himself to the discussion of Hume's philosophical views, but finds it necessary to defend his "moral character"
(A746/B774). Kant insists that Hume is "blameless", even though he
tried

> to undermine, through far-fetched subtleties so elaborately thought
> out, the conviction which is so comforting and beneficial for mankind,
> that their reason has sufficient insight for the assertion and for the
> determinate conception of a supreme being. (A745/B773)

We should not conclude that Kant is stepping outside the bounds of
philosophy in this passage, though he leaves strict logical argumentation
behind. His defence of rational faith must be understood historically.
Indeed, Kant goes out of his way to emphasize the historical character of
reason. Commentators, especially in the English-speaking world, commonly forget that Kant made a sharp distinction between the "understanding" on the one hand, and "reason" on the other. This distinction,
which underlies the large division of the first *Critique* into the Transcendental Analytic and Transcendental Dialectic, is fundamental; for Kant
thinks that, while the understanding allows of "a logic of truth" (A62/B87),
reason does not. While the Analytic is about that "massive central core of
human thinking which has no history",[28] the Dialectic is about something
that has a definite history. The final chapter of the *Critique* is entitled
'The history of pure reason'. If we take this characterization of reason as
"historical" seriously, we must also recognize that it is subject to change
and can develop in different ways. Though its development may proceed
in accordance with certain principles, it would be difficult to predict its
actual course in history. Just like any other human ability, it may improve
when it is properly tended, or it may deteriorate when it is neglected. In
fact, according to Kant, reason is one of the most fragile of human
abilities. A rational outlook is not easily won, and can be easily lost.

If we want to see Kant's critical enterprise as he saw it, we must
understand it first and foremost as a stage in this so-called "history of
pure reason". The *Critique of pure reason*, no less than the other two
Critiques, is intended to contribute to the further development of the
rational outlook of humanity. Kant's criticism of Hume's philosophy
must be understood primarily in this context. It is not narrowly focused

on the problem of causality; it is concerned with the wider problem of rational faith. Kant did not merely oppose Hume with theoretical arguments designed to prove him wrong once and for all. Rather, he appealed to "needs of reason" that have a definite historical background and hence may change. Though Kant believed that these needs result from a practical reason which does not change, he tried to show that failure to satisfy them will undermine rationality itself. Rational faith is "the foundation of further employment of reason" (*Critique of practical reason*, p. 247). Moreover, "the primacy of the pure practical reason in its association with speculative reason" also has consequences for his theoretical arguments (p. 223). They cannot be as strong as they are often made out to be. They must ultimately be reduced to what Kant calls "the modest language of a rational belief."[29]

V

I doubt that Kant's arguments would have been sufficient to require Hume to modify his position on religious faith. There is no reason to think that Hume would have found major problems with Kant's first argument, showing that our need for unity "naturally" leads us to assume that there is an intelligent source of the universe. After all, Hume himself wrote at the beginning of *The natural history of religion* that the "whole frame of nature bespeaks an intelligent author; and no rational enquirer can, after serious reflection, suspend his belief a moment with regard to the primary principles of genuine Theism and Religion" (NHR 309). Though Hume found it difficult to accept that this belief is historically founded on rational considerations, he might still have accepted the belief itself.

However, Hume would certainly not have accepted Kant's more substantive claims about God. Kant's moral argument for the existence of God reveals a radical difference between the Kantian and the Humean view which is ultimately founded on their different conceptions of reason. Whereas Hume never failed to draw attention to his belief that reason ultimately is "a species of instinct or mechanical power" (E 108), and was not given to a very exalted view of human nature, Kant adamantly insisted that reason is what makes us special and gives us a worth higher than anything else in this world. Whereas Hume based his view of morals on a "pleasing sentiment of approbation" (E 289), Kant regarded such a sentiment as disguised self-love. For him, only pure autonomous reason can reveal who we really are or, perhaps better, who we should aspire to be. For Hume, this ideal would have appeared empty, and Kant would have appeared to him as one of those who "exalt our species to the skies, and represent man as a kind of human demigod, who derives his origin from heaven, and retains evident marks of his lineage and descent" (Ess.

80). He rejected this angelic conception of human nature. But if Kant's emphasis on an autonomous reason would have struck Hume as too exalted, he would have rejected Kant's political argument as requiring too much philosophical cunning. Kant seems to have believed that, without the incentives of pure and rational principles, we would fall prey to egoism, and that we could be disinterested only in so far as we are rational. Our empirical or non-rational nature was for him essentially characterized by self-interest. It could thus not lead to anything of moral worth. But such a philosophy of pure self-interest was no more than a satire for Hume (E 302). Neither Kant's "enthusiastic" rationalism, nor his pessimistic empirical psychology, is "a true delineation or description of human nature".[30]

NOTES

1. There is a historical case to be made that Hume actually had an influence on this Kierkegaardian conception, at least indirectly. For it can be shown that his discussions of belief in the *Treatise* and *Enquiry* deeply influenced Hamann and Friedrich Heinrich Jacobi in their conception of faith. Jacobi especially liked to talk of a *salto mortale* into faith; and Kierkegaard knew both Hamann and Jacobi. For more on Hume and Hamann, see Philip Merlan, 'From Hume to Hamann', *Personalist* 32 (1951), 11–18; 'Hamann et les dialogues de Hume,' *Revue de métaphysique* 59 (1954), 285–9; 'Kant, Hamann–Jacobi and Schelling on Hume,' *Rivista critica di storia di filosofia* 22 (1967), 343–51.

   This interpretation would also serve to make Hume a sceptic in the way in which Bayle and others before him were sceptics. For an exploration of these issues see especially the works of Richard Popkin and Terence Penelhum. Seen in this context, it is not surprising that this passage has given rise to speculations about Hume's own religious beliefs.

2. For an incisive caricature of the "Barthian Protestant", see A. N. Prior, 'Can religion be discussed?', in *New essays in philosophical theology*, ed. A. G. N. Flew and A. C. MacIntyre (London 1955), 1–11. The character whom Prior calls the "Modernist Protestant", who is inspired by such theologians as Paul Tillich and Rudolf Bultmann, would seem to have to agree to Hume's theory of faith.

3. This does not mean that it cannot be explained in some way. Hume himself gives psychological (or naturalistic) and historical explanations of religion. However, these do not amount to justifications. They lead to further indictments, as we shall see. I should add that Hume's arguments relate to a religion that involves belief in a personal Deity. I shall not consider what he might have to say about non-theistic religions such as Buddhism and Confucianism.

4. Immanuel Kant, *Critique of pure reason*, tr. N. Kemp Smith (London 1933), Bxxx.

5. Kant, 'What is orientation in thinking?', in *Critique of practical reason and other writings in moral philosophy*, tr. L. W. Beck (Chicago 1949), pp. 293–305, esp. 300–301.

6. Kant, *Prolegomena to any future metaphysics*, tr. L. W. Beck (Indianapolis 1950), pp. 5–9, esp. pp. 8–9.

7. E. C. Mossner, *Life of David Hume*, 2nd edn (Oxford 1980), p. 597. J. Noxon suggests that "Hume spent more of his pages on the topic of religion than on any other" ('Hume's concern with religion', in *Hume's many-sided genius*, ed. K. R. Merrill and R. S. Shahan (Norman, OK 1976), p. 59).

8. See, for instance, G. J. Nathan, 'The existence and nature of God in Hume's theism', in *Hume: A re-evaluation*, ed. D. W. Livingston and J. T. King (New York 1976), 127–49. Terence Penelhum's subtle analysis of this issue also sees Hume's agnosticism tempered by the realization that sceptical arguments are psychologically impotent. See Penelhum's *Hume* (London 1975); 'Hume's skepticism and the *Dialogues*' in *McGill Hume studies*, ed. D. F. Norton and others (San Diego, CA 1979), 253–78; and *God and skepticism* (Dordrecht 1983). It appears to me that all such arguments wrongly presuppose that Philo always speaks for Hume in the *Dialogues*. For criticism of these views, see Noxon, 'Hume's concern with religion', and K. E. Yandell, 'Hume on religious belief', in *Hume: A re-evaluation*, 109–25. See also J. C. A. Gaskin, *Hume's philosophy of religion*, 2nd edn (London 1988), pp. 126ff.

9. My discussion is restricted to Hume's account of the effects of modern religion. I shall say nothing about pre-Christian beliefs.

10. D 225. See also 'Of superstition and enthusiasm', Ess. 73f.: "Weakness, fear, melancholy, together with ignorance, are, therefore, the true sources of SUPERSTITION."

11. NHR 361. For a dialectical interpretation of the "essential and universal properties of human nature", see M. Kuehn, 'Hume's antinomies', *Hume studies* 9 (1983), 25–45.

12. Hume, 'Of suicide', Ess. 577f.: "One considerable advantage, that arises from philosophy, consists in the sovereign antidote, which it affords to superstition and false religion. All other remedies against that pestilent distemper are vain, or, at least, uncertain." Cf. E 12.

13. D 219. See also NHR 330–31, and Mossner, pp. 306–7; 'Of suicide', Ess. 577ff., and 'Of superstition and enthusiasm', Ess., p. 77, where superstition and enthusiasm are characterized as "the corruptions of true religion". For a more positive evaluation of Hume's conception of "true religion", see D. W. Livingston, *Hume's philosophy of common life* (Chicago 1984), pp. 173–86; *id.*, 'Hume's conception of true religion', in A. G. N. Flew and others, *Hume's philosophy of religion* (Winston-Salem, NC 1986), 33–73.

14. The formulation is taken from Nathan, p. 148. See also Gaskin, pp. 219–29.

15. D 220. This is very similar to what Hume said in an unpublished preface to volume II of the *History* (Mossner, pp. 306–7).

16. Kant wrote that "for its own sake morality does not need religion at all" (*Religion within the limits of reason alone*, tr. T. M. Greene and H. H. Hudson (New York 1960), p. 3).

17. See J. H. Stuckenberg, *Life of Immanuel Kant* (London 1882), p. 352.

18. See M. Kuehn, 'Kant's transcendental deduction: A limited defense of "Hume's principle"', in *New essays on Kant*, ed. B. den Ouden (Bern 1987), 47–72.

19. W. H. Walsh says that "if a term is to be meaningful, according to the Kantian account, it must be possible to point to something in experience that corresponds to it, or at the very least to find some counterpart for it in experience, in the way in which we can find experiential counterparts for the pure categories in their schemata" ('Kant's moral theology', *Proceedings of the British Academy* 49 (1963), p. 264). What Walsh calls a "meaningful term" is

called by Kant a "concept that possesses objective reality", or one that has "real possibility" as opposed to merely logical possibility. And objective reality or real possibility always presupposes that a "corresponding intuition can be found", at least in principle. If it is impossible, in principle, to find a corresponding intuition, then the term is void and without meaning for Kant. Today, this is sometimes referred to as "Kant's principle of significance", and it is understood as a part of Kant's theory of meaning. Though it may be somewhat anachronistic to attribute to Kant a theory of meaning in the modern sense, I believe Walsh is essentially correct.

20. *Critique of practical reason*, p. 236.
21. If we accept the view of recent commentators who claim that Hume held a form of "attenuated theism", Kant would be wrong in thinking that Hume sought to undermine deism. For this view of Hume as an attenuated theist, see the work of Yandell and Gaskin, cited above.
22. 'Orientation', p. 298. He makes the same point, though not as clearly, in his *Prolegomena*, p. 110.
23. 'Orientation', p. 298.
24. *Critique of practical reason*, pp. 227–8. Kant hints at this argument in the *Prolegomena* as well: see pp. 109–10.
25. For such a view, see especially A. W. Wood, *Kant's moral religion* (Ithaca, NY 1970), and Walsh. For a critique of this view, see M. Kuehn, 'Kant's transcendental deduction of God's existence as a postulate of pure practical reason', *Kant-Studien* 76 (1985), 152–69.
26. *Critique of practical reason*, p. 234. Kant is quick to point out that, while these postulates "do not extend speculative knowledge, they give objective reality to the ideas of speculative reason in general (by means of their relation to the practical sphere), and they justify it in holding to concepts the possibility of which it could not otherwise even venture to affirm".
27. *Religion within the limits of reason alone*, p. 5.
28. See P. F. Strawson's *Individuals* (London 1964), pp. 10, 247.
29. *Prolegomena*, p. 25. This appears to bring Kant closer to Hume's Philo, who declares in the *Dialogues* that "reasonable men may be allowed to differ, where no one can be positive" (D 128).
30. Kant's revolutionary zeal would probably have looked too "enthusiastic" to the more conservative Hume. Though he might have admitted that it might lead to something good in the long run, he would have remained sceptical – or so it seems to me.

Index

Abbott, W. R., 199n.
Abercrombie, George, 19n.
Aberdeen
  Burgh of, 2; Earl of, *see* Gordon, William;
    universities at, *see* King's College; Mar-
    ischal College
ability, natural, 25, 36
  vs moral virtue, 60, 64, 72, 79n., 161
Addison, Joseph, 204
Advocates
  Faculty of, 5, 14, 19n.; Library, 14
agnosticism, 241, 254n.
Ahl, F. M., 57n.
Alembert, Jean le Rond d', 136n.
Alexander of Abonuteichos, 195n.
ambition, 31, 43, 44, 46, 110, 111, 231–3,
    235, 236
analogy, 133, 162, 181, 222n., 248
analysis, method of, 126–7
anatomy, 128, 131
  of the mind, 35, 38, 39, 61, 120, 123,
    126–7, 132, 134, 135n., 136n., 213–14
ancients, 26, 33, 161, 202–3, 213, 214
Anderson, William, 18n., 21n.
anger, 111
animal nature, compared with human, 28,
    122, 134, 135n., 138n.
animal spirits, 26, 105, 128–30, 131, 138n.,
    235n.
Annandale, Marquis of, *see* Johnstone,
    George
Annet, Peter, 200n.
anthropomorphism, 246, 248
antiquaries, 124, 174
Appendix (*Treatise*), 51–3
approbation, moral, 27, 30, 31, 35–6, 39,
    42, 57n., 59, 60, 64–73, 77–8n., 79n.,
    98, 114–16, 215, 232
  causes of, 34, 60, 62, 65, 66, 69–73, 76,
    79n., 80n., 96, 114, 116, 215
Aquinas, Thomas, *see* Thomas Aquinas
Arbuckle, James, 56n.

Arbuthnot, Alexander, 20n., 21n.
Arbuthnot, John, 5th Viscount, 1
Arcemboldi, Bishop of Genoa, 228
Árdal, P. S., 109, 118n.
Argathelians, 1–14, 16, 17n., 18–19n., 21n.
Argyll, Dukes of, *see* Campbell, Archibald;
    Campbell, John
Aristotle, 88, 106, 117n., 145, 147, 150
Arnauld, Antoine, 141
  on faith, 177; on judgement, 197–8n.; on
    knowledge, 177; on miracles, 178–9,
    183, 192; on probability, 176–9, 180,
    181, 193
Arnot, Hugo, 19n.
art classique, 207
assent, 74, 128, 189
  Locke on, 150–51, 158n., 180–82; Wilkins
    on, 175–6; *see also* belief
association of ideas, *see* idea(s), association
    of
atheism, atheists, 4, 10, 14, 37, 198n., 208,
    217, 223n.
attraction, 224–5
attributes
  moral, 160–62, 165–6, 168, 169n., 249;
    natural, 160–63, 165–6, 169n.; *see also*
    virtue(s)
Augustine, Bishop of Hippo, 56n., 178–9,
    197n., 237, 237–8n.
Augustinianism, 27, 56n.
authority, and belief, 175, 177, 181, 184,
    185, 197–8n.
avarice, 28, 31, 46, 113

Bacon, Francis, Baron Verulam, xiv, 8,
    120–21, 122, 123–4, 126, 127, 134,
    135n., 137n., 198n.
Baier, A. C., 80n., 109, 118n.
Baillies of Jariswood, 19n.
Balfour, James, Jnr, of Pilrig, 9, 25, 84
banks, 4, 10, 18n.
Barfoot, M., 56n., 135n., 139n.

Barthians, 239, 253n.
Bayle, Pierre, xvi, 27–9, 30, 40, 53, 54n., 55n., 56n., 163, 169n., 198n., 230, 237, 237n., 238n.
Baynes, T. S., 197n.
Beauchamp, T. L., 144–5, 157n.
Beccaria, Cesare, 76n.
Becket, Thomas à, xvi, 231–3, 236
belief, 142, 149, 152–4, 171, 172, 175, 177, 180–81, 198n.
  Hume's theory of, 31–2, 46, 52–3, 128, 161, 190, 230; proportionality of, 175–6, 179, 180, 187, 189–91; rational, 172, 240, 248–52; religious, 172, 183, 219, 222n., 224, 226–7, 229, 230–34, 236, 239–41, 243, 244, 248–9, 251–2, 253n., 254n.; *see also* assent; evidence, weight of; faith
benevolence, 34–5, 36, 40, 41, 63–4, 67, 77n., 78n., 92, 107–8, 111, 114, 121, 160, 162, 165, 166, 168, 189
  Butler on, 80n., 106–8, 118n.; divine, 37; Hume vs Hutcheson on, 34–7, 40–42, 47–51, 63–4, 67, 77, 78n., 80n., 114; and justice, 47–51; *see also* desire(s); passion(s)
Bentham, Jeremy, xiii, 58–61, 64, 67, 72, 73–6, 76n., 77–8n., 82n.
  on extrinsic grounds, 58, 74; Hume's influence on, 60; on moral despotism, 74–5
Berkeley, George, 77n., 126, 131, 137n., 138n., 204–6, 220n., 221n.
Bernard, C. J., xv–xvi, 196n., 200n.
Bernier, François, 33, 55n.
Bible, 89, 171, 172–3, 176, 182, 184, 188, 197n.
bills of mortality, 161, 167, 168n.
Blair, Hugh, 186, 191–3, 200n.
Bogle, George, of Daldowie, 18n.
Bolam, C. G., 196n.
Bossuet, Jacques-Bénigne, 197n.
Boswell, James, 241
"boundary principle", 247
Bourgogne, Duc de, 208
Boyle, Robert, 32, 56n., 120, 198n.
Boyle Lectures, 33, 199n.
Bricke, S., 22n.
Briggs, William, 138n.
Brisbane, Thomas, MD, 18n.
Brown, John, 77n.
Browne, John, 221n.
Browne, Peter, 137n.
Bryson, G., 138n.
Buckle, S., 83, 102n., 103n.
Buffon, Comte de, *see* Leclerc, Georges Louis

Buickerood, J. G., 135n.
Bultmann, R., 253n.
Burke, Edmund, 192
Burnett, James, Lord Monboddo, 124
Burns, R. M., 117n., 195n., 196n.
Bute, Earl of, *see* Stuart, John
Butler, Joseph, xiv, 80n., 105–10, 111, 112, 114, 115, 116, 117, 117n., 118n., 120, 121–2, 124, 126, 127, 134, 135n., 136n., 137n., 168n., 200n.
  on habits, 105, 106–8, 115; on moral character, 106–8, 116

Caesar, Julius, 53
calm passion, *see* passion(s), calm
Calvin, Jean, xvi, 237, 237–8n.
Calvinism, 174, 177
"Cambuslang wark", 18n.
Campbell, Archibald, 1st Earl of Ilay and 3rd Duke of Argyll, 1–12, 14–17, 17–18n., 19n., 20n., 21n., 22n.
Campbell, Archibald, of Succoth, 17n.
Campbell, John, 2nd Duke of Argyll, 2, 4, 6, 7, 9, 10, 18n.
Campbell, John, 4th Duke of Argyll, 16
Campbell, Principal Neil, 15, 17n., 18n., 21n.
canon, 119–20, 122, 127, 130, 133–4
Capaldi, N., 135n.
Carre, George, of Nisbet, 6
Carrive, P., 221n.
Cartesianism, xiv, 87, 158n., 171, 177, 197n.
  see also Descartes, René
Cato, 49, 53, 57n.
causation, causality
  belief in, 23; evidence for, 243; as philosophical relation, 142–3; as principle of association, 30, 46, 190, 224–5; and probability, 32, 105, 116, 140, 195, 241, 252; and property, 32, 56n.; and theology, 241, 243, 249, 252; *see also* probabilistic reasoning
cause(s), 41, 44, 172, 180, 182, 190, 194, 195, 198n., 200n., 214, 215, 217, 224, 225, 241
  discovery of, 43; efficient, 127–32; final, 35, 77, 163, 223n.; natural, 163; occasional, 129, 138n.; of the universe, 33, 161, 163, 166–8, 243, 248–9
certainty, 86, 128, 142, 147–9, 167, 172, 175, 179, 180, 184, 188 (*see also* demonstration)
  moral, 171, 173, 176, 178, 179, 184
Chambers, Ephraim, 138n.
Chandler, Samuel, 200n.
character, 73, 109, 121, 129, 178–9, 197n., 205, 210, 231–4

moral, xiv, 24, 26, 34–6, 40–42, 44–7,
52, 59, 60, 64, 65, 70, 73, 75–6, 78–9n.,
80n., 81n., 98, 105–18, 161, 196n.; and
moral approval, 77–8n., 116; in philo-
sophical dialogue, 204–11, 213, 220n.,
222n.; religious, xvi, 228–37
Charles, Dauphin, 233–4
Checkland, S. G., 18n.
Chillingworth, William, 172
Christianity, *see* religion, Christian
Chrysostom, 197n.
Cicero, 20n., 26–9, 33, 36, 38, 49, 55n.,
77n., 204, 206–7, 220n., 221n., 222n.,
238n.
Clarke, Samuel, 24, 40–42, 74, 77n., 78n.,
169n., 199n., 241
"Cleanthes", 162, 163, 206, 217–18, 222n.,
244
Cleghorn, William, 8–10, 13, 14, 20n.
Clephane, John, MD, 15
Clow, James, 15–16
Coleman, D., 80n.
Colliber, Samuel, 169n.
Collingwood, R. G., 196n.
concomitant ideas, *see* idea(s), concomitant
conjunction, constant, 32, 107, 112, 116,
143, 148, 153–4, 180, 189–90, 199
conscience, 78n., 117, 208
consent, 43, 89–93, 95
consequence(s), unintended, 95–7, 99
contiguity, 30, 46, 143–4, 190, 224, 230
contract(s), 46, 48–9, 50–51, 91, 92
convention(s), 27–32, 28–9, 34, 43–4, 46,
49–50, 51, 64, 91–3, 95–6, 102, 103n.,
114, 228
   and repeated experience, 113
Conway, Francis Seymour, 1st Earl of Hertford, 16
Conway, Gen. Henry Seymour, 16
Coombe, William, 220n.
Cooper, Anthony Ashley, 3rd Earl of
Shaftesbury, xv, 8, 120, 135n., 202–5,
207–12, 213, 214, 218, 219–20n., 221n.,
223n.
Cosh, M., 19n.
Courts of Session and Justiciary, 2, 19n.
Coustures, Jacques, Baron de, 27–9, 55n.
Coutts, James, 21n.
Coutts, John, Lord Provost, 4–14, 18n., 21n.
Cowley, Abraham, 120
Craig, John, 200n.
Craigie, Robert, of Kilgraston and Glen-
doick, SCJ, 2, 17n.
Craigie, Thomas, 20n., 21n.
Crawford (Crawfurd), Earl of, *see* Lindsay,
John
creation, 33

credulity, 178, 190
criticism, 165
   biblical, 172, 197n.
Crousaz, Jean-Pierre de, 54n.
Crown, the, 2-4, 11, 14
Crusades, 236
Cudworth, Ralph, 197n.
Cullen, William, MD, 15, 21n., 22n.
Cumberland, Richard, 58, 76n.
Cuming, Patrick, 5, 12, 14, 18n.
custom, xiv, 105, 108–10, 112–13, 115–17,
117n., 122, 125, 128, 130, 190, 225–6,
240
   see also habit
Cyrenaics, 35

Dalrymple, John, 2nd Earl of Stair, 1, 7
Dante Alighieri, 176, 197n.
Darwall, S. L., xiii
Daston, L., 196n., 197n.
deduction, xiv, 85–6, 141–2, 144–6, 148,
151, 157n., 158–9n., 169n., 215
deism, 10, 14, 173, 218–19n., 244–5, 246–7,
255n.
"Demea", 162, 206, 217–18, 222n.
demonstration, 85–6, 99, 103n., 140–48,
155, 157n., 158n., 159n., 169n., 171–2,
180, 186, 249
   see also certainty; science(s)
Descartes, René, xiv, 126, 127, 128–9, 130,
131, 133–4, 135n., 137–8n., 141, 157n.
design, 33, 34, 47, 50, 85–6, 96, 162, 200n.,
216, 221n., 246, 248
desire(s), xiv, 28, 31, 46, 59, 62, 72, 75,
77n., 78n., 80n., 98, 109, 110–12, 114,
118n., 229, 232, 233, 237, 237–8n.,
242
dialogue(s), xv, 201–23
   "authorless", 202, 205, 207, 209, 211,
212–13, 218; comic, 204; conventions
of, 205–6; of the dead, 208, 219–20n.;
historicity of, 204, 209; methodical use
of, 212, 217, 218; as natural way of
philosophising, 201–3, 211; pedagogical, 208; philosophical, 203–5, 208–9,
218; and religious exposition, 204, 206,
208, 212; rhetorical use of, 212, 217,
218; therapeutic, 209
Dick, Robert, 18n., 21n.
Dijksterhuis, E. J., 56n.
Diodorus Siculus, 28
disciplinary matrices, 119
Dominicans, 228–30
doubt
   religious, 33, 162, 175, 186, 189, 231,
244; *see also* scepticism
Dulles, A., 196n.

Dundas, Robert, of Arniston, Jnr, SCJ, 2, 12, 14, 17n., 19n., 20n., 21n.
Dunlop, Alexander, 18n.
Dunois, Comte de, 191

Eddy, D. D., 221n.
Edinburgh
  Burgh of, 4, 5, 10, 11, 168; constitution ("set") of, 4, 18n.; *literati*, 2, 16, 168n.; ministers of, 1, 10–13, 15, 16, 20n.; Philosophical Society, 20n.; Town Council, 3, 4–5, 8–9, 11–13, 19n., 20n., 21n.; University, 1, 3, 4, 6–8, 9, 17n., 18–19n., 20n., 25, 32–3, 54, 56n., 139n., 172
education, 92, 115, 190, 219n., 225
Elibank, Baron, *see* Murray, Patrick
Elizabeth, Queen, 175
Elliot, Gilbert, Lord Minto, SCJ, 2, 10, 20n.
Elliot, Gilbert, of Minto, MP, 21n., 222n.
Emerson, R. L., xii, 17n., 19n., 20n., 21n.
emotion(s), 105, 107, 109, 110, 111, 114, 189, 235
  see also passion(s)
empiricism, 23–4, 25, 86–8, 94–6, 103, 131, 246, 247, 253
enthusiasm, xvi, 172, 181–2, 196n., 228, 229, 242, 253, 254n., 255n.
Epictetus, 112
Epicurus, Epicureanism, xiii, 26–35, 46, 49, 50, 53, 54–5n., 56n., 138n., 163, 222n., 243
epigraph (*Treatise*), 53
Errol, Earl of, *see* Hay, Charles
Erskine, Charles, Lord Tinwald, SCJ, 2, 11–12, 20n., 21n.
Erskine, John, of Carnock, 19n.
esteem, *see* fame
Eucharist, 177, 181, 196–7n.
Eusebius, 178
Evangelicals, 17n.
evidence, 106, 122, 123, 141, 171, 173, 174, 175, 176, 179, 181, 186, 191–3, 198n., 199n., 173, 175–6, 225, 240
  weight of, 150, 173, 175–6, 179, 181–2, 183, 187–8, 192, 199n.; *see also* probability; proof; testimony
evil, problem of, xv, 160–70, 216
exemplars, 119
experience, xiv, 26, 29–31, 33, 36, 42, 46, 112, 113–14, 116–17, 143–4, 146, 149, 152–6, 158n., 161, 163, 173–4, 180, 183, 185, 187, 188–9, 197n., 198n., 199n., 226–7, 240–41
  contrariety to, 179, 180, 181, 182, 189, 194, 198n.; contrariety distinguished from non-conformability, 185, 194; and

convention, 113; limits of, 241, 243, 245, 247; religious, 172, 188–9, 234
experiment, contrary, 189
experimental method, xii, 27, 29–33, 52–3, 87–8, 103n., 120–21, 123, 127, 136n., 140, 156, 168n., 189, 214–15, 218–19, 244
  see also Newtonian method; philosophy, experimental
explanation, xiii, 90–93, 102n., 104n., 154, 226, 242
external world, 199–200n.
eyewitnesses, *see* testimony

faith, xvi, 72, 162, 172, 174, 177, 196n., 199n., 237n., 239–40, 242, 246, 248, 250–51, 252
  historical, 197n.; irrational, 239; rational, 240, 252; *see also* belief
fame, 31, 32, 43, 46, 49, 118n., 229, 232, 233
fear, 31, 107, 111, 114, 118n., 231
fellow-feeling, 96–7
Fénelon, François, 208–9, 219–20n., 221n.
Ferguson, Adam, 21n., 25, 133
Feyerabend, P., 101, 104n.
fideism, 239, 253n.
Findlater and Seafield, Earl of, *see* Ogilvie, James
Fleck, L., 102n.
Fleetwood, William, 182
Fletcher, Andrew, of Saltoun, Lord Milton, SCJ, 2, 6, 7, 10, 15, 17n., 18n., 19n., 21n., 22n.
Flew, A. G. N., 158n.
Flinn, M., 168n.
Flood, the, 184, 198n.
Fogelin, R. J., 146, 158n.
Fontenelle, Bernard, 219–20n., 221n.
Forbes, D., 83, 102n., 103n.
Forbes, Duncan, of Culloden, Lord President, SCJ, 2, 193
Forbes, William, 18n.
Fordyce, David, 219n.
Forrester, James, 219n.
Frankena, W. K., 77n.
free-thinking, 206, 250

Garlies, Lord, *see* Stewart, Alexander
Gaskin, J. C. A., 169n., 196n., 237n., 254n., 255n.
Gassendi, Pierre, 27–9, 30, 33, 55n., 56n., 197n.
Gay, John, 77n.
Gibbon, Edward, 192
Gilpin, W., 220n.
Glanvill, Joseph, 120, 135n., 175, 197n., 198n.

Glasgow
  Burgh of, 2, 10, 16; Presbytery, 14, 15;
    University, 1, 3–4, 9, 10, 14–16, 17n.,
    18n., 20n., 21n., 33
glory, *see* fame
God, 31, 227
  agency of, 85, 172, 174, 181, 182, 183,
    185, 186, 195, 198n., 199n.; attributes
    of, xv, 33, 37, 160–63, 165–6, 169n.,
    172, 196n., 217–18, 222n., 227, 246–7,
    249; existence of, 33, 206, 217, 219,
    222n., 240, 244, 246, 248–9, 254n.; will
    of, 34, 37, 77n., 87–8, 90, 99, 126, 183
Good, H., 221n.
goodness
  moral, 59, 61–3, 66, 73, 76, 77n., 80n.;
    natural, 59, 60, 61, 73, 75; *see also*
    virtue(s)
Gordon, William, 2nd Earl of Aberdeen, 1
government, 31, 32, 34, 44, 46, 49, 88, 89,
    92, 101, 103n.
Gowdie (Goldie), John, 18n.
grace, 34, 174, 196n., 244–5
Graham, James, 2nd Duke of Montrose, 1,
    5, 15, 16, 17n., 21n.
Graham, James, of Easdale, 19n.
Graham, John, of Dougalston, 18n.
Graham, Mungo, of Gorthy, scj, 2
Grant, A., 19n.
Grant, F. J., 19n., 21n.
gravity, 198n.
Green, T. H., 106
Grose, T. H., 106
Grotius, Hugo, xiii, 36, 47, 48, 49, 57n.,
    83–95, 102, 102n., 103n., 104n., 113,
    118n., 197n.

Haakonssen, K., 83, 93–4, 95–7, 102, 102n.,
    104n.
habit(s), xiv, 70, 97, 105–18, 122, 129–30,
    190
  active vs passive, 105–8; *see also* custom
Hacking, I., 157n.
Haddington, Earl of, *see* Hamilton, Thomas
Hamann, Johann Georg, 239, 253n.
Hamilton, Alexander, MD, 9
Hamilton, Bailie Gavin, 3–4, 9–12, 14, 17n.
Hamilton, Robert (Edinburgh), 9, 17n.
Hamilton, Robert (Glasgow), 3, 18n., 21n.
Hamilton, Thomas, 7th Earl of Haddington,
    6
Hamilton, Principal William, 9
Hamilton, William, of Airdrie, 9
happiness, 26, 29, 47, 59, 62, 64, 70, 76n.,
    78n., 80n., 81n., 110–12, 114, 118n.,
    161, 162, 166, 249
  greatest, 58, 63, 76n.

Harrison, R., 82n.
Hartley, David, 127
hatred, 30, 45, 46, 50, 65–6, 68, 72, 80n.,
    111, 227
Hay, Charles, 13th Earl of Errol, 1
Hay, John, 4th Marquis of Tweeddale, 1–5,
    8, 10, 12, 13, 17n., 19n., 20n., 21n.
Hay, Thomas, of Huntington, 2, 5, 12, 13,
    17n., 19n., 20n., 21n.
Henderson, Robert, 20n.
Henry II, 231–3
Herbert, Edward, of Cherbury, 220n., 221n.
Hertford, 1st Earl of, *see* Conway, Francis
    Seymour
Hippocrates, 137n.
Hirschman, A. O., 103n., 104n., 112–13,
    118n.
history, xi–xii, xv–xvi, 42, 119, 123–4
  historical method, xv, 123, 173–6, 179–81,
    183, 187, 197n., 198n., 200n.; mixed,
    123–4; natural, xii, xiv, 120–27, 203;
    see also philosophy, and Hume's *History*
Hobbes, Thomas, 24, 25, 27, 28, 31, 33,
    34, 46, 54, 86–7, 89, 92, 113, 118n.,
    121, 189
Home, Henry, Lord Kames, scj, 2, 6, 12,
    13, 19n., 35, 106, 124, 125, 164
Home, John, 21n.
Homer, 211
Hooke, Robert, 139n.
Hope, John, 2nd Earl of Hopetoun, 1
Hope, V. M., 78n.
Horace, 27, 28, 31, 36, 47, 49, 55n., 57n.,
    210, 221n.
Houyhnhnms, 98
Huguenots, 196n.
human nature, *see* nature, human
Hume, David, *passim*
  biography, xii–xiii, 1–22, 25–6, 32–3, 106,
    160, 163–4, 169n., 172, 191–2; charges
    against his philosophy, 10, 11, 12, 14,
    21n., 25; literary genres, xv, 165,
    201–23; manuscripts, xiv–xv, 160–70;
    revisions to first *Enquiry* 195n.; revi-
    sions to *Treatise* xiii, xv, 38–9, 46, 51–4,
    57n., 164, 171; writing conventions,
    163, 168n., 169n.
Hume, Hugh, 3rd Earl of Marchmont, 1,
    6, 19n.
Hurd, Richard, 203–4, 206, 219n.
Hurlbutt, R. H., 220n., 221n., 223n.
Hutcheson, Francis, xiii, 10, 11, 17n., 18n.,
    20n., 56n., 57n., 58–67, 74, 75, 76n.,
    77n., 78–9n., 79–80n., 82n., 83, 99,
    104n., 105, 106, 117n., 118n., 120, 133,
    139n., 164, 213
  on approbation as a simple idea, 59, 61,

62, 78n.; on benevolence, 34–5, 40, 41, 63–4, 77n., 78n., 111, 114; on calm desire and the passions, 110–12; on Epicureanism, 33–5; and Hume, 4, 5, 10, 14, 23–54, 64–73, 76, 110–12, 114, 161, 165, 169n., 170n.; on love, 35, 62, 72, 110–11; on moral choiceworthiness, 63; on moral goodness, 59, 61–2; on moral sense, xiii, 24, 34, 37, 39, 44–5, 50, 59, 61–4, 65, 67, 74, 78n., 79–80n., 114; on natural goodness, 61; on public sense, 62, 64, 78n.; reaction to Bk II of the *Treatise* 35–8; and Reformed theologians, 34, 37; on rights, 34, 47–51, 63–4
hypocrisy, 230–36
see also self-deception

idea(s)
 abstract, 137n.; of approbation (Hutcheson), 59, 61, 62; association of, 30, 43, 46, 52, 68, 72, 107, 115, 126, 128, 130, 136n., 144, 154, 189–90, 225–6, 230, 237n. (*see also* causation; contiguity; resemblance); comparison of, 142, 147; concomitant (Hutcheson), 24, 44–5, 52–3; in Descartes, 137–8n.; and impressions, 30–32, 39, 41, 44, 45, 49, 52, 53, 66, 73, 82n., 121, 130–32, 189; intermediate, xiv, 141, 142, 147–51, 153–6, 158n., 180; relations of, 40–41, 141, 142–3, 145, 244; theory of, 127, 130–32, 133; *see also* imagination
Ilay, 1st Earl of, *see* Campbell, Archibald
illation, 150, 158n.
imagination, xvi, 30, 32, 50–52, 71, 128–9, 144, 154, 161, 167, 189, 190, 220n., 224–7, 228, 230, 237
impression(s), 30–31, 39, 41, 44, 49, 52, 68, 79, 82n., 107, 128, 130–32, 143, 161, 167, 189, 190, 226, 230
 see also idea(s), and impressions
Indian prince, 194, 200n.
induction, xiv, 123, 127, 140, 157n., 158n., 214
 see also probabilisitic reasoning
Inglis, Sir John, 20n.
intelligence, 160–61, 165, 200n.
interest(s), 31–2, 43–4, 46, 49, 51, 79n., 96, 103n., 110, 118n., 172, 175, 176, 179, 181, 183, 197–8n., 229, 231–2
 as calm and violent passions, 112; public, 47, 49, 57n., 80n., 91, 94, 96, 97, 99, 114–15; self, 42–3, 57n., 95–6, 98, 112–13, 116–17; *see also* patronage; self-love
introspection, 123, 126
intuition, 142–4, 147, 151, 155, 159n.

Inverary, 10, 19n.
'is-ought', 24, 94, 169n.

Jacobi, Friedrich Heinrich, 253n.
Jacobites, 2, 6, 11
Jacobson, A. J., 158n.
Jansenism, 177–8, 193
Jesus Christ, 174, 184, 195
Jews, 173
Joan of Arc, xvi, 191, 231, 233–4, 236
Johnstone, George, 3rd Marquis of Annandale, 6, 12, 19n.
Johnstone, Sir James, of Westerhall, 6, 12, 19n.
Johnstone, John, MD, 18n.
Jolley, N., 139n.
Jones, P. H., 196n., 238n.
judgement(s)
 of fact, 115, 148–9, 150, 175, 176, 179, 180, 186, 187, 190, 197–8n.; moral, 23, 30, 43–4, 54n., 61, 65–6, 68, 73, 79, 107, 112, 115–16; and the general point of view, 32, 47, 70–71; and the "narrow circle", 70–71, 80–81; natural, 226
Jupiter Ammon, oracle of, 53
justice, xiii, 27–9, 39, 41, 44, 45, 49, 52, 53, 67, 68, 84, 87, 91–101, 103n., 104n., 106, 109, 112–15, 168n., 242
 and benevolence, 47–51; origin of, 83–4, 95–7, 102, 110, 136n.
justification, xiii, 89–93, 95–8, 100–102, 104n.

Kames, Lord, *see* Home, Henry
Kant, Immanuel, xvi, 104n., 239–55
 on autonomous reason, 252; on causation, 241; on faith, 240, 244–53; on the history of reason, 251–2; on "Hume's principle", 245, 247, 248, 254n., 255n.; on "Hume's problem", 241, 248; on the need of reason, 248–50; on the principle of significance, 255
Ker, John, 19n.
Kerr, John, 1st Duke of Roxburghe, 1, 7
Kierkegaard, Søren, 253n.
King, William, 169n., 219n.
King's College, Aberdeen, 3, 126, 127
Kippis, Andrew, 20n.
Kirk, the, 3, 5, 7, 11, 13, 14, 16
Kirkpatrick, William, 18n.
Kivy, P., 138n.
knowledge, 103, 142, 147–53, 171–2, 177
 limits of, 122, 240, 245
Kuehn, M., xvi, 254n., 255n.
Kuhn, T. S., xiv, 119–20, 134, 135n.

Labienus, 53, 57n.

Labrousse, E., 55n., 56n.
Latimer, J., 168n.
latitudinarians, 172, 175–6
Laudan, L. L., 136n.
Law, Edmund, 169n.
Law, Prof. William, 12, 84
Law, William, of Elvingstone, 12, 21n.
law(s), 29, 89–90, 95–6, 174, 180, 186, 187, 197n.
    see also natural law; nature, law(s) of
Leclerc, Georges Louis, Comte de Buffon, 136n.
Leechman, William, 4, 14, 15, 17n., 18n., 19n., 21n.
Leibniz, Gottfried Wilhelm, 104n., 141
Leidhold, W., 82n.
Leslie, John, 10th Earl of Rothes, 1
liberty, 6–7, 34, 242, 250–51
Lindsay, Hercules, 21n.
Lindsay, I. G., 19n.
Lindsay, John, 10th Earl of Crawford, 1, 21n.
Livingston, D. W., 103n., 136n., 254n.
Locke, John, xiv–xv, xvi, 40, 42, 47, 51, 61, 86, 103n., 113, 120, 121–2, 124, 126–7, 128–32, 133–4, 135n., 136n., 137n., 138n., 139n., 140–41, 142, 147–52, 152–3, 155–7, 157n., 158n., 159n., 190, 197n., 200n., 225–6, 237n., 241
    on causality, 153, 180; on demonstration, 147–8, 149; on faith, 172; on historical probability, 177, 179–83, 185–6, 191, 193, 198n., 200n.; on miracles, 181–3, 196n., 198n.; on opinion, 150, 152–4, 158n., 180, 190; on probabilistic reasoning, 148–52, 157n., 180–81; on reasonableness in morals, 40, 42, 47, 51; on sensitive knowledge, 184, 199n.
logic, 21n., 141, 148, 164, 176–7, 197n., 251
Loudoun, John, 18n.
love, 28, 30, 35, 45, 46, 50, 62, 65–7, 68, 69, 72–3, 75–6, 78n., 80n., 81n., 82n., 110–11, 166, 227, 233, 235
    see also interest(s); self-love
Lucan, 53, 57n.
Lucian, 195n., 203, 204, 219–20n., 221n.
Lucretius, 27, 28, 33
Luther, Martin, xvi, 229–30, 235, 237n.
Lyttelton, George, 195n., 220n.

M'Cosh, James, 132, 138n.
Machiavelli, Niccolò, 236
MacIntosh, J. J., 138n.
MacIntyre, A. C., 96–7, 104n., 157n.
Mackenzie, Kenneth, 5

Mackie, J. D., 4, 18n.
Mackie, J. L., 158n.
MacLaurin, Colin, 2, 8
MacLaurin, John, 12, 17n., 18n.
Macpherson, James, 191–2, 200n.
madness, 189, 225, 237n.
Maimonides, 196n.
Malcolm, C. A., 18n.
Malebranche, Nicolas, xiv, xvi, 126, 127, 128, 129, 130, 131, 133, 134, 138n., 141, 225, 226, 237, 237n., 238n.
Malherbe, M., xv, 222n.
man, *see* nature, human
Mandeville, Bernard, 24, 40, 56n., 104n., 120, 209, 220n., 221n.
Manichaeans, 169n.
manners, 191–3, 203, 205, 210–11
Marchmont, Earl of, *see* Hume, Hugh
Marischal College, 3, 20n., 139n.
martyrdom, Hume's explanation of, 230, 231
Marxism, 84, 101–2
mathematics, 40, 165, 175, 180, 200n.
matter, 163, 198n.
Maxwell, Sir John, Lord Pollock, scj, 15, 21n.
Mayo, T. F., 54n.
melancholy, 164, 167
memory, 173, 224
    see also imagination
mercantilism, Hume's opposition to, 6
merit, 215
Merlan, P., 253n.
metaphysics, 24, 35, 38, 132, 138n., 241, 243, 245, 247
method, experimental, *see* experimental method
Michael, E. and F. S., 138n.
Middleton, Conyers, 196n., 197n.
Mill, J. S., 63
Millar, John, 125
Milton, Lord, *see* Fletcher, Andrew
mind, 131, 163, 164, 172, 190
    natural history of, 120–27, 203; philosophy of, xii, xiv, 172; science of, 120–39; *see also* anatomy, of the mind
miracle(s), xv, 141, 149, 161, 164, 171–200, 239
    contrary, 187; definition of, 179, 183, 185, 199n.; evidence for, *see* testimony, criteria for assessment; function of, 172–3, 176, 183
Mitchell, Sir Andrew, MP, 2, 8, 17n., 20n.
Moderates, 16, 17n., 20n.
moderns, 29, 53, 203, 204, 210–11, 213, 215
Montesquieu, Charles de Secondat, 118n., 125, 137n.

Montrose, Duke of, *see* Graham, James
Montucla, Jean-Étienne, 125
Moor, James, 20n., 21n.
Moore, J. W., xiii, 4, 18n., 83, 102n., 104n., 111, 118n.
moral judgement, *see* judgement(s), moral
moral realism, 24, 44–5
moral sense, *see* sense(s), moral
moralist(s), 29, 33, 35, 38, 39
  ancient, 26, 27, 33, 55n.
morals, xiii, xvi, 27–9, 33–5, 40–41, 105, 165, 172, 210, 214–15
  and religion, 34, 36–7, 52–3, 234–7, 242, 244–5, 248–52
More, Hannah, 160, 168n.
More, Henry, 174–5, 197n., 220n., 221n.
More, Martha, 160, 168n.
Morthland, Charles, 18n.
Moses, 174, 184, 196n.
Mossner, E. C., 21n., 136n., 137n., 169n., 221n., 254n.
motive(s), 28, 36, 37, 38, 40, 41, 47–8, 49–51, 57n., 58, 59, 60, 62–3, 64, 67, 68–9, 75, 76, 77–8n., 79n., 82n., 95, 98–9, 107, 108, 114, 178, 179, 242
Muirhead, George, 8, 16, 20n.
Munro, N., 18n.
Murdoch, A., 17n., 19n.
Mure, William, of Caldwell, MP, 6, 10, 17n., 19n., 164
Murray, Patrick, 5th Baron Elibank, 11, 12
mysteries, 177, 184

Nadler, S. M., 139n.
Nathan, G. J., 254n.
'natural', meaning of, 34, 35, 38, 77n., 124–5
natural history, *see* history, natural
natural law (moral/legal contexts), xiii–xiv, 58, 76–7n., 83–95, 99, 101–2, 103n., 104n.
natural lawyers, 83–5, 91–2, 95, 97, 99–102, 103n., 104n.
natural philosophy, *see* philosophy, natural
naturalism, 23
naturalistic fallacy, 24
nature, 35, 90, 92, 103n., 203
  contrariety to, 174, 182, 185, 193, 195, 198n., 199n.; course of, 172, 174, 180–83, 185–6, 196n., 198n., 199n.; human, 83–7, 89–95, 101–2, 189 (*see also* science(s), of man); law(s) of, 93, 179, 181, 183, 185, 187–8, 194, 196n., 199n. (*see also* natural law); state of, 28, 34, 87, 89, 93, 113; uniformity of, xiv, 172, 180, 186, 194, 216
necessity, 28, 43, 48, 115, 124, 136n., 144–5, 155, 158n., 176

Newhall, Lord, *see* Pringle, Sir Walter
Newton, Sir Isaac, 119, 120, 127, 135n., 137n., 138n.
Newtonian method, 125, 127, 132, 136–7n., 139n.
Newtonianism and natural religion, 8
Nicole, Pierre, 176
Nietzsche, F., 237n.
Norton, D. F., 24, 44–5, 54n., 56n., 57n., 82n., 138n., 169n.
Noxon, J., 135n., 136n., 254n.

obligation, 31, 34, 37, 44, 46, 47–9, 68, 74, 83, 84, 90, 92
observation, 29–30
Ogilvie, James, 5th Earl of Findlater, 2nd Earl of Seafield, 1
optics, 107, 115, 131–2, 226
order, 163
  natural, 125
Origen, 197n., 200n.
Ossian, xv, 191–3, 200n.
Oswald, James, of Dunnikier, MP, 6
Owen, D. W. D., xiv–xv, 158n., 198n.

pain, *see* pleasure and pain
"Palamedes", 94, 216
Palladini, F., 55n., 103n.
"Pamphilus", 201, 202, 205–7, 212, 215, 216–17, 222n.
paradigmatic texts, 119, 124
Pâris, Abbé François de, 193, 195–6n.
Parsons, Philip, 220n.
Pascal, Blaise, 104n., 177
passion(s), 31, 36, 39, 42, 43–4, 45, 48–9, 50–51, 52, 54, 56n., 57n., 65–6, 68, 70, 77n., 79n., 81n., 82n., 87, 95, 98, 181, 183, 189, 190, 192, 198n., 227, 230, 233, 234–7, 237n., 238n.
  Butler on, 107, 121; calm, 78n., 105, 109–10, 112–15; causes of, 50, 69, 235; and interest, 44, 112–13, 118n.; opposition of, 228, 230; and reason, 40, 109, 237, 238n.; violent vs calm, 31, 46, 109–10, 112–13; *see also* ambition; anger; fear; hatred; interest; love; self-love
Passmore, J. A., 157n., 196n.
patronage, 1-22
Paul, Apostle, 195n., 197n.
Peach, John, 160
Pearce, Zachary, 200n.
Pelham, Henry, 22n.
Pelham, Thomas, 1st Duke of Newcastle, 22n.
Penelhum, T. M., 117n., 118n., 253n., 254n.
personal identity, 51–2

Phillipson, N. T., 133, 136n., 138n., 139n.
"Philo", xv, 162–3, 206, 218, 220–21n.,
222n., 242–4, 254n.
philosophy
easy, 201, 213–14, 217; experimental, 67,
106, 120; history of, xi– xii, 119; and
Hume's *History*, xv–xvi, 224, 228–34,
236; and literary form, 201–19; moral,
xii–xiv, 22–54, 172, 202, 213; natural,
165, 206; obscure and abstruse, 214,
216–18, 243
Physiological Library, 32–3, 56n.
Pinkerton, J. M., 19n., 20n.
Plato, 189, 197n., 203, 204, 210
pleasure and pain, xiii, 108, 111, 161, 168
degree vs frequency of, 161, 162, 166–8,
169n.; and moral judgement, 61, 65–6,
68, 73, 79
Plutarch, 26
pneumatology, 164, 170n.
poetry, 190, 191–3, 200n., 210, 217
politics, xii, 1–21, 165
Pollock, Robert, 20n.
Polybius, 197n.
polytheism, 124, 196n., 226–7
Pope, Alexander, 135n.
Pompey, 53
Popkin, R. H., 196n., 253n.
Popper, K. R., 101
Porterfield, William, 138n.
Port-Royal *Logic*, 141, 176–80, 182, 184,
197n., 198n.
Potter, Michael, 18n.
prayer, 174, 227, 244
Price, J. V., 219n., 221n., 223n.
Price, Richard, 74
pride, 30, 32, 43, 44, 45, 46, 49, 65–6, 69,
72, 80n., 82n., 232, 235
Priestley, Joseph, 127
Pringle, Francis, 7, 19n.
Pringle, John, MD, 7–9, 11, 19n., 20n., 84
Pringle, Robert, 7
Pringle, Sir Walter, Lord Newhall, SCJ, 19n.
Pringle, Walter Torsonce, 19n.
Prior, A. N., 24, 54n., 253n.
Prior, Matthew, 219n.
probabilistic reasoning, xiv, 140–57, 157n.,
158n., 159n., 161, 178–9, 180–81, 198n.
see also causation, causality
probability, xv, 106, 161, 172, 173, 186,
193–5, 200n.
antecedent and consequent, 178; Arnauld
on, 176–9, 180, 181, 193; Craig on,
200n.; Locke on, 140, 148–52, 155,
157n., 177, 179–83, 185–6, 191, 193,
198n., 200n.; philosophical and unphilosophical, 190, 194; Wilkins on, 175

prodigies, 177, 189, 194
progress, natural, 124, 125
projection, 226–7
promise(s), 43–4, 48–9, 83, 84, 91, 92, 101,
113
proof, 122, 147–50, 153, 155, 158n., 168,
180, 181, 183, 185–91, 199n., 213–14,
218, 243, 246, 249
defined, 186; degrees of, 186; Locke on,
158n., 180–81, 199n.; opposed by
proof, 185–8
property, 28, 30, 32, 34, 43, 44, 46, 48–9,
50–51, 56n., 83, 88–92, 103n., 113–14
Protestantism, 171–3, 174, 178, 179, 196n.,
226, 228–31, 253n.
providence, 13, 51–2, 174
psychophysiology, xiv, 128–30, 225, 234–7
Pufendorf, Samuel, xiii, 31, 34, 36, 47, 48–9,
55n., 56n., 57n., 83–4, 86–8, 90, 94–5,
99–100, 102, 103n., 104n.
Pye, Samuel, 220n.

Radbill, S. X., 20n.
Ramsay, Michael, 55n., 169n.
Raphael, D. D., 23–4, 44, 54n., 56n.,
78n.
Raynor, D. R., 4, 18n.
reason, xiv, 160–61, 164, 165, 169n., 177,
178, 198n., 199–200n., 225–6, 244–5,
251–2
and morality, 38–9, 39–44, 215; and the
passions, 40, 109, 237, 238n.; and religion, 171–2, 239, 240, 244–5, 248–9,
251, 252–3; scepticism with regard to,
190; things above, 172, 177, 184,
199–200n.; things contrary to, 181–2,
184, 190
reasoning, 140–57
see also demonstration; probabilistic reasoning
Reformation, 173, 196n., 228–30
Reid, Thomas, xiv, 25, 74, 119, 120, 125–7,
130–32, 133, 134, 135n., 136–7n.,
138n., 139n.
religion, xii, xv–xvi, 171–2, 186, 224–38,
239, 241–4, 246–53
cause(s) of, 214, 216, 224, 228, 242, 253n.;
Christian, 171–3, 176, 179, 182, 184,
188, 197n., 234–7, 239–40, 242 (*see
also* Protestantism; Roman Catholicism); Islamic, 235–6; natural, xv, 8,
32–3, 165, 170n., 171–2, 183, 195,
206–7; and rationality, xvi, 8, 171–2,
229–31, 239–45, 252; revealed, 32–3,
169n., 171, 172–3, 174, 196n.; true,
244, 252, 254n.; *see also* morals, and
religion; revelation

resemblance, 30, 32, 46, 69, 142, 155, 190, 225, 227, 230
resurrection, 195
revelation, 172, 174, 181, 182, 184, 222n., 229–30
rhetoric, and philosophy, 170n., 201–5, 212, 217, 218, 222–3n.
  distinguished from philosophy, 161, 165, 167
right(s), 34, 47–51, 63–4, 90, 103n.
Roberts, W., 168n.
Robertson, William, 2
Roebuck, John, 160
Roman Catholicism, 171, 172–3, 177, 179, 183, 196–7n., 228–30, 231, 235, 236, 238n.
  see also Dominicans; Jansenism
Rosenberg, A., 144–5, 157n.
Ross, I. S., 21n., 56n.
Rosse, George, 18n., 21n.
Rothes, Earl of, *see* Leslie, John
Roxburghe, Duke of, *see* Kerr, John
Ruat (Rouet), William, 16, 20n., 21n.

St Andrews University, 3, 7, 19n., 20n.
St Clair, Gen. James, 16
St Evremond, Charles de St Denis, Seigneur de, 27, 28, 55n.
Scanlon, T. M., 58, 77n.
scepticism, sceptic(s), xiii, 5, 8, 10, 11, 14, 24, 26, 33, 37, 39, 40–41, 53–4, 54–5n., 56n., 83, 112, 161, 162, 164, 171, 172, 173, 186, 199–200n., 203–4, 206, 241, 245, 253n., 254n., 255n.
  see also virtue(s), sceptical ideas of
science(s), xii, 86, 100, 102n., 103n., 164–5, 247
  of man, 29–30, 106, 164, 203, 213; of the mind, 119, 127–32; *see also* demonstration
Scot, William, of Bristo, 102n.
Scott, David, of Scotstarvit, MP, 19n.
Scott, Robert, 2
Scott, W. R., 117n.
Sedgwick, R. R., 17n., 18n., 19n.
self-deception, 230–34
  see also hypocrisy
self-love, 48, 55n., 79–80n., 95–6, 111, 197–8n., 252
  see also interest, self
Seneca, 26, 112
sense(s), 164, 176, 177, 184–5, 188–9, 199n.
  moral, xiii, 24, 34, 37–8, 39–40, 44–7, 50, 59, 61–4, 65, 67, 74, 77n., 79–80n., 114, 211, 215; public, 62, 64, 78n.
sentiment(s), 23, 36–7, 39, 42, 44, 45, 47, 52, 57

Sessions, W. L., 223n.
Shaftesbury, 3rd Earl of, *see* Cooper, Anthony Ashley
Shaw, J. S., 17n., 18n., 19n., 20n., 22n.
Sheffield, John, 220n.
Sher, R. B., 4, 18n., 20n., 133, 139n.
Sherlock, Thomas, 200n.
Sibbald, Sir Robert, 124
Simson, Robert, 2, 18n., 21n., 22n.
sin, 34, 237, 237–8n.
Skelton, Philip, 200n.
Smith, Adam, 15, 16, 21n., 25, 124–5, 136n.
Smith, James, 18n.
Smith, N. Kemp, 23–4, 25, 44, 54n., 56n., 77–8n., 138n., 163
Smith, Robert, 138n.
Smollett, Tobias, 2
Society of Writers to the Signet, 19n.
Socrates, 137n., 210
Spinoza, Baruch, 87–8, 103n.
Sprague, E. D., 220n.
Sprat, Thomas, 120, 135n.
Squadrone, 1–15, 17n., 18n., 19n., 20n.
Stafford, F. J., 200n.
Stair, Earl of, *see* Dalrymple, John
Stephen, L., 200n.
Steuart, Robert, 32, 56n., 139n.
Steuart, Sir James, 118n.
Stewart, Alexander, Lord Garlies, later 6th Earl of Glasgow, 10, 16
Stewart, Archibald, Lord Provost, 4, 6, 7, 10, 13, 14, 18n., 19n., 21n.
Stewart, Dugald, 125, 133, 136n., 137n.
Stewart, John, 19n.
Stewart, M. A., xv, 4, 18n., 111, 118n., 169n., 196n.
Stillingfleet, Edward, 176, 184, 196n., 197n., 198n., 199n.
Stoicism, Stoics, xiii, 26–7, 36, 39, 49–50, 53, 55n., 111–12, 118n., 169n., 172, 198n.
  Christian, 37, 111–12
Stove, D. C., 144–5, 157n., 158n.
Stratonicians, 163, 169n.
Strawson, P. F., 255n.
Stroud, B., 77n., 78n., 80n., 146, 158n.
Stuart, John, 3rd Earl of Bute, 6
Stubbes, George, 220n.
Stuckenberg, J. H., 254n.
suicide, 184
superstition, 181, 184, 190, 214, 228, 230, 232, 235, 236, 242, 244, 254
sympathy, 29, 35, 36, 44–7, 57n., 67–73, 99, 229–30, 233–4

testimony, xv, 121, 149, 173–8, 180–94, 197n., 198n., 199n., 200n.

criteria for assessment of, 175, 176, 177–8,
    180–81, 186–9, 191–2; external circum-
    stances, 178, 180, 193; internal circum-
    stances, 177–8, 180, 192–3
theism, 160–63, 165, 172, 183, 196n., 241–2,
    246, 249, 252, 255
Thomas Aquinas, 85, 88, 103n., 197n.
Thomson, J., 21n.
Thomson, James, 2
Thucydides, 174, 197n.
Tiberius, 180
Tillich, P., 253n.
Tillotson, John, 172, 173, 176, 184–5, 196n.,
    199n., 200n.
Tindal, Matthew, 219n.
Trail, Robert, 20n.
transubstantiation, 176, 177, 184–5, 199n.,
    200n.
Tullideph, Thomas, 3, 17n.
Turnbull, George, 2, 139n.
Tweeddale, Marquis of, *see* Hay, John

understanding, faculty of, 23, 39–40, 42,
    54, 105, 152, 156, 214, 220n., 226, 243,
    245–6, 251
utilitarianism, xiii, 58–82, 77n.
    philosophical, 58, 60, 61, 64, 68, 75–6
utility, 27, 29, 31, 34, 36, 43, 45–6, 47, 49,
    55n., 60, 73–4, 75, 91–2, 94, 96, 115,
    162
    principle of, 58, 62–3, 73–4, 76n., 77–8n.

vice, 45, 68, 79n.
    see also virtue(s)
Vico, Giambattista, 104n.
virtue(s), 6, 23–4, 30, 34, 35–50, 52, 53,
    54, 55n., 94, 97, 99, 102n., 106–8,
    160–62, 165, 169n., 215, 235–6
    artificial, 27–9, 35–6, 38–9, 44, 69–70,
    91–3, 95–7, 99, 103n., 104n.; Epicurean
    ideas of, 26, 27–9, 33–5, 49, 50, 53,
    54n., 57n.; monkish, 235–6, 242; moral,
    vs natural ability, 60, 64, 72, 79–80;
    natural, 27–9, 34, 38–9, 47, 70–72, 92;
    and philosophy, 111–12; sceptical ideas

of, 26, 27, 33, 40–41, 46, 48, 49, 50,
    54n., 56n., 57n.; Stoic ideas of, 26, 36,
    39, 49, 50, 53; "Warmth in the Cause
    of", 19n., 35, 61, 77n.; *see also* ability;
    attributes; character, moral

Walbank, F. W., 197n.
Wallace, Robert, 2, 13, 14, 16, 20n.
Walpole, Sir Robert, 2, 6–7, 18n., 19n.,
    237n.
Walsh, W. H., 254–5n.
Walton, C., 136n.
Ward, Seth, 197n.
Watts, Isaac, 198n., 200n.
Webster, Alexander, 12–13, 16
Webster, John, 197n.
West, Gilbert, 200n.
Westerman, P. C., xiii, 102n.
Whelan, F. C., 78n.
Whichcote, Benjamin, 78n.
Whigs, 1, 2, 6
White, R., 223n.
Whitson, T. B., 17n.
Wilkins, John, 172, 175–6, 198n., 199n.
will, 89, 91, 103n., 111, 113, 126
    effect of custom on, 105, 108–10, 111
Willis, Thomas, 138n.
Wilson, M. D., 157n.
Wishart, Principal William, Jnr, 1, 5, 8,
    9–10, 12–14, 18n., 20n., 21n.
witchcraft, 175, 197n.
Wodrow, Robert, 19n., 174, 196–7n.
Wollaston, William, 40–42
Wood, A. W., 255n.
Wood, N., 135n.
Wood, P. B., xiv, 136n., 137n.
Woolston, Thomas, 200n.
Wootton, D., 117n., 195n., 196n., 197n.,
    200n.
Wright, J. P., xiv, 128, 136n., 137n., 138n.,
    237n.

Yalden-Thomson, D. C., 105, 117n.
Yandell, K. E., 254n., 255n.
Yolton, J. W., 133, 139n., 157n.